PLANS AND DETAILS FOR CONTEMPORARY ARCHITECTS: BUILDING WITH COLOUR

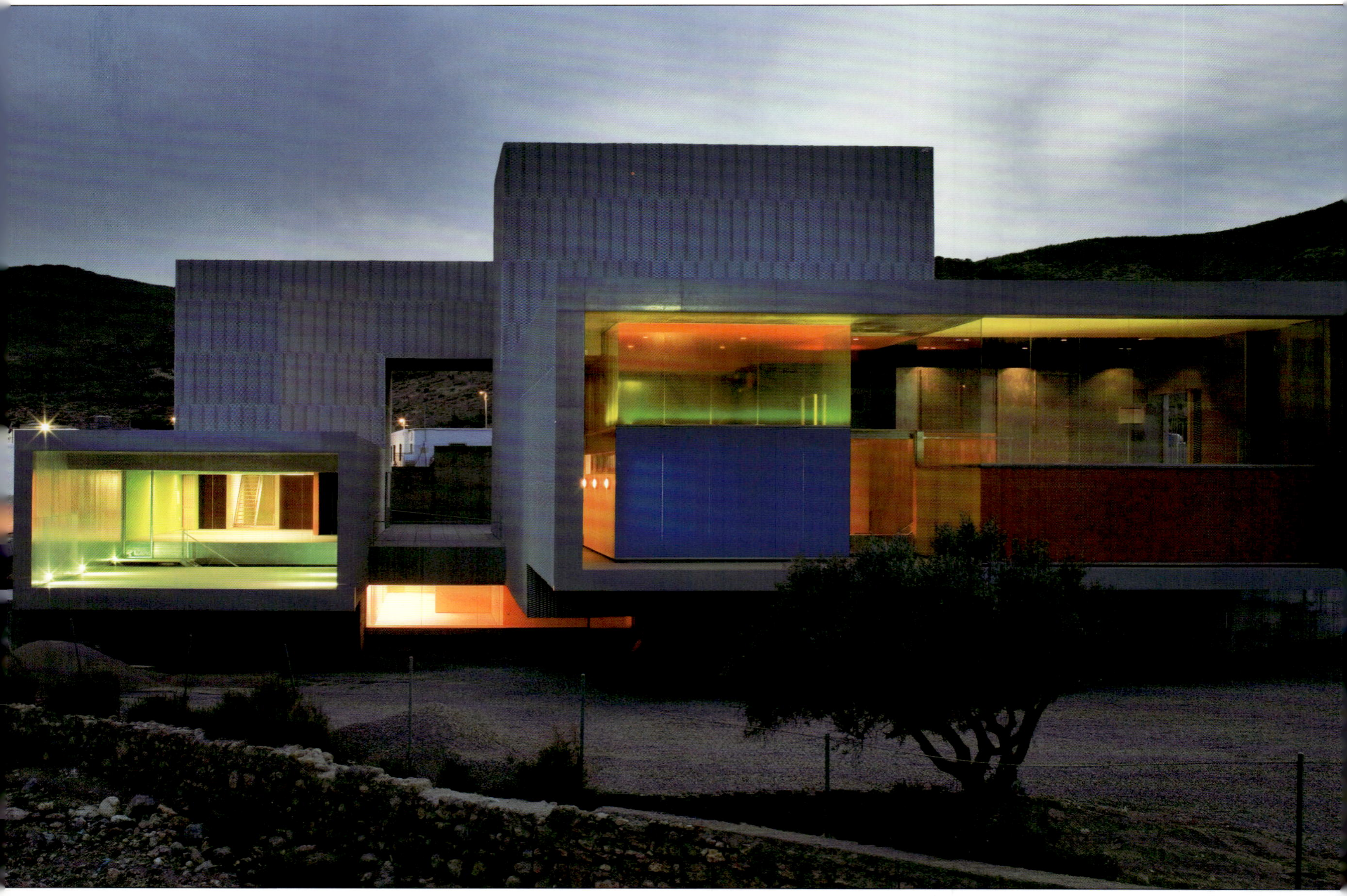

PLANS AND DETAILS FOR CONTEMPORARY ARCHITECTS: BUILDING WITH COLOUR

EDITED AND DESIGNED BY **THE PLAN**

Thames & Hudson

CONTENTS

006 Colour in Contemporary Architecture
by Michael Webb

008 Architecture and Colour
by Francesco Pagliari

044 "Els Colors" Nursery School
Barcelona, Spain
RCR Aranda Pigem Vilalta Arquitectes

056 Clapham Manor School
London, UK
dRMM Architects

064 Ørestad College
Copenhagen, Denmark
3XN

118 Fire and Police Station
Berlin, Germany
Sauerbruch Hutton Architects

126 Diagnostic and Therapeutic Centre, CEDT
Daimiel, Spain
estudio.entresitio

136 The Public – West Bromwich, UK
Alsop Architects

182 New Terminal T4 Barajas Airport
Madrid, Spain
Richard Rogers Partnership – Estudio Lamela

198 Soccer City Stadium
Johannesburg, South Africa
Boogertman + Partners Architects

208 Agbar Tower
Barcelona, Spain
Ateliers Jean Nouvel and b720 Arquitectos

010 Tamsa Offices
Veracruz, Mexico
Caruso-Torricella Architetti

020 2 Harbour Buildings
Münster, Germany
Bolles+Wilson

032 Condominium Trnovski Pristan
Ljubljana, Slovenia
Sadar Vuga Arhitekti

078 University Library
Utrecht, The Netherlands
Wiel Arets Architects

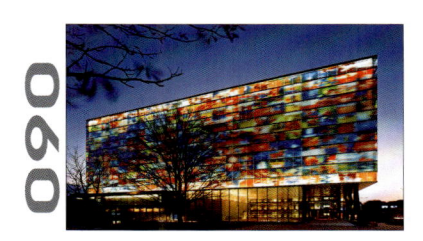

090 Netherlands Institute for Sound and Vision
Hilversum, The Netherlands
Neutelings Riedijk Architects

106 Theatre and Music Centre
Níjar, Spain
MGM – Morales Giles Mariscal

148 Santa Caterina Market
Barcelona, Spain
Miralles Tagliabue Arquitectos

158 Flower Market
Barcelona, Spain
Willy Müller Architects

168 St Giles Court Development
London, UK
Renzo Piano Building Workshop

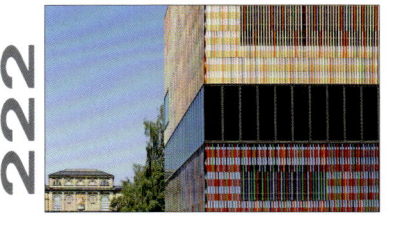

222 Brandhorst Museum
Munich, Germany
Sauerbruch Hutton Architects

234 **Project Credits**

COLOUR IN CONTEMPORARY ARCHITECTURE

Architects have employed colour, often with great audacity, for at least three millennia, but little of this work survives. Pigments fade, tastes change, and history is rewritten. When a Bavarian prince became the first king of a newly independent Greece in 1833, he decreed that the sun-bleached ruins of the Athenian Acropolis should be stripped of later additions, and the sanitized Parthenon took its place as the defining symbol of the classical world. Traces of the brilliant colours that once highlighted its marble carvings were ignored or expunged. A later generation of romantics scrubbed and refaced Gothic cathedrals. Le Corbusier entitled a book *When the Cathedrals were White*. In fact they were originally polychromatic, and remain so wherever medieval stained glass survives.

The early modernists were similarly traduced in succeeding decades. Black-and-white photography barely hinted at their varied palettes, and the myth of a purist white architecture took hold and lives on in the buildings of Richard Meier. The shock of the new returns when one explores the Berlin housing estates of Bruno Taut and his contemporaries, recently restored to the joyful exuberance they had in the late 1920s. The interior of the reconstructed house in Dessau that Paul Klee and Wassily Kandinsky shared during their Bauhaus years employs twenty-three distinct tones. Walking into the Café Aubette in Strasbourg, a three-dimensional painting by Theo van Doesburg working in collaboration with Hans and Sophie Arp, is to immerse oneself in a geometric field of primary colours. Every year a few more modern classics regain their vibrant hues.

Increasingly, contemporary architects are adding colour to their vocabulary of design. For some it is their signature. From the Pompidou Centre on, Richard Rogers has employed primary hues to articulate boldly expressed steel structures. Jean Nouvel uses colour in a theatrical way and has a special fondness for leading one from dark shadowy spaces into an explosion of red. Sauerbruch Hutton, an Anglo-German partnership based in Berlin, draws on a spectrum of assertive and subtle tones for the glass panels that compose their façades. All three are represented in this selection of nineteen primarily European projects. In some, colour is the primary theme, in others it is merely an accent. But, dominant or subordinate, understated or aggressive, colour is the spice in the stew, enhancing the flavour of the other ingredients.

A few projects stand out from the rest for their creative use of colour to reduce mass, proclaim purpose, or orientate users. In the first category is the Condominium Trnovski Pristan, which makes a significant contribution to the eclectic townscape of Ljubljana, the pocket capital of Slovenia. In a city of Austrian Secession buildings and the Mannerist masterpieces of Joze Plecnik, Sadar Vuga has pixelated the façades so that they seem to dissolve around the jutting balconies.

In contrast, the extension to the central fire and police station in Berlin stands out from the banality of the new government enclave. The Chancellor's house and federal offices are puffed-up monuments of mediocrity, as dispiriting as Albert Speer's grandiose plan for Germania, though mercifully smaller in scale. Sauerbruch Hutton have taken the red of the fire service and the friendly green of the police and have wrapped their functional concrete building in glass panels of those colours, mingling them at the centre to emphasize the interdependence of these two public services. Nothing could be simpler or more legible. To identify the Netherlands Institute for Sound and Vision in Hilversum,

Neutelings Riedijk has wrapped a container with a screen of coloured relief glass that abstracts memorable images broadcast by Dutch television. In the consistency with which a single envelope expresses the programme of the building it recalls an earlier work by the same firm: the Veenman printing works in Ede, with its lettered façade. It reaches out to the street and casts a magical play of coloured light across the atrium by day. To complement this 21st-century version of a stained glass window, corridors are painted scarlet and framed by a grid of dark brick to pull colour into the heart of the building.

Barcelona is the city of Antoni Gaudí, who carried the Catalan tradition of colour and ornament to a peak of invention. His writhing, brilliantly tiled façades express the spirit of place and inspired the tragically short-lived Enric Miralles and Benedetta Tagliabue, who now directs his office. The Santa Caterina Market was the first major work she undertook after his death: a reconstruction of her neighbourhood shopping centre. Its undulating roof is best seen from surrounding apartment buildings, but it can be glimpsed from the Plaça Nova at the heart of the Gothic Quarter. What first appears to be an abstract composition of brilliant colours was derived from pixelated photographs of the produce that is sold beneath the beams of the ceiling vault.

Ateliers Jean Nouvel and b720 Arquitectos' multicoloured glass and concrete Agbar Tower soars above the Diagonal, midway between the city centre and the new waterfront commercial zone. The tower, which houses the offices of Barcelona's water company, alludes to the bowed spires of Gaudí's Sagrada Família, and coincidentally to Foster & Partners' Swiss Re in the City of London. The surface is clad with corrugated aluminium panels, pixelated in red, blue and white to evoke fire, water and steam. This stylized depiction of a geyser is diffused by an outer membrane of translucent glass louvres.

A pair of linear terminals, designed by Richard Rogers Partnership and Estudio Lamela, have tripled the capacity of Madrid's Barajas Airport and transformed its image. Tapered steel Y members with concrete footings support an undulating steel-framed roof, within and around the perimeter. Abundant natural light, warm materials and a spectrum of colours humanize the experience of walking through these extended spaces. It remains a tedious chore, especially when one has to change from the domestic to the international terminal, but colour enlivens the journey and points the way. Yellow at the mid-point, the concourses intensify to orange-red at one end and blue-purple at the other, as though a rainbow were carrying passengers to the planes.

Michael Webb

ARCHITECTURE AND COLOUR

Colour and architecture are very special bedfellows. In the contemporary mindset, colour does not seem to be the result of designer whim. Nor is it seen automatically as a mere decorative element or as a way of making single elements stand out from their backdrop, in accordance with conventional pictorial traditions. In modern architecture, colour is all about experimenting with materials, creating interconnection between different volumes of an organic whole, or the contrary, identifying a particular component as an element apart. Colour can be used to establish a hierarchy among disparate parts or to signal continuity. It makes statements and highlights particular features. It follows volumes as they develop and determines materials. In short, colour has become architectural composition.

Colour may be used to underline the materiality of architectural forms through our perception of density, brilliancy or nuanced hues Whether marked by vaguely romantic or classical overtones, colour can work in two ways: accentuating the dynamic functions of a group of architectural volumes, or imparting a sense of measured stability where priorities, scale and functions are clearly and uncompromisingly defined.

The role of colour in connecting or separating interior and exterior is complex too. Whether applied to public or private space, colour can be used to signal distance, to the point of antagonism, between two separate worlds, or – when outside surfaces resonate with the colour schemes of their interior counterparts – emphasize continuity.

Colour, volume, materials and luminosity are all part of a whole. Colour becomes a sort of catalyser enhancing architectural structure. Amid the vast spaces of the New Terminal T4 Barajas airport designed by Richard Rogers, colour plays an important role in signage. It also imparts identity and helps create aesthetically pleasing environments. As well as unequivocally signalling the different spatial functions, the colour sequence on the structural steel elements and metal beams on the intrados of the roof gives a sense of one single, all-embracing volume. Externally, the rhythmically graduated colours on the structural steel pillars running the entire length of the fronts converge to yellow, clearly signposting the main entrance.

Symbolic and innovative use of colour is also evident in the Netherlands Institute for Sound and Vision by Neutelings and Riedijk. Appropriately in a television broadcasting building where image is "content", image and colour become architectural form. The outer envelope is turned into a coloured image thanks to hundreds of glass panels forming a vitreous ceramic screen on to which are projected as many images, single frames or abstract renderings of film or video footage. The images lend the elevations an immaterial quality. Beams of coloured light pierce the spaces inside, reverberating on coloured mosaic wall surfaces and other wall cladding materials. At night, when lit from within, the building stands out as a transparent volume.

When colour and material work in symbiosis, the architecture they serve is not only immediately recognizable but also distinctive – perhaps even beyond the original intention of the author. The complex curved roof of Barcelona's Santa Caterina Market, covered by a mosaic of ceramic tiles in a graduated range of sixty-five shades, has become the hallmark of the building refurbished by Enric Miralles and Benedetta Tagliabue. Just a glimpse of a section of the roof as it juts out over the building is enough to bring to mind the widely publicized aerial views of the entire roof span. Here colour is not just symbolic for this building. It stands for a cultural heritage where light has always been a component part of "decoration".

Similarly, Sauerbruch Hutton's Berlin fire and police station uses colour as symbol and message. The elevation is given a dynamic quality as the brilliant glazed colours veer from green to red as the operable glass brise-soleil panels proceed horizontally up the building, overlapping like shingles. Looking at the building returns an image similar to when you catch a glimpse of a passing object. The use of colour blurs the material confines of the architecture. Close up, the building reflects its surrounds; from afar the reflections become abstract shapes. The Utrecht University Library by Wiel Arets is another example of colour used as a means of abstraction and symbol. The architecture itself expresses the different types of knowledge contained in a library: the contrasting elements of concentration and communication. The same contrast is echoed by the opposing textures and materials used to develop the precise geometry of the elevations. With the addition of colour, they become a vehicle of the abstract. The external cladding alternates concrete panels with black relief finishes and stretches of screen-printed operable glass panels whose stylized plant motifs allow only limited views of the interior. Light reverberates in different ways on the façades. The transparent segments are punctuated by the opaque black areas, while the distinctive mouldings are especially assertive under artificial light. Inside, the same abstraction is pursued. Beams and wall sections in black finish and fair-faced concrete contrast vibrantly with the red rubber tabletops. Everything works to underline the irreconcilable distinction between silence and speech in the temple of the written word.

Colour glimpsed through transparent surfaces is also used by Entresitio to offset and enliven the rigorously geometric volumes of the Diagnostic and Therapeutic Centre in Daimiel, Spain. The brilliant red folded sheet steel cladding the brick walls is softened by an outer envelope of micro-perforated steel mesh, giving the building a fabric-like appearance.

The residential building Trnovski Pristan in Ljubljana designed by the Slovenian practice Sadar Vuga demonstrates how the use of a medley of elements sets the scene for decided colour strategies. Large black metal mouldings at the windows make the lights seem larger and contrast to great effect with the façade cladding, an outer envelope of multi-coloured ceramic tiles on an aluminium frame. As a result, the façade looks like a screen with moving coloured pixels interrupted by the bold strokes of the mouldings. The overall impression is of a clearly visible stack of storeys in a dematerialized volume.

Sauerbruch Hutton's architecture for Munich's Brandhorst Museum leans towards the phantasmagoric. Located in a district home to several monumental 19th-century museum buildings, this latest addition has adopted colour as a way of standing out. On the exterior, an array of hollow coloured slats bathe the façade with coloured light making the Brandhorst a distinctive landmark. In contrast, the discreet, muted interiors take a back seat to the works of art.

Similarly, Renzo Piano has transformed an office block in St Giles, London, into a fragmented iridescent complex. The extruded vitrified ceramic tile cladding in six colours brings out to great effect the different volumes comprising the whole complex and clearly indicates the different functions catered for within.

At Barcelona's nursery school "Els Colors", colours teach. Glazed walls of laminated glass are enhanced by a sandwich film of yellow, green, orange and red. As well as offering visual and sensory stimulation to the young pupils, the riotous colours give depth to an essential architecture made up of a series of simple, almost stark, volumes. Brilliantly coloured glazed walls segment and dematerialize this sequence of juxtaposed volumes. They are punctuated by a series of opaque galvanized slabs that further enhance the visual and perceptive experience.

Colours can also convey a sense of tension and the ineffably lightweight. Agbar Tower, one of Barcelona's new iconic buildings, designed by architect Jean Nouvel and the b720 Arquitectos practice, soars up in a multitude of colours, cladding materials and layered envelopes. The undulated aluminium sheet steel modules come in twenty-five irregularly arranged colours moving from earthy red through to sky blue. The same colours are repeated on the inner steel slab modules. The resultant colour map is muted and blurred by an outer envelope of laminated glass, making the tower seem an almost impalpable presence despite its imposing volume. From a distance, it seems to rise into nothing, its steel and transparent glass dome blending with the colour of the sky.

Francesco Pagliari

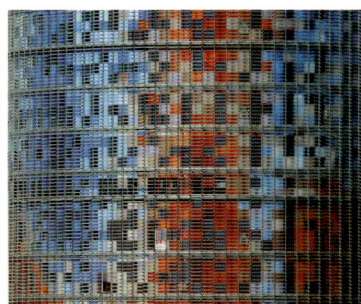

TAMSA OFFICES – VERACRUZ, MEXICO
CARUSO-TORRICELLA ARCHITETTI

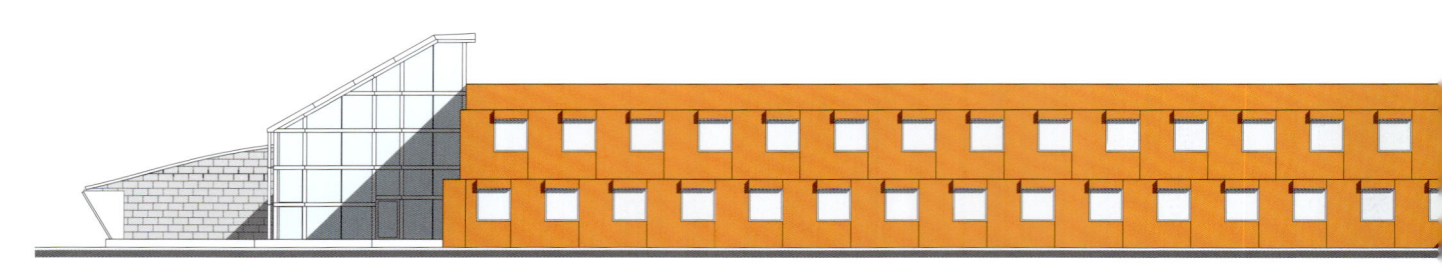

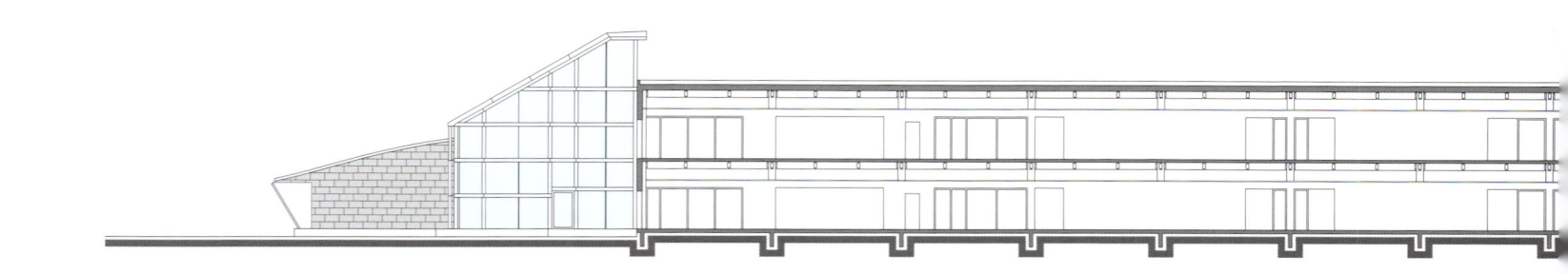

■ South Elevation – Scale 1:400

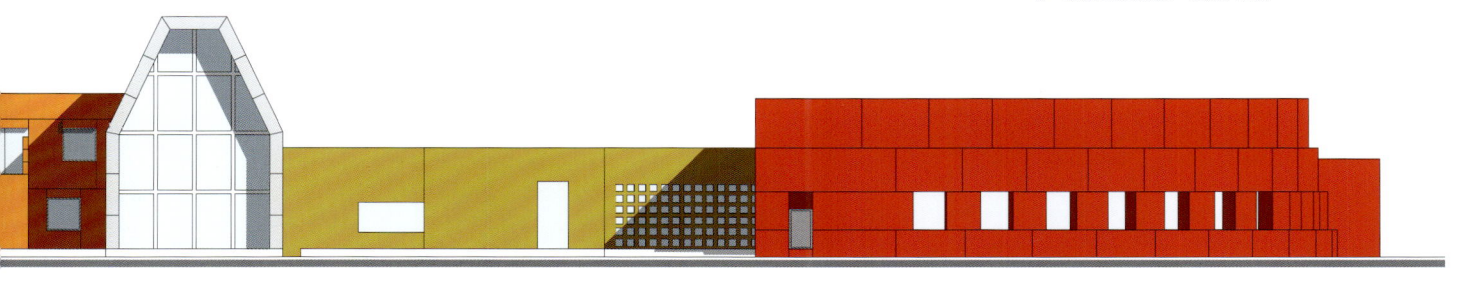

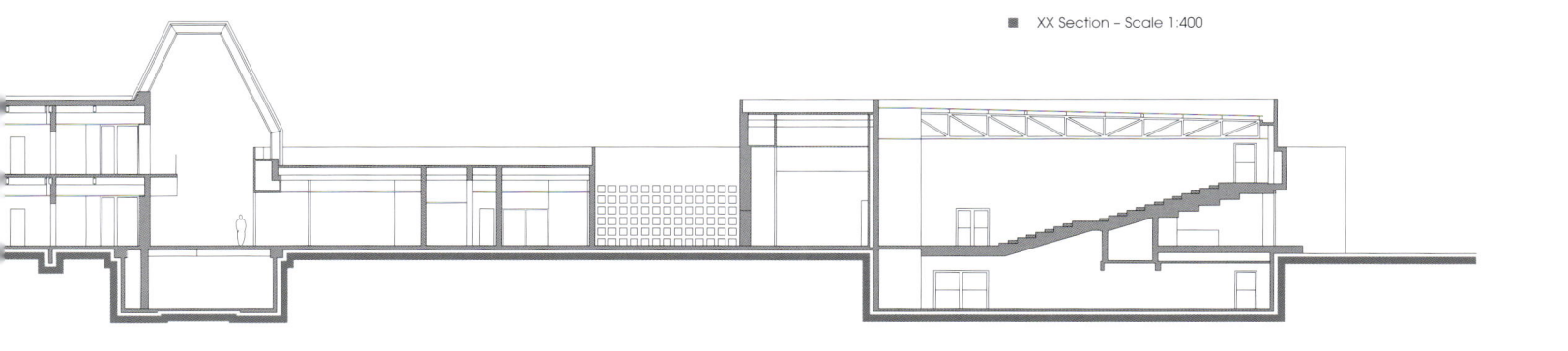

■ XX Section – Scale 1:400

■ North Elevation – Scale 1:400

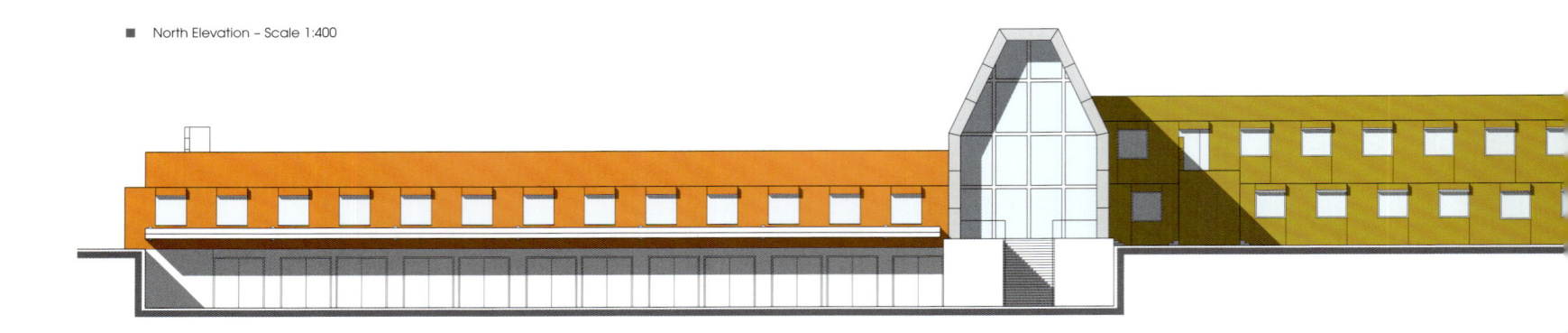

The project for the Tamsa offices in Veracruz, Mexico, focused on three key elements: delivering modern, functional offices; retaining the essential flavour of Mexican culture, and capturing the iconic essence of the country's landscapes and architectures, from pre-Hispanic and Hispanic through to contemporary vernacular building styles. The complex comprises six buildings: a distribution mall; a services facility – with reception, bank, travel agency and auditorium – and four office buildings. All the technical services and equipment are housed underground in a basement that mirrors the ground plan.

Pivotal to the project, the large mall presents as a gateway into the factory from the outside world. It is also a distribution corridor leading off to the buildings on either side. Its long, constant width is topped by an upper trapezoidal section. While typically state-of-the-art in its design, the roof's shape also recalls an archetypal cavern of the Cumaean Sibyl, corridors leading into the pyramids, or even a Maya arch. The mall's metal structure is clad externally with zinc-titanium panels and internally with plasterboard.

The continuous surfaces are broken only by narrow windows reaching to the roof that cast long strips of intense luminosity onto the corridor below. The mall's shape and size immediately denote it as the main public space of the complex. The buildings accessed from it have reinforced concrete frames, while their walls are built in the local tradition and jut out into the mall by about a metre.

The basic element of the façade is the typical "L"-shaped element of the "almenas", the jointly decorative and defensive crenellation that topped pre-Hispanic buildings in the region of Veracruz. The sequence of these elements creates the window spaces. In the two-storey buildings, the two rows of "L"-shaped elements are set in staggered fashion, highlighting the motif to great effect. Also in the Mexican tradition, every building is painted a different colour with no concern for gradual colour grading.

The two two-storey buildings on the left of the mall house the offices. The buildings end in glazed stairwells and are connected by a passage and the metal panelling and glazing structure of the cafeteria. On the right, the mall leads to a building that houses a bank, travel agency and auditorium in that order. The other two buildings are the senior management offices and the IT service unit.

The auditorium is a typical, well-shaped quarter circle. The internal walls are clad in perforated aluminium sound-proofing panels. The foyer has a large glazed wall, while a masonry wall with square-shaped openings serves both as a sun screen and an enclosure for an exhibition area of Mexican art. On display are "Judas" and other typical Mexican figures, made out of papier mâché by Mexican artist Spindola, who also created the "alebrijes" skeletons hanging from the mall ceiling.

A large 3 x 9 m (10 x 25 ft) "Mensaje" by Goeritz in perforated gilded sheet steel hangs in the auditorium foyer above the entrance door and near the staircase in untreated oxidized sheet steel. Two other works by Goeritz grace the entrance to the senior management offices: one, a circle, and the other, a huge square of gold leaf.

■ East Elevation – Scale 1:400

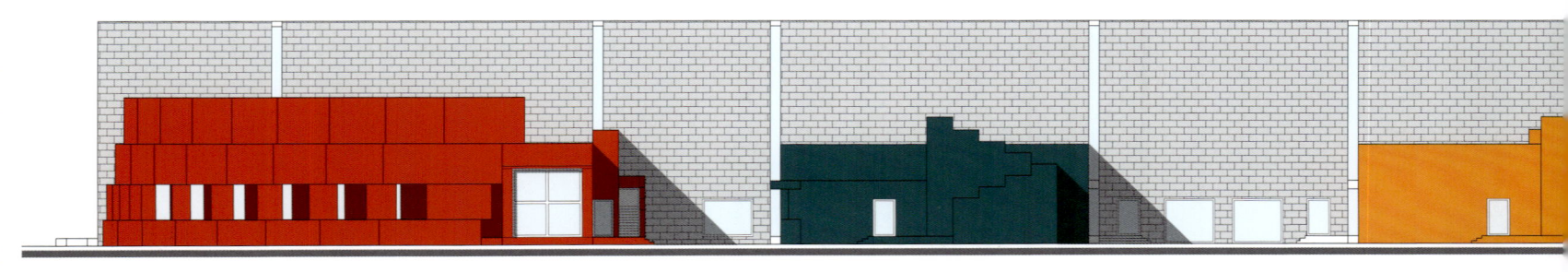

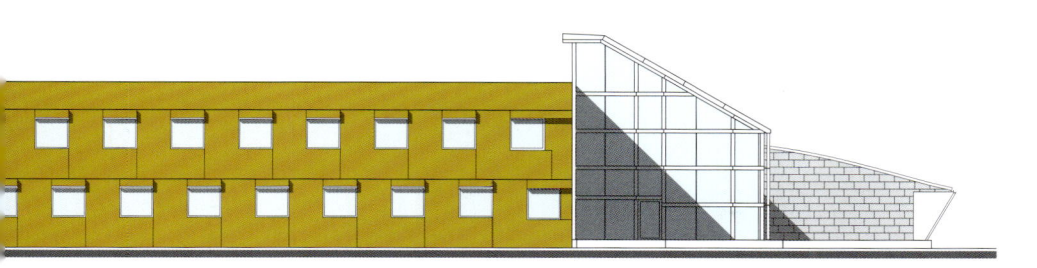

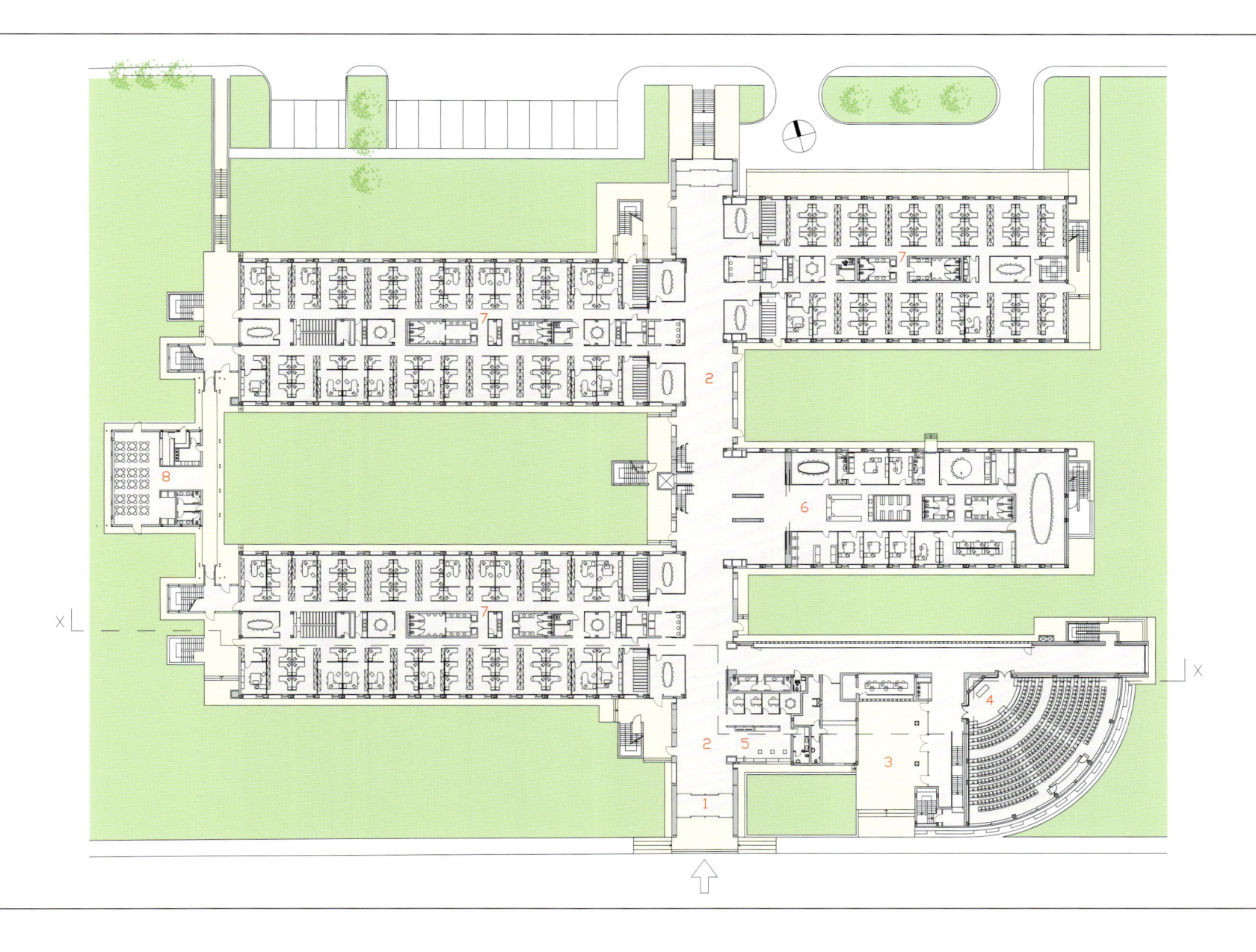

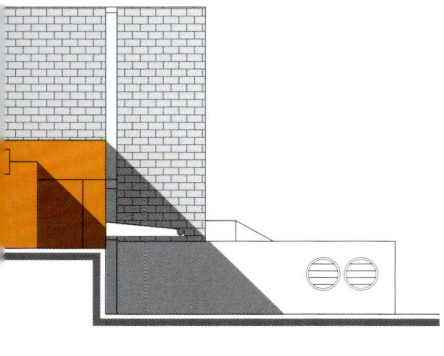

Ground Floor Plan – Scale 1:800

1. Main Entrance
2. Mall
3. Auditorium entrance
4. Auditorium
5. Services area (Reception Desk, Bank, Travel Agency)
6. Management
7. Offices
8. Cafeteria

013 / Caruso-Torricella

014 / Tamsa Offices

■ Complex's Chromatic Range

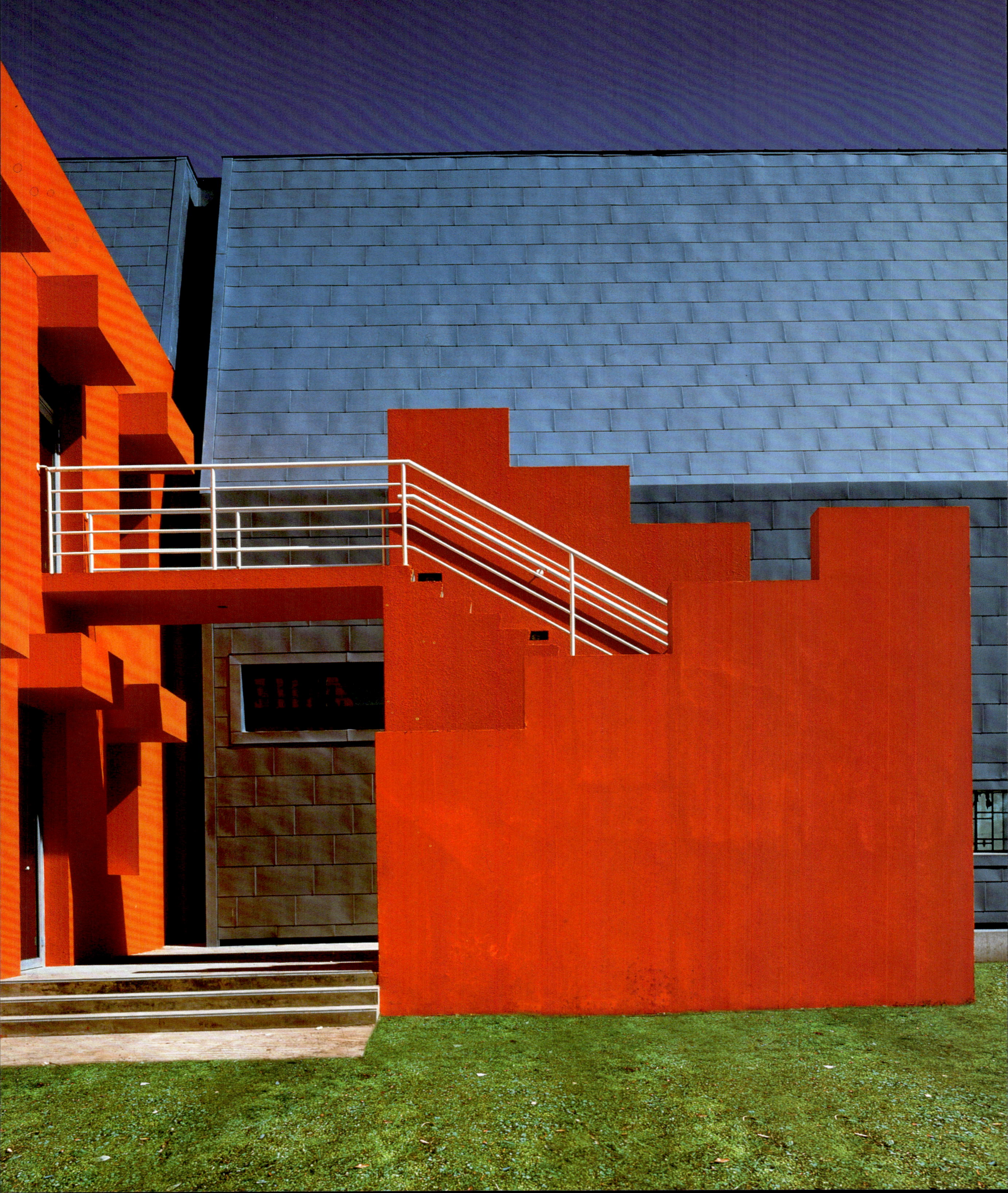

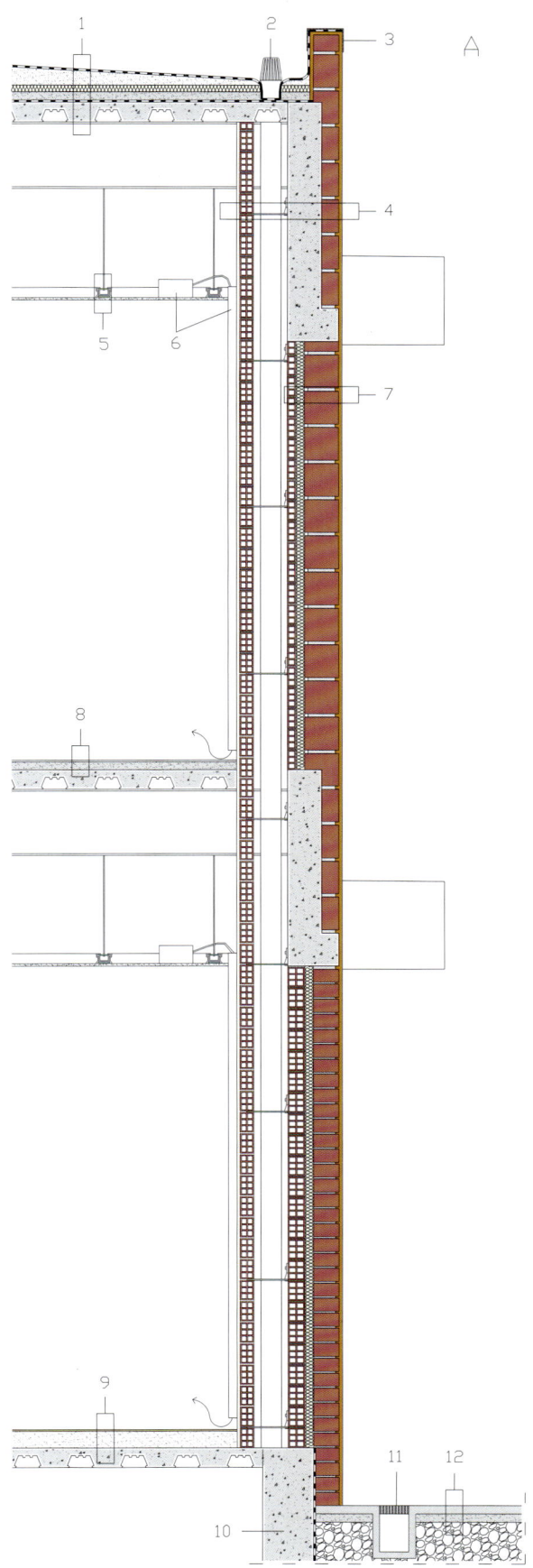

**DETAILS A, B: OFFICE FAÇADE
VERTICAL SECTIONS – SCALE 1:40**

1. Waterproofing membrane, screed forming 2% slope, 1 5/8" (40 mm) board insulation, 2" (50 mm) screed, vapour barrier, pre-cast 4 3/4" (120 mm) reinforced concrete slab, 15 3/4" (400 mm) h. steel I-beam (parallel to plane of section)
2. Rainwater collection and filtering system
3. Steel flashing
4. Colour-washed plaster render, 4" (100 mm) masonry blocks, 7 7/8" (200 mm) reinforced concrete structure, tie rod, 7 7/8" (200 mm) air space, downspout (parallel to plane of section), 3 1/8" (80 mm) perforated masonry blocks, render
5. False ceiling formed by Plafond Armstrong 5/8" (15 mm) fibreglass panels on frame of aluminium profiles suspended from beam by tie rods
6. Installation space
7. Colour-washed plaster render, 7 7/8" (200 mm) masonry blocks, 2" (50 mm) board insulation, 2" (50 mm) perforated masonry blocks
8. Carpet floor covering, 2" (50 mm) screed, pre-cast 4 3/4" (120 mm) reinforced concrete slab
9. Resin flooring, 4" (100 mm) screed, pre-cast 4 3/4" (120 mm) reinforced concrete slab
10. Reinforced concrete edge
11. Steel grille over drainage well
12. 2" (50 mm) concrete sheets, 2" (50 mm) concrete screed, gravel layer
13. Steel C-profile trim
14. Steel flashing, render, 3 1/8" (80 mm) screed, 8 5/8" (220 mm) perforated masonry block infill, 7 7/8" (200 mm) reinforced concrete shelf, colour-washed plaster render
15. Steel drip moulding
16. Fibreglass closure panel on frame of steel box profiles
17. Fixed 1/4 – 5/8 – 1/8 + 1/8" (6 – 16 – 4 + 4 mm) aluminium double glazing unit
18. Sill formed by sheet steel, sloping screed, reinforced concrete beam

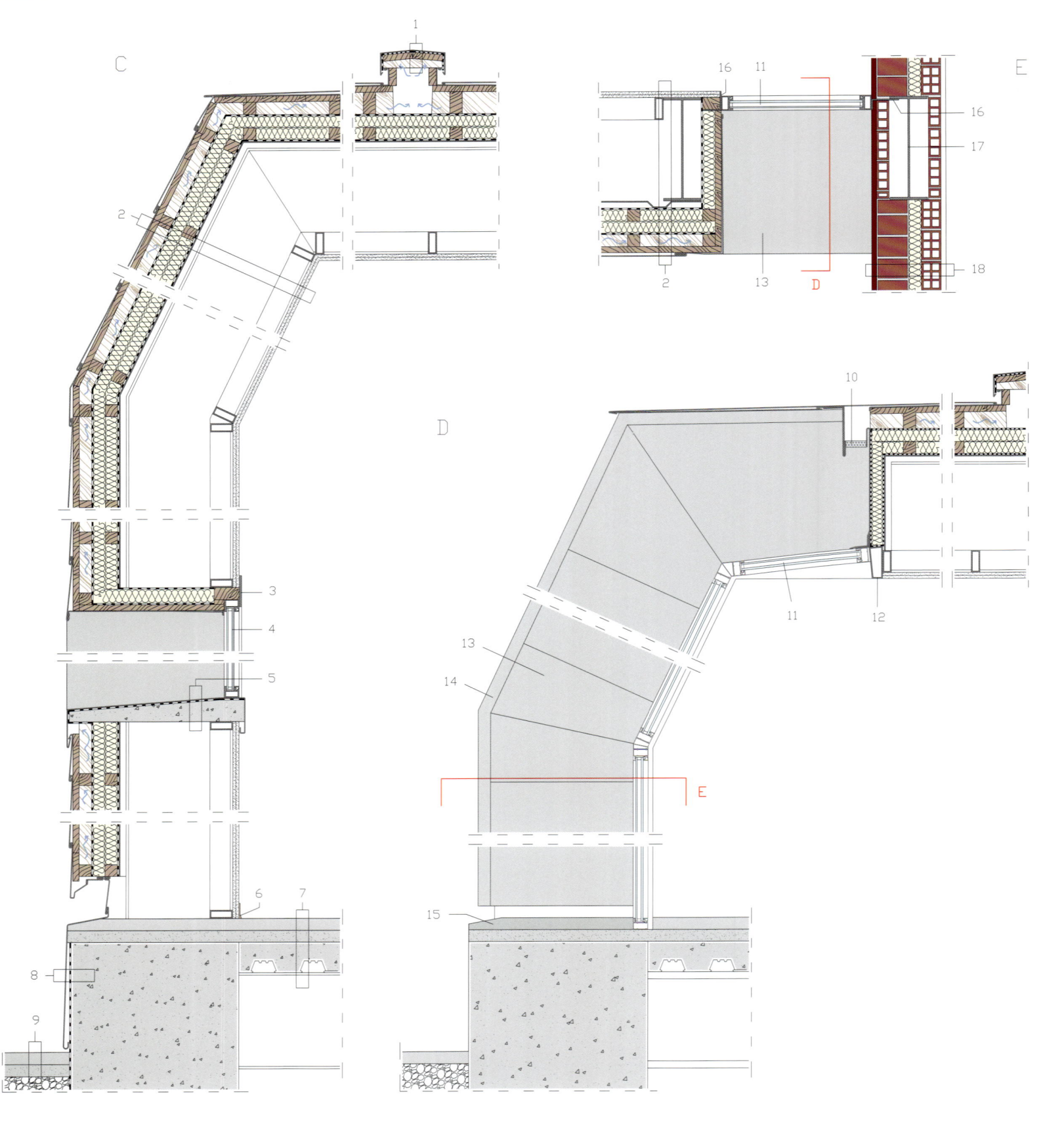

DETAILS C, D, E: MALL SHELL VERTICAL AND HORIZONTAL SECTIONS SCALE 1:20

1. Ventilated ridge formed by Rheinzink shingles, waterproofing membrane, 1" (25 mm) timber battens, wood beam (parallel to plane of section)
2. Rheinzink 1" (25 mm) shingle cladding, timber battens, frame of 2" (50 mm) wood, waterproofing membrane, 2" (50 mm) board insulation, 2" (50 mm) board insulation with frame of 2 x 2" (50 x 50 mm) timber, vapour barrier, 1 1/4" (30 mm) corrugated sheeting, 17 3/8" (440 mm) steel I-beam, frame of 3 1/2 x 1 3/8" (90 x 35 mm) steel box profiles supporting cladding, interior wall covering formed by double 1" (25 mm) gypsum board
3. Aluminium cornice
4. 1/4 – 5/8 – 1/8 + 1/8" (6 – 16 – 4 + 4 mm) aluminium double-glazing unit
5. Sill formed by Rheinzink shingles, waterproofing membrane, reinforced concrete bracket
6. Timber skirting
7. Floor in 2" (50 mm) smooth concrete tiles, 2" (50 mm) screed, pre-cast 4 3/4" (120 mm) reinforced concrete slab, 15 3/4" (400 mm) steel I-beam (parallel to plane of section)
8. Rheinzink shingle cladding, waterproofing membrane, reinforced concrete foundation
9. 2" (50 mm) concrete sheets, 2" (50 mm) concrete screed, ballast layer
10. Insect screen
11. Window in 1/4 – 5/8 – 1/8 + 1/8" (6 –16 – 4 + 4 mm) aluminium double glazing
12. Galvanized steel box profile supporting window
13. Rheinzink shingle cladding (parallel to plane of section)
14. Rheinzink angle trim (parallel to plane of section)
15. Exterior stone slab footing
16. Steel L-profile cover
17. 17 3/8 x 5 7/8" (440 x 150 mm) steel I-beam
18. Colour-washed plaster render, 3 1/8" (80 mm) perforated masonry blocks, 2" (50 mm) board insulation, 5 1/8" (130 mm) masonry blocks, render

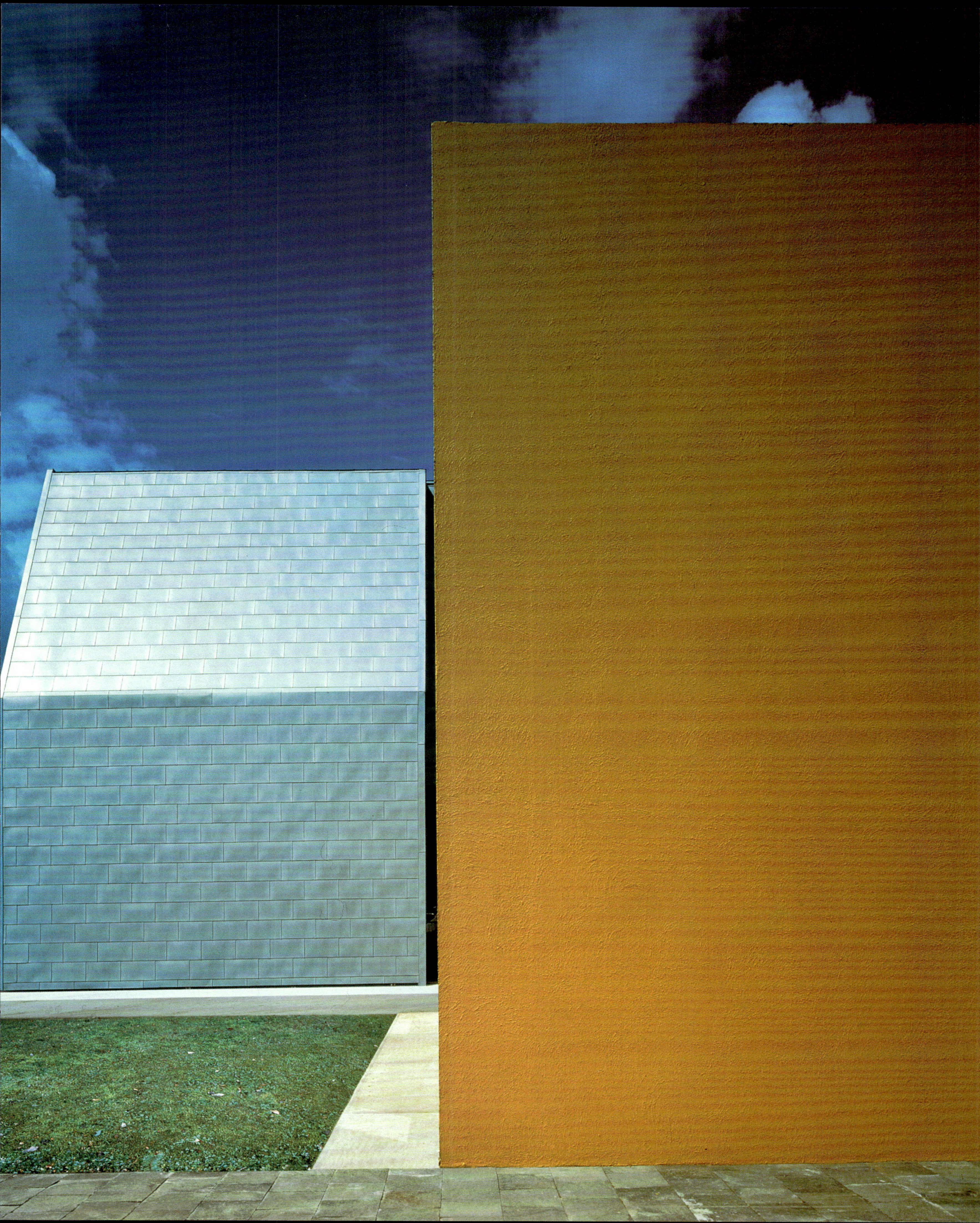

2 HARBOUR BUILDINGS – MÜNSTER, GERMANY
BOLLES+WILSON

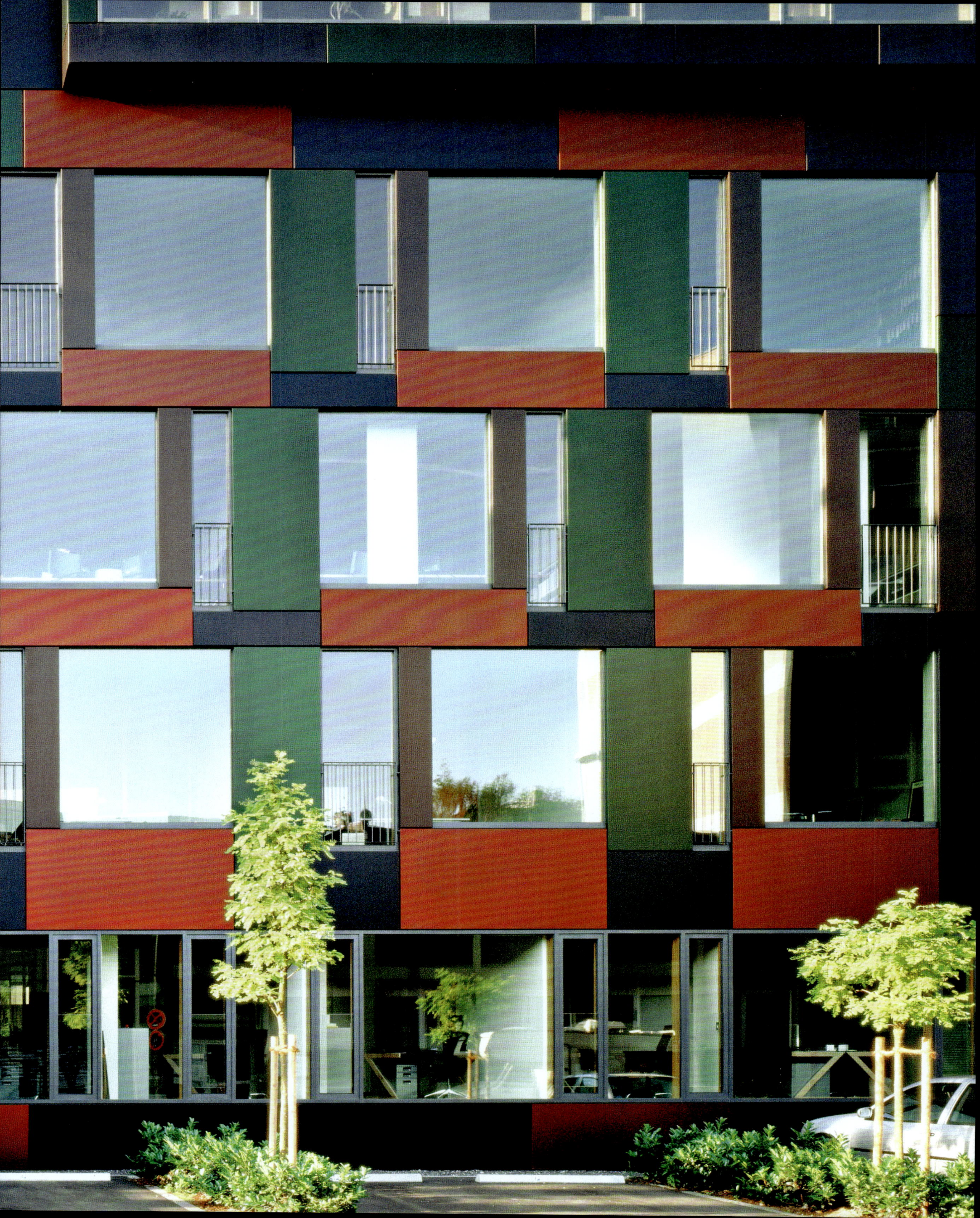

■ Third Floor Plan – Scale 1:400

1. Hall
2. Offices
3. Toilets
4. Lift
5. Garage Ramp
6. Restaurant
7. Meeting Room

■ Ground Floor Plan – Scale 1:400

North Elevation – Scale 1:400

Urban and architectural renewal has transformed Münster's canal-harbour into a typical post-industrial neighbourhood. The loft floor plan of the new buildings at numbers 14 and 16 have the same functional versatility as the warehouses that populated this area and the same expressive elevations looking south over the canal or north onto the street.

No. 14 is a sharply sculptured building. Large windows with flush mounted blinds and brick cladding create deliberately flat, linear surfaces. Inside, the loft layout does not constrain interior usage. The stairwell and lift shaft rise centrally on the north façade. Plant and services are grouped in a central column.

No. 16 has façades of different styles and a roof garden. The south-facing elevation overlooking the harbour is characterized by the horizontal lines of glass-fronted balconies running the full length of the building. The projecting fourth floor balcony adds a further horizontal note. The wide glazed surfaces are shielded by a series of modular louvres that create an intermediate space between inside and out.

The north, street-side elevation is a mosaic of glass squares – either fixed or operable – and anodized aluminium slabs whose muted colours change with the light. The flat façade is relieved by a box volume cantilevering out from the first floor to signpost and provide a protective canopy for the main entrance.

The box's glazed sides and fair-face concrete interior provide an ideal showcase for art installations. The 22-metre-deep building houses one or two units per floor, alternating enclosed cells and open spaces. Service boxes are fitted centrally against the walls of the short side.

The last two floors are occupied by the Bolles+Wilson practice. Walls and all ceilings, without cable ducts, are in fair-face concrete and offer uniform, reflecting surfaces for freestanding lighting. Partition walls are in frosted glass. A curved, acoustically insulated, wooden wall (made magnetic by a hidden metal undersheet) leads to the meeting room. The first four (splayed) steps of the stairs invite the visitor into a miniature architectural promenade.

The thermal insulation and deep floor plan are just two of the features that ensure minimal heat loss in winter and heat gain in summer. A cool water circulation system activates the building mass and regulates extreme summer temperatures.

In winter, the hot water heating system rarely has to kick in on account of the highly efficient thermal insulation.

South Elevation – Scale 1:400

■ XX Section – Scale 1:400

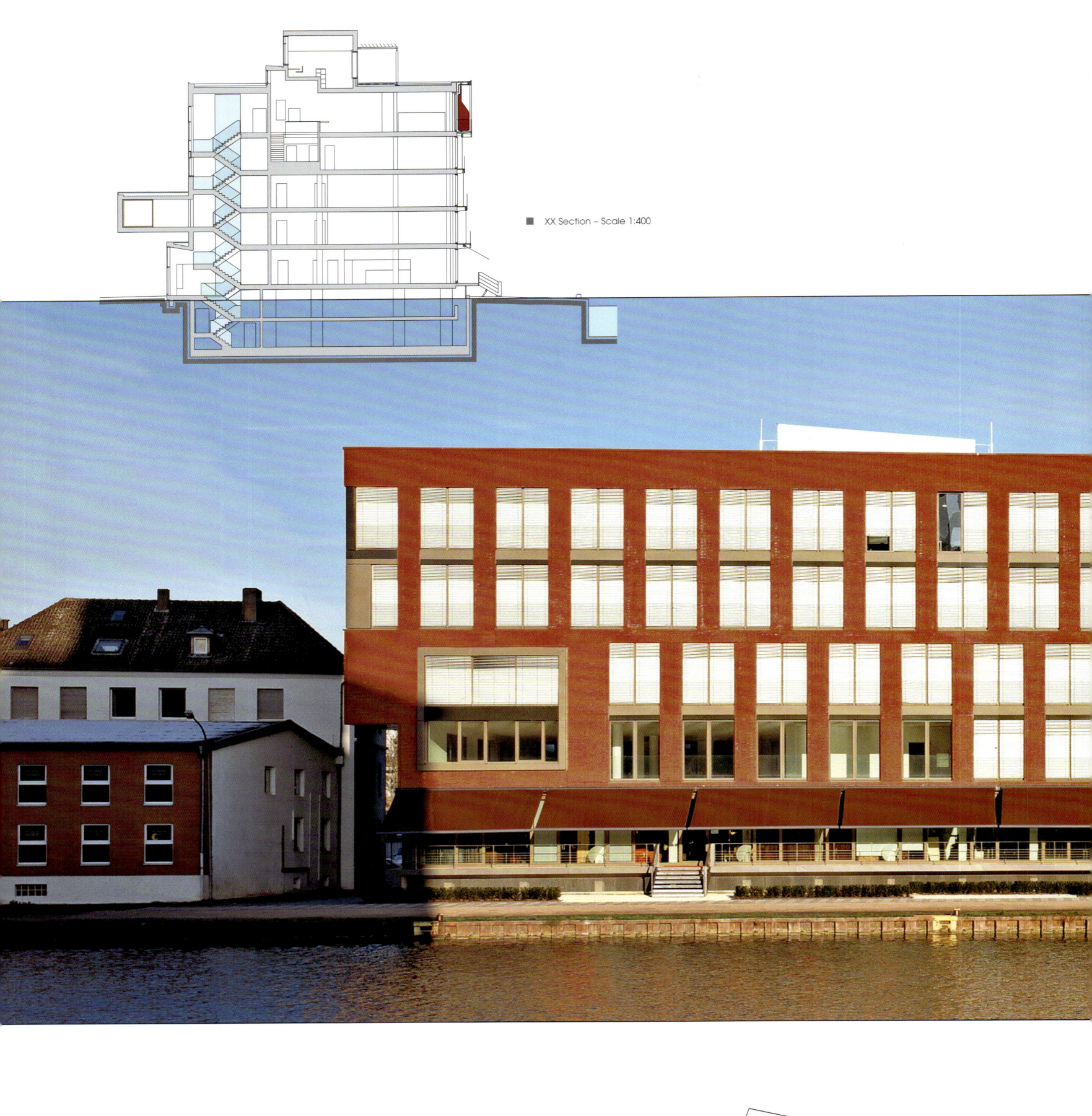

■ South Elevation – Scale 1:1000

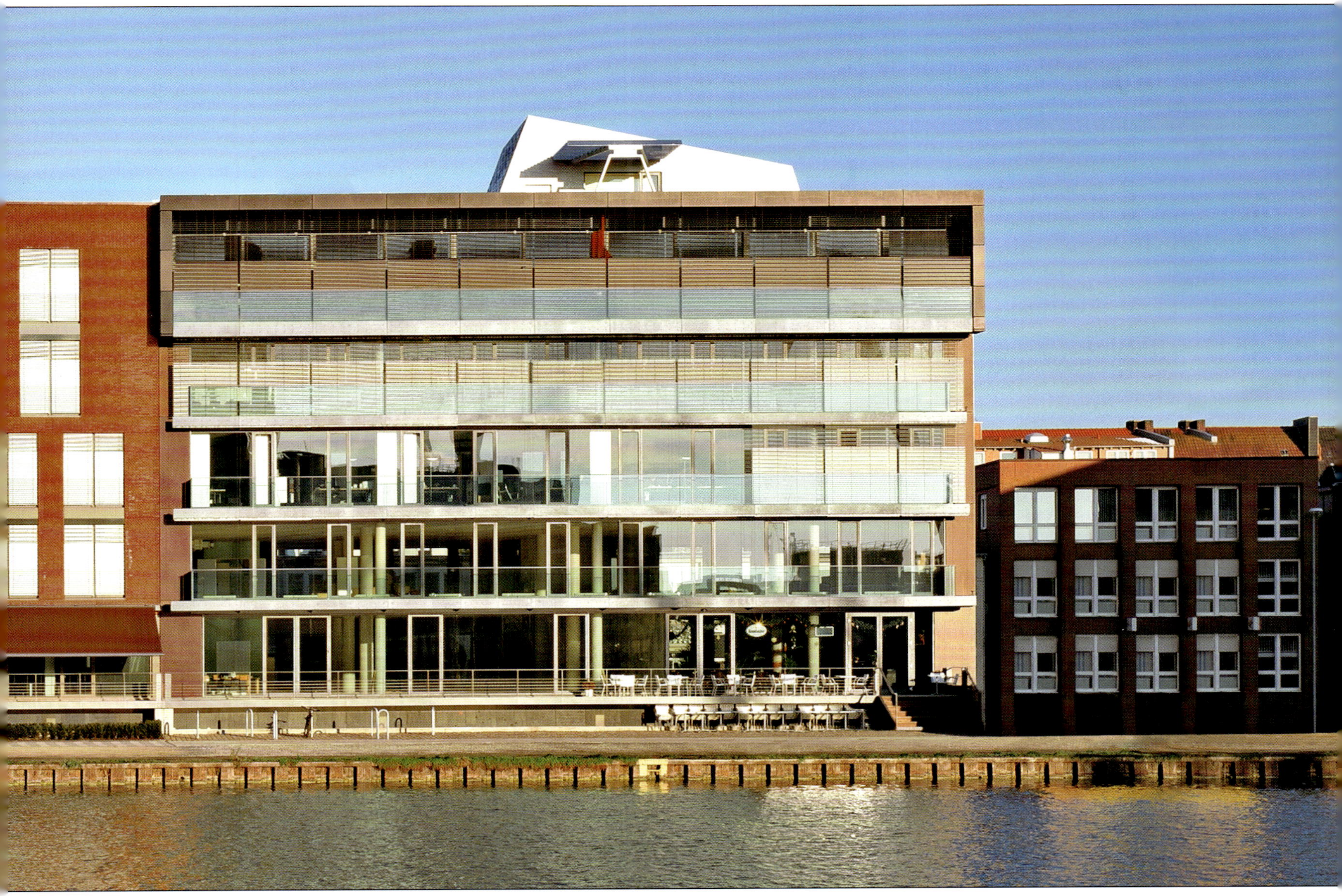

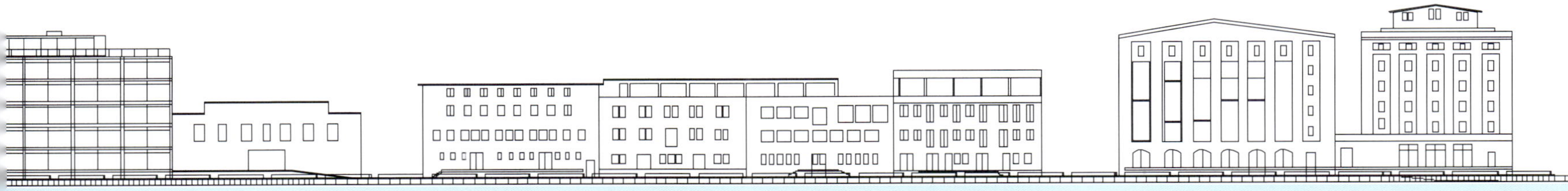

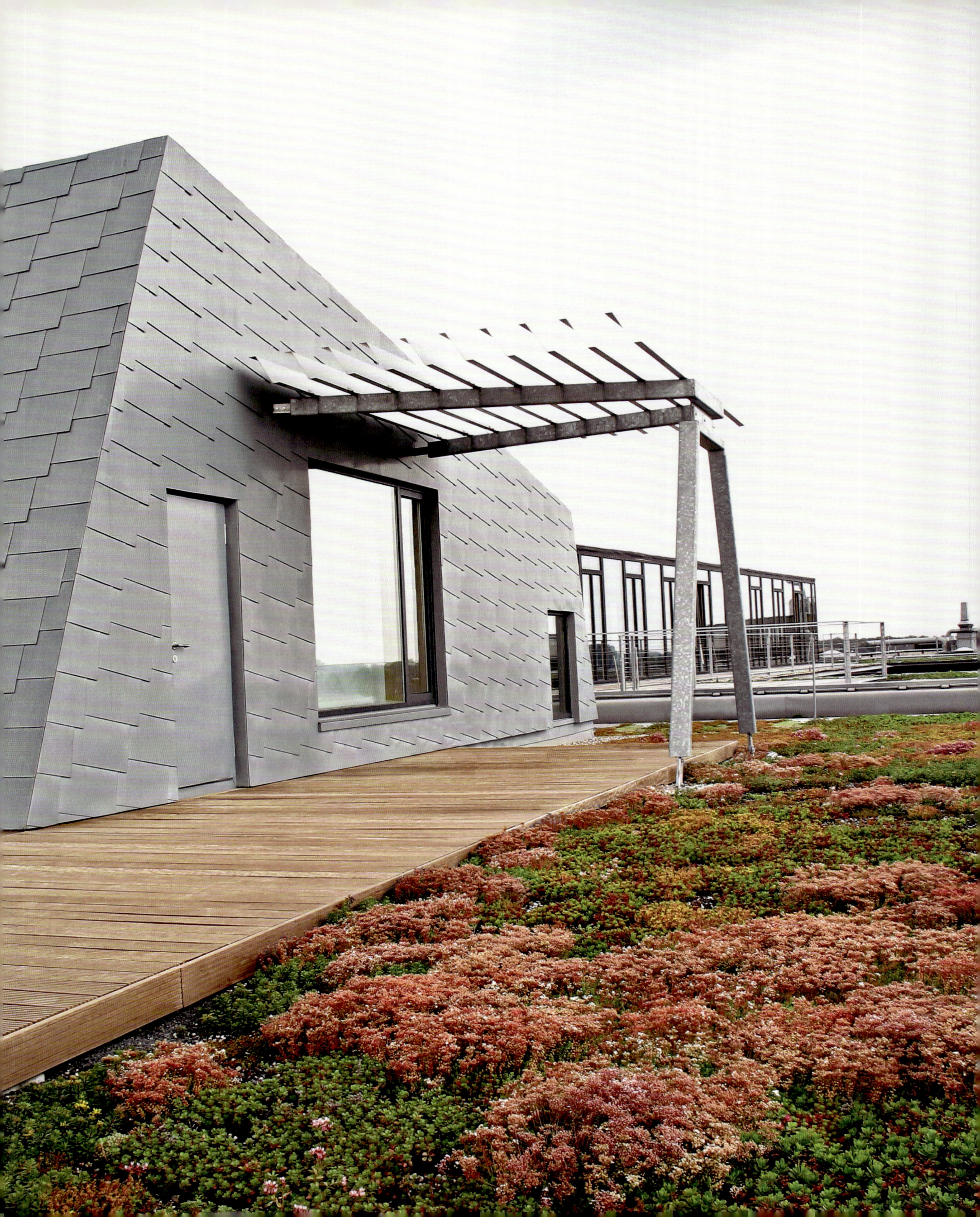

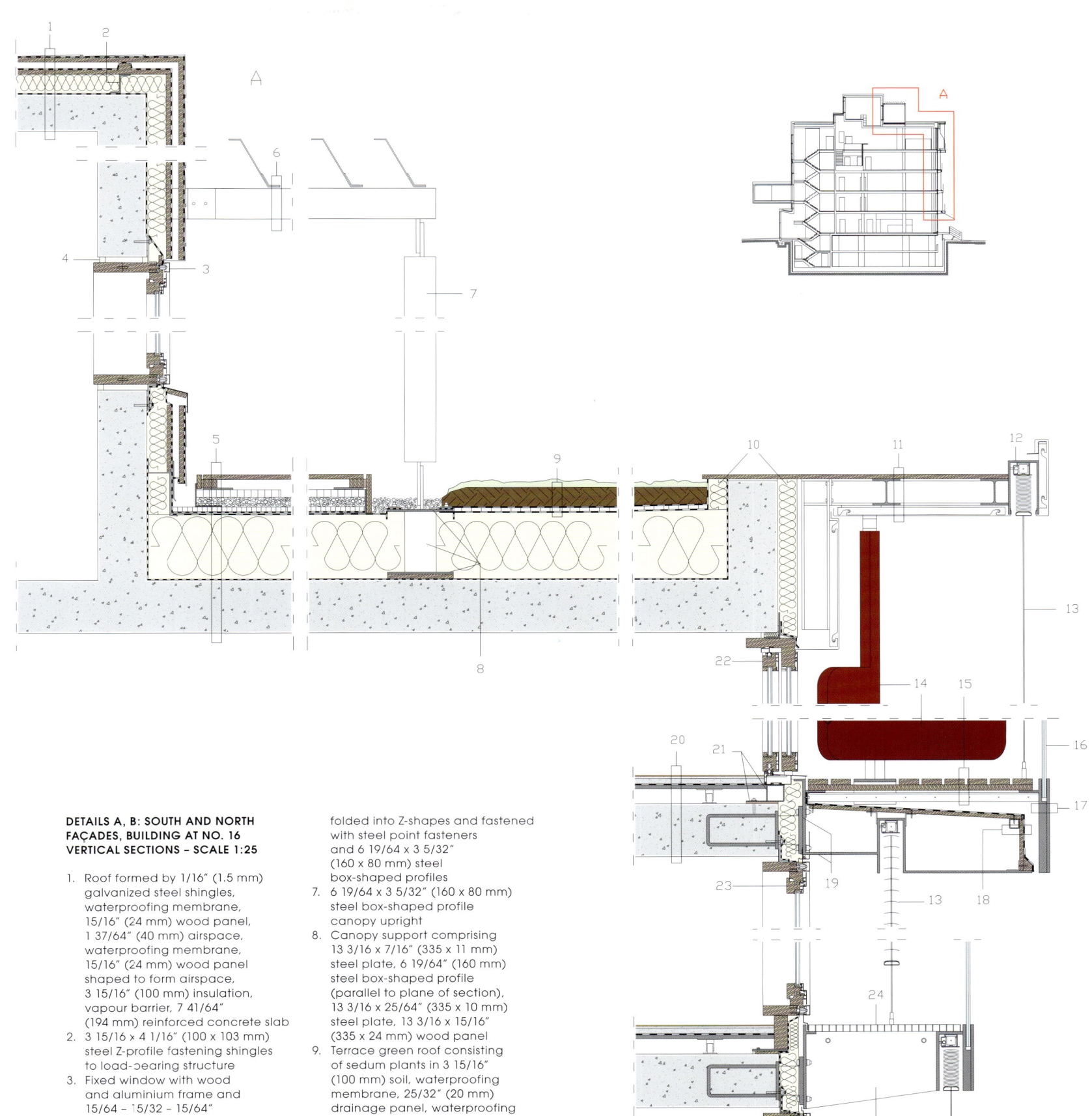

DETAILS A, B: SOUTH AND NORTH FAÇADES, BUILDING AT NO. 16 VERTICAL SECTIONS – SCALE 1:25

1. Roof formed by 1/16" (1.5 mm) galvanized steel shingles, waterproofing membrane, 15/16" (24 mm) wood panel, 1 37/64" (40 mm) airspace, waterproofing membrane, 15/16" (24 mm) wood panel shaped to form airspace, 3 15/16" (100 mm) insulation, vapour barrier, 7 41/64" (194 mm) reinforced concrete slab
2. 3 15/16 x 4 1/16" (100 x 103 mm) steel Z-profile fastening shingles to load-bearing structure
3. Fixed window with wood and aluminium frame and 15/64 – 15/32 – 15/64" (6 – 12 – 6 mm) double glazing
4. 1 3/16" (30 mm) thick silicone sealing acting as vapour barrier
5. Terrace roof comprising 63/64" (25 mm) wood decking with 2 3/4 x 1 49/64" (70 x 45 mm) wood joists, 5 29/32 x 25/64" (150 x 10 mm) steel plate, 4 23/32" (120 mm) double aluminium grille containing 1 31/32" (50 mm) ballast layer with 5 5/16 x 4 51/64" (135 x 122 mm) steel L-profile closure, double waterproofing membrane, 13 35/64" (344 mm) insulation, vapour barrier, 11 1/64" (280 mm) reinforced concrete slab
6. Canopy formed by series of 13/64" (5 mm) aluminium slats folded into Z-shapes and fastened with steel point fasteners and 6 19/64 x 3 5/32" (160 x 80 mm) steel box-shaped profiles
7. 6 19/64 x 3 5/32" (160 x 80 mm) steel box-shaped profile canopy upright
8. Canopy support comprising 13 3/16 x 7/16" (335 x 11 mm) steel plate, 6 19/64" (160 mm) steel box-shaped profile (parallel to plane of section), 13 3/16 x 25/64" (335 x 10 mm) steel plate, 13 3/16 x 15/16" (335 x 24 mm) wood panel
9. Terrace green roof consisting of sedum plants in 3 15/16" (100 mm) soil, waterproofing membrane, 25/32" (20 mm) drainage panel, waterproofing membrane
10. 3 15/16" (100 mm) thick board insulation
11. 29/32" (23 mm) wood roof, frame of HEA 140 steel beams supporting projecting volume, 25/64" (10 mm) airspace, 1/16" (1.5 mm) anodized sheet aluminium cladding with hidden steel fastening system
12. 11 7/64 x 6 7/64" (282 x 155 mm) steel C-profile supporting sliding sunblinds
13. Aluminium sliding sunblinds with retraction system and 13/64" (5 mm) Ø metal cable guide
14. Divider made of steel box-shaped profiles with

027 / Bolles+Wilson

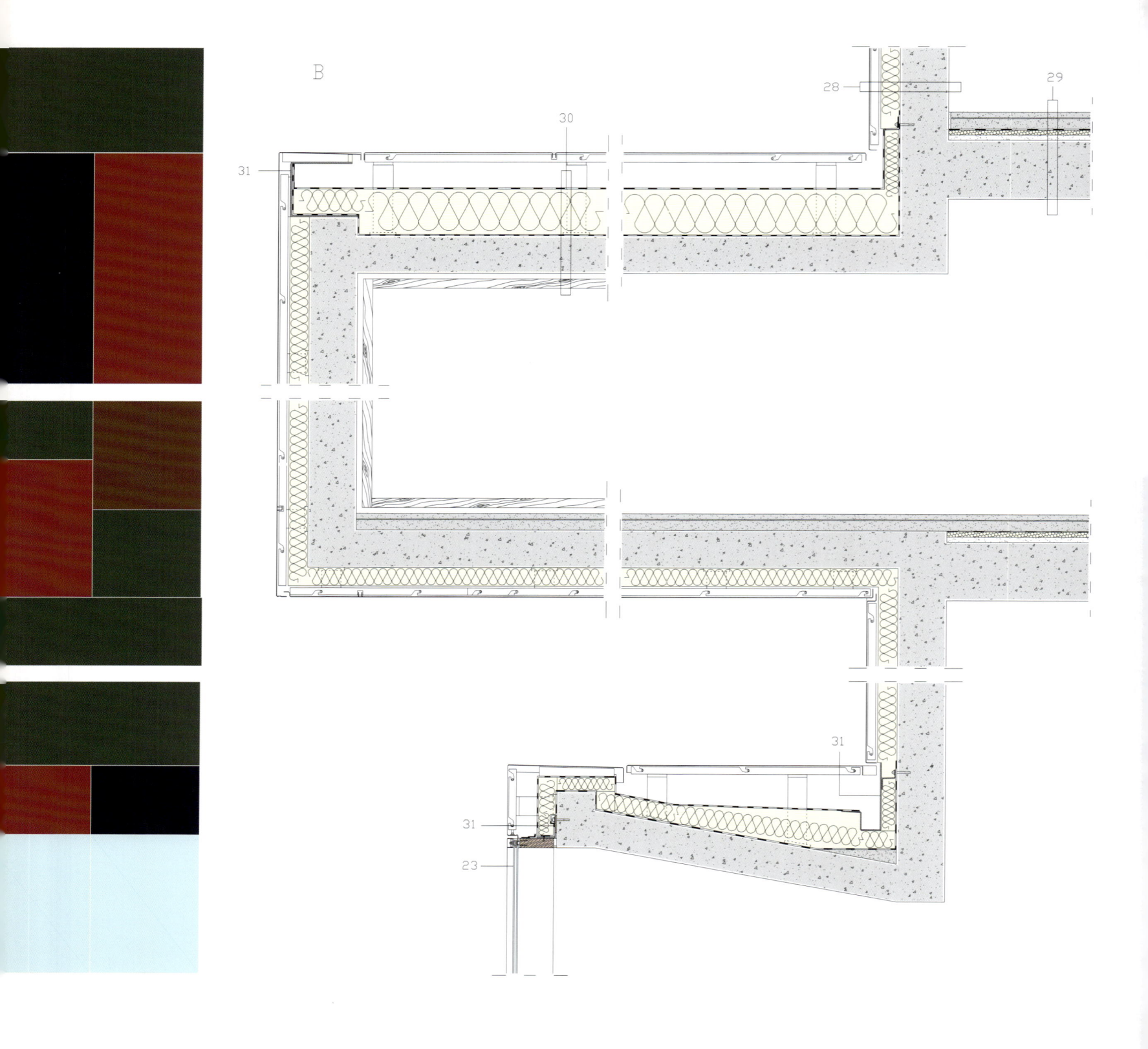

two-tone sheet metal finish
15. 3 15/16 x 1 3/16" (100 x 30 mm) wood decking, 1 3/16" (30 mm) wood joists, 33/64" (13 mm) airspace, 1 57/64" (48 mm) steel T-profile support
16. 25/32" (20 mm) thick laminated glass balustrade
17. 19/32" (15 mm) steel plate finish and steel profile supporting balustrade
18. 1 31/32 x 1 31/32" (50 x 50 mm) steel box-shaped profile, 25/32" (20 mm) wood panel, waterproofing membrane
19. Shaped steel plates anchoring exterior projecting volume to slab
20. 13/64" (5 mm) carpeting, 25/64" (10 mm) layer of glue, 1 29/64" (37 mm) anhydride screed, waterproof PE film, 45/64" (18 mm) load-bearing steel plate with steel supports, 3 5/32" (80 mm) airspace for acoustic insulation, 11 1/64" (280 mm) reinforced concrete slab
21. 3 35/64 x 3 35/64" (90 x 90 mm) steel box-shaped profile and 11/64" (4.5 mm) steel plate connecting window door frame to slab
22. Sliding window door with wood and aluminium frame and 15/64 – 15/32 – 15/64" (6 – 12 – 6 mm) double glazing
23. Fixed window with wood and aluminium frame and 15/64 – 15/32 – 15/64" (6 – 12 – 6 mm) double glazing
24. 1 3/8" (35 mm) thick galvanized steel grille
25. Steel bracket supporting balcony anchored by steel plates to load-bearing structure
26. Roller blind and tube fixed to balcony
27. 8 21/32 x 3 15/16" (220 x 100 mm) steel box-shaped profiles and 10 15/64 x 25/64" (260 x 10 mm) steel plate supporting roller blind tube
28. 1/16" (1.5 mm) multicoloured anodized aluminium façade cladding with hidden steel fasteners, 3 15/16" (100 mm) board insulation, 63/64" (25 mm) reinforced concrete structure
29. 1 3/16" (30 mm) concrete panel flooring, 13/64" (5 mm) mortar layer, 2 11/64" (55 mm) concrete screed, waterproof PE film, 1 3/16" (30 mm) acoustic insulation, 1 3/16" (30 mm) layer filling of rigid expanded polystyrene, 12 21/64" (313 mm) reinforced concrete slab
30. Roof cladding support comprising 4 3/32 x 4 3/32" (104 x 104 mm) steel box-shaped profile joists, 5 19/32" (142 mm) airspace, waterproofing membrane, 9 27/32" (250 mm) insulation, vapour barrier, 7 7/8" (200 mm) reinforced concrete slab, wood fixed window frame
31. Steel profiles of various sizes connecting cladding to load-bearing structure

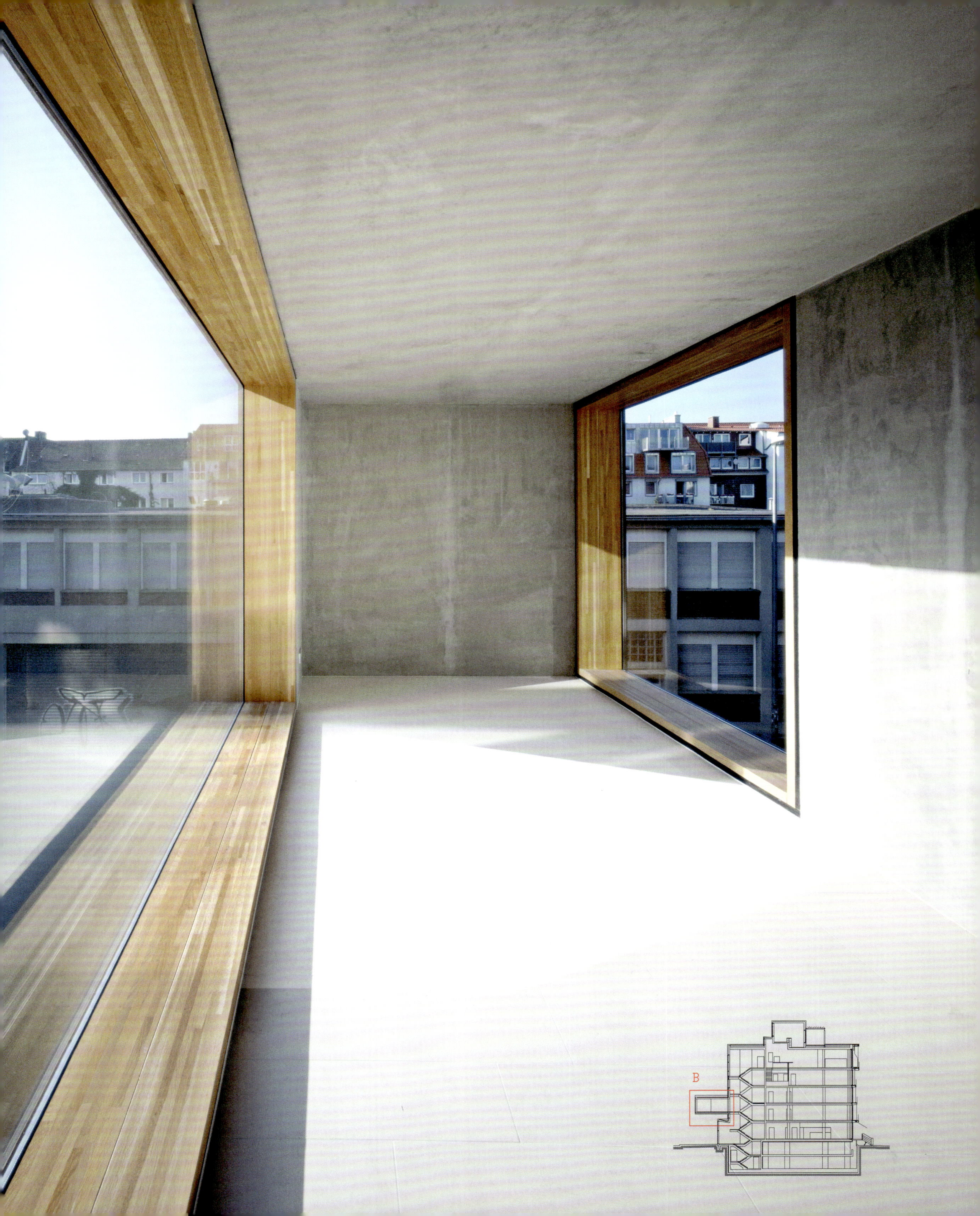
B

krukenkamp am kai

DETAIL C: NORTH FAÇADE, BUILDING AT NO. 14
VERTICAL SECTION - SCALE 1:25

1. Parapet comprising 1 3/8" (35 mm) solid bricks, 3 5/32" (80 mm) pre-cast concrete panel, 3 35/64" (90 mm) airspace, waterproofing membrane, 3 15/16" (100 mm) board insulation, vapour barrier, 9 27/32" (250 mm) reinforced concrete structure, vapour barrier, 25/64" (10 mm) board insulation, waterproofing membrane, 1 3/16" (30 mm) airspace, 13/64" (5 mm) sheet aluminium flashing
2. Steel support for aluminium flashing, waterproofing membrane, 1 3/16" (30 mm) thick double wood panel
3. 3 15/16" (100 mm) ballast layer, 63/64" (25 mm) Zinco Floradrain drainage panel, Sarnafil film, 8 37/64" (218 mm) insulation on slope for drainage, vapour barrier, 9 27/32" (250 mm) reinforced concrete slab
4. Steel L-profiles of different sizes fastening cladding system to load-bearing structure
5. 15/64" (6 mm) thick glass parapet
6. 1/16" (1.5 mm) aluminium flashing
7. Heating system radiator
8. 1/16" (1.5 mm) thick profiled sheet aluminium sill
9. 1 31/32" (50 mm) ballast layer, 63/64" (25 mm) Zinco Floradrain drainage panel, Sarnafil film, 10 15/64" (260 mm) max. insulation on slope for drainage, vapour barrier, 11 1/64" (280 mm) reinforced concrete slab, 3 15/16" (100 mm) board insulation
10. Cladding in 4 17/32" (115 mm) solid brick with supporting 3 5/32 x 8 5/64" (80 x 205 mm) concrete flange
11. 1/16" (1.5 mm) anodized sheet aluminium cladding with hidden steel fasteners
12. 2 23/64 x 13/64" (60 x 5 mm) steel plate and 11 39/64 x 4 13/32" (295 x 112 mm) and 3 15/16 x 2 23/64" (100 x 60 mm) coupled steel L-profiles fastening cladding to load-bearing structure
13. Continuous glazed façade with aluminium frame and 15/64 – 15/32 – 15/64" (6 – 12 – 6 mm) double glazing
14. Coupled 8 15/64 x 3 1/32" (209 x 77 mm) steel L-profile and 3 15/32 x 3/8" (88 x 9.5 mm) steel plate connecting glazed façade frame to ground slab
15. Earth, 3 15/16" (100 mm) board insulation, vapour barrier, 11 13/16" (300 mm) reinforced concrete structure, 1 31/32" (50 mm) board insulation, earth
16. 6 19/64 x 4 23/32" (160 x 120 mm) rainwater drain
17. 1 31/32" (50 mm) thick concrete pavement

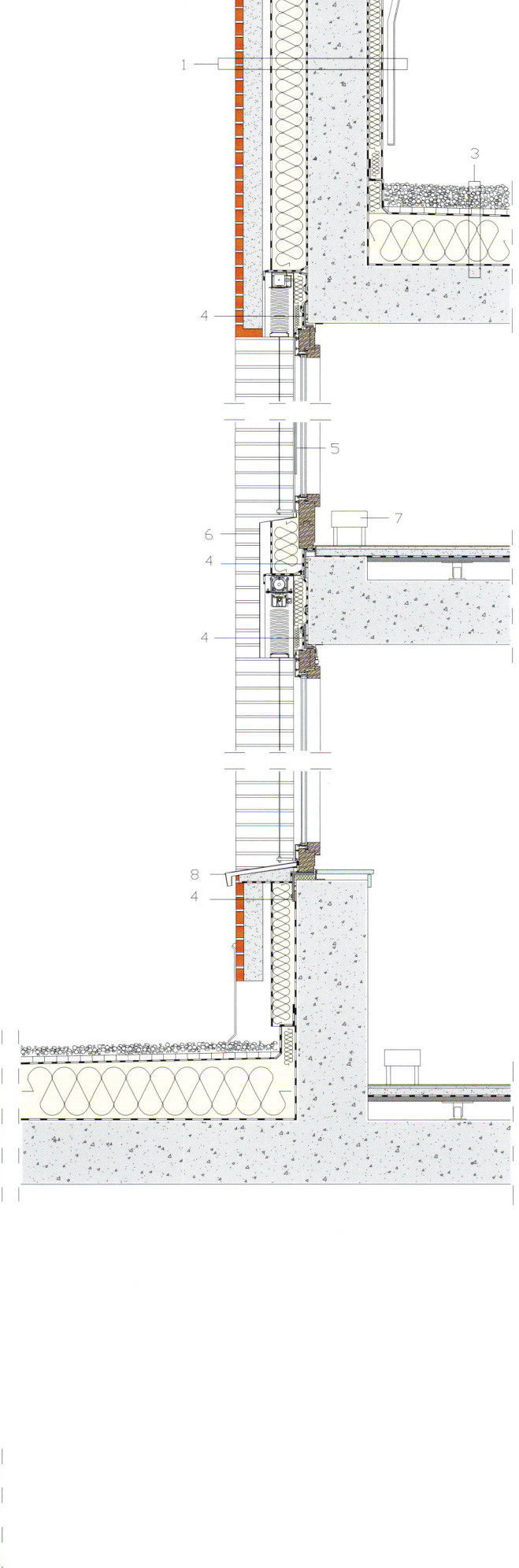

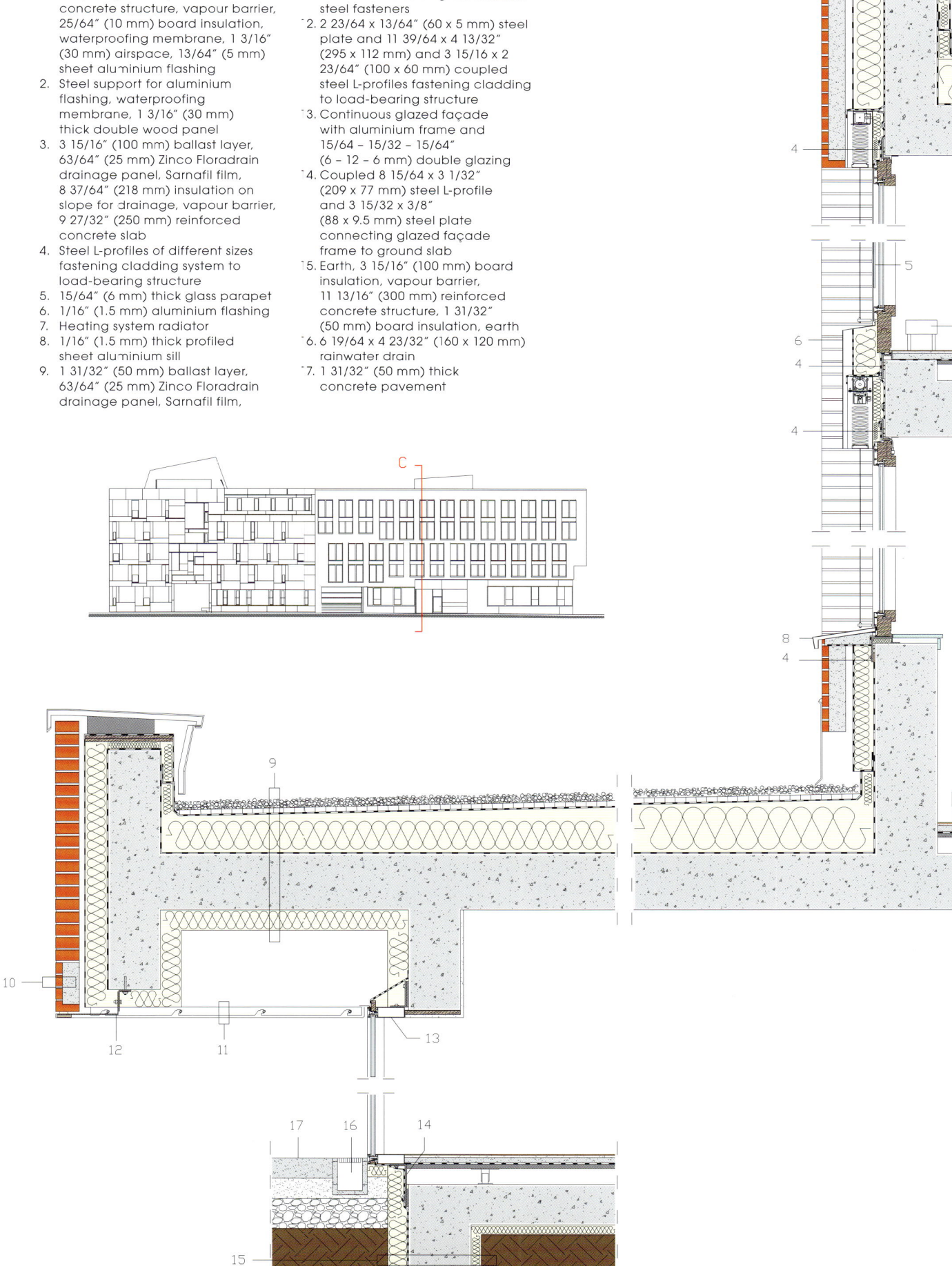

Bolles+Wilson

CONDOMINIUM TRNOVSKI PRISTAN
LJUBLJANA, SLOVENIA

SADAR VUGA ARHITEKTI

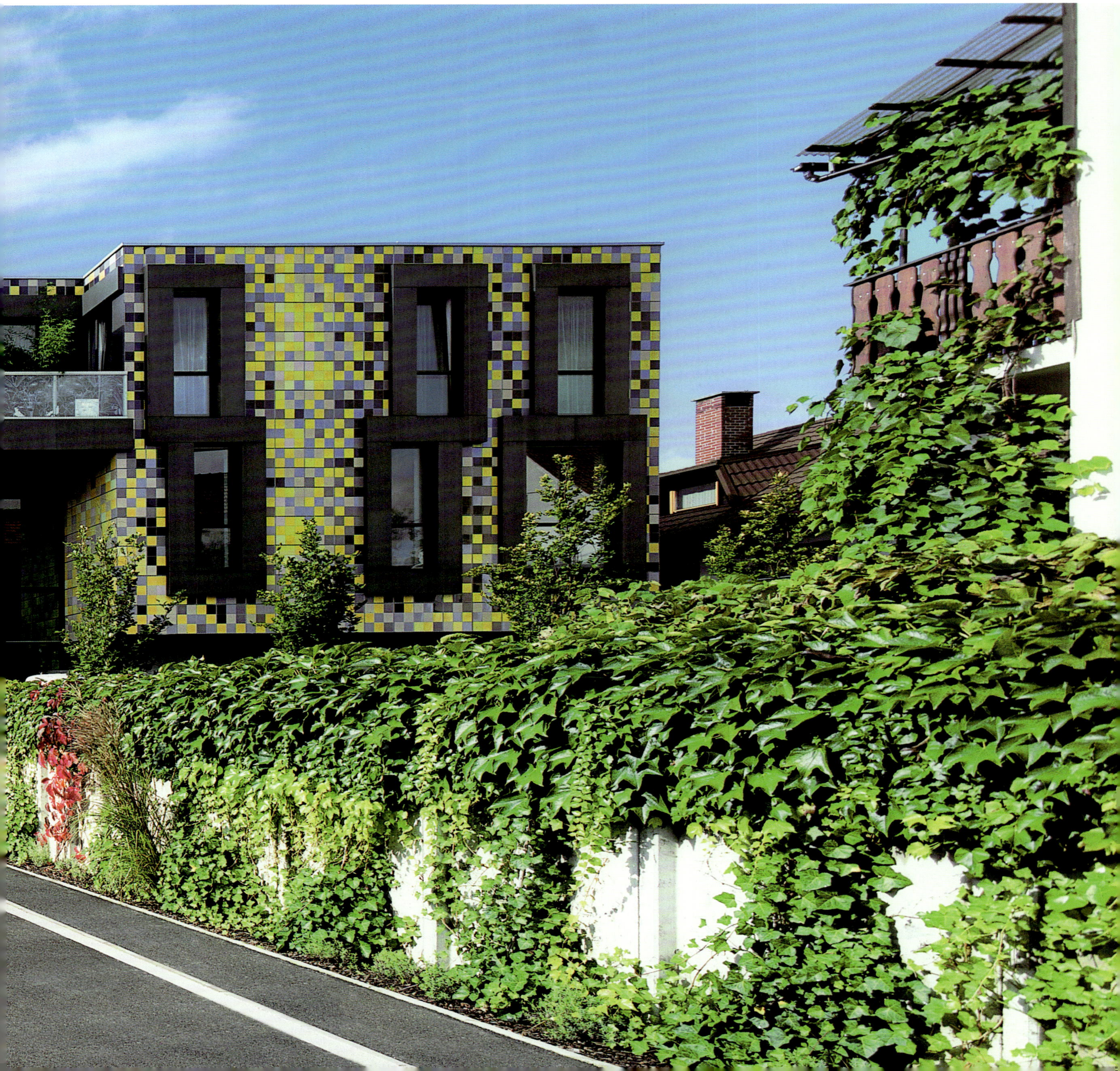

The Trnovski Pristan apartment building in Ljubljana, Slovenia, is sited near the Ljubljanica river amidst luxuriant vegetation. Comprising fifteen apartments of differing typologies, the building is a dynamic series of irregular, segmented volumes. Irregularity of shape is heightened by the apparently random array of large garden-balconies. The underlying architectural programme is to create a symbiotic link between this striking volume and its internal and external environments.

To do this, young architects Sadar Vuga have created huge, "blown-up" windows, jutting balconies and communal transition areas like the atrium and winter garden. Stylized natural forms decorate the glazed façade and parapets, while the communal garden interconnects with the private space of the balconies. The interconnection continues into the apartments themselves.

Typically, Sadar Vuga have discarded conventional technical, topological and typological definitions in favour of explicit architectural "formulae" to express their conceptual purpose. The outsized windows with their black metal frames define space and disrupt volumetric proportions, seemingly placing the structural frame over, and not under, the whole building.

The multi-coloured, "pixelated", ceramic mosaic cladding of the façade lends a further dynamic quality to the architecture. The brighter (yellow) "pixels" blend with the "natural pixels" of the leaves on trees in the garden and along the path. Façade colours have been carefully graduated, with black shades closest to the dark window frames. During the day when the glass darkens on exposure to sunlight, the black wall softens the stark shapes of the dark window frames.

■ Site Plan – Scale 1:2000

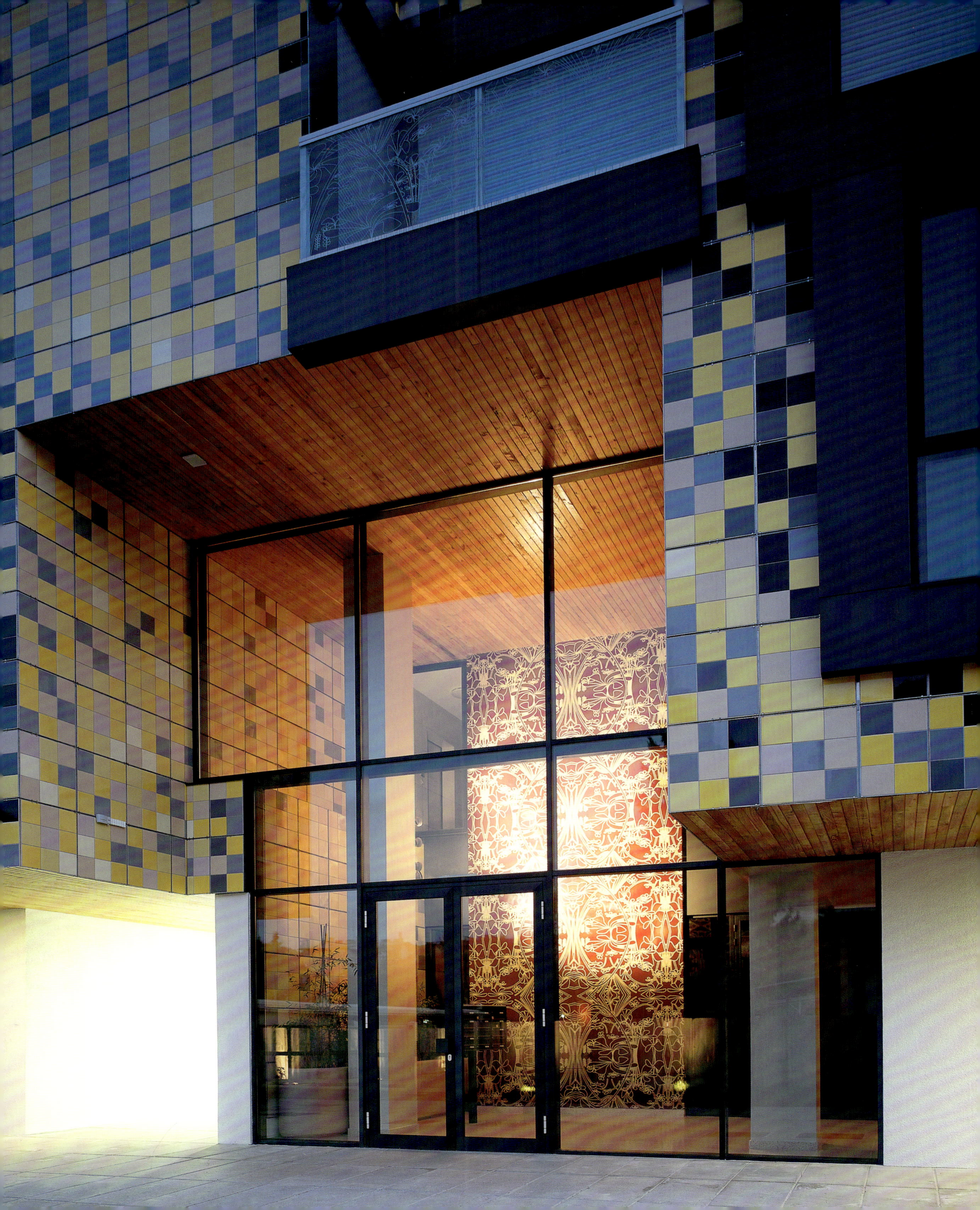

036 / Trnovski Pristan

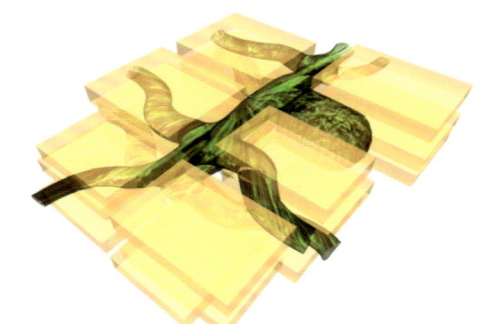

■ Design Schemes for Space Distribution

■ Wall Tile Colour Arrangement: Study

037 / Sadar Vuga

South-West Perspective

North-West Perspective

038 / Trnovski Pristan

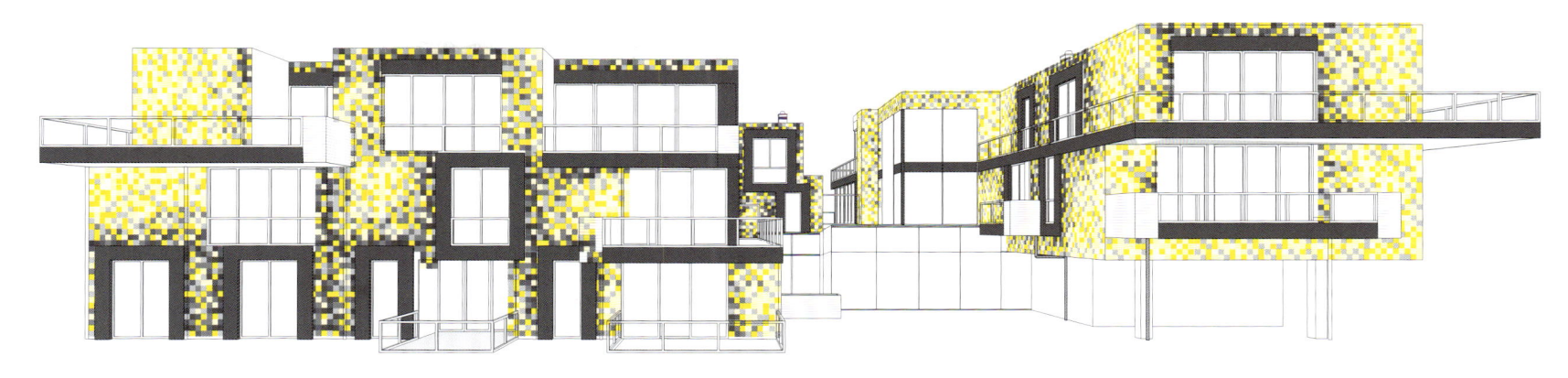

■ South-East Perspective

■ North-East Perspective

■ Ground Floor Plan - Scale 1:300

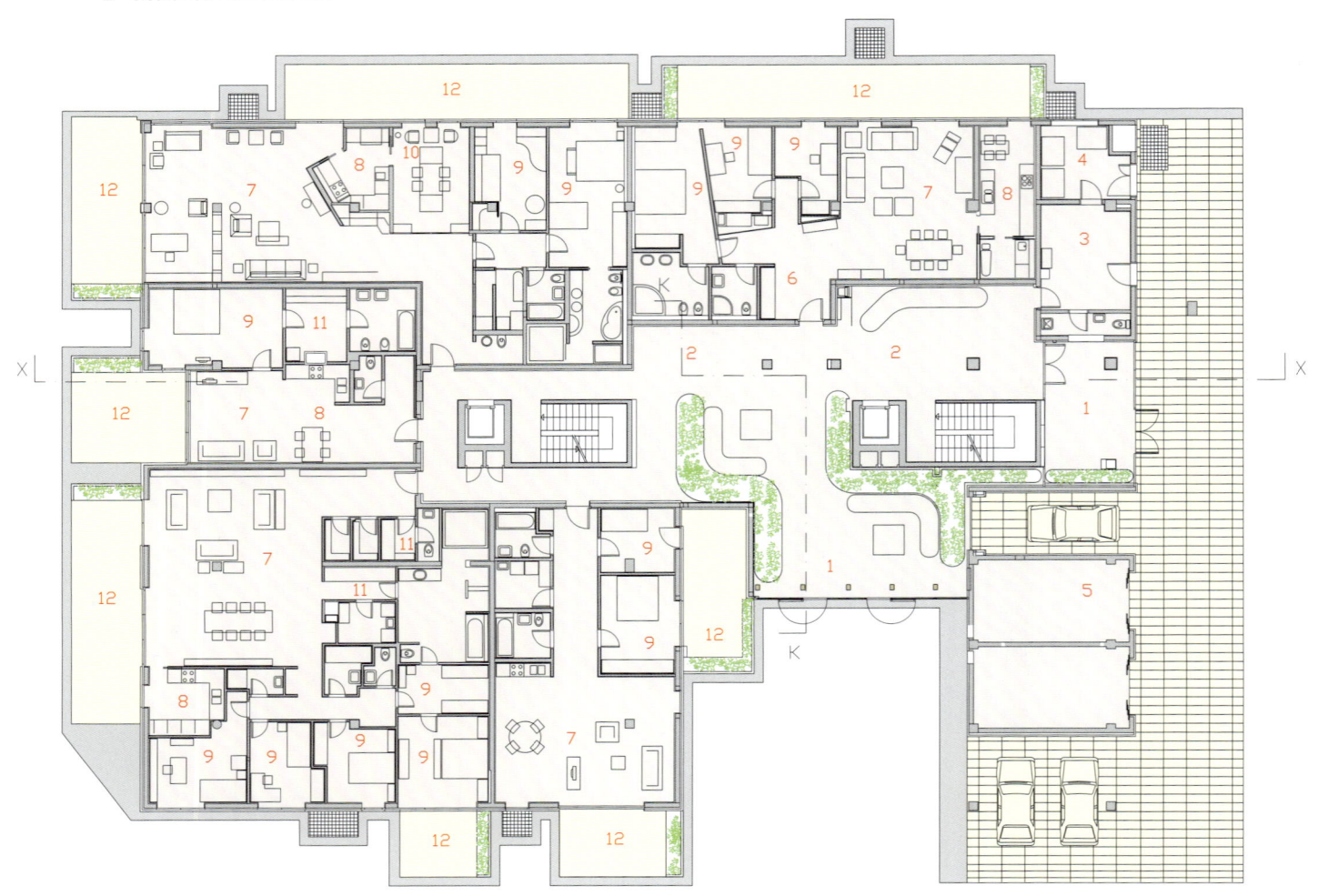

1. Lobby
2. Winter garden
3. Storage
4. Plant room
5. Garage
6. Entrance
7. Living room
8. Kitchen
9. Bedroom
10. Dining room
11. Wardrobe
12. Terrace
13. Study

■ XX Longitudinal Section - Scale 1:300

■ First Floor Plan – Scale 1:300

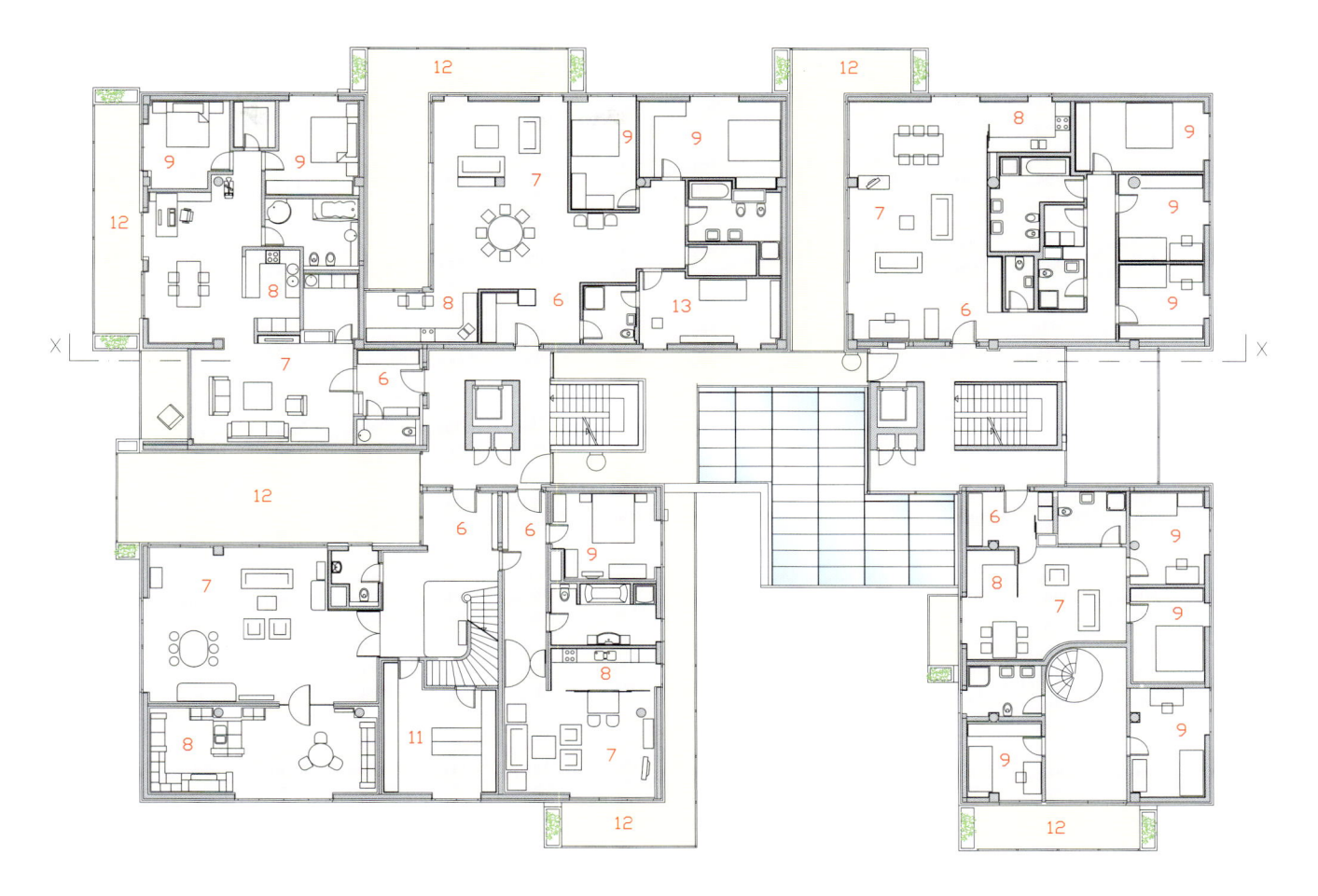

■ Second Floor Plan – Scale 1:300

041 / Sadar Vuga

**DETAIL A: EXTERNAL FAÇADE
VERTICAL SECTION – SCALE 1:20**

1. Metal flashing
2. Wood supporting flashing
3. Ceramic tile cladding on aluminium plate support, frame in steel C-profiles, 3 5/32" (80 mm) insulation, 7 7/8" (200 mm) reinforced concrete structure, waterproofing membrane, 3 11/32" (85 mm) insulation, 25/32" (20 mm) teak panel
4. Steel plate for fixing cladding to structure
5. Black metal cornice
6. Motorized roller blind
7. Schüco Aluminium frame with 5/32 – 5/8 – 5/32" (4 – 16 – 4 mm) double glazing
8. Flooring formed by ceramic tiles, layer of glue, screed on 1% slope, double waterproofing membrane, 3 15/16" (100 mm) polystyrene thermal insulation, waterproofing asphalt membrane, 11 1/64" (280 mm) reinforced concrete slab
9. False ceiling formed by double 63/64" (25 mm) gypsum board panels on framework of steel omega profiles
10. Glass parapet
11. Frame in box-shaped profiles supporting parapet
12. Stainless steel rainwater drain
13. Steel filtering grille
14. Pavement formed by ceramic tiles, layer of glue, screed on 1% slope, 1 3/16" (30 mm) insulation, double waterproofing membrane, 9 21/32" (245 mm) reinforced concrete slab, 2 3/4" (70 mm) insulation, 1 3/16" (30 mm) acacia panel
15. Steel L-profile supporting window frame
16. Radiant tube heating system
17. Parquet flooring, layer of glue, 1 31/32" (50 mm) screed, 3 5/32" (80 mm) polystyrene thermal insulation, 9 27/32 – 11 13/16" (250 – 300 mm) reinforced concrete slab
18. 3 15/16" (100 mm) thick insulation
19. Ceramic tile cladding on aluminium plate support, frame in steel C-profiles, 2 3/4" (70 mm) insulation, reinforced concrete beam
20. 1 3/16" (30 mm) thick acacia finishing panel

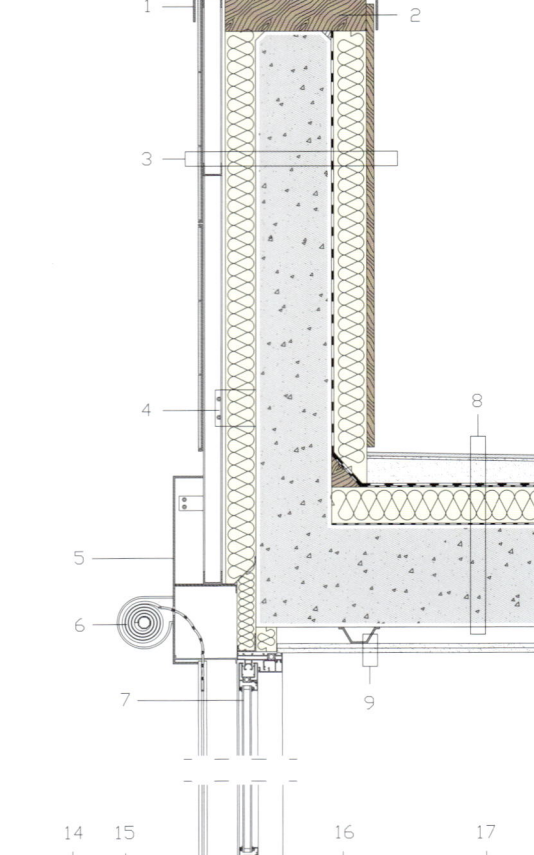

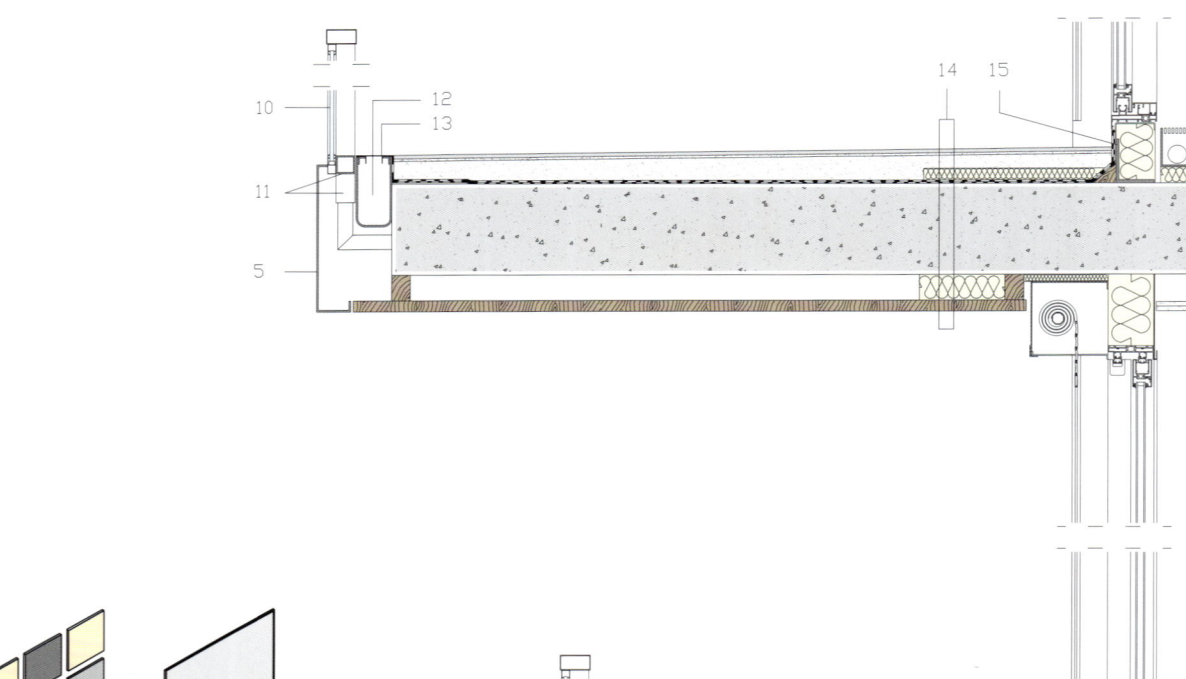

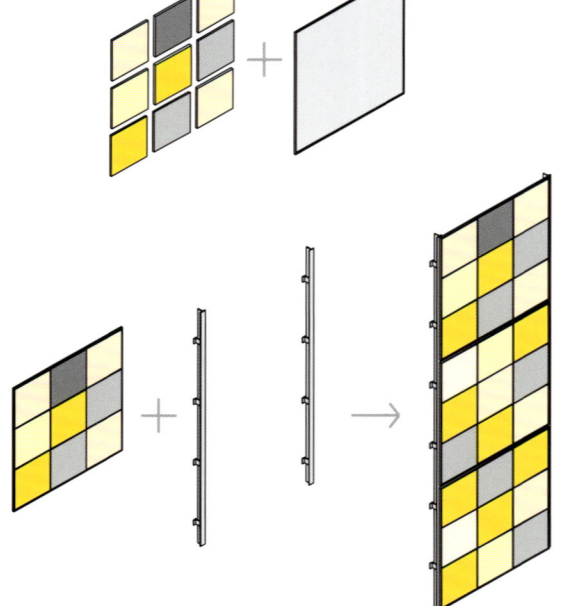

■ Façade Panel Construction Layout

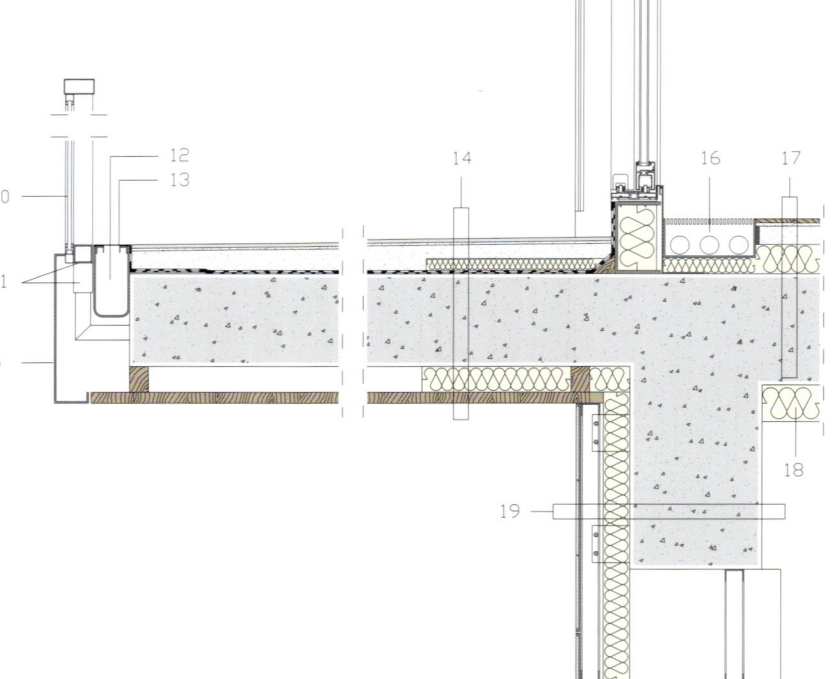

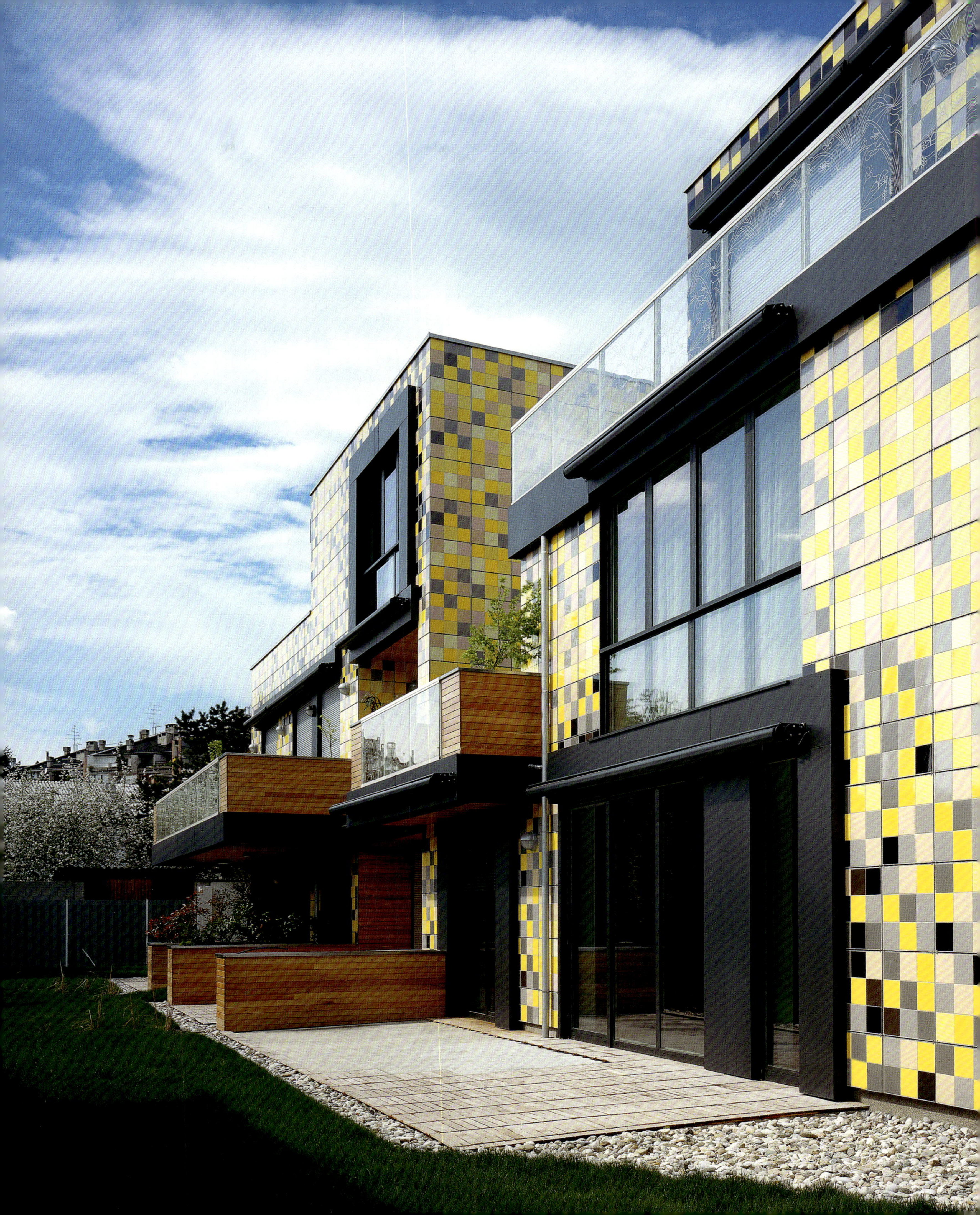

"ELS COLORS" NURSERY SCHOOL
BARCELONA, SPAIN

RCR ARANDA PIGEM VILALTA ARQUITECTES

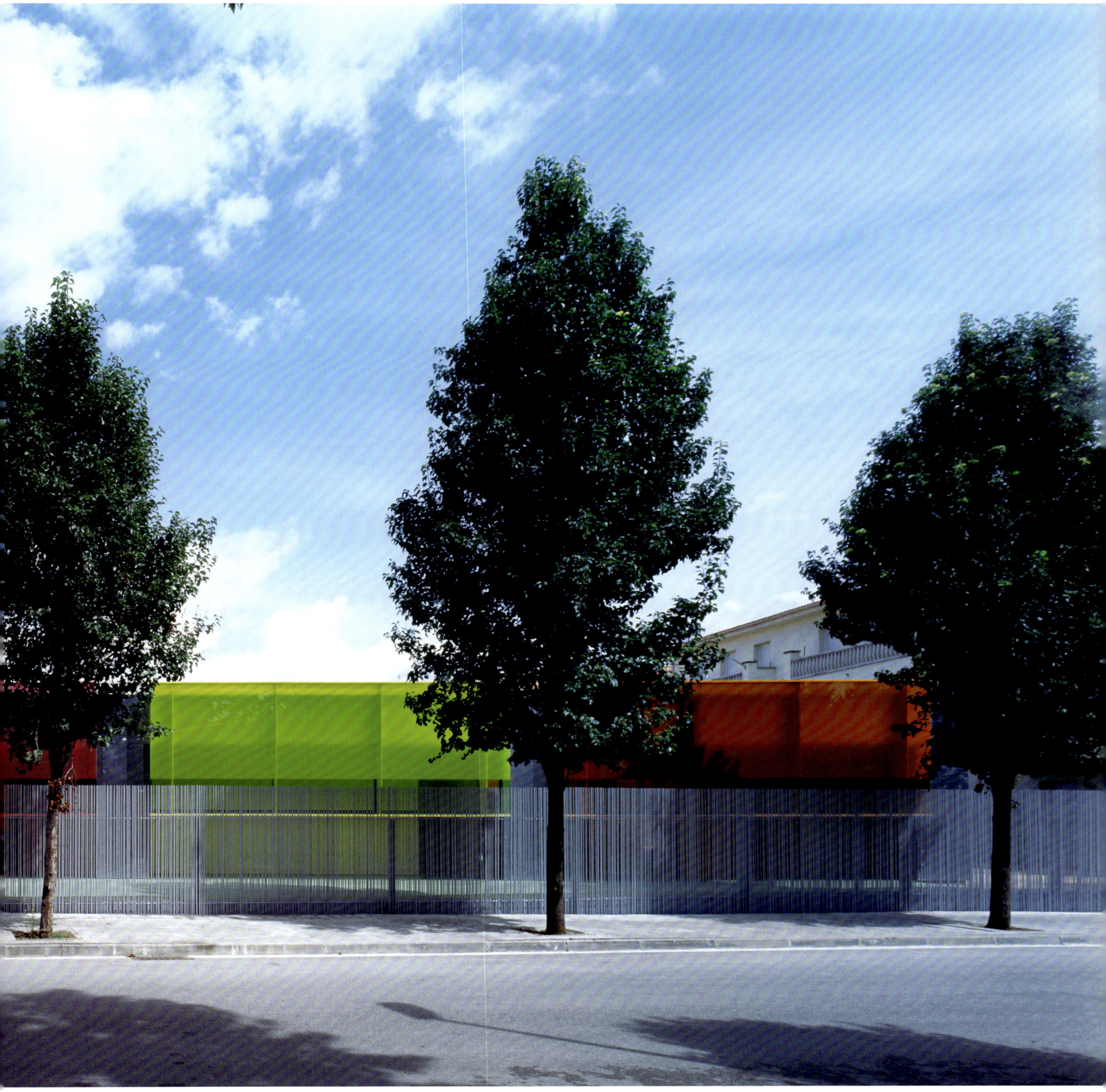

The architecture of the nursery school in Manlleu is one of straight lines. Two long, low blocks are linked by a third transverse element to create an enclosed outdoor space. The multi-purpose connecting structure is the core of the whole complex. As well as containing the entrance atrium, a staircase to the upper level, and an open, covered walkway between the two blocks, it formally separates the "classrooms" – divided according to the needs of the various age groups – from the collective areas, services, kitchen, storeroom, laundry and bathrooms. Throughout, the brilliant colours – yellow/green, orange, red and blue – of the façade cladding and glazing highlight the juxtaposition of volumes. The overall effect is of an architectural ensemble that appears more complex than it really is, an interesting reflection on RCR's projects.

The main entrance is located on the side of one of the longitudinal buildings in line with the connecting block. It is marked out by a massive canopy extending from the floorslab. A bold orange wall anchored to the end of the canopy creates a protected enclosure. The sequence of rooms for babies up to one year is accessed from a side corridor, while the areas for the 1–2 and 2–3 year olds are set on either side of a central corridor.

Directly above the main entrance and atrium, a box-shaped upper floor houses the staff common room and director's office. The complex is fenced off by an elegant metal grille whose closely set vertical members provide protection but do not block the view to the outside. Similarly, the glazed curtain walling does away with closed interiors. This, together with the colour scheme and the alternation of transparent and opaque surfaces, is designed to enhance the youngsters' perception of complex spatial, and interpersonal, relationships.

The structural frame is a mix of vertical steel elements and concrete floorslabs. The façades are partly clad in zinc galvanized metal sheets in deliberate contrast to the coloured glazing. At night, these opaque sections make the intense sequence of coloured glass even more striking.

False ceilings and partition walls are in plasterboard. Inside, the linoleum flooring is the same shade of green throughout, while outside, synthetic carpeting creates the same visual continuity on the horizontal as the curtain walling does on the vertical.

Areas with high moisture content, like the kitchen and bathrooms, have been waterproofed with a layer of PVC.

Ground Floor Plan – Scale 1:250

1. Entrance Portico
2. Atrium
3. Storeroom
4. Kitchen
5. Dormitory
6. Storeroom for Teaching Material
7. Bathrooms
8. Multipurpose Room
9. Veranda
10. Classrooms

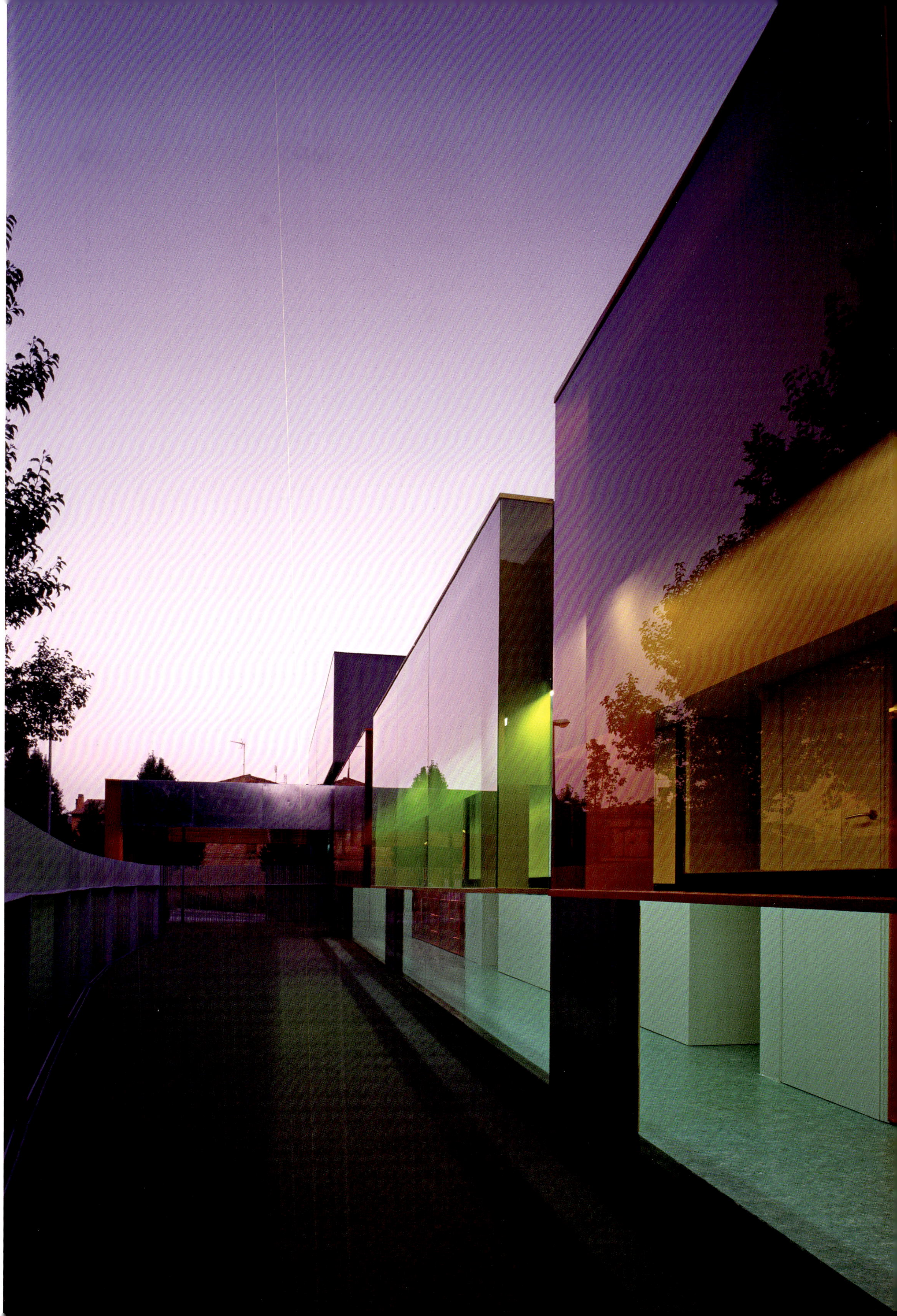

South-West Elevation – Scale 1:200

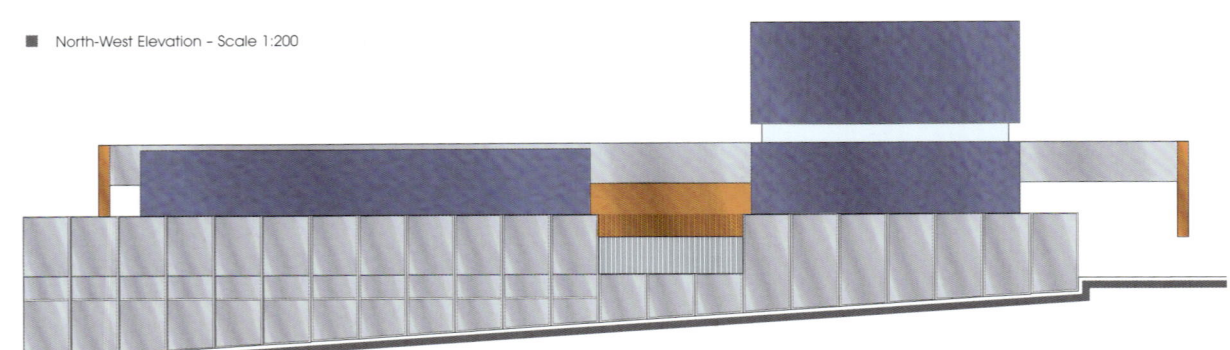

North-West Elevation – Scale 1:200

048 / "Els Colors"

■ XX Cross Section – Scale 1:200

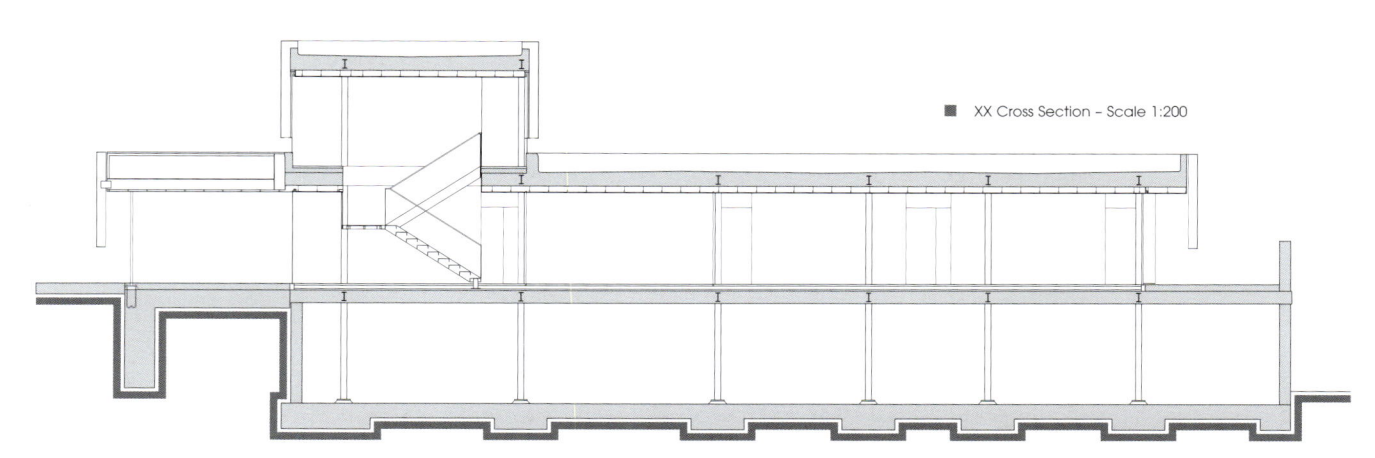

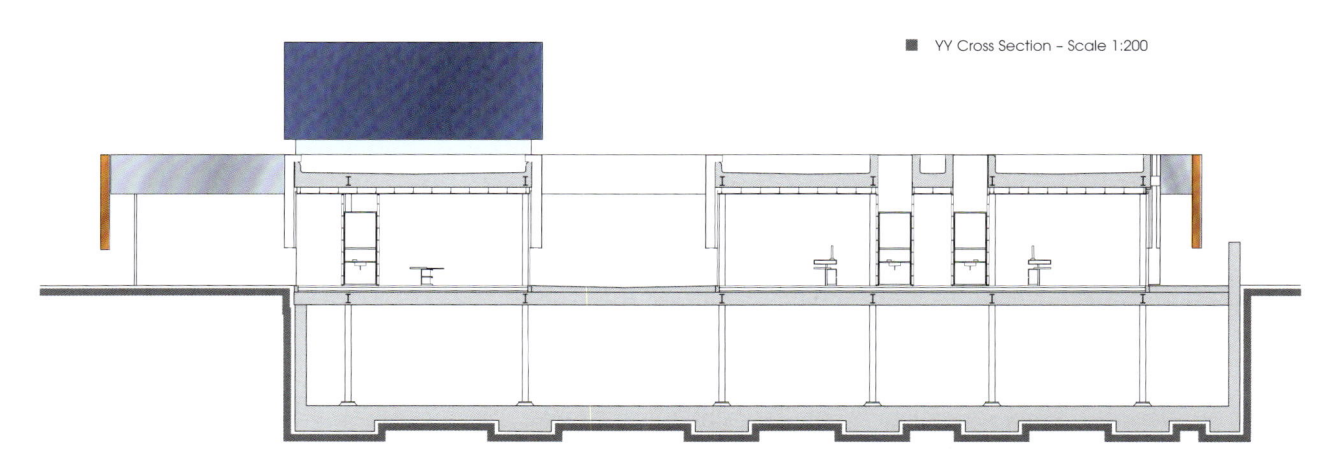

■ YY Cross Section – Scale 1:200

049 / RCR

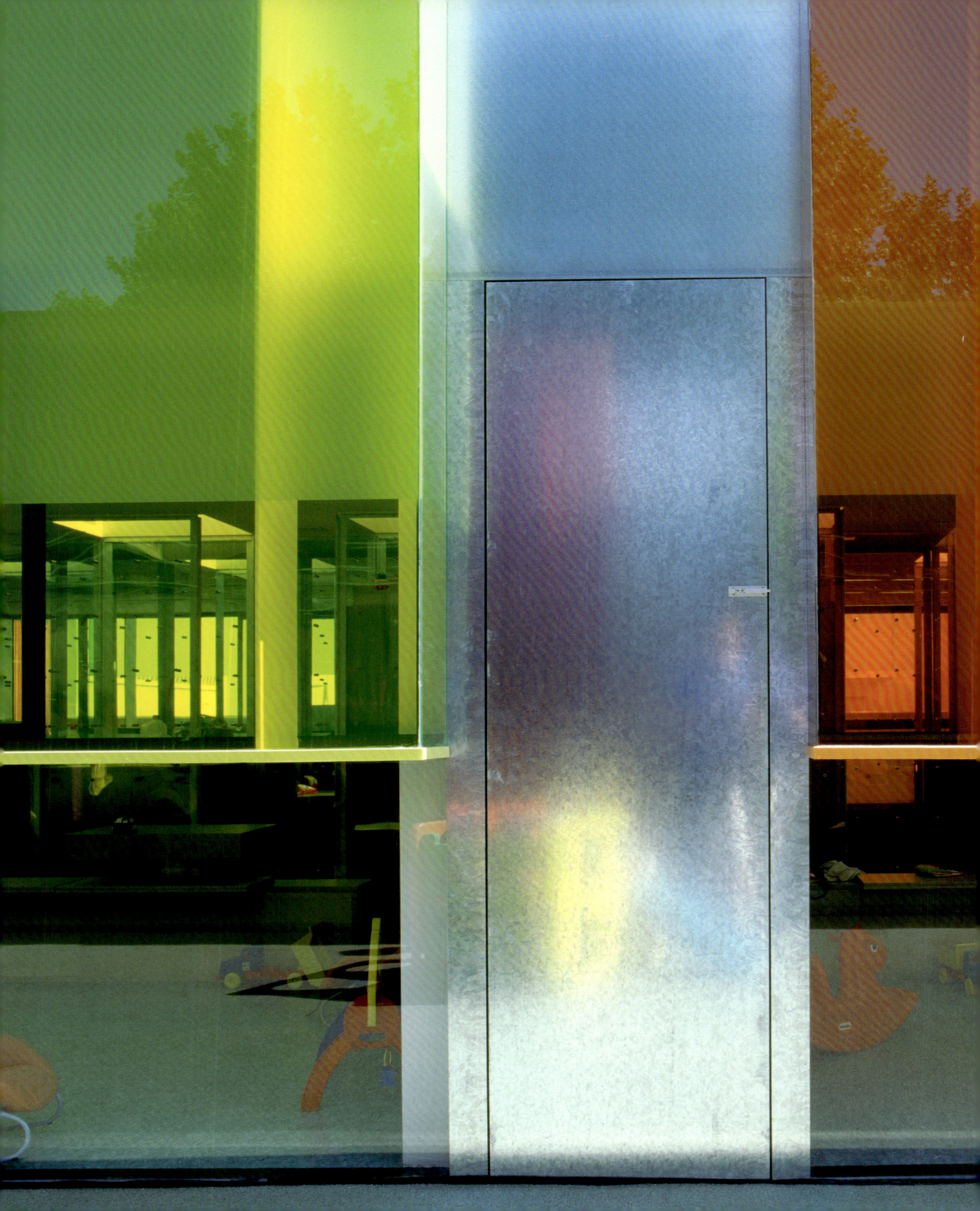

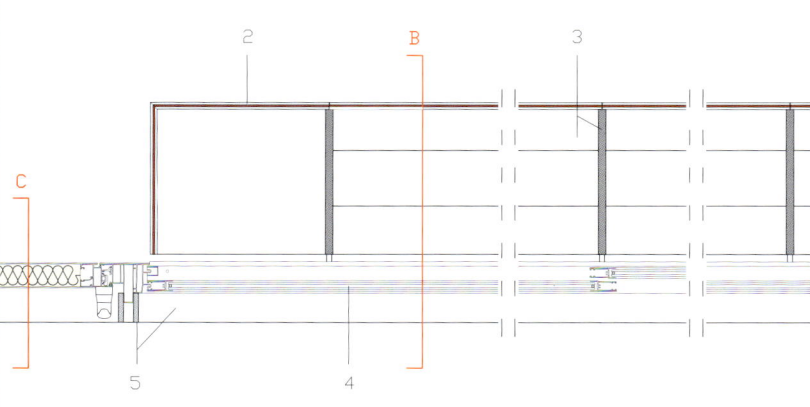

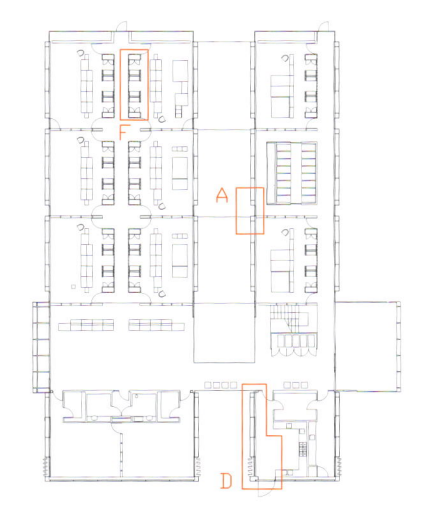

**DETAILS A, B, C, D, E:
CONSTRUCTION SYSTEM
VERTICAL AND HORIZONTAL SECTIONS
SCALE 1:15**

1. Entrance door consisting of sheet aluminium sandwiching fibreglass insulation and aluminium frame
2. Continuous glazed façade with solar filter formed by 1/16 + 1/16" (5 + 5 mm) partially frosted laminated glass sandwiching coloured PVB film
3. Lacquered aluminium structure supporting façade formed by upper and lower 11 7/8 x 5 7/8" (300 x 150 mm) vertical and horizontal plates
4. Continuous glazed façade formed by 1/8 – 1/4 – 1/8" (4 – 6 – 4 mm) aluminium double glazing units
5. Lacquered aluminium vertical and horizontal profiles securing façade
6. HEB 160 beam
7. Partition in classrooms formed by 3/4" (20 mm) gypsum board, frame of vertical and horizontal wood
8. Ballast layer, waterproofing membrane, 2 3/4" (70 mm) fibreglass board insulation, foamed concrete screed forming 1.5% slope, 13 3/4" (350 mm) reinforced concrete slab, false ceiling comprising gypsum board on frame of aluminium C-profiles
9. Masonry block perimeter wall
10. Steel L-profile cover
11. Aluminium cornice
12. Waterproofing membrane
13. Steel L-profile supporting façade
14. Steel plates anchoring façade to supporting structure
15. Fibreglass insulation layer
16. Fluorescent tube
17. Ventilation inlet
18. Continuous glazed façade formed by 1/16 + 1/16" (5 + 5 mm) partially frosted laminated glass sandwiching coloured PVB film
19. Floor consisting of linoleum, screed, screed with embedded radiant heating, 2" (50 mm) insulation layer, reinforced concrete slab
20. Lacquered steel threshold fixed to concrete edge
21. Paving consisting of rubber sheets, screed, waterproofing membrane, foamed concrete screed forming 1.5% slope, reinforced concrete slab
22. Door with 1/16 + 1/16" (5 + 5 mm) partially frosted laminated glass sandwiching coloured PVB film, frame of 4 x 1 5/8" (100 x 40 mm) aluminium box profiles, sheet aluminium
23. 3/4" (20 mm) plastered gypsum board, wall in thermal-insulated 9 3/8" (250 mm) masonry blocks, 3/4" (20 mm) gypsum board with enamel paint finish
24. Lacquered wood door
25. Gypsum board with painted enamel finish, wall in masonry blocks
26. PVC flooring

052 / "Els Colors"

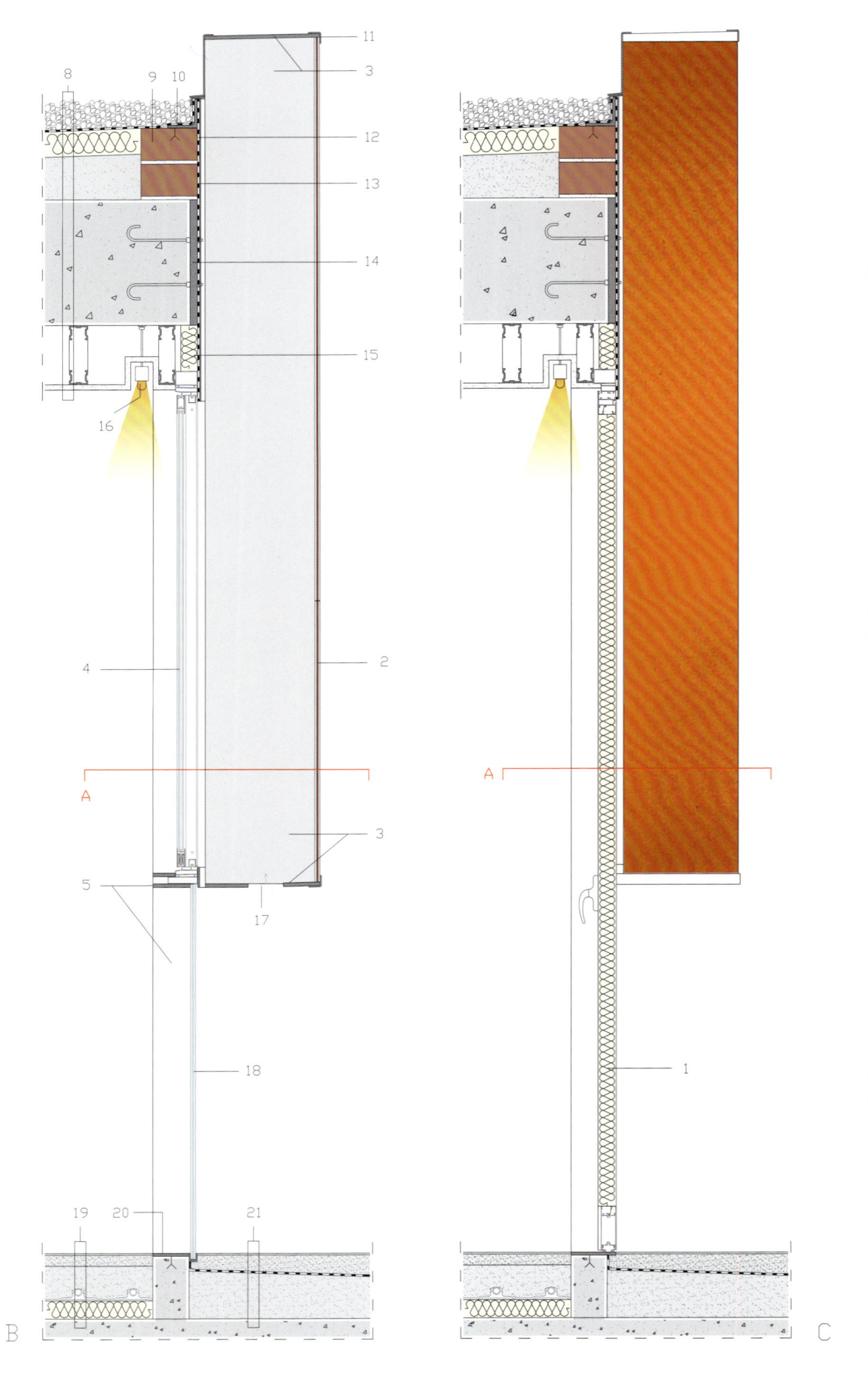

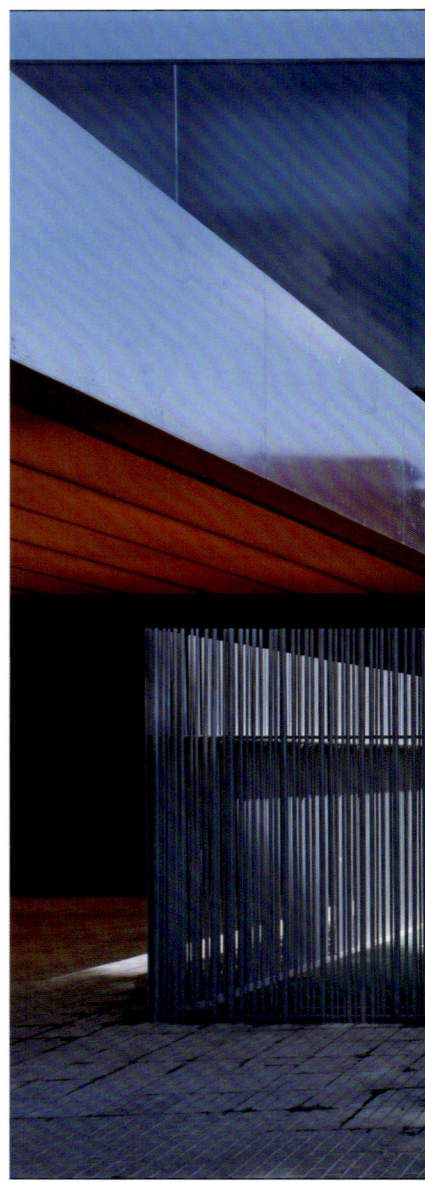

053 / RCR

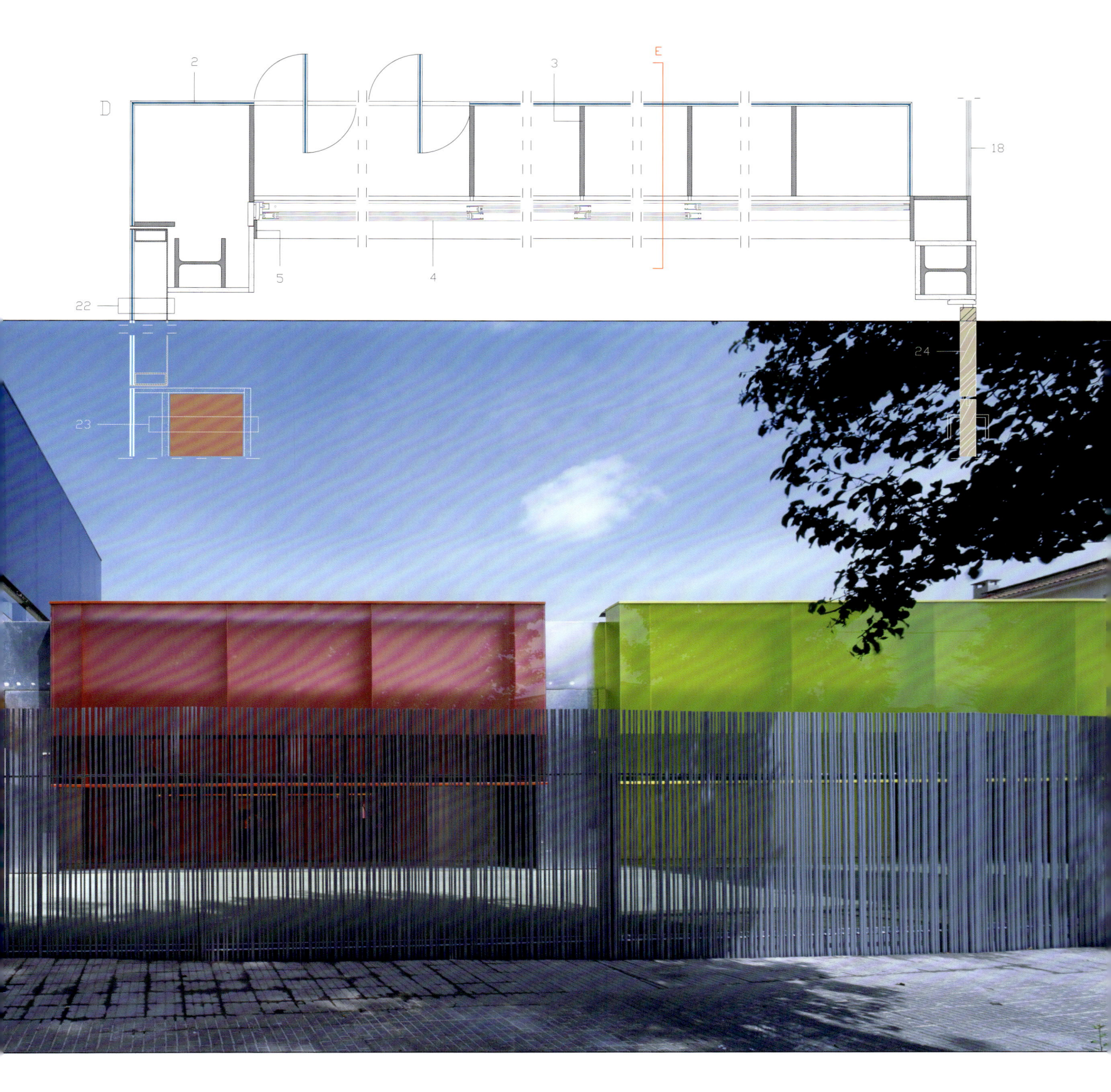

054 / "Els Colors"

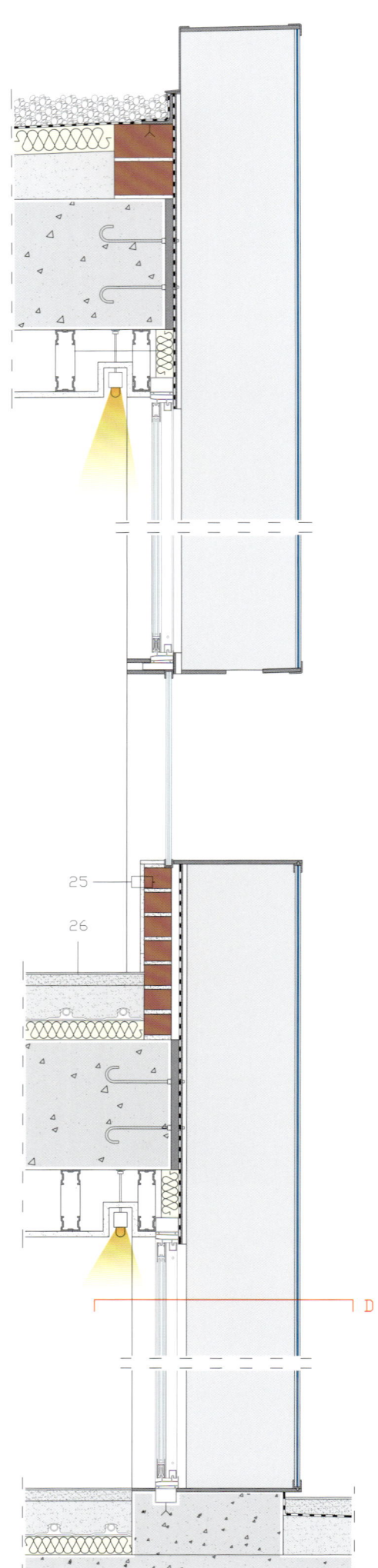

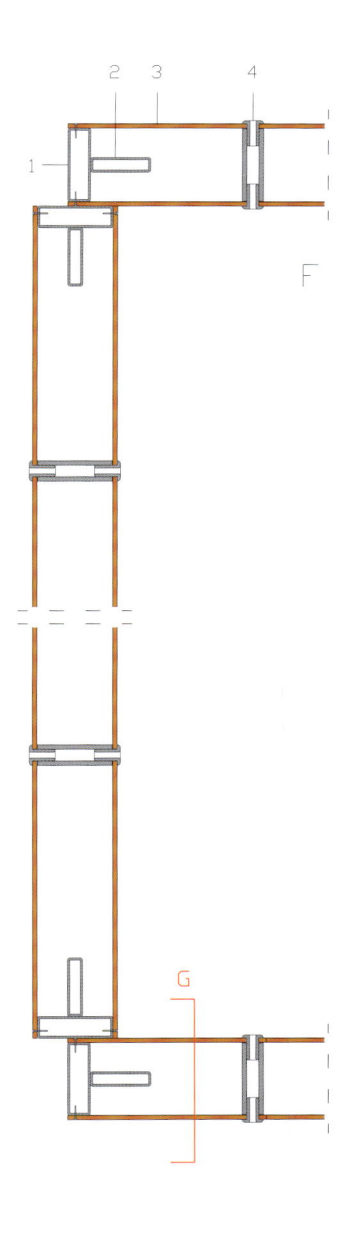

DETAILS F, G:
INTERIOR TRANSPARENT PARTITIONS
HORIZONTAL AND VERTICAL SECTIONS
SCALE 1:5

1. Lacquered 2 x 5/8 x 1/16"
   (50 x 15 x 1.5 mm) aluminium
   box profile supporting wall
2. Lacquered reinforcing
   1 5/8 x 3/8 x 1/16" (40 x 10 x 1.5 mm)
   aluminium box profile
3. Transparent wall formed
   by coloured 1/8" (3 mm)
   methacrylate panels
4. Jointed steel pin and cylinder
   connecting panels
5. Connection between walls and
   false ceiling and floor consisting of
   3/4 x 3/8 x 1/16" (20 x 10 x 1.5 mm)
   aluminium box profiles and
   3/4 x 3/4" (20 x 20 mm) L-profiles
6. Lacquered 1 1/4 x 1 1/4"
   (30 x 30 mm) aluminium box profile
   supporting false ceiling and wall
7. False ceiling consisting
   of 5/8" (15 mm) gypsum board
   with enamel paint finish

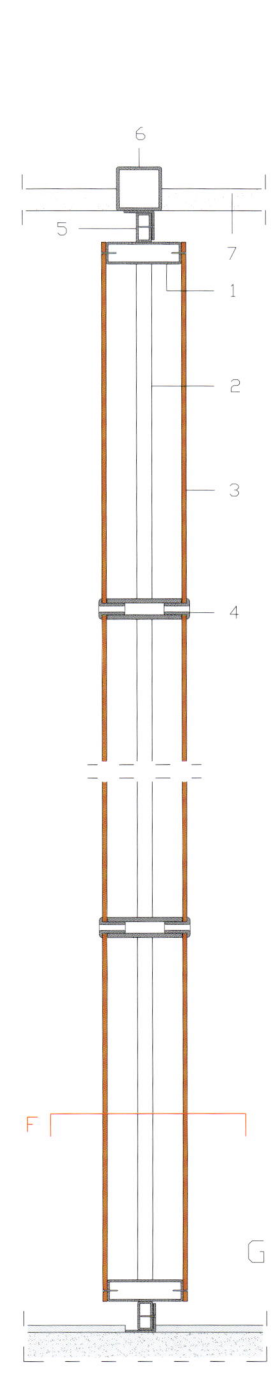

CLAPHAM MANOR SCHOOL – LONDON, UK
DRMM ARCHITECTS

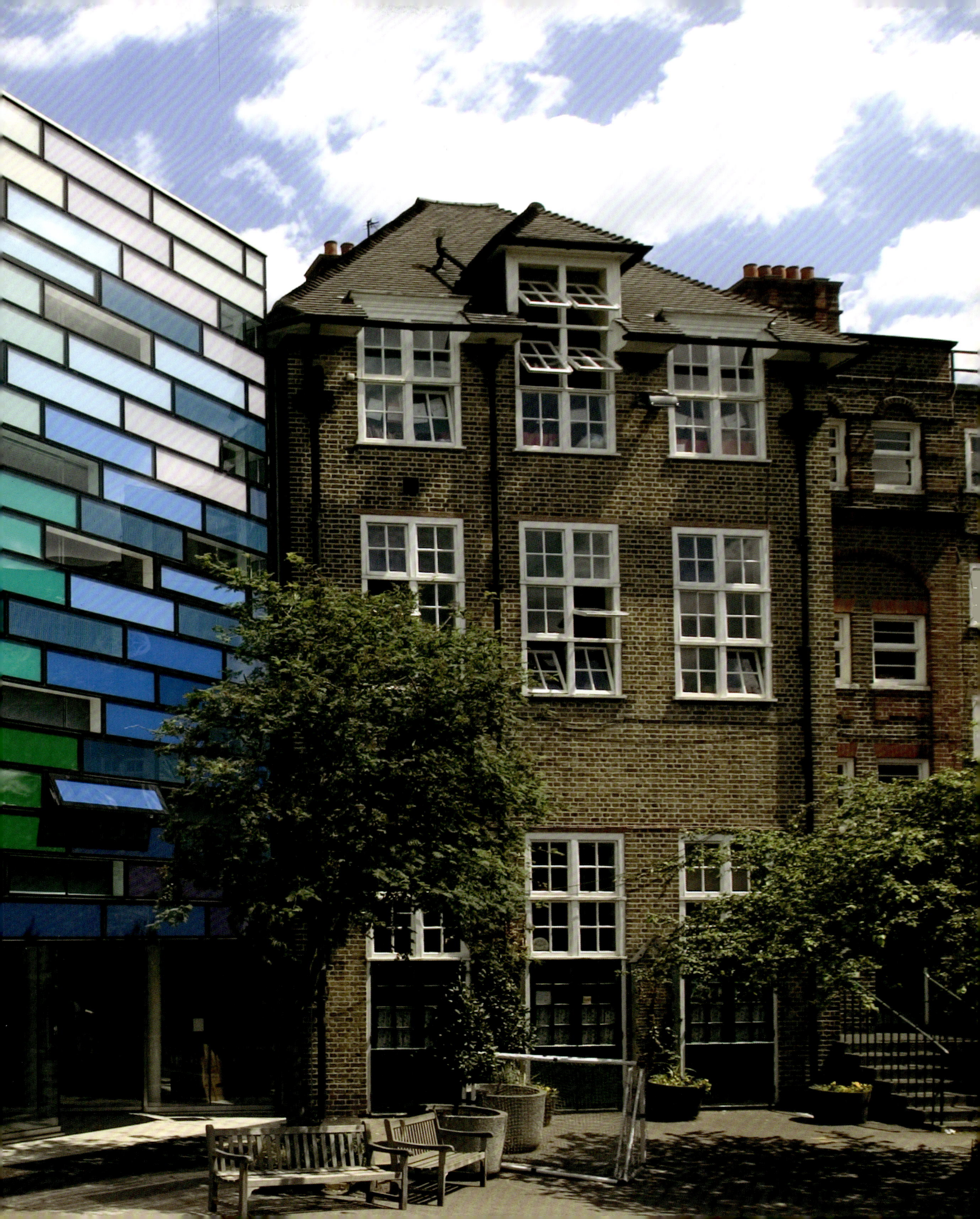

■ North Elevation – Scale 1:300

■ East Elevation – Scale 1:300

■ Ground Floor Plan – Scale 1:400

1. Main Pupil Entrance
2. Parent / Visitor Entrance
3. Playground Entrance
4. Reception Area
5. Administration
6. Meeting Room
7. Kitchenette
8. Medical Room
9. Classroom

■ First Floor Plan – Scale 1:400

058 / Clapham Manor

South Elevation – Scale 1:300

West Elevation – Scale 1:300

Adding onto Victorian buildings is both a source of debate and a fact of life in London, where 19th-century brick structures make up a significant proportion of the housing stock. But when you are dealing with a public building, and a beloved primary school that has received awards for excellence (despite cramped conditions), the pressure to keep to old forms is pronounced. However, it is also true that the public and planning departments can be more forward-thinking than they are often given credit for. The new addition to Clapham Manor primary school in south London by dRMM Architects makes a point both for bold gestures and a considered approach in the face of historic buildings. Looking at the site, which had not only a Victorian schoolhouse but also another protected building on the other side, lead architect Philip Marsh quickly decided against a homage to the past. Headteacher Brian Hazell, who has been at the school for twenty-five years, agreed. 'I love the old building,' he says, 'but I felt we needed a new modern space for the staff and for the children. We didn't want some kind of historic pastiche.' Instead Marsh designed a building that stands proudly in the new century, with glass curtain walls that form a brightly coloured mosaic 'loop' around the new structure. At first glance, the new wing looks like a stand-alone piece of architectural deviation, with its angular multi-coloured glass façade sitting hard up next to the three-storeys of old brick and white-painted sash windows. But a closer look reveals a similar pattern in the panes of coloured glass to the shape and rhythm of the brick. Standing in front of the two buildings, which are joined by a transparent glazed link, visitors can also appreciate a similarity of scale and volume. And, as Marsh points out, 'curtain walls are not new, they were used a lot in postwar school buildings, but now technology has moved on.' The glass panels all measure the same 505 x 200 mm (19 1/8" x 7 7/8") but there are three variations: tinted, fritted and clear. The coloured sections are backed with insulation and some are top-hung windows that can open to allow for ventilation, without being a danger to children.

In other ways, too, the glazing system is much more than just a bright, playful skin: the architects used the patterns of the glass grid to create an array of surfaces and fittings on the interior of the building. The benefits of the curtain walls are immediately apparent inside the new ground-floor entrance/reception area, classrooms, dance studio, art room and meeting rooms. As one would expect with this much glass, these are flooded with light, but it is a controlled effect, tempered by the colouring of the glass and by sections of the grid that have been filled in with wood panels and with sections covered in colourful pinboard, so that student work can be easily displayed without damaging wall surfaces. The use of perforated board on ceilings and perforated veneer on some sections of walls, alternating with unpainted concrete alongside the window grid, make for a pleasant material variation especially in the entrance atrium. Too often the modern love of glass and hard surfaces creates an echoing, impersonal space, but here, the acoustics have been tamed, so that the sound of children moving through the corridors can be lively without feeling chaotic.

Despite the dynamic interior solutions, it is the use of colour that marks this building out, a feature that seems risky in this tight context of low-rise brick, but has proved to be more popular than anyone expected. The palette was chosen, Marsh explains, to reflect some of the existing colours around the site (though in brighter tones), such as the red and yellow that refer to the brick on the old building. On another side, greens link to the soft landscape, and, the architect adds, "the desire to have more soft landscape". Blues gesture towards the sky, and all of the colours become paler as they go up, "so that the building sort of dematerializes towards the top". Both headteacher and architect were impressed by the positive reception of the finished building and the amount of support they received from local people and planning agencies. "It's amazing", says Marsh, "the number of emails I've received from people praising the building. You don't often get that sort of reaction." Whatever one feels about the importance of historic preservation, it is easy to see that this bright insertion has been an uplifting experience for the neighbourhood. Maybe the enthusiastic response says something about the feelings that well-designed educational spaces can elicit, or about the potential for improvement of young minds when faced with bold and inventive surroundings.

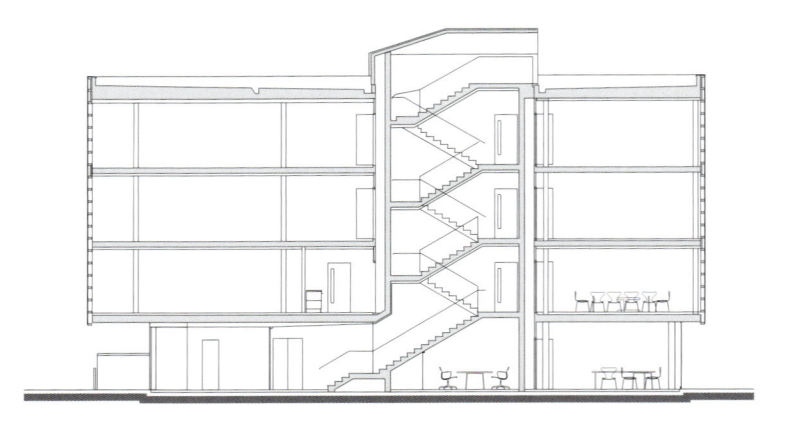

■ XX Section – Scale 1:300

060 / Clapham Manor

■ YY Section – Scale 1:300

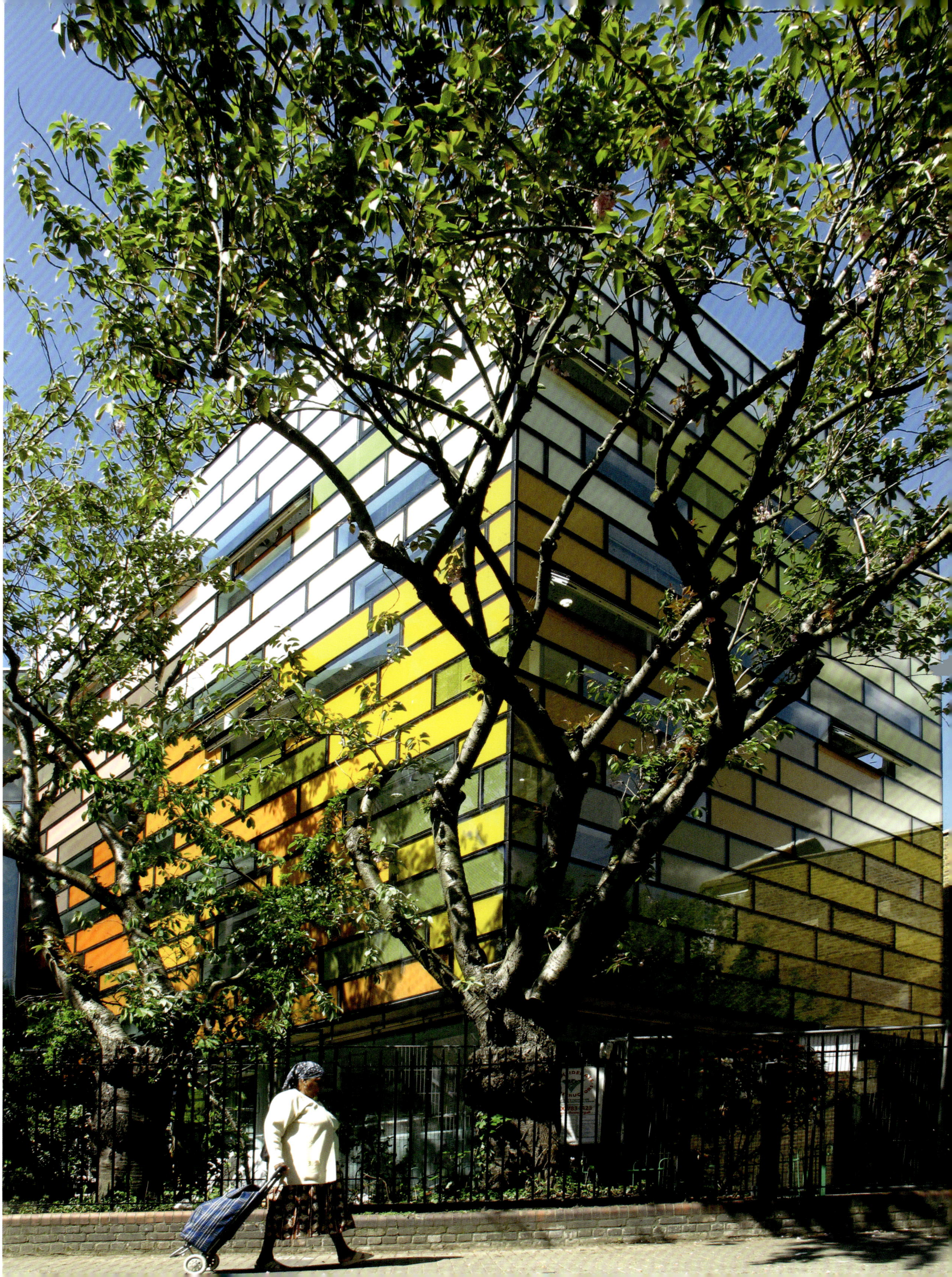

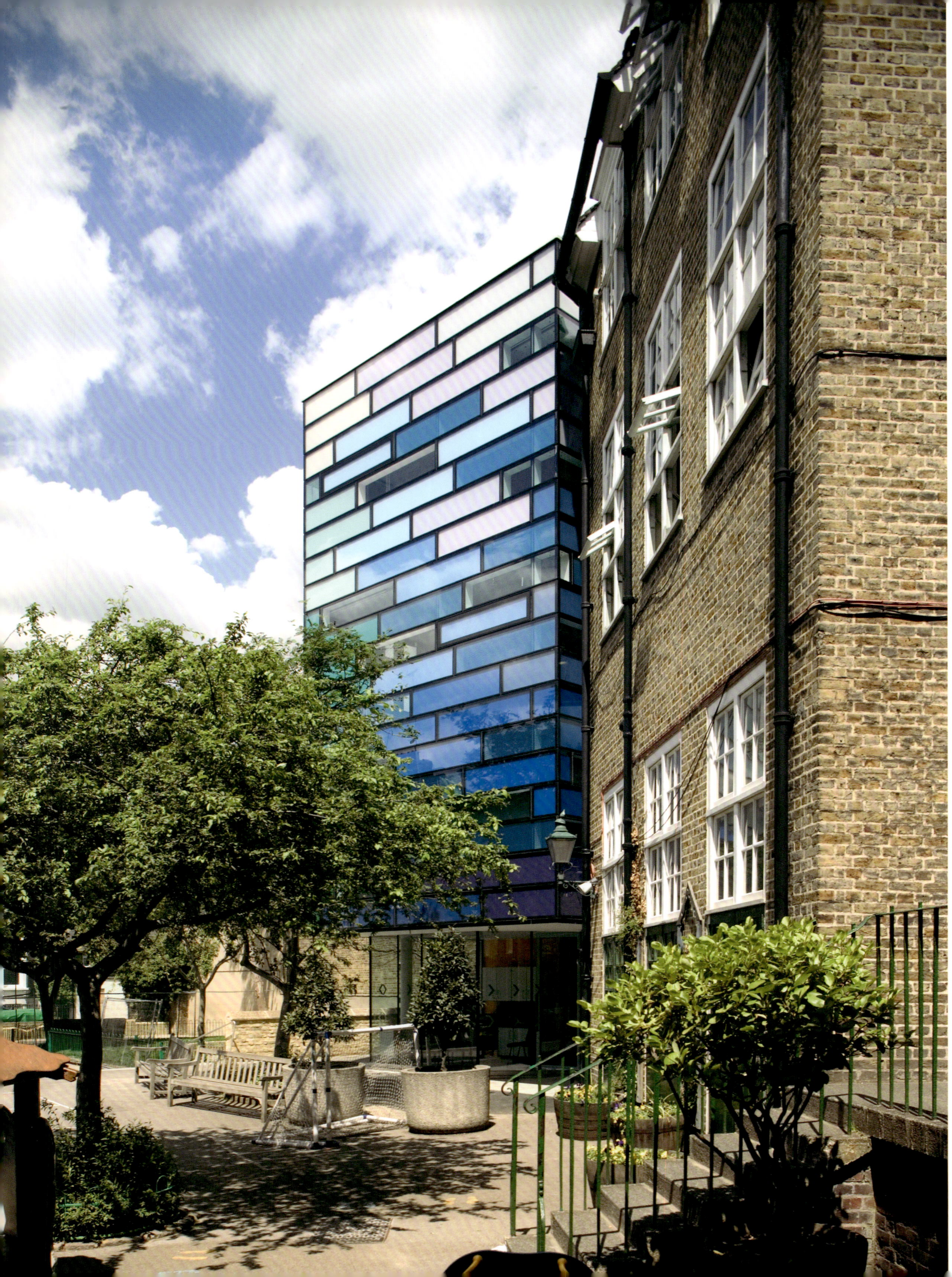

DETAIL A: POLYCHROME FAÇADE
VERTICAL SECTION – SCALE 1:25

1. Roof comprising waterproofing membrane, triple insulation layer forming 1% slope, vapour barrier, 9 1/8" (230 mm) cast-in-place reinforced concrete slab
2. Double waterproofing membrane sandwiching steel flashing, 1 5/8" (40 mm) board insulation, vapour barrier, 3/4" (18 mm) plywood panel
3. Façade formed by horizontal and vertical steel box profiles with Schüco 1/4 – 7/8 – 1/4" (6 – 22 – 6 mm) aluminium double-glazing units with opaque polychrome glass, 4" (100 mm) board insulation, 2" (50 mm) airspace, 5 7/8" (150 mm) reinforced concrete structure
4. 1/4 – 7/8 – 1/4" (6 – 22 – 6 mm) double-glazing unit with semi-transparent silk-screened coloured glass
5. Adjustable sun shading
6. Installation housing in 1/2" (12 mm) thick plywood panels
7. False ceiling consisting of 1/2" (12.5 mm) acoustic board insulation in perforated gypsum board on aluminium C-profiles and tie rods suspended from slab
8. Interior wall covering of classrooms consisting of 3/4" (18 mm) plywood panels for posting displays with coloured felt finish, steel L-profile support, double 2 + 2" (50 + 50 mm) board insulation
9. Rubber flooring, 3/4" (18 mm) plywood board support, levelling layer, 1 3/8" (35 mm) floor heating, vapour barrier, 9 1/8" (230 mm) reinforced concrete slab
10. Transom window with exterior 1/8 – 3/4 – 1/8" (4 – 18 – 3 mm) double glazing with opaque polychrome glass and plywood panels with interior felt finish in aluminium frames
11. 1/4 – 7/8 – 1/4" (6 – 22 – 6 mm) transparent double glazing
12. Steel flashing
13. Exterior false ceiling consisting of double 1" (25 mm) gypsum board on steel C-profiles and tie rods suspended from slab, 2" (50 mm) board insulation
14. Steel Z-profile fastening glazed façade to supporting structure
15. Continuous glazed façade with 1/16 – 5/8 – 1/16" (5 – 15 – 5 mm) double-glazing units on steel U-profiles with insulation
16. Steel threshold
17. Steel Z-profile securing continuous façade to slab
18. Resin flooring, 2 3/4" (70 mm) screed, 1 3/8" (35 mm) floor heating, waterproofing membrane, cement and sand screed, 4" (100 mm) ballast layer, earth
19. Paving in 2" (50 mm) concrete blocks, 2" (50 mm) screed, ballast layer

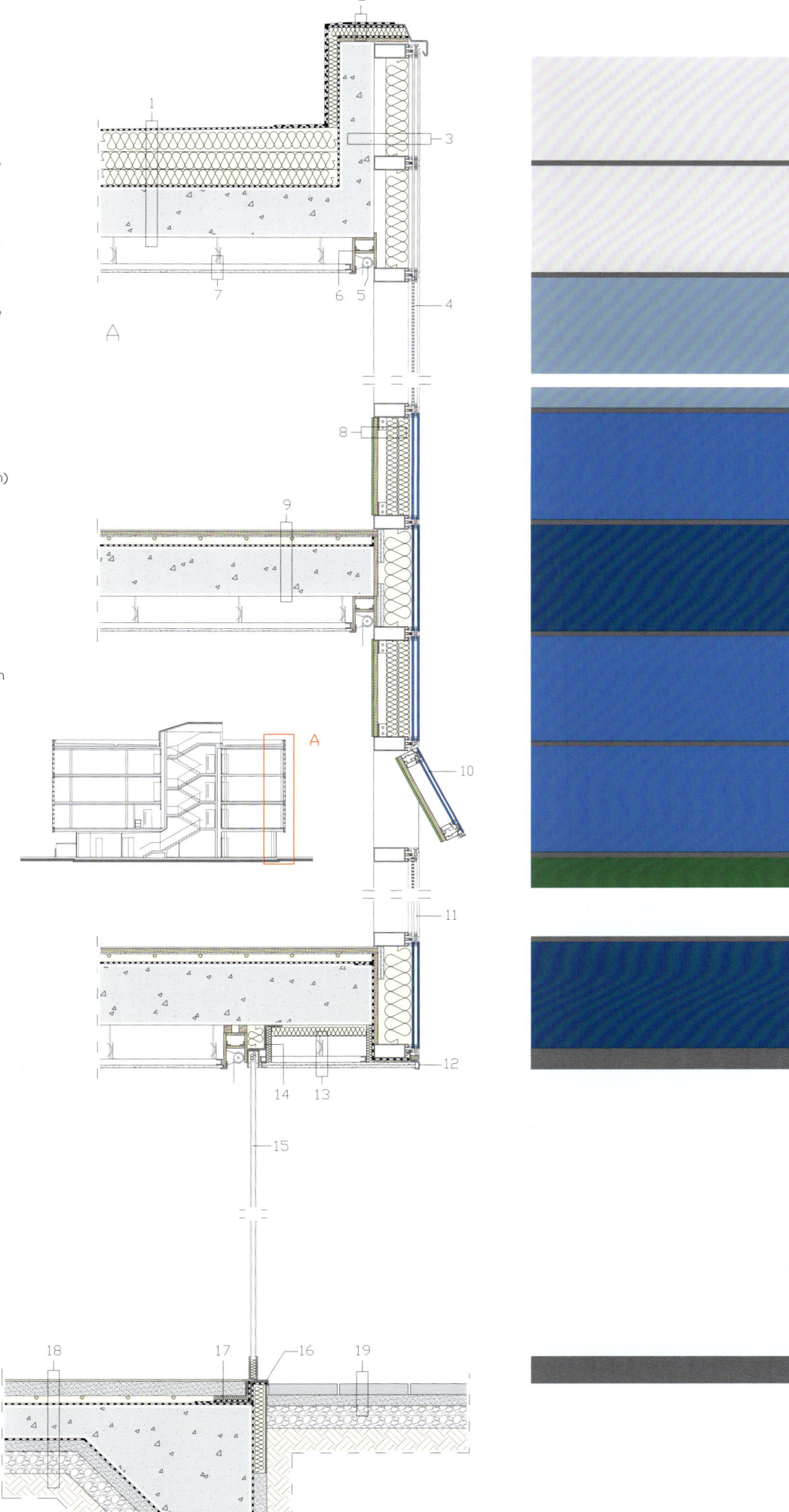

ØRESTAD COLLEGE – COPENHAGEN, DENMARK
3XN

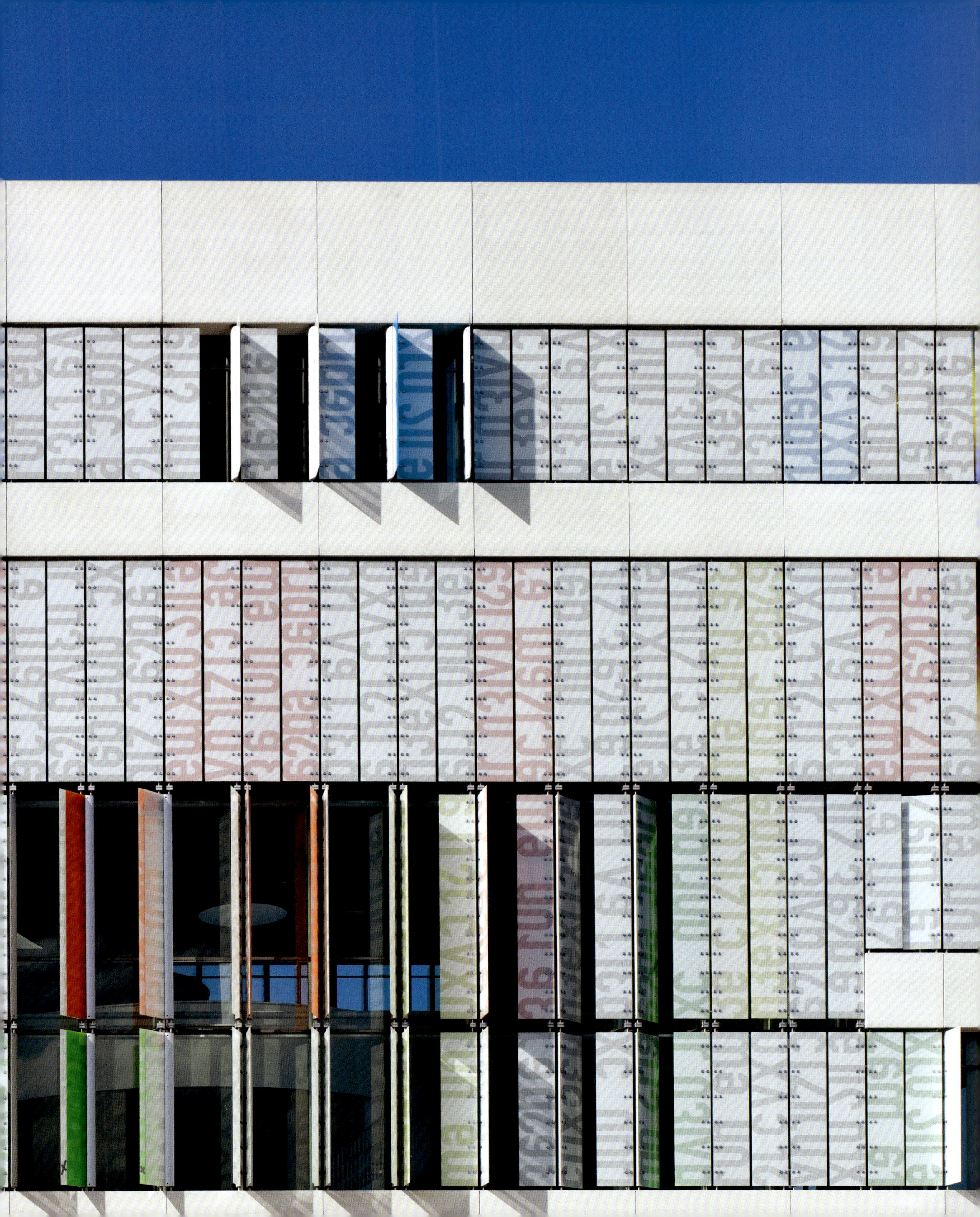

066 / Ørestad College

■ East Elevation – Scale 1:400

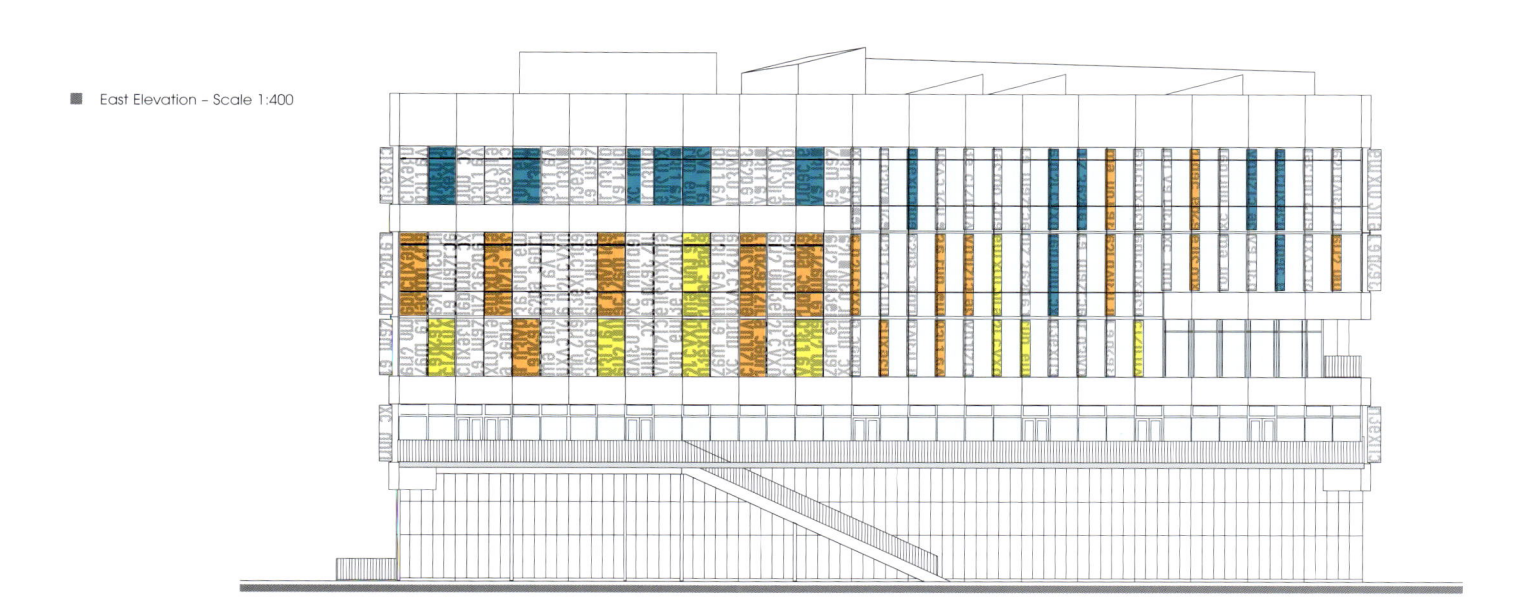

The Ørestad College commissioned by the city of Copenhagen is the result of a restricted-entry ideas competition won by architectural practice 3XN in 2003. The architecture mirrors Denmark's new approach to higher education facilities, the areas of free-flowing circulation and aggregation matching the organizational flexibility of the educational system.

The building's structure is clearly visible behind transparent glazed elevations that also reveal the interior layout. The horizontal floor bands are intermittently broken, marking double or triple interior volumes that lend movement to the whole building.

On the exterior, vertical blades in semi-transparent coloured glass act as brise-soleil and project beams of changing coloured light onto the inside. On the interior, the key node is the intersection of floors and a large central staircase spiralling upward to a roof terrace. On the plan, the four aboveground floors resemble a series of boomerangs set in staggered fashion around the axis of the staircase. In this way spaces and volumes open out from the ample stairway, creating a functional and perceptive dynamic. Environments for study, meeting, teaching and socializing flow on from one another, defined by the shape, quality and furnishings attributed to each spatial distribution. Every aboveground floor is an integrated study area equipped for interdisciplinary learning, while common services like the gym and library have been placed below grade. The building's structural frame is not a regular grid module. Hinged to the floors departing from the central staircase, three large cylindrical elements near the outer perimeter serve as "structural columns". These, together with other smaller pillars, connect to the horizontal structures and distribute the loads. The cylinder structures contain accessory stairs linking all floors. The different functions of the succession of open and closed spaces are evidenced by variation of the materials used. At the stair access and landings, the magnesite flooring gives way to the same wood as the steps. The railings are also in wood.

The cylindrical "island" volumes dedicated to study and meetings comprise thick insulated walls with micro-perforated sliding panels to allow for a variety of uses.

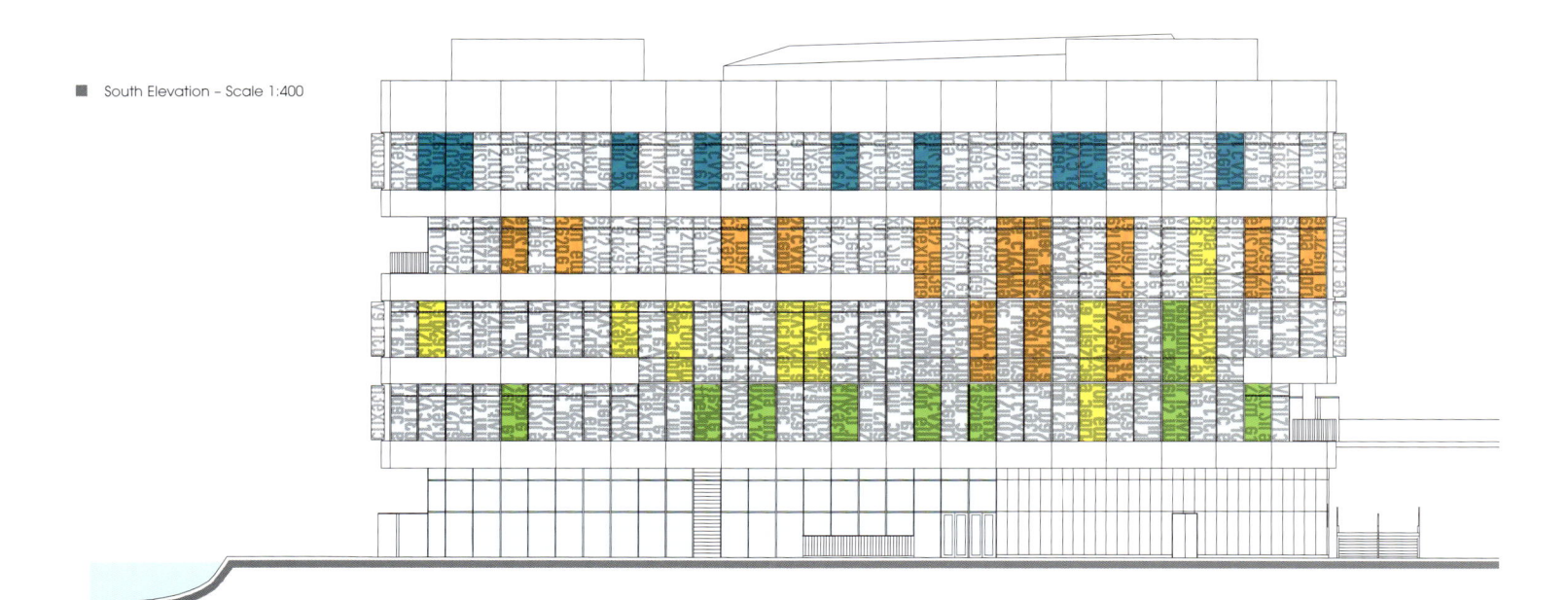

■ South Elevation – Scale 1:400

Site Plan - Scale 1:7000

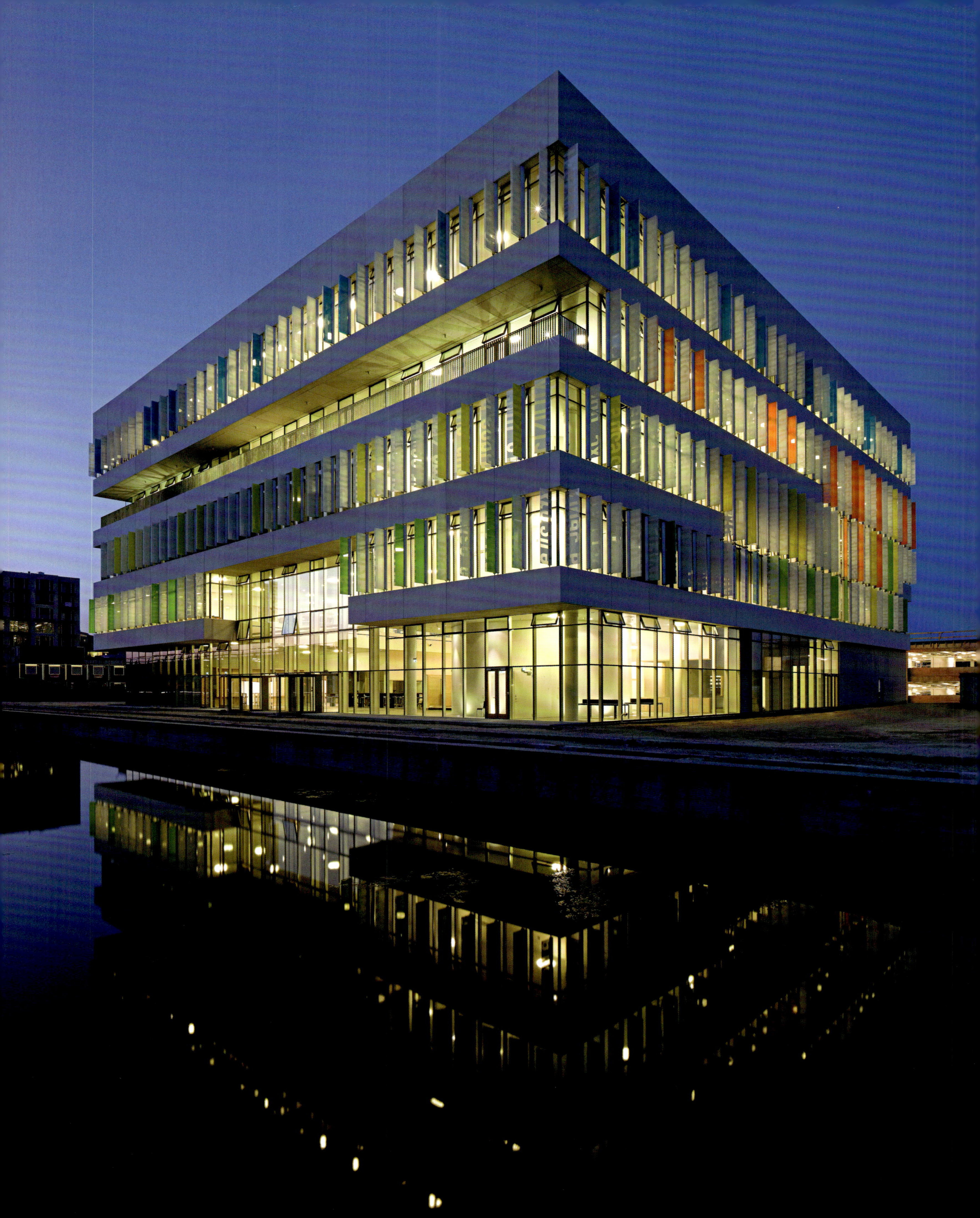

■ First Floor Plan – Scale 1:400

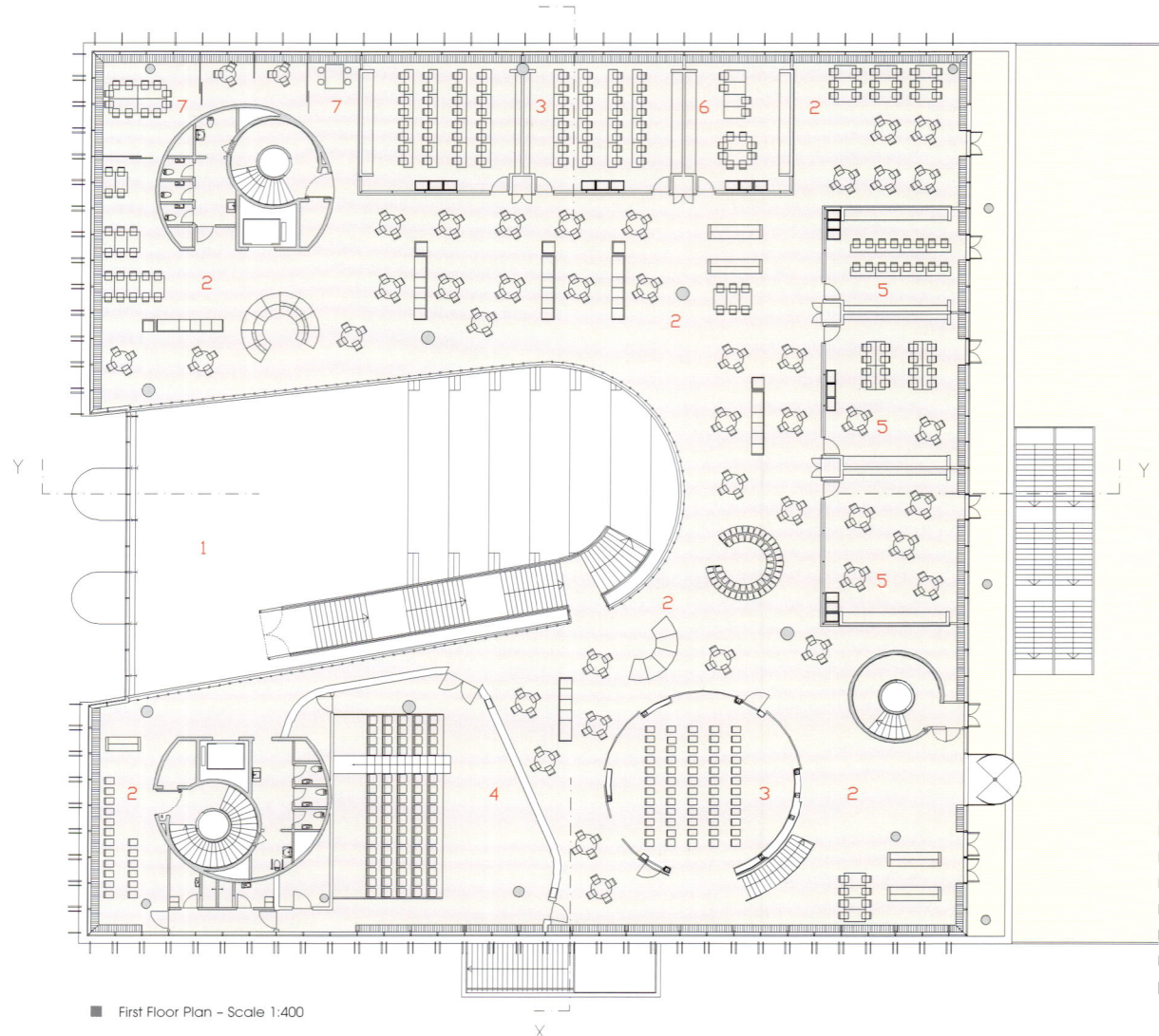

1. Hall
2. Relaxation and Study Area
3. Lecture Hall
4. Multi-Functional Room
5. Study Room
6. Staff Room
7. Administration

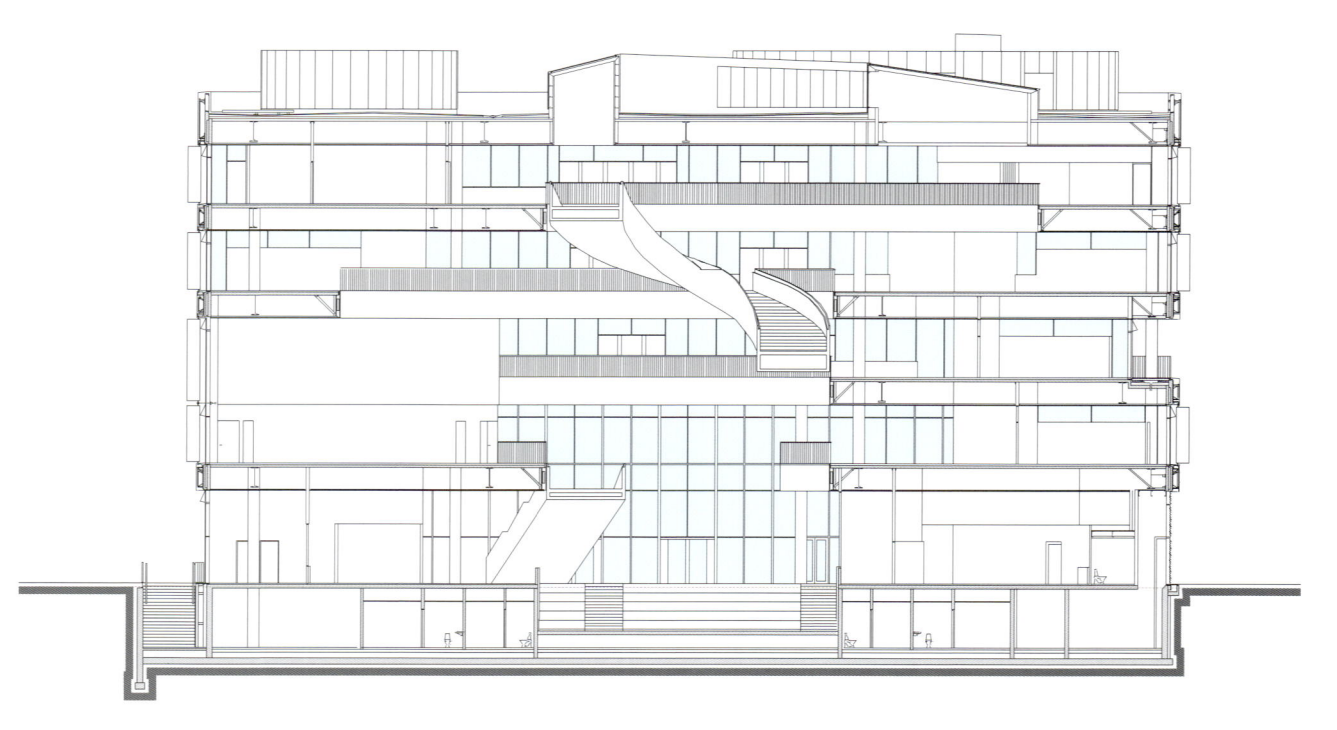

■ XX Section – Scale 1:400

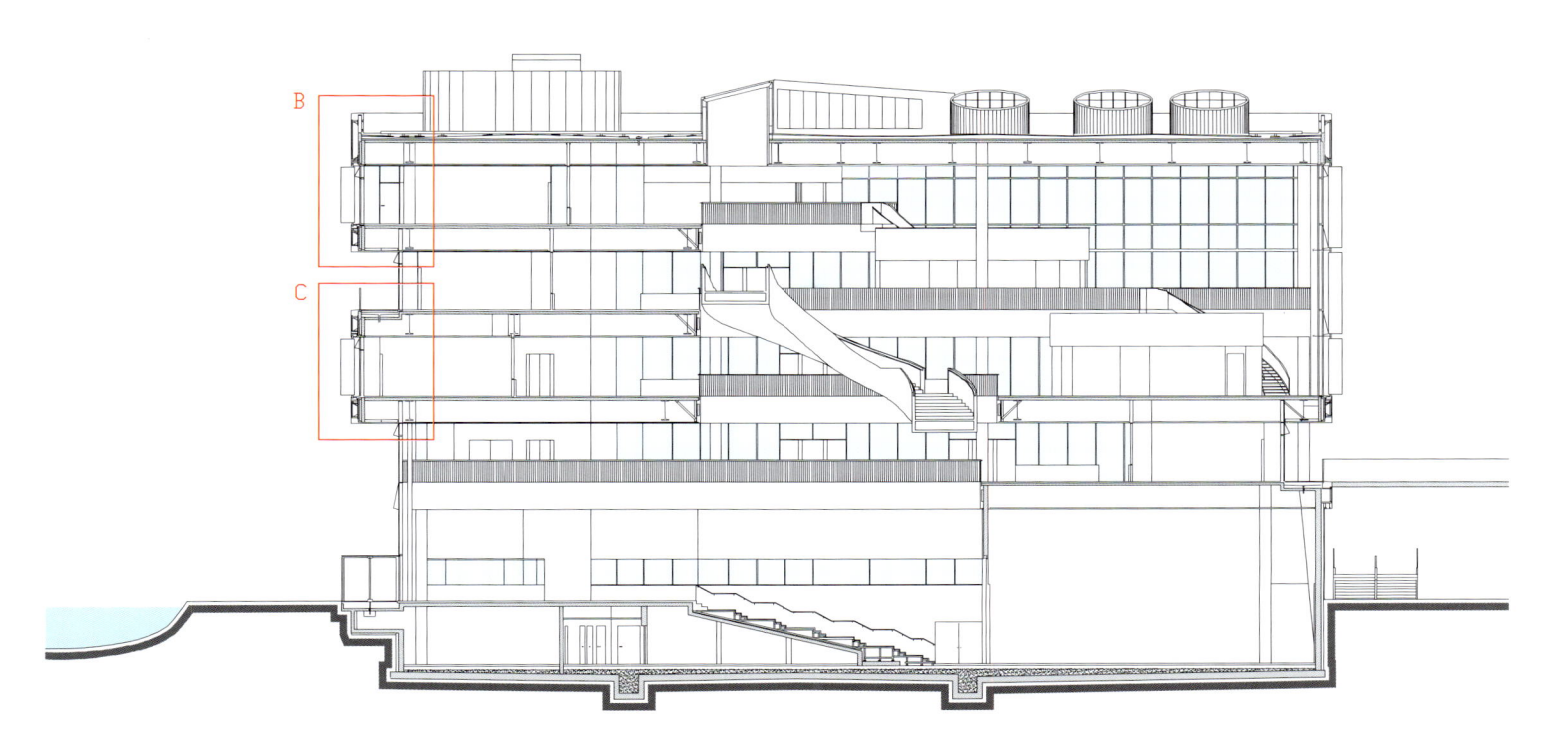

■ YY Section – Scale 1:400

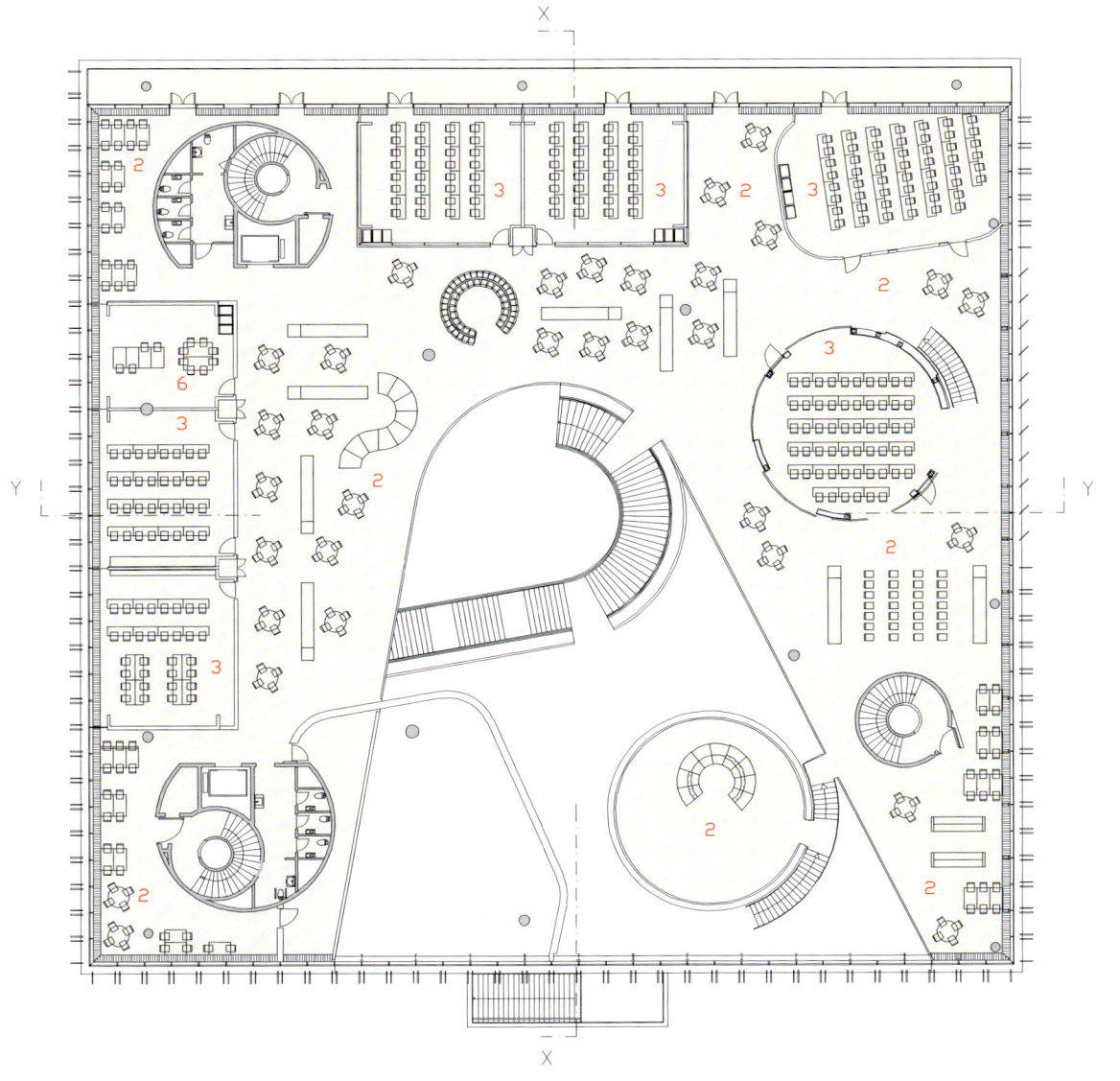

■ Second Floor Plan – Scale 1:400

071 / 3XN

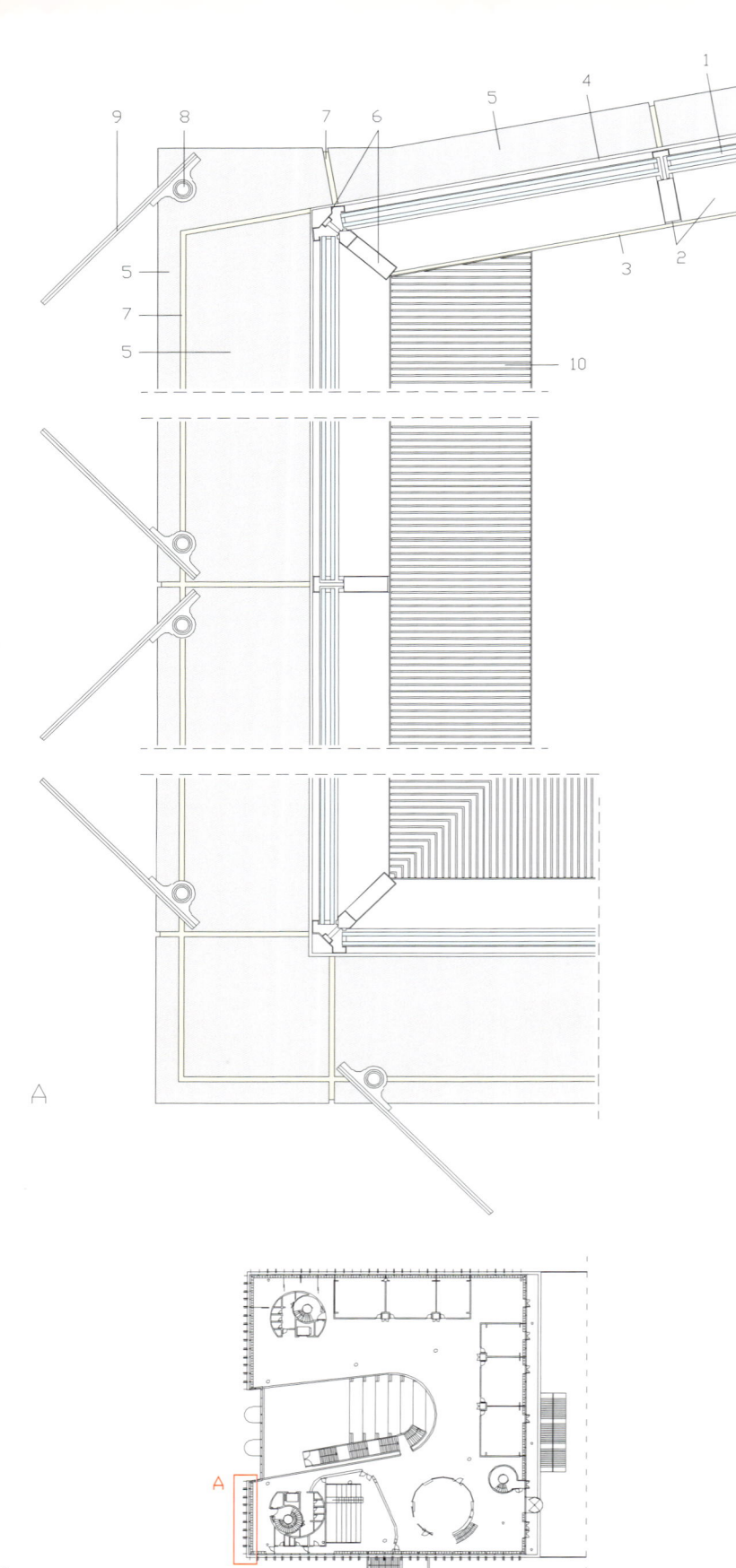

DETAIL A: FAÇADE
HORIZONTAL SECTION – SCALE 1:20

1. Façade system formed by 15/32 – 5/8 – 15/32" (12 – 16 – 12 mm) aluminium double-glazing units
2. Frame supporting façade formed by 5 29/32 x 1 31/32" (150 x 50 mm) aluminium box-shaped profiles
3. 25/64" (10 mm) thick Neoprene elastic joint
4. Aluminium guide finishing
5. 15/32" (12 mm) thick fibrocement cladding
6. System of aluminium angle profiles supporting façade
7. 19/32" (15 mm) thick expansion joint
8. 3 5/32" (80 mm) steel shaft for supporting and adjusting direction of louvres
9. 118 7/64 x 27 9/16 x 5/8" (3000 x 700 x 16 mm) adjustable louvres in coloured silk-screened glass
10. Ventilation system aluminium grille

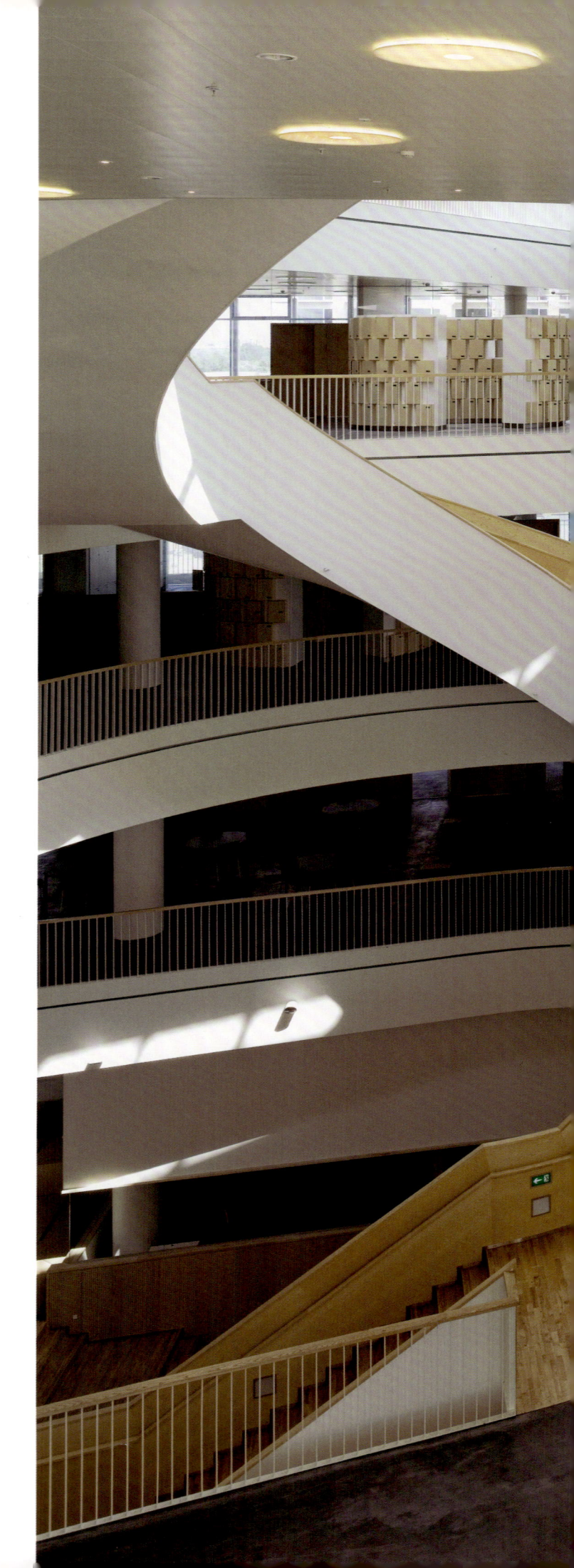

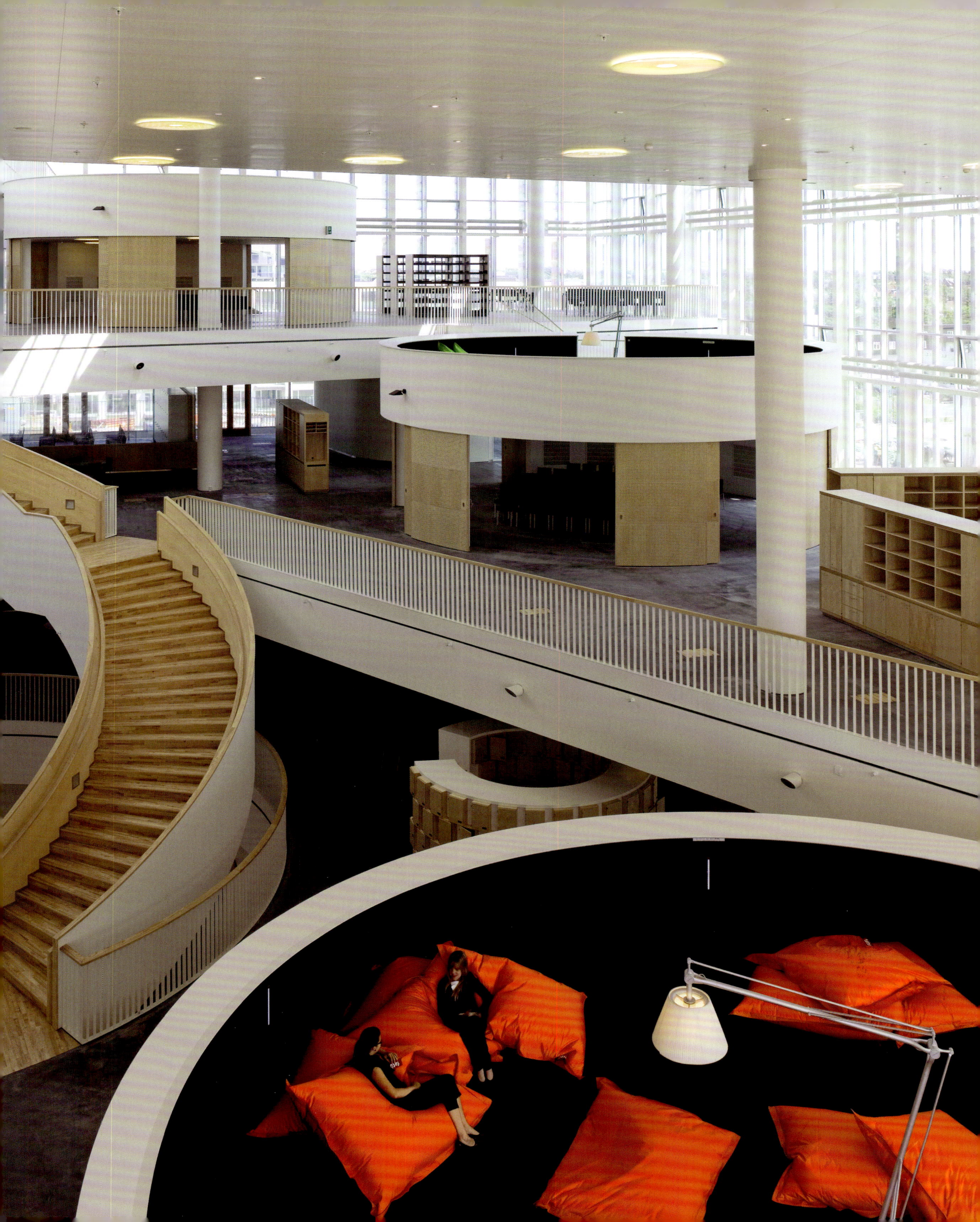

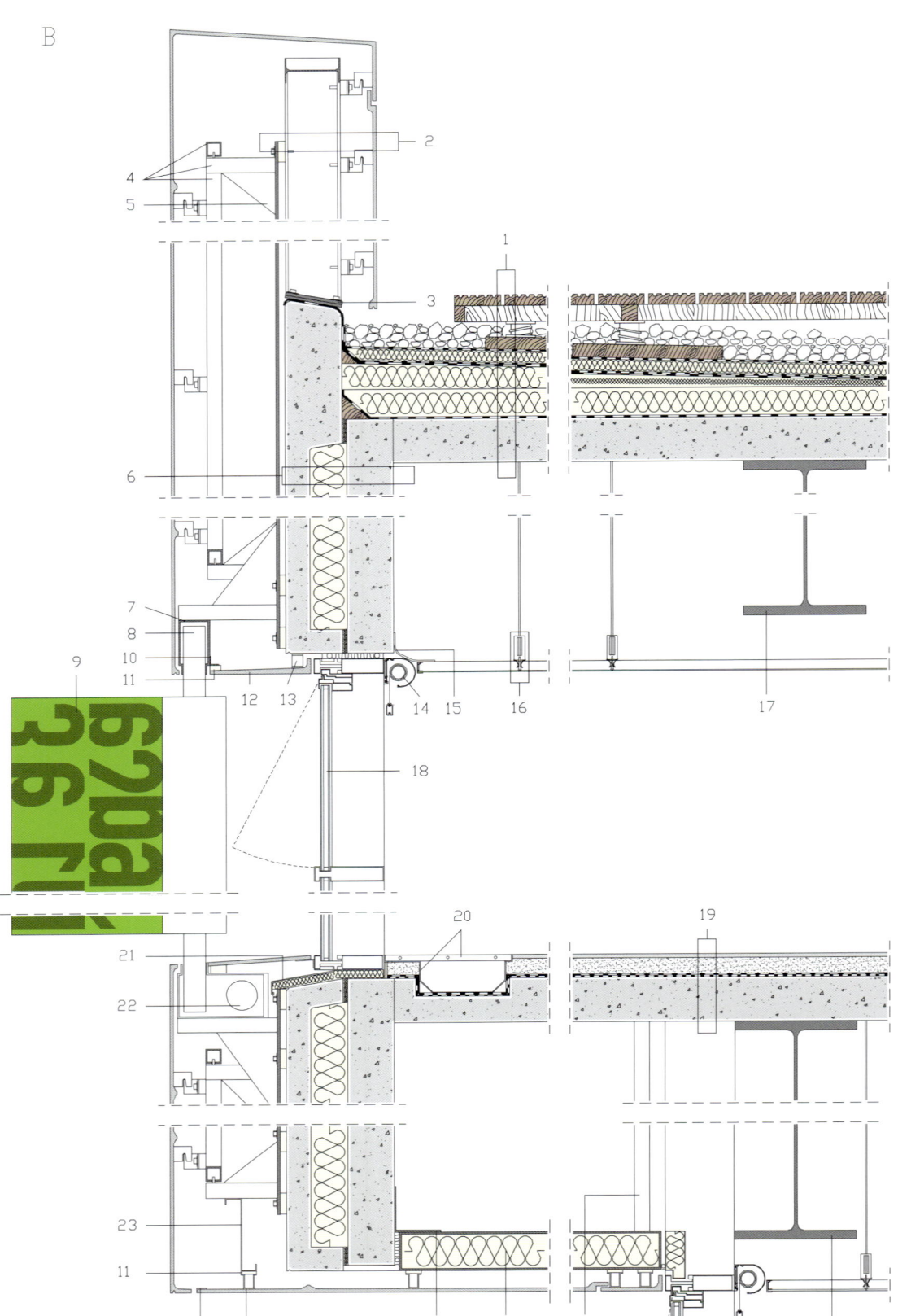

**DETAILS B, C: FAÇADE
VERTICAL SECTIONS – SCALE 1:20**

1. Exterior decking in 1 3/8" (35 mm) wood boards, 2 23/64" (60 mm) wood bearers and joists, ballast layer, joint for adjusting height, 1 37/64" (40 mm) wood panel base, waterproofing membrane, 1 37/64" (40 mm) board insulation, double waterproofing membrane, layer of insulation on 1% slope, 3 15/16" (100 mm) board insulation, vapour barrier, 5 29/32" (150 mm) reinforced concrete slab
2. 15/32" (12 mm) fibrocement cladding, fastening system, 7 3/32 x 3 5/32" (180 x 80 mm) steel double T-section beam supporting façade cladding system, Neoprene joint, 25/64" (10 mm) steel plate
3. Steel plates anchoring beam to load-bearing structure
4. Frame of 1 31/32 x 1 31/32" (50 x 50 mm) box-shaped profiles supporting fibrocement panels
5. Steel reinforcing bracket
6. Pre-cast concrete panel, 4 23/32" (120 mm) board insulation, 5 29/32" (150 mm) reinforced concrete structure
7. 7 3/32 x 3 35/64" (180 x 90 mm) aluminium U-profile
8. 3 5/32" (80 mm) steel shaft supporting and for adjusting direction of louvres
9. 118 7/64 x 27 9/16 x 5/8" (3000 x 700 x 16 mm) adjustable louvres in coloured silk-screened glass
10. Steel L-profile anchor
11. Neoprene elastic joint
12. Fibrocement panel closing off space
13. Steel C-profile anchoring fibrocement panel to load-bearing system
14. Roller blind
15. Non-woven membrane
16. False ceiling formed by sheet aluminium on steel C-profiles and

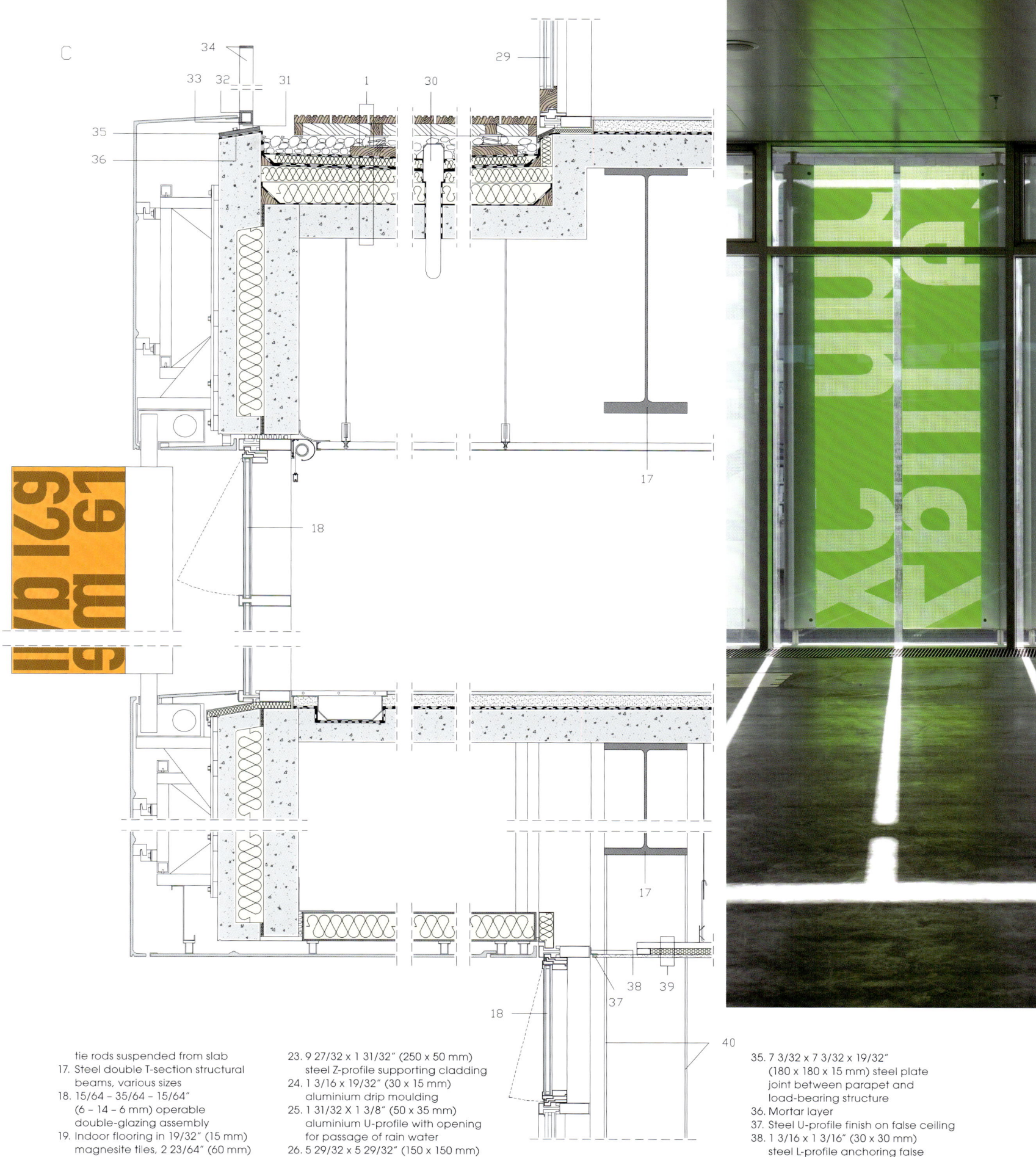

tie rods suspended from slab
17. Steel double T-section structural beams, various sizes
18. 15/64 – 35/64 – 15/64" (6 – 14 – 6 mm) operable double-glazing assembly
19. Indoor flooring in 19/32" (15 mm) magnesite tiles, 2 23/64" (60 mm) anhydrite-based levelling screed, double acoustic membrane, 5 29/32" (150 mm) reinforced concrete slab
20. Ventilation system aluminium grille and duct
21. Aluminium flashing
22. Motorized system for adjusting louvres
23. 9 27/32 x 1 31/32" (250 x 50 mm) steel Z-profile supporting cladding
24. 1 3/16 x 19/32" (30 x 15 mm) aluminium drip moulding
25. 1 31/32 X 1 3/8" (50 x 35 mm) aluminium U-profile with opening for passage of rain water
26. 5 29/32 x 5 29/32" (150 x 150 mm) steel L-profile supporting false ceiling
27. 5 1/8" (130 mm) false ceiling formed by aluminium panels with insulation
28. 1 31/32 x 1 31/32" (50 x 50 mm) steel box-shaped profile supporting false ceiling
29. Wood door with 5/16 – 45/64 – 5/16" (8 – 18 – 8 mm) double glazing
30. Rainwater drainage system
31. Steel plate joint
32. 2 23/64 x 2 23/64 x 25/64" (60 x 60 x 10 mm) steel U-profile supporting parapet
33. 1 37/64 x 25/64" (40 x 10 mm) steel bar joint
34. Parapet formed by 2 23/64 x 25/64" (60 x 10 mm) steel profiles
35. 7 3/32 x 7 3/32 x 19/32" (180 x 180 x 15 mm) steel plate joint between parapet and load-bearing structure
36. Mortar layer
37. Steel U-profile finish on false ceiling
38. 1 3/16 x 1 3/16" (30 x 30 mm) steel L-profile anchoring false ceiling to window frame
39. False ceiling formed by 31/64" (12.5 mm) gypsum board, acoustic insulation, supporting frame in 1 1/16 x 2 23/64" (27 x 60 mm) C-profiles fixed to slab by tie rods
40. IPE 360 steel structural beam

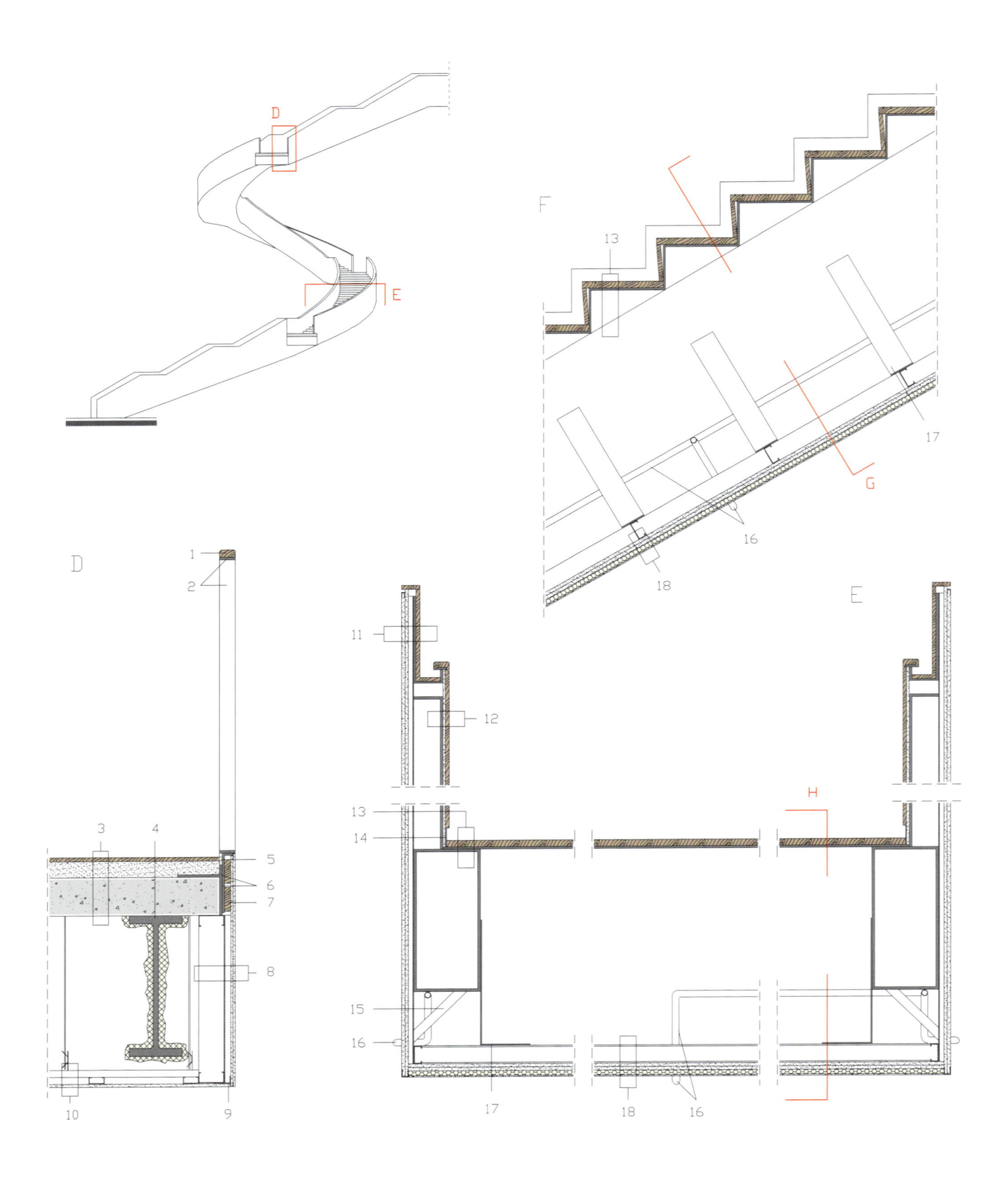

**DETAILS D, E, F: MAIN STAIRCASE
VERTICAL SECTIONS – SCALE 1:20**

1. Ash handrail
2. Parapet in 2 23/64 x 25/64" (60 x 10 mm) steel profiles
3. Floor in 19/32" (15 mm) ash boards, 2 9/16" (65 mm) screed, 5 29/32" (150 mm) reinforced concrete slab
4. 21 21/32" (550 mm) h. steel double T-section beam with spray-applied fireproofing
5. Flexible joint
6. System of steel profiles supporting parapet
7. Wood spacer
8. 45/64" (18 mm) double gypsum board, 63/64" (25 mm) corrugated sheeting, frame of 3 15/16 x 1 37/64" (100 x 40 mm) steel C-profiles supporting false ceiling
9. 2 23/64 x 1 3/16" (60 x 30 mm) steel L-profile trim
10. False ceiling formed by 33/64" (13 mm) gypsum board, supporting frame of steel 2 23/64 x 1 1/16" (60 x 27 mm) C-profiles on tie rods suspended from slab
11. 1 1/32" (26 mm) double gypsum board, 25/32" (20 mm) corrugated sheeting, 25/64" (10 mm) profiled steel plate, 19/32" (15 mm) ash panelling
12. 19/32" (15 mm) ash panelling, 25/64" (10 mm) gypsum board, 25/64" (10 mm) profiled steel plate
13. 63/64" (25 mm) ash tread, 5/16" (8 mm) steel profile supports, 22 3/64 x 9 27/32" (560 x 250 mm) steel box-shaped profile
14. Steel skirting
15. Reinforcing steel box-shaped profile
16. Water fire-extinguishing system
17. 19 11/16 x 7 7/8" (500 x 200 mm) steel L-profile supporting false ceiling
18. 5/32" (4 mm) plaster layer, 25/32" (20 mm) acoustic insulation, 1 1/32" (26 mm) double gypsum board, frame in 2 3/4 x 1 3/16" (70 x 30 mm) steel C-profiles

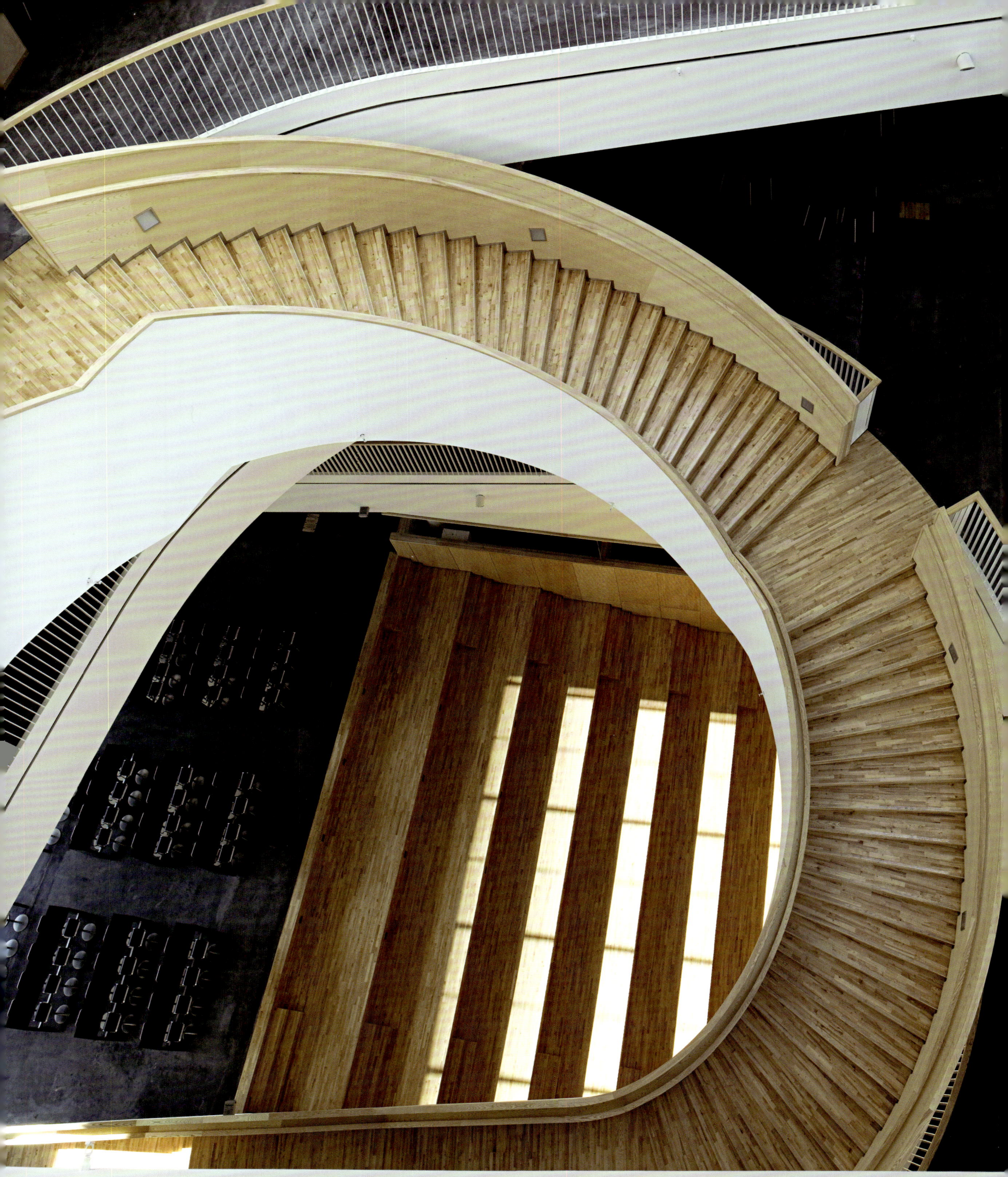

UNIVERSITY LIBRARY
UTRECHT, THE NETHERLANDS

WIEL ARETS ARCHITECTS

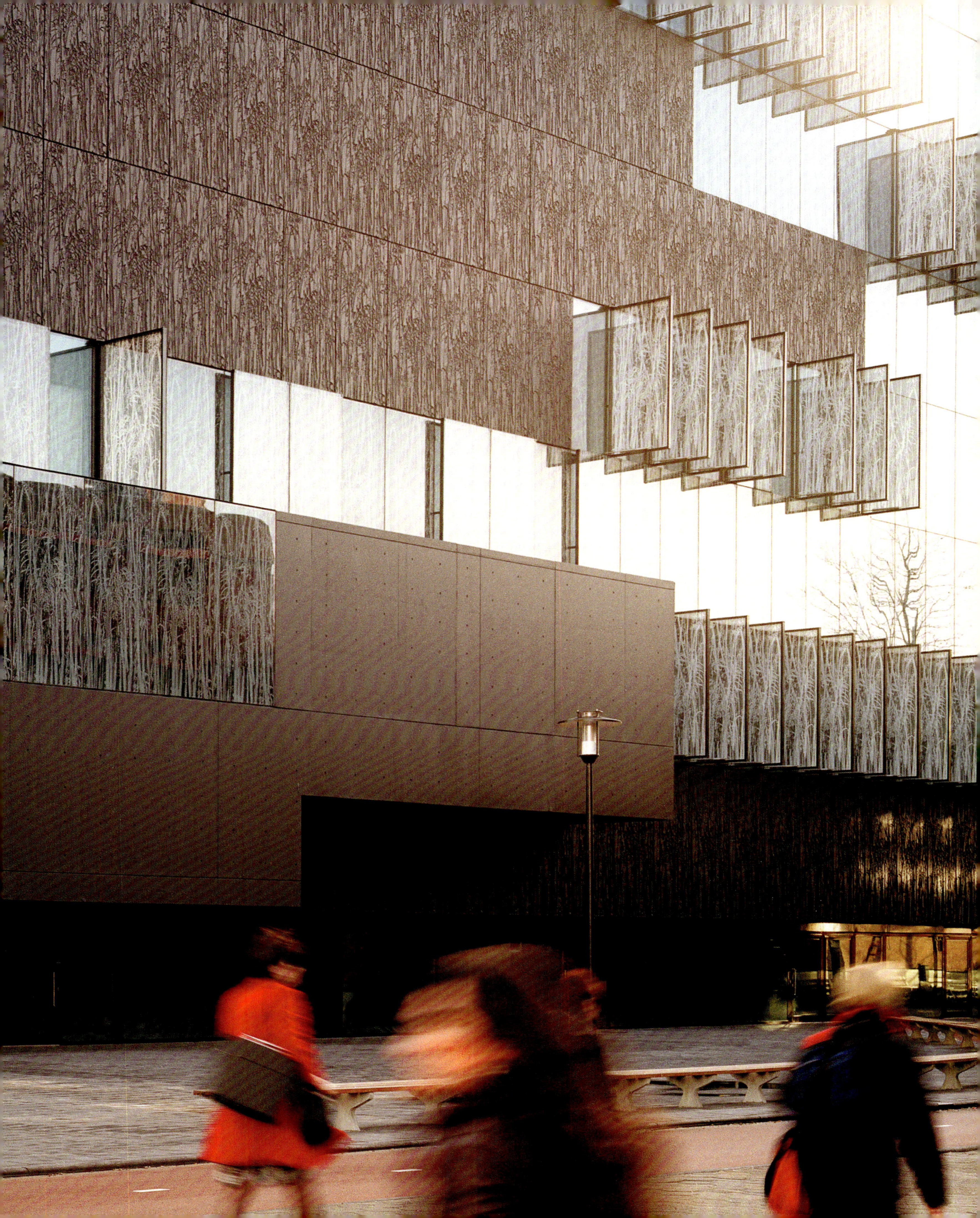

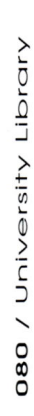

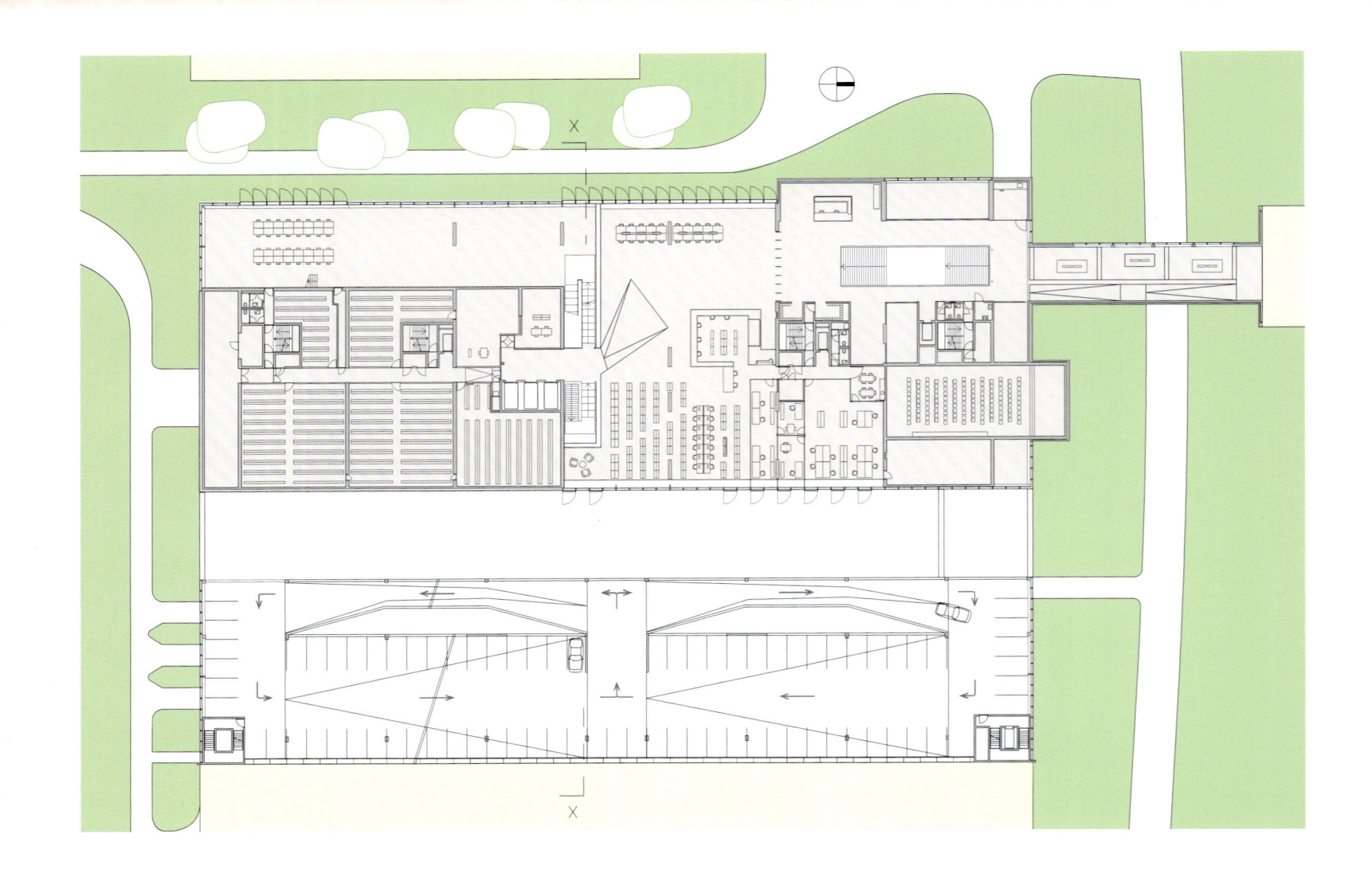

■ First and Sixth Floor Plan - Scale 1:800

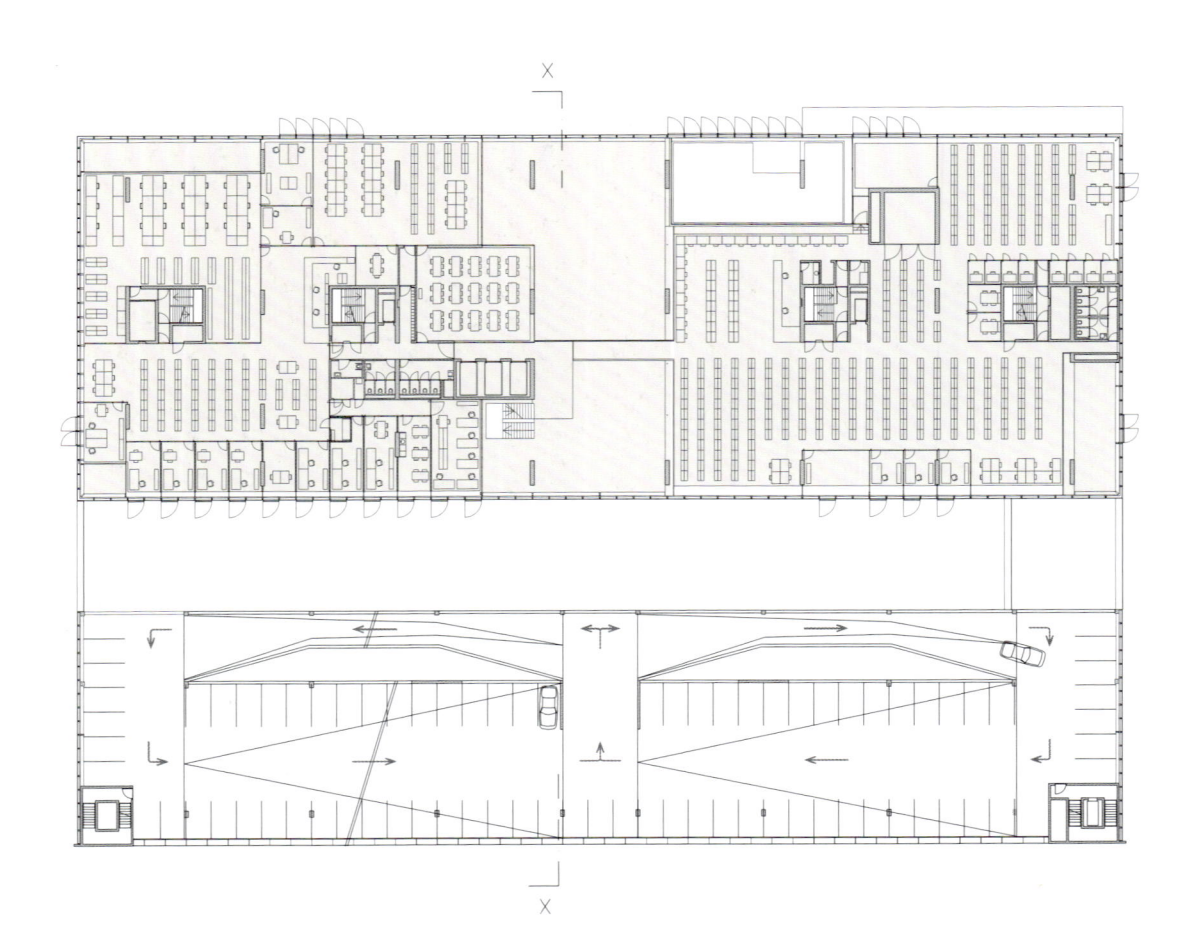

080 / University Library

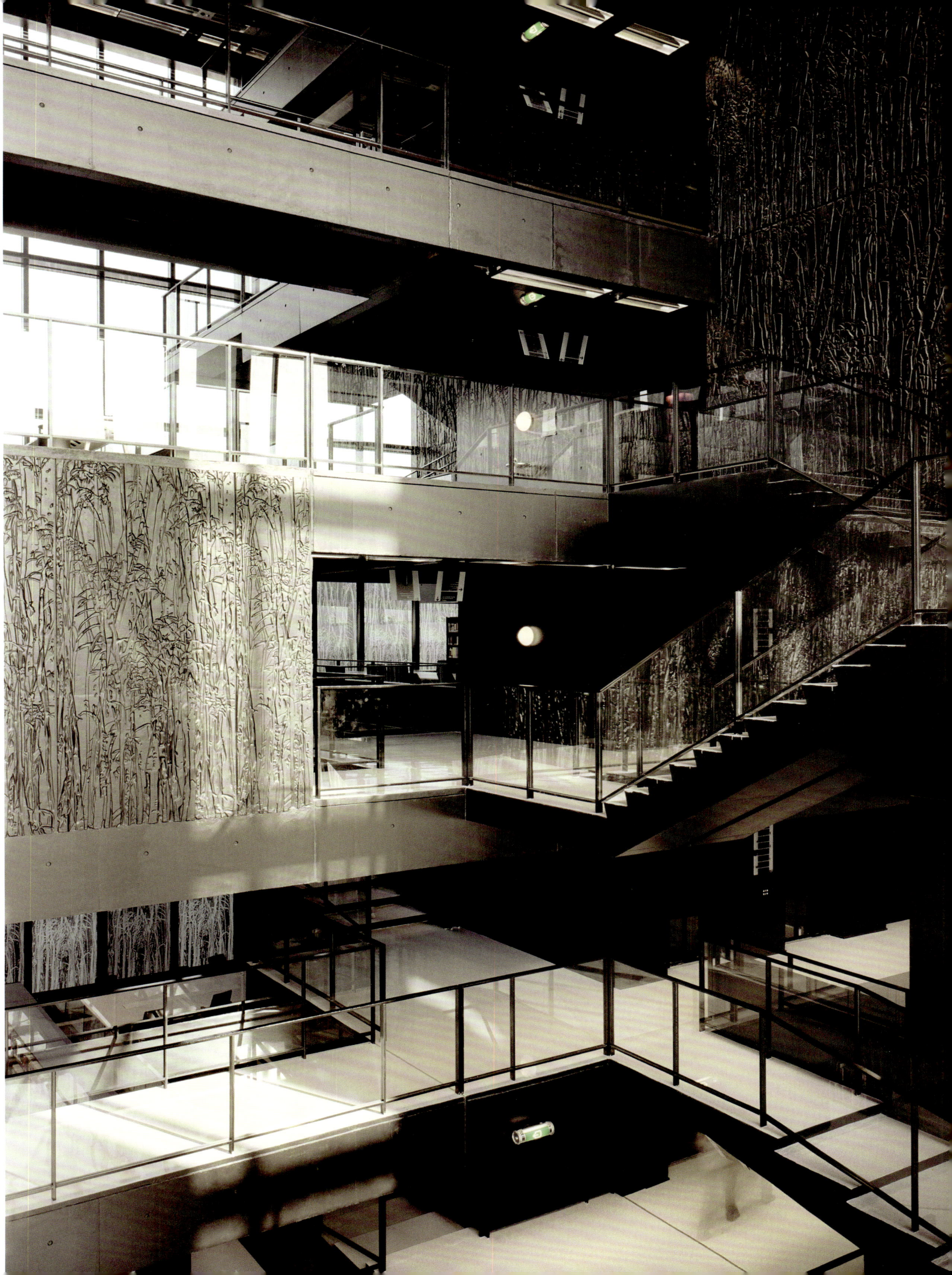

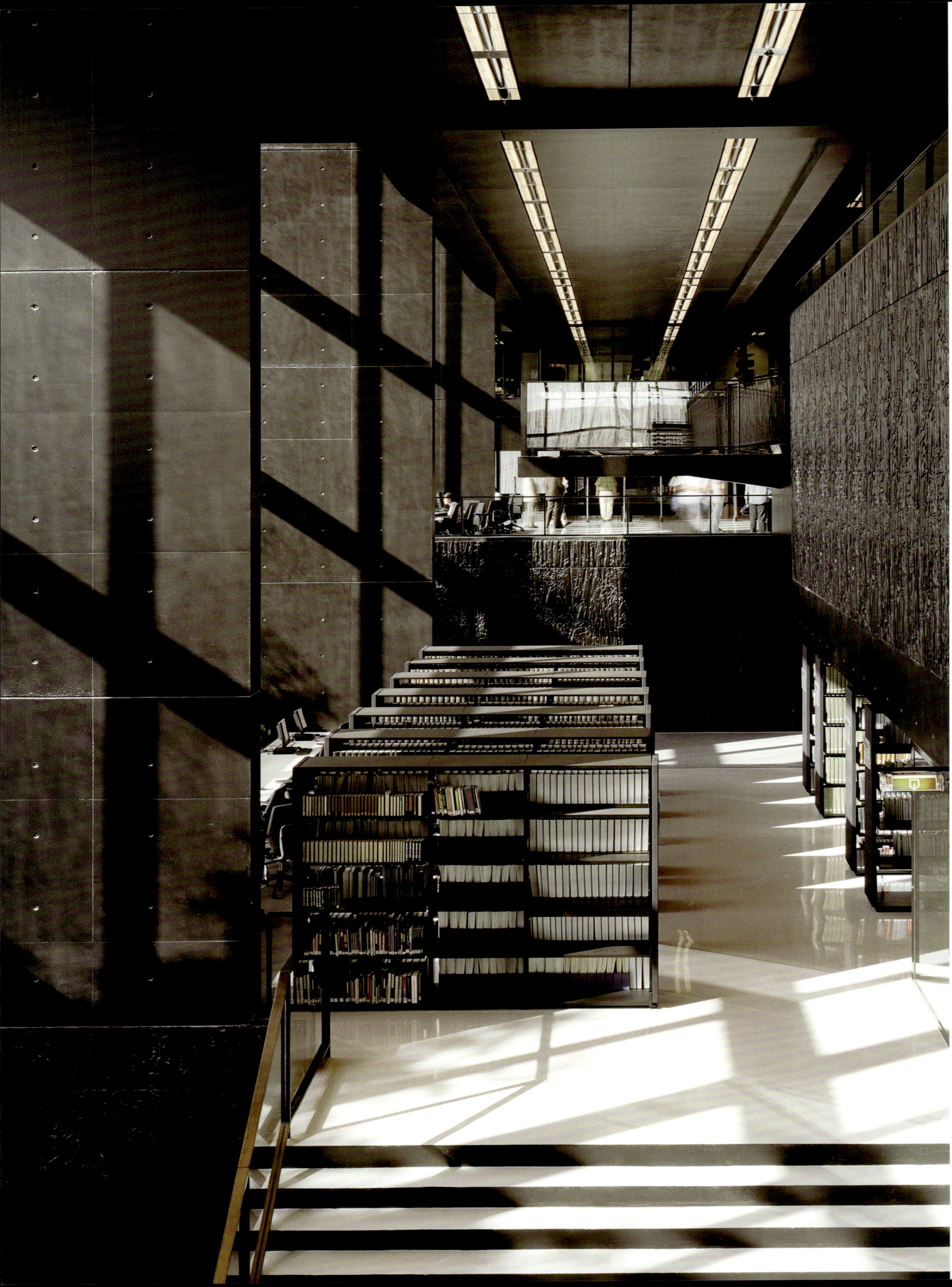

XX Section – Scale 1:800

Reminiscent of a flight data recorder, Utrecht University Library is more than a place where people can consult books – it is a place where they can work in concentrated fashion, but also meet people without the need for any other stimuli except the atmosphere that the building radiates.

Floating like clouds, the book depots divide the space into zones, and are interconnected by stairs and slopes.

The depots in black patterned concrete on which the reading rooms rest are encased by a partly double-glazed façade to which a silk-screened design has been applied to let in natural light. The glass façade also encloses the car park like a smooth skin, making it an integral part of the complex.

On one side is the university site where the view from the raw interior offers a filtered prospect of the open countryside around; on the other is the view of the long slopes beside the inner courtyard which act as blinds filtering the view of the car park. Based on the idea that silent communication is important in a building where there is hardly any talking, the atmosphere is determined, with an emphasis on creating a sense of security. This was essential in the choice of a black interior. A light, shiny floor provides enough reflection of natural or artificial light to illuminate some of the 4.2 million books to be found on the open shelves, while the long white tables make reading a book or consulting electronic information possible without excessive strain.

The individual workplace with full facilities is the key element. They have been positioned in such a way that the user's choice of workplace determines the degree of communication with other users. Absorption versus confrontation, working in a concentrated way versus communication: these are the main premises in this library where also the infrastructure has more than one function.

This also informs the circulation route which leads to the bar, lounge area, reception corner (cocktail corner), auditorium and desks, all of which are highlighted with red rubber. Other facilities such as shops add a further dimension to the route, breaking down the monofunctionality of the library programme.

084 / University Library

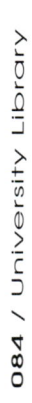

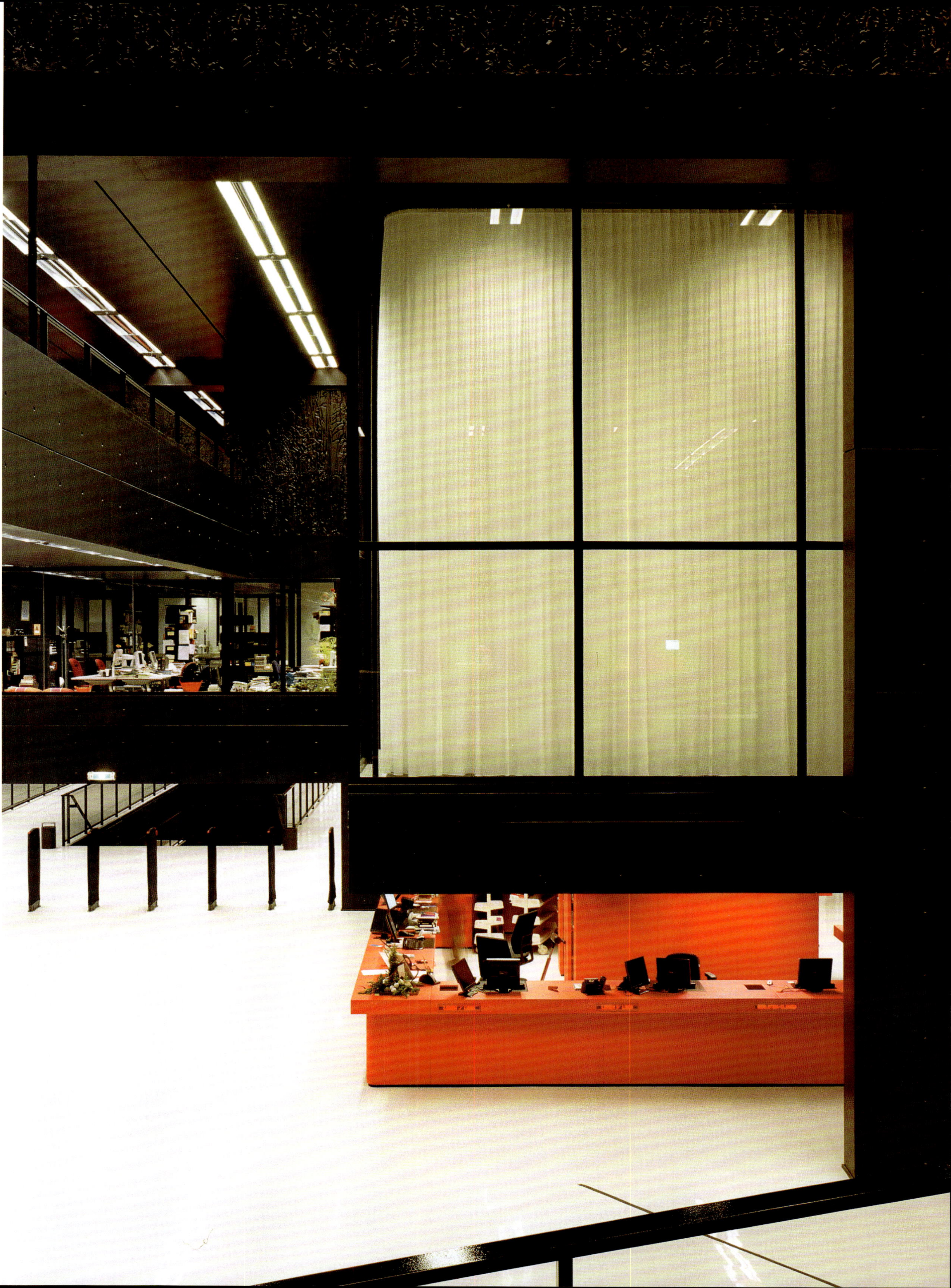

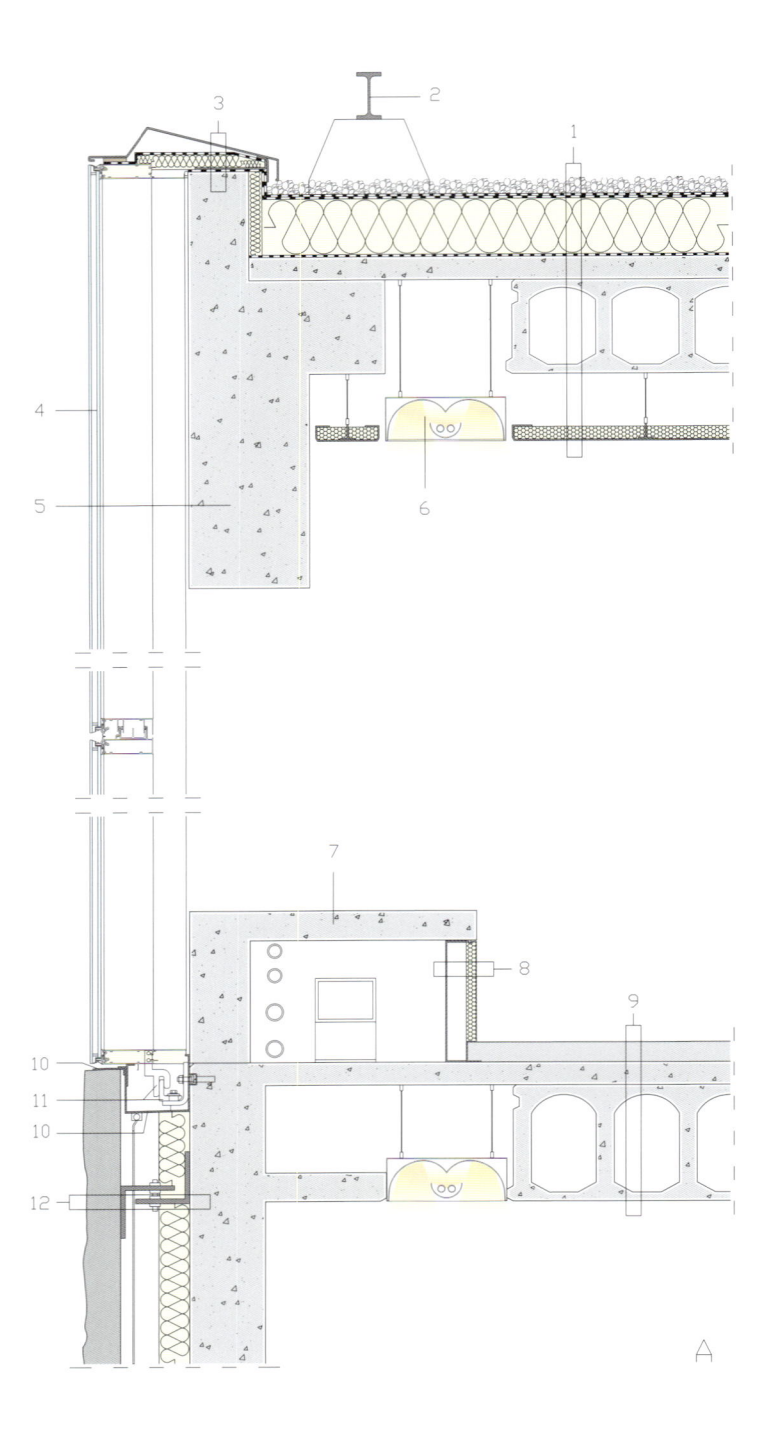

**DETAILS A, B, C:
CONSTRUCTION SYSTEM
VERTICAL SECTIONS – SCALE 1:25**

1. Roof comprising ballast layer, double waterproofing membrane, 7 7/8" (200 mm) board insulation, vapour barrier, 3 1/8" (80 mm) reinforced concrete slab, pre-cast 12 1/2" (320 mm) reinforced concrete slab, false ceiling formed by 2" (50 mm) aluminium panels with acoustic insulation on tie rods suspended from slab
2. IPE 160 beam anchoring façade maintenance system
3. Aluminium flashing, waterproofing membrane, 2" (50 mm) board insulation, aluminium L-profile, waterproofing membrane, reinforced concrete edge
4. Continuous glazed façade formed by 5/16 – 3/4 – 3/8" (8 – 18 – 10 mm) aluminium double-glazing units with thermal insulating glass
5. Reinforced concrete beam painted black
6. Reflected lighting
7. Installation space cover in reinforced concrete painted black
8. Aluminium profile, acoustic insulation, supporting aluminium C-profile
9. Floor in 2 3/4" (70 mm) concrete tiles with epoxy finish, 3 1/8" (80 mm) reinforced concrete slab, pre-cast 15 3/4" (400 mm) reinforced concrete slab
10. Aluminium profile
11. Steel brackets securing glazed façade to supporting structure

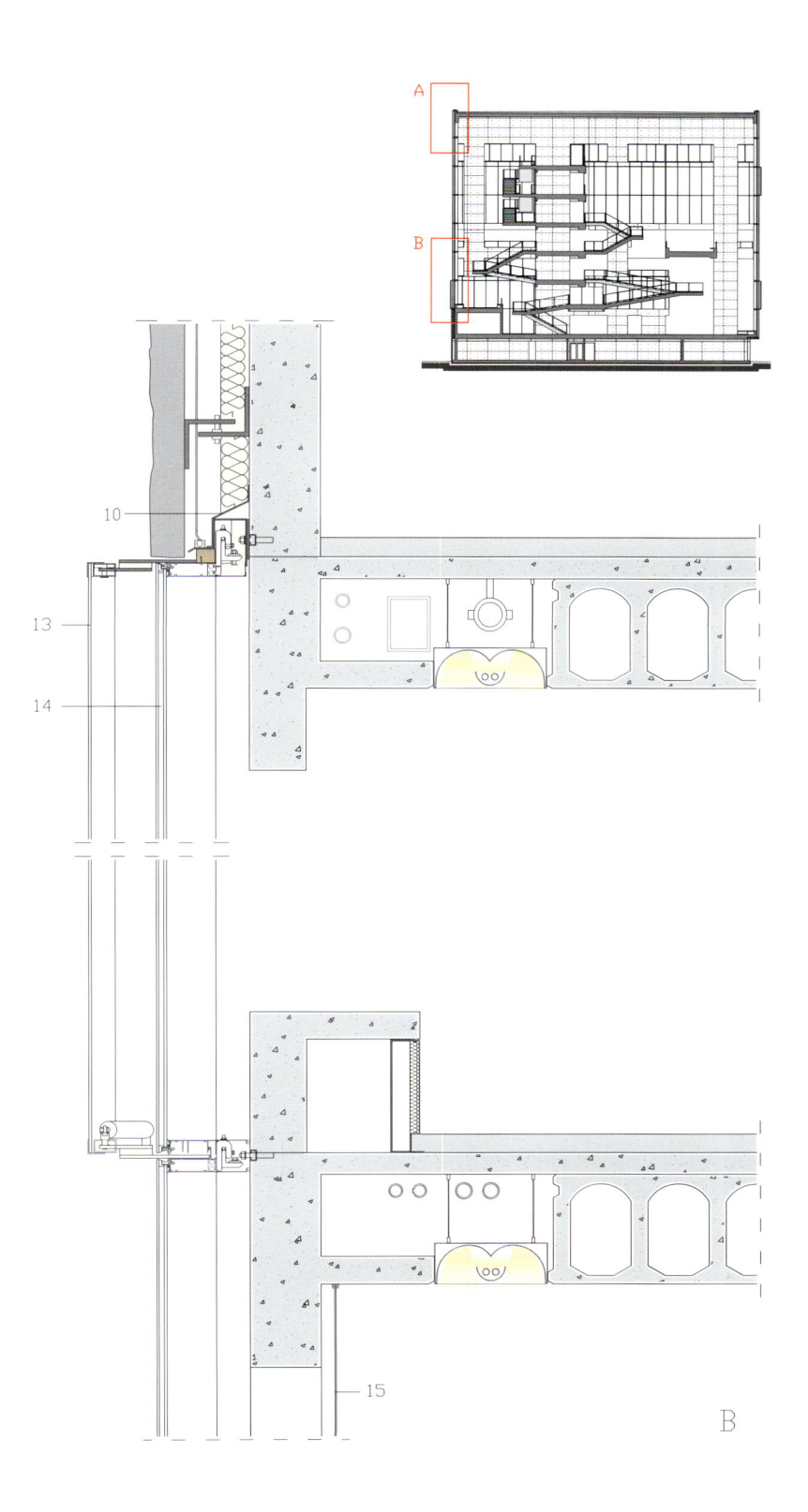

12. Pre-cast concrete panel with textured finish painted black, structure of 7 1/8" x 7 1/8" (180 x 180 mm) steel L-profiles securing panel to supporting structure, steel tie rod bracing, 4" (100 mm) board insulation, 9 3/8" (250 mm) reinforced concrete structure
13. Silk-screened glass in aluminium frame with automatic movement based on position of sun
14. Continuous glazed façade formed by 5/16 – 3/4 – 3/8" (8 – 18 – 10 mm) aluminium double-glazing units with thermal insulating glass
15. Sun blind
16. Suspended floor in 2" (50 mm) concrete tiles painted black, height adjustable joints, polystyrene board insulation on 1.5% slope, waterproofing membrane, 16 1/8" (410 mm) reinforced concrete beam
17. Aluminium flashing
18. 5 7/8" (150 mm) cladding painted black, 7 1/8" (180 mm) board insulation, 9 3/8" (250 mm) reinforced concrete structure
19. Floor in 2 3/4" (70 mm) concrete tiles with epoxy finish, 11" (280 mm) reinforced concrete slab, 3 1/8" (80 mm) board insulation, 7 7/8" (200 mm) cladding in reinforced concrete painted black
20. Steel casing, 4" (100 mm) board insulation
21. Aluminium casing, aluminium L-profile support
22. 1/8 – 1 – 1/8" (4 – 25 – 4 mm) aluminium double-glazing unit

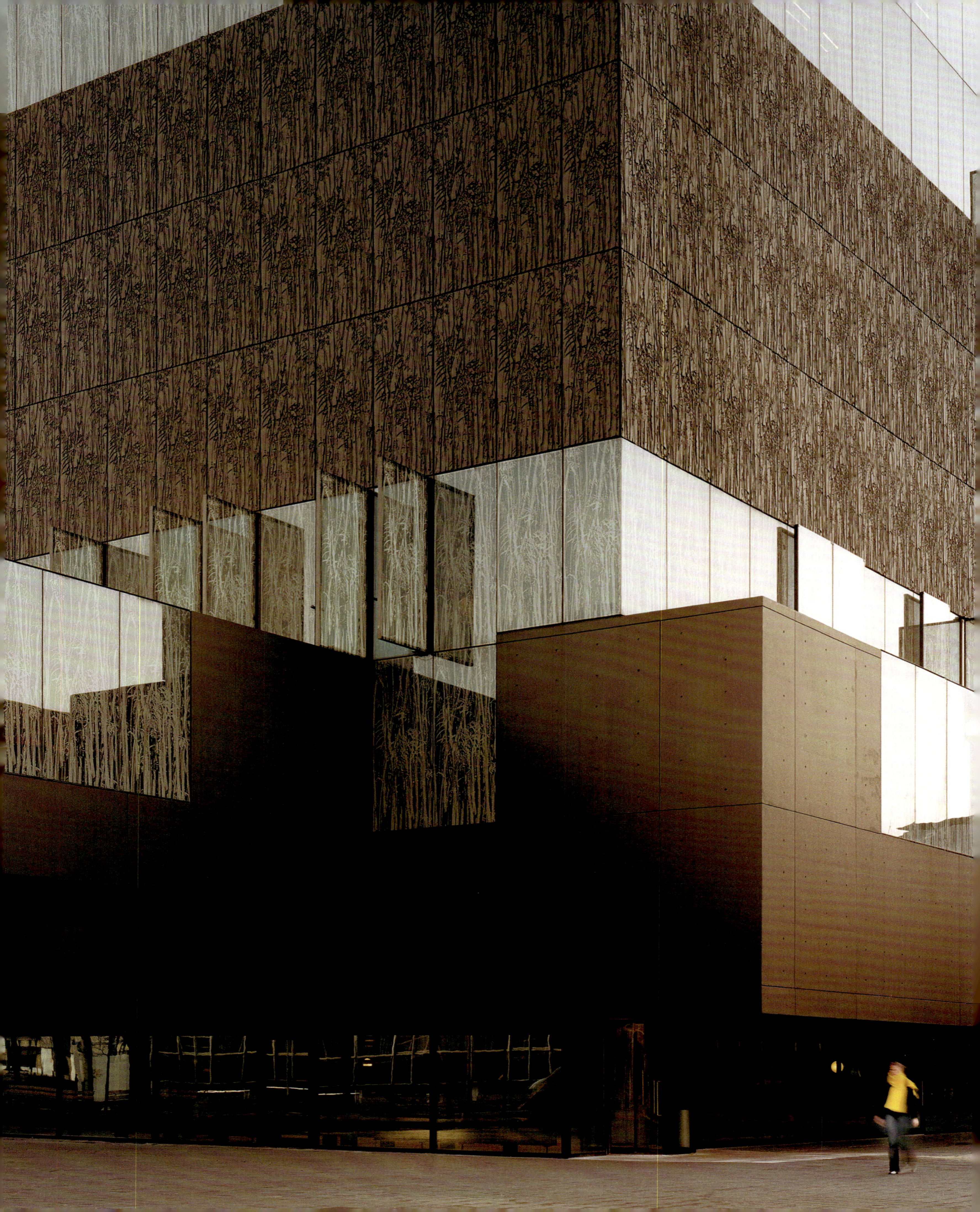

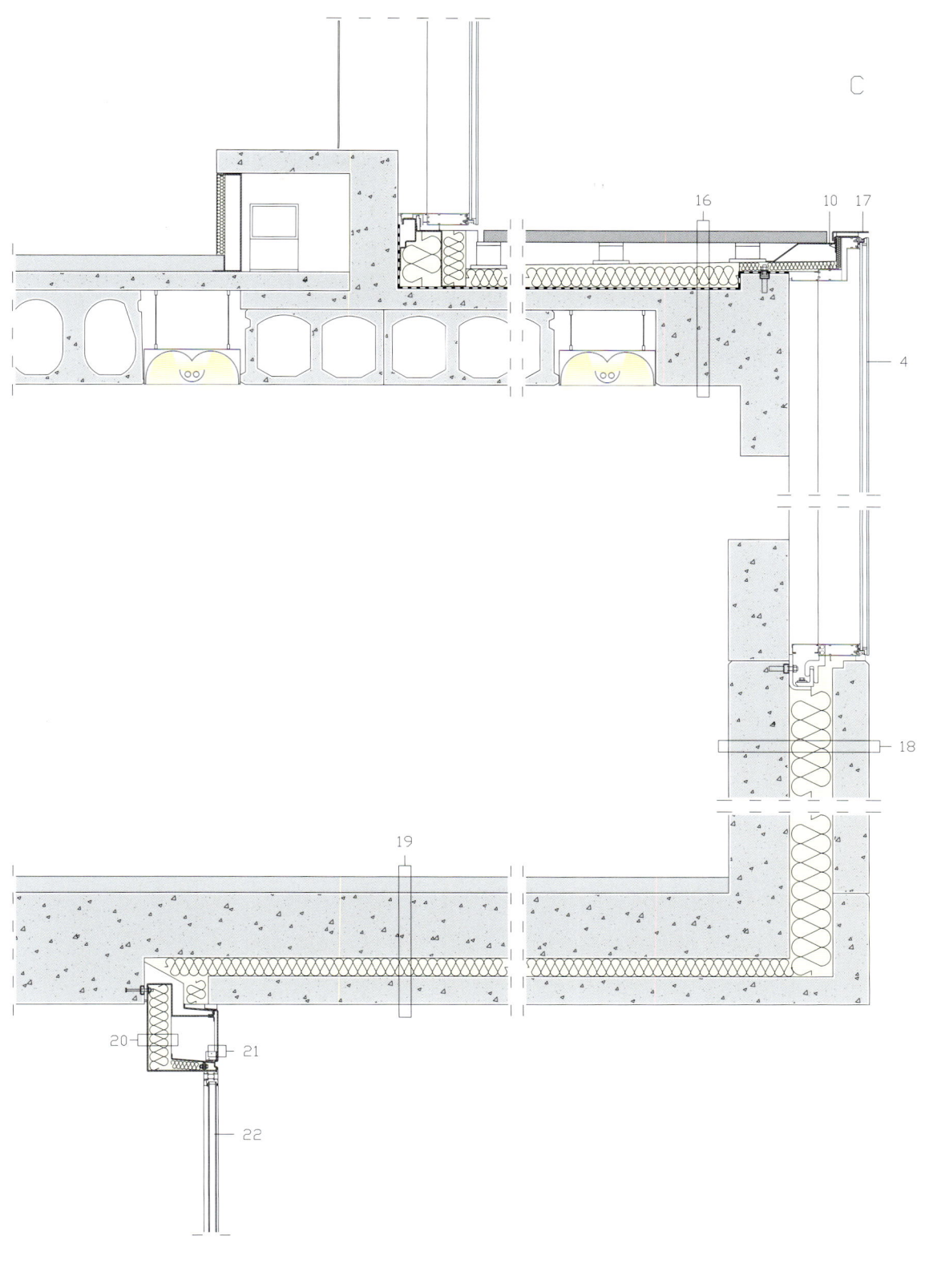

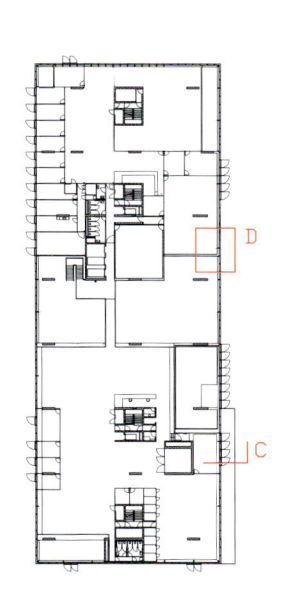

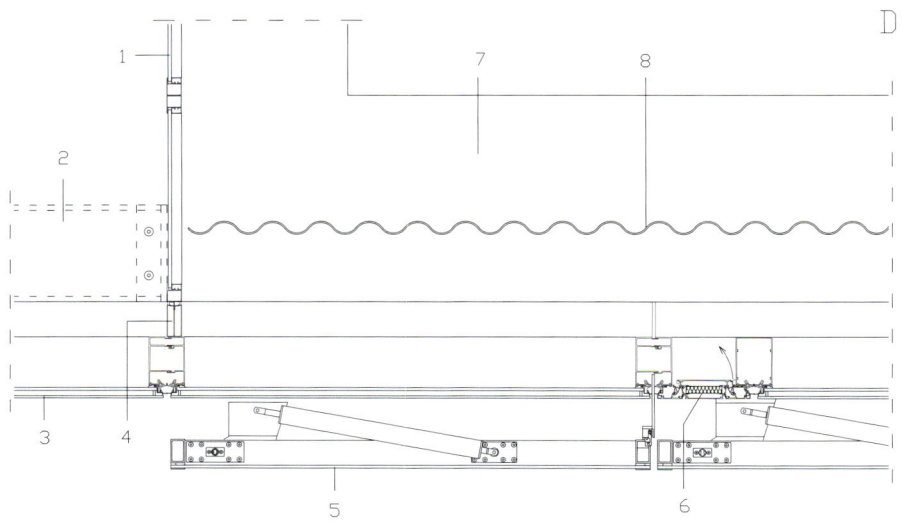

DETAIL D: FAÇADE
HORIZONTAL SECTION – SCALE 1:25

1. Glazed interior wall with aluminium frame
2. Steel beam supporting façade panels
3. Continuous glazed façade formed by 5/16 – 3/4 – 3/8" (8 – 18 – 10 mm) aluminium double-glazing units with thermal insulating glass
4. Steel profile with thermal insulation between façade and glazed interior wall
5. Silk-screened glass in aluminium frame with automatic movement based on position of sun
6. Manually operated ventilation panel with thermal insulation
7. Concrete installation space cover (parallel to plane of section)
8. Sunblind

NETHERLANDS INSTITUTE FOR SOUND AND VISION
HILVERSUM, THE NETHERLANDS

NEUTELINGS RIEDIJK ARCHITECTS

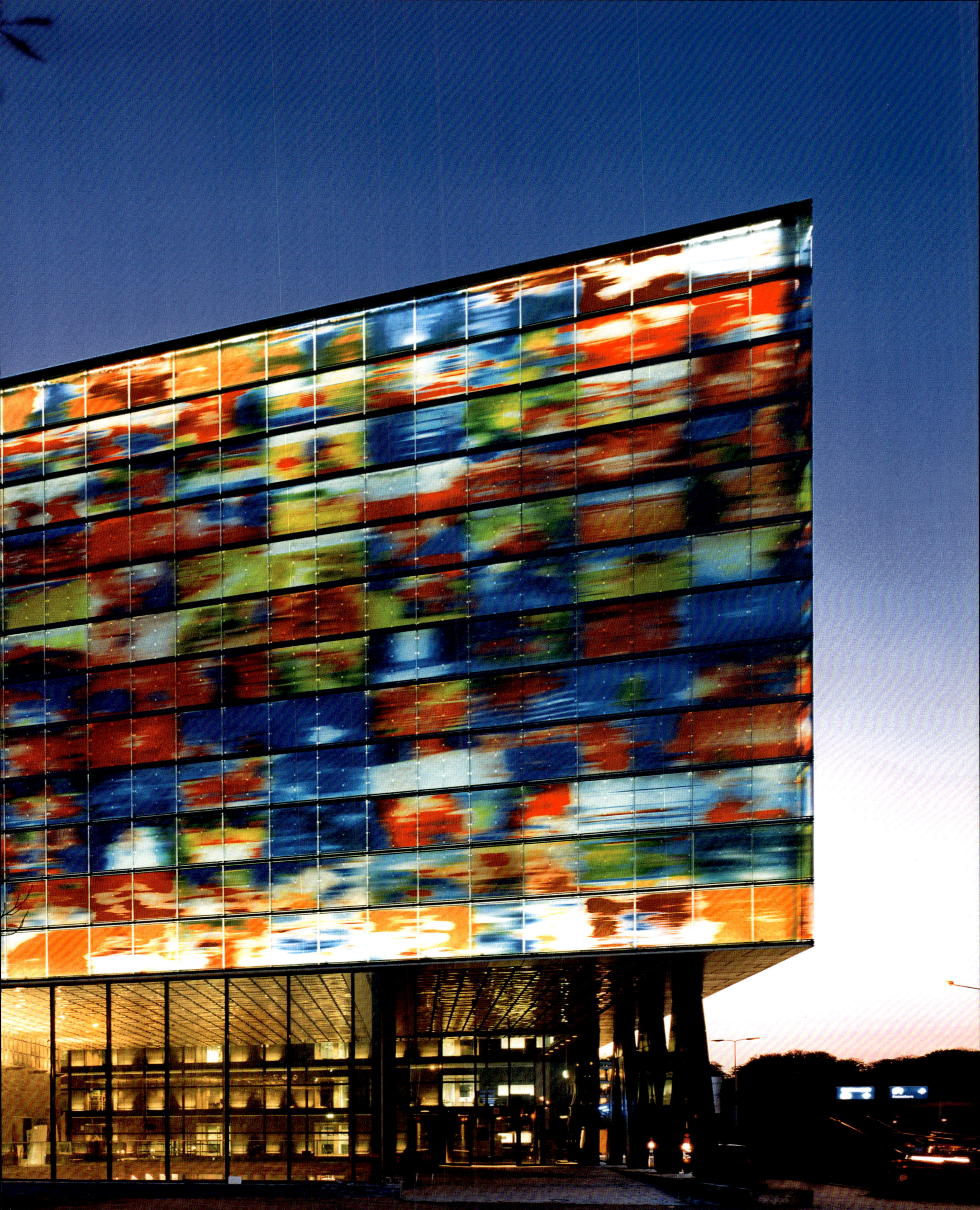

Today architecture is image. We may bemoan the fact that experience is less and less a part of how a landscape is perceived and understood, but it's also true that most of what we know comes to us via images: from the television screen, advertising posters or glimpsed through the windows of a moving car. This was the premise for Willem Neutelings and Michiel Riedijk's design for the Netherlands Institute for Sound and Vision (Nederlands Instituut voor Beeld en Geluid) in Hilversum. The building houses the country's entire national radio and television archive, offices, and an area called "Media Experience" where the public can get a hands-on understanding of how a TV studio works. The Institute has been designed as the monumental entrance to a quarter grouping Holland's television studios. Called Media Park, it is the site of the splendid building of broadcaster VPRO – the first ever project by architectural practice MVRDV (1993 – 1997).

By applying images to the Institute's glazed façade – some 748 photo frames – Riedijk has turned it into a huge kaleidoscope. Colours are filtered as if through the window of a giant Gothic cathedral. Special application technology makes each image resemble a sort of bas-relief, distinguishable, however, only under certain conditions of light or distance. This vibrant coat of many colours transforms the building into a brilliantly distinctive urban landmark. The outside is just the tip of the iceberg though.

Inside, a densely organized series of diverse volumes contrasts markedly with the flat outer façades. Neutelings and Riedijk had the brilliant idea of splitting the overall volume into two equal parts: the underground levels to house the huge archive and, from the ground level up, areas open to the public – exhibition spaces, offices and service zones like the atrium, restaurant, auditorium, shop and toilet facilities. Although distinct, each area converges on the great central cavity. Hugging the sides of this gaping hole, the stacked corridors plunge, in Dantesque Inferno style, five storeys below ground.

Soaring upwards are the stepped volumes of the exhibition hall, meeting rooms, and restaurant "sloping gently down" towards a glazed façade overlooking the garden. Each section is code-clad: stone with orange-backed apertures for the archive, and glass for the offices, with aluminium cladding reminiscent of a '70s Paco Rabanne creation. The stepped and sloping geometries of archive, south-facing restaurant and west-facing exhibition hall allow light to penetrate the depths of the building.

The overall result is one of surprising sculptural spaces that lend the building its inimitable character. With the Netherlands Institute for Sound and Vision, the architects have overturned their characteristic style of creating urban landmarks signalled by their unmistakeable shape. Although highly distinctive, the Institute's façades are regular. It is inside that the architects' articulated spatial distributions are given full rein. The contrast between the angular external elevations, the ethereal quality of the aboveground elements, and the solid materiality of the underground structures is immediately apparent from the atrium.

The building's structural frame enhances the contrast. The exhibition space is supported by just three elements: two pillars visible on the façade (three upside-down Vs), and a central element. The 54 m (177 ft) façade of exhibition hall and office block to the west is one huge, top-hung, glazed curtain wall. The dramatic effect of the coloured light streaming through the glazing further highlights the ineffable lightness of the whole construction.

This unique building successfully combines incompatible opposites: the need to protect some 700,000 hours of highly sensitive archival film material, and the exuberantly spectacular scenario required of a place like "Media Experience" where each section is distinct yet visible. In keeping with their well-honed practice, Neutelings and Riedijk have laid out a succession of environments designed to present contrasting perceptual impressions. The entrance bridge over the archive hollow takes the visitor towards the enormous exhibition hall, on to the auditorium and finally to the restaurant. Neutelings and Riedijk allow images to caress surfaces while their architecture provides an awesome spatial experience.

■ Ground Floor Plan – Scale 1:500

1. Entrance
2. Central Hall
3. Central Info and Ticket Desk
4. Restaurant
5. Shop
6. Offices
7. Terrace
8. Temporary Exhibition
9. Computer Room
10. Auditorium 1
11. Auditorium 2

■ Second Floor Plan – Scale 1:500

■ First Underground Floor Plan – Scale 1:500

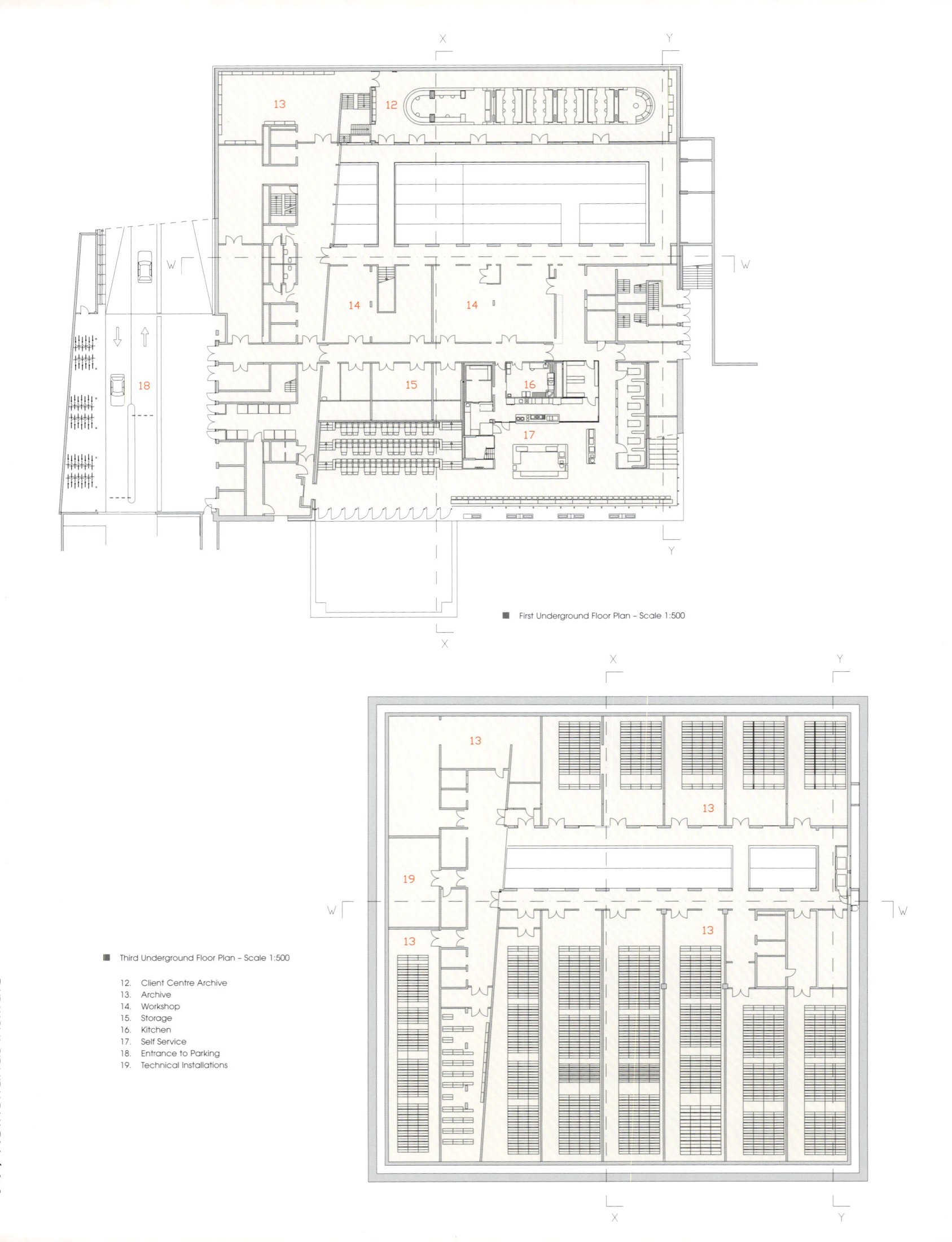

■ Third Underground Floor Plan – Scale 1:500

12. Client Centre Archive
13. Archive
14. Workshop
15. Storage
16. Kitchen
17. Self Service
18. Entrance to Parking
19. Technical Installations

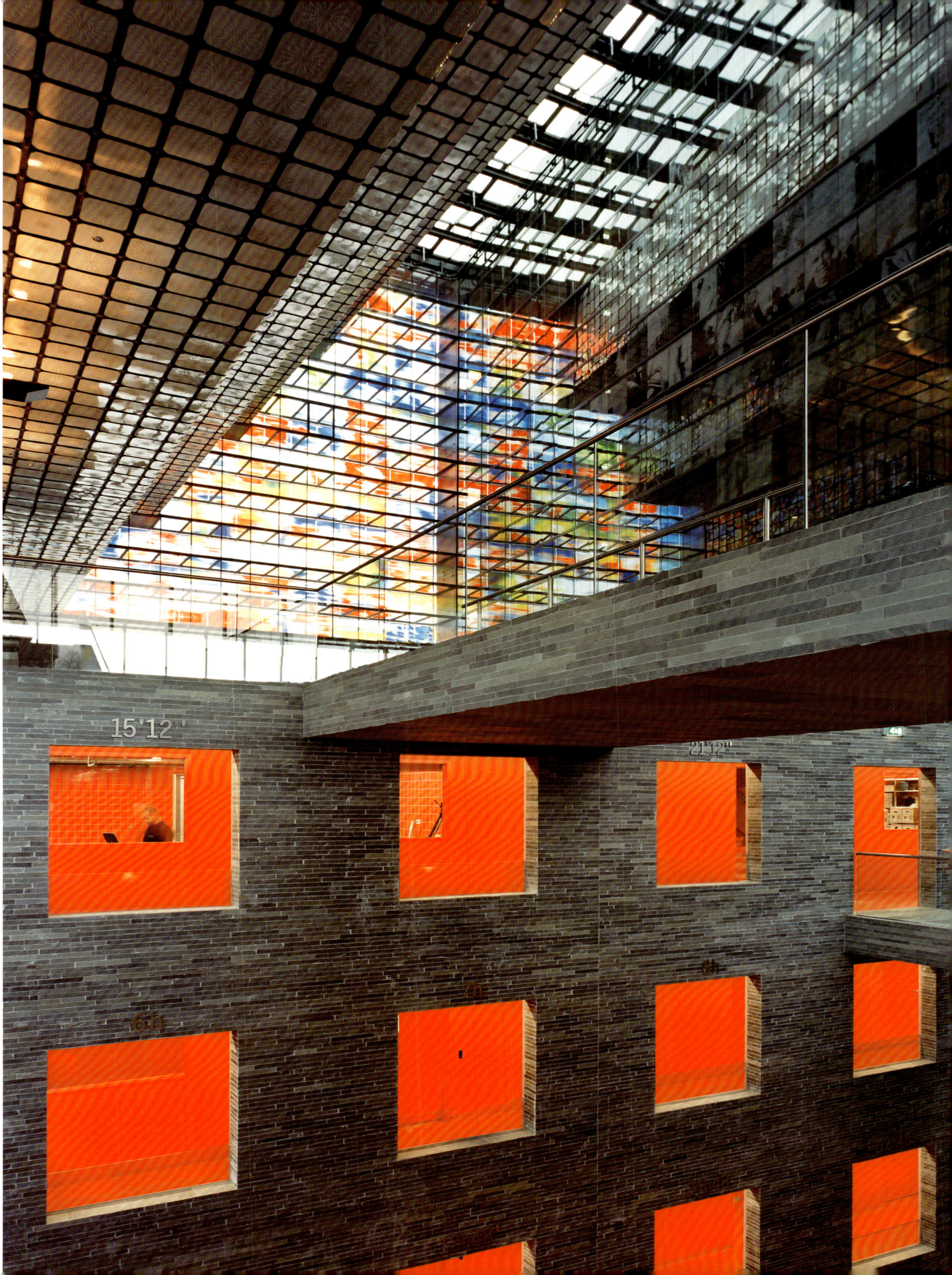
15'12"
21'12"

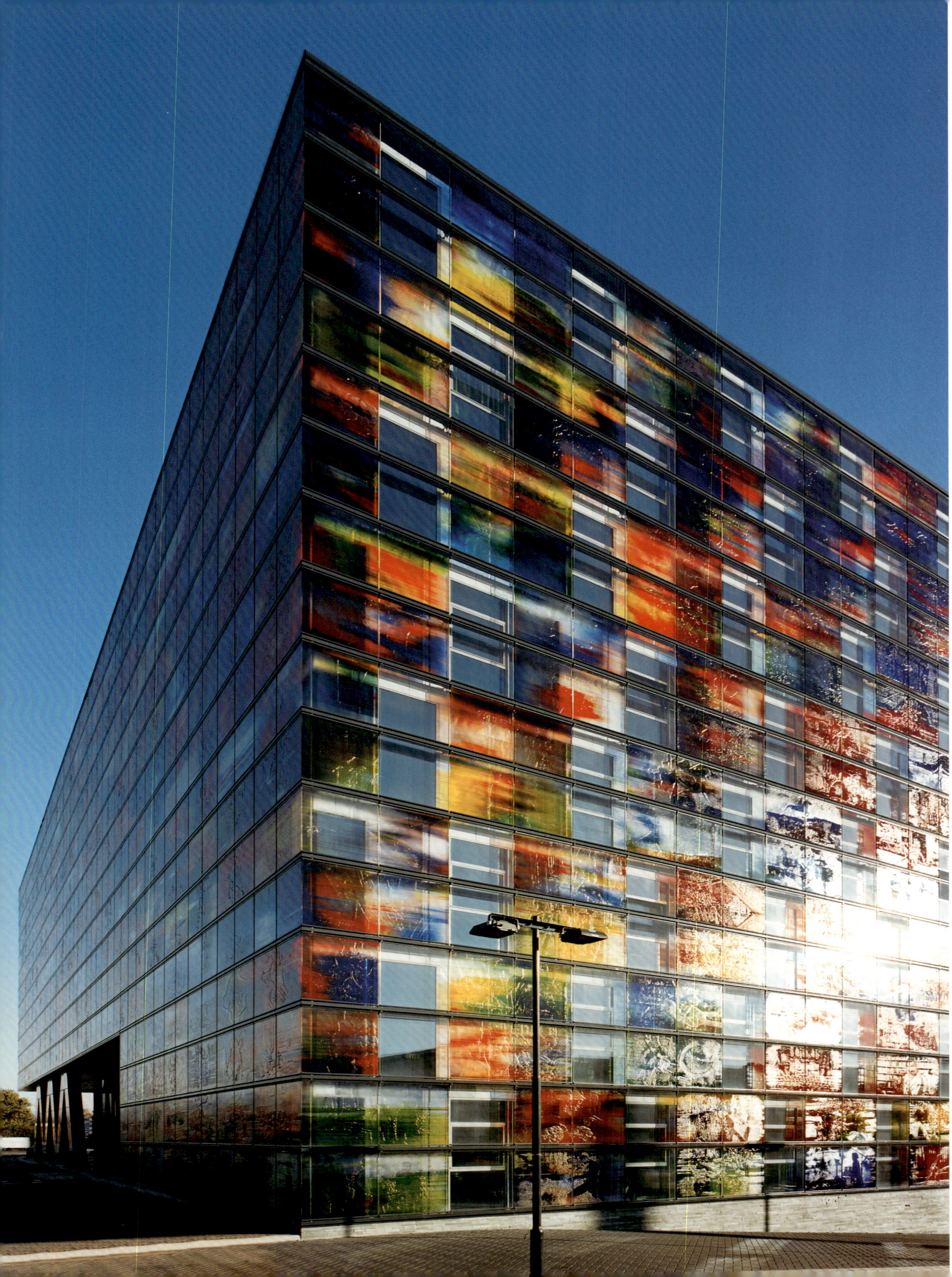

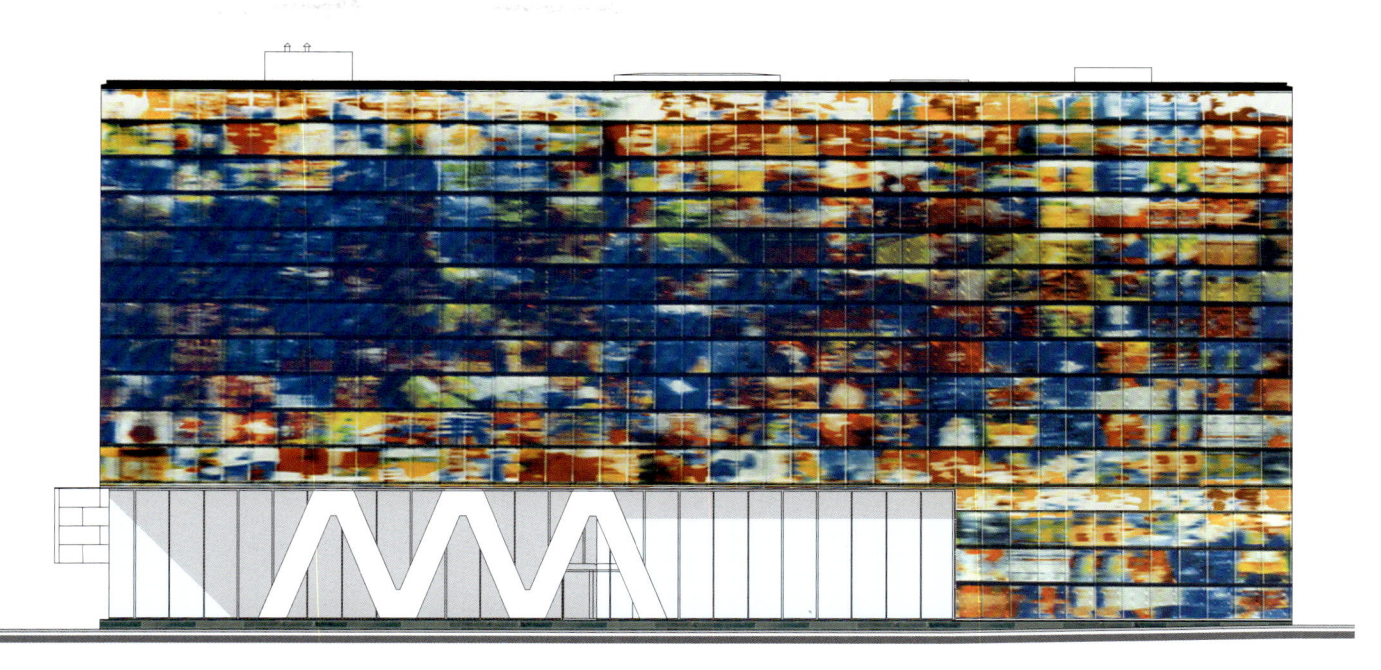

■ East Elevation – Scale 1:350

For the glass façade of the Netherlands Institute for Sound and Vision in Hilversum, we were looking for a way to translate some original TV-images taken from the archives into sustainable coloured high-relief glass panels. What we sought to achieve was the quality of light-transmitting cathedral windows, not just a piece of glazed and mirrored technology but a lightly tactile surface.

To make the façade, it took us and Jaap Drupsteen three years, in collaboration with a research team from TNO Eindhoven and Saint-Gobain, who developed an entirely new production line. The result was 748 coloured high-relief images, applied to more than 2100 glass panels.

The challenge lay in incorporating a wide range of televised images in the façade, forming a random selection from the Institute's archives. In manufacturing the panels we opted, for reasons largely of durability, for a stained-glass technique in which a ceramic paste is applied to glazed panels by means of a specially designed printer.

Drupsteen transferred the manipulated video stills to the panels, a completely digital operation allowing him, theoretically, to transfer an unlimited number of different images at no additional cost. Much more difficult was the process of creating relief, which relies on the principle used in slumping glass.

After choosing a video still, Drupsteen milled its positive images into an MDF panel with a CNC (computer numerical control) milling machine. He then placed the wood panel, coated on one side in ceramic paste, on the sand mould in an oven heated to 820° C. At this temperature the paste burned the image into the glass, and the glass panel softened enough to take on the shape of the mould.

The result was a coloured, high-relief glass pane that is UV resistant and incorporates long-term durability.

Neutelings Riedijk Architects

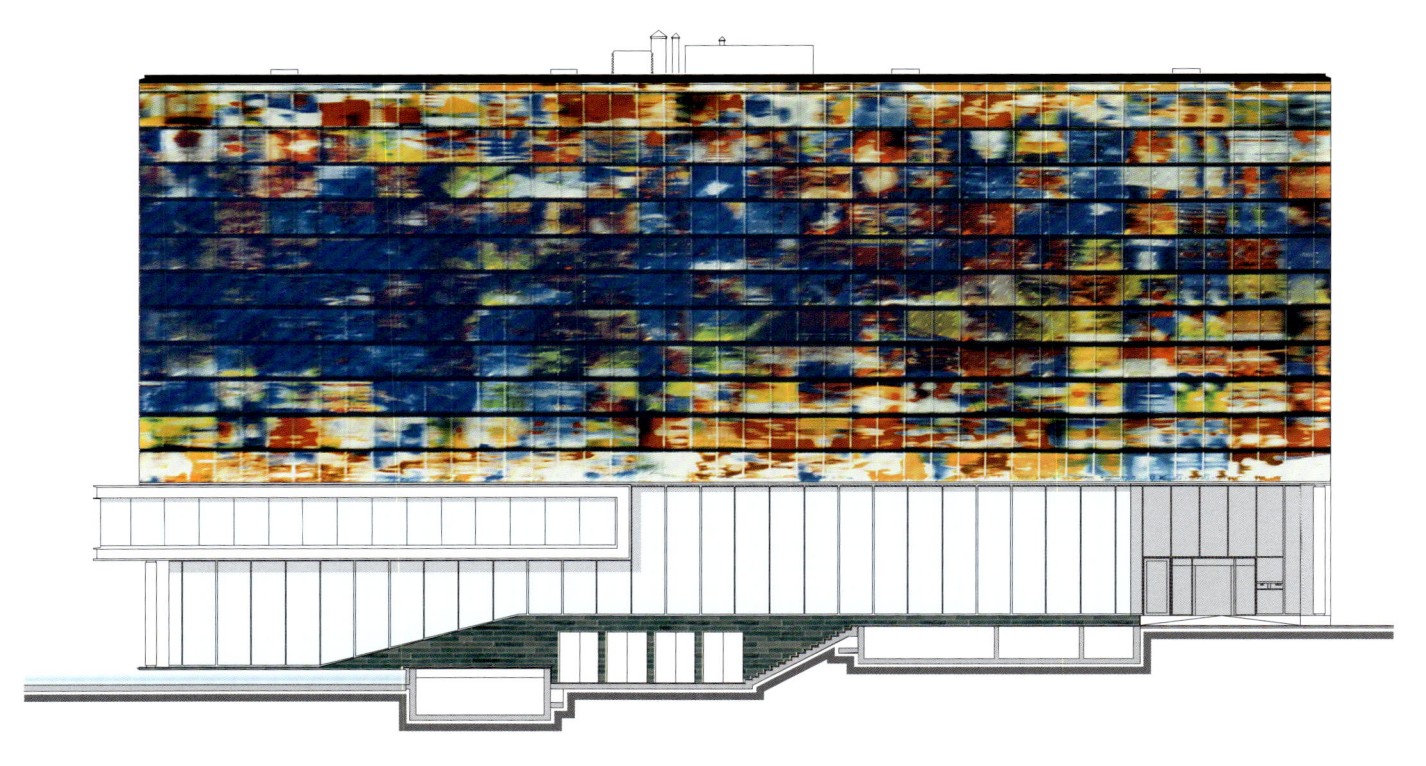

■ South Elevation – Scale 1:350

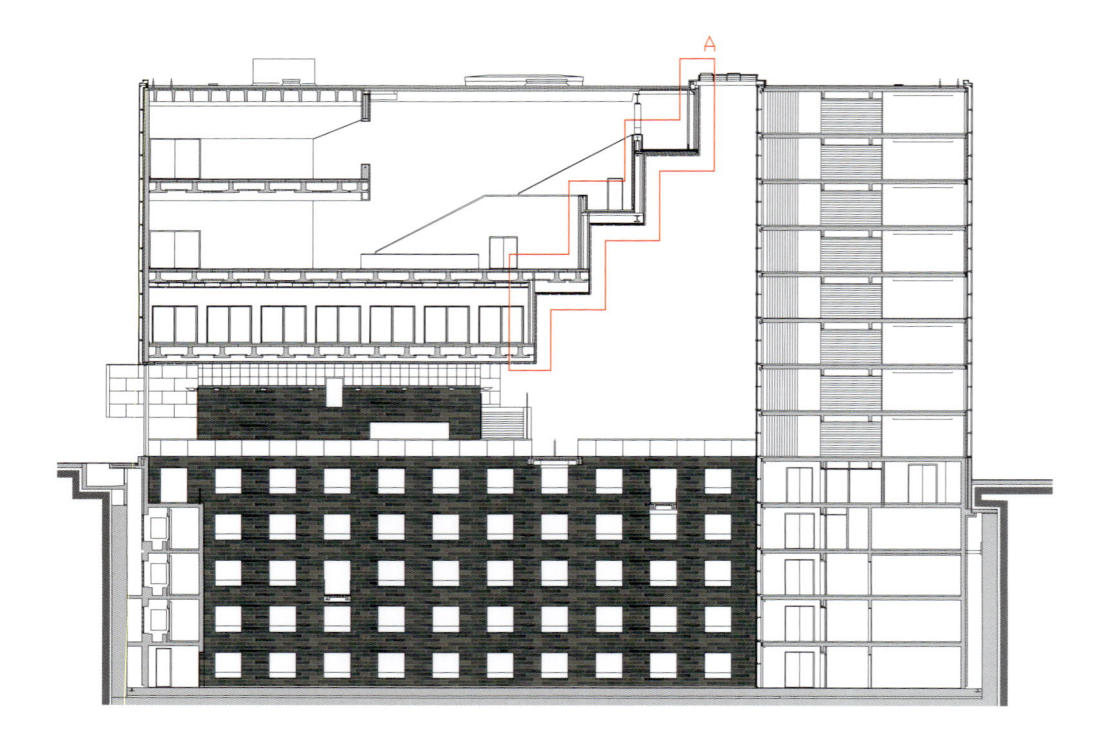

■ WW Cross Section – Scale 1:500

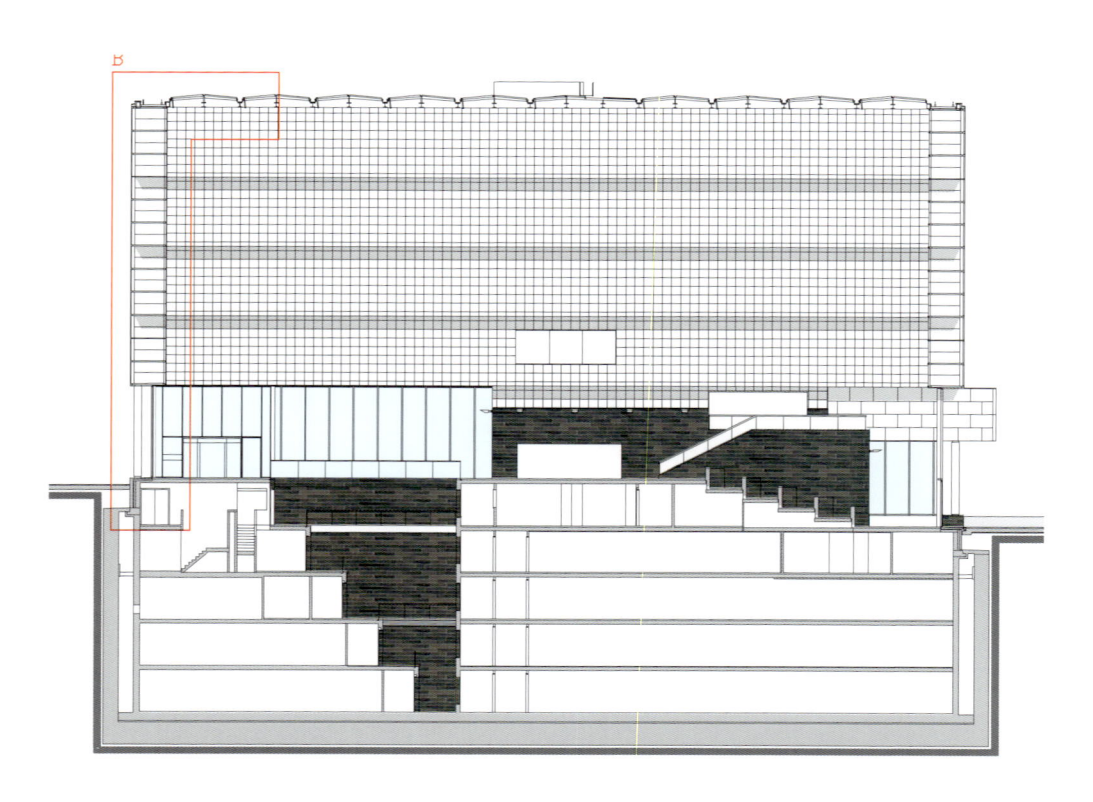

■ XX Longitudinal Section – Scale 1:500

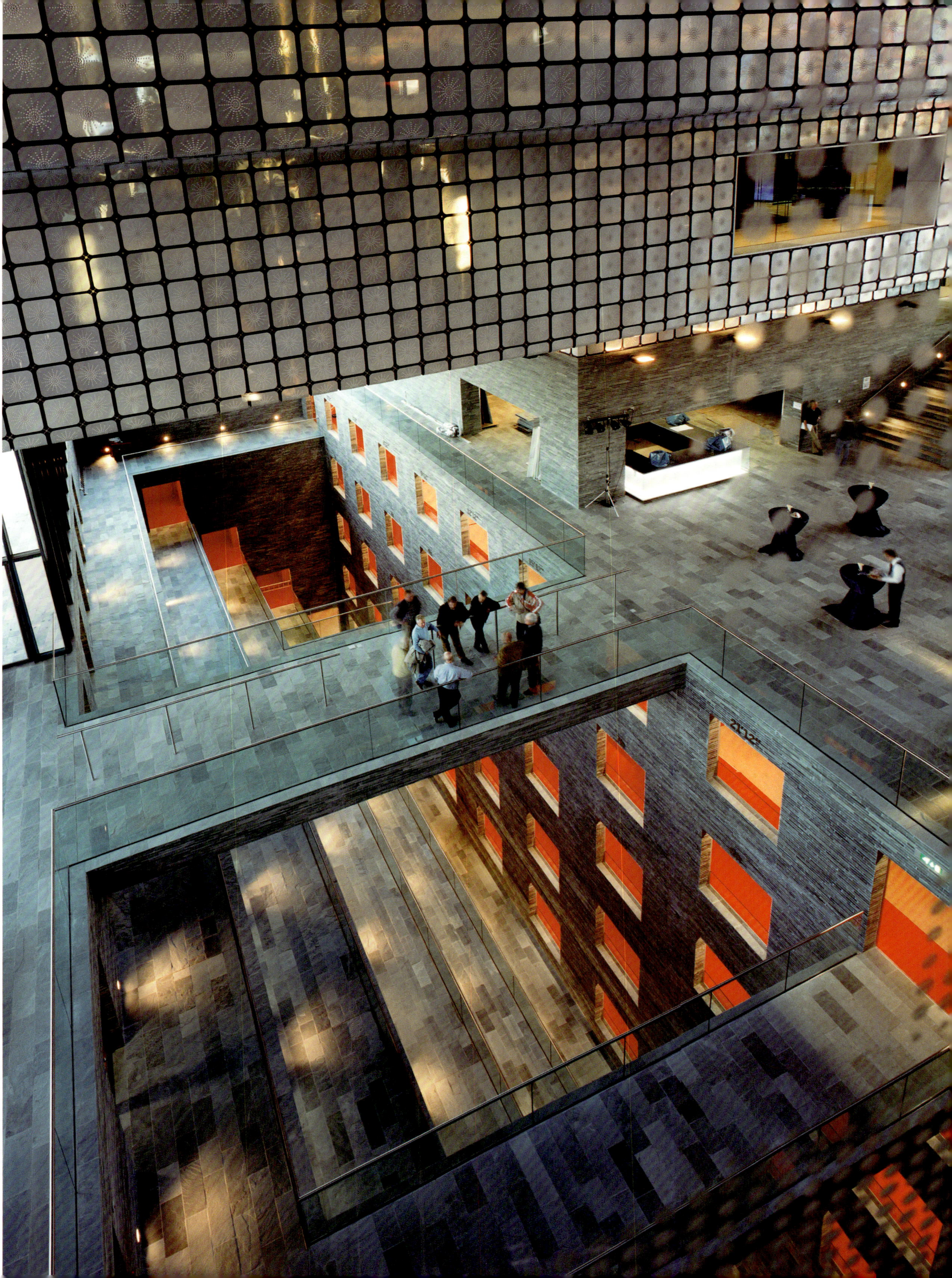

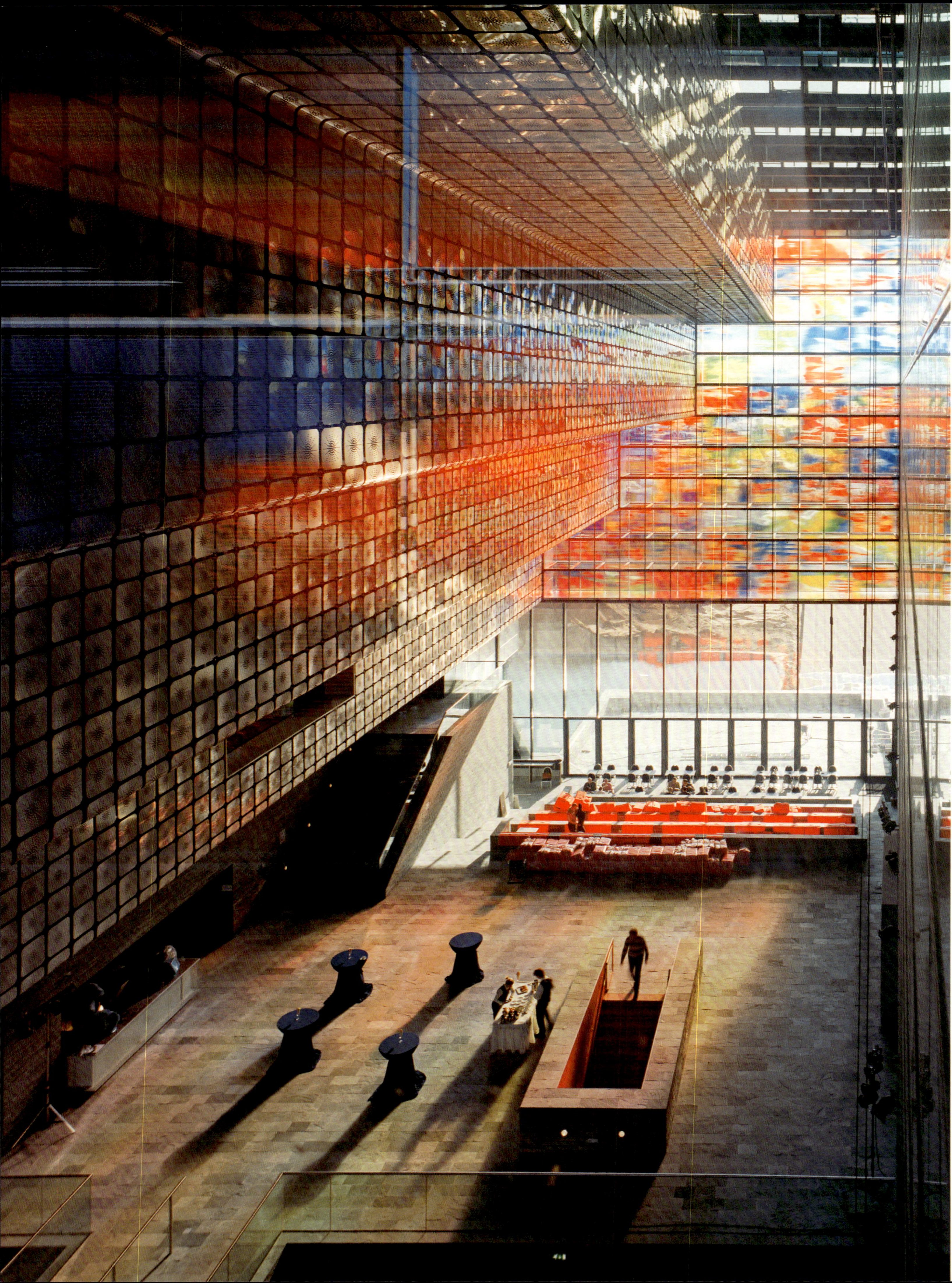

DETAIL A – INTERIOR FAÇADE ON ATRIUM
VERTICAL SECTION – SCALE 1:20

1. IPE 180 tracks for roof cleaning system on supporting system of box-shaped structural work
2. Fixed steel double-glazed skylight with 25/64 – 25/64 – 25/64" (10 – 10 – 10 mm) safety glass and sun filter
3. 7 3/32" (180 mm) Ø ventilation shaft
4. Steel ventilation grille
5. 3 55/64" (98 mm) thermal insulation board, 4 23/32" (120 mm) sprayed lightweight concrete fill over corrugated sheeting
6. 4 23/32 x 3 5/32" (120 x 80 mm) steel L-profile closure
7. Roof structural frame comprising HEB 300 beams (parallel to plane of section)
8. Secondary roof framework of HEA160 beams
9. System for anchoring aluminium panels comprising stainless steel spring and stainless steel rod fixed to 3 35/64 x 1 31/32" (90 x 50 mm) wood battens
10. 5/64" (2 mm) perforated aluminium panel, black polyester acoustic insulating fabric, 1 31/32" (50 mm) mineral wool acoustic insulation, double 63/64" (25 mm) gypsum board panel, finish in insulation material on steel C-profiles
11. Smoothed and painted plaster, 31/64" (12.5 mm) gypsum board panel, 45/64" (18 mm) multilayer wood panel, finish in insulation material on 3 15/16" (100 mm) steel C-profiles
12. Wood closing batten fixed to steel profiles
13. Cabling space incorporated into wall
14. Steel structure supporting wall
15. Resin finish with concave skirting board, 13/64" (5 mm) radius
16. 5/64" (2 mm) resin flooring, 3 5/32" (80 mm) lightweight concrete screed, 4 23/32" (120 mm) sprayed lightweight concrete fill over corrugated sheeting, frame in steel 3 15/16" (100 mm) C-profiles
17. 1/16" (1.5 mm) sheet steel cladding
18. 1/16" (1.5 mm) sheet steel parapet capping glued to 15/32" (12 mm) fibrocement support, 45/64" (18 mm) anchoring profile, 45/64" (18 mm) multilayer wood panel, 3 15/16" (100 mm) steel C-profile, acoustic insulation filling
19. 5/64" (2 mm) resin flooring, 3 5/32" (80 mm) lightweight concrete screed, 4 23/32" (120 mm) sprayed lightweight concrete fill over corrugated sheeting, frame in steel 6 11/16" (170 mm) C-profiles
20. 6 19/64" (160 mm) Ø ventilation shaft
21. HEA 400 steel beam supporting floor

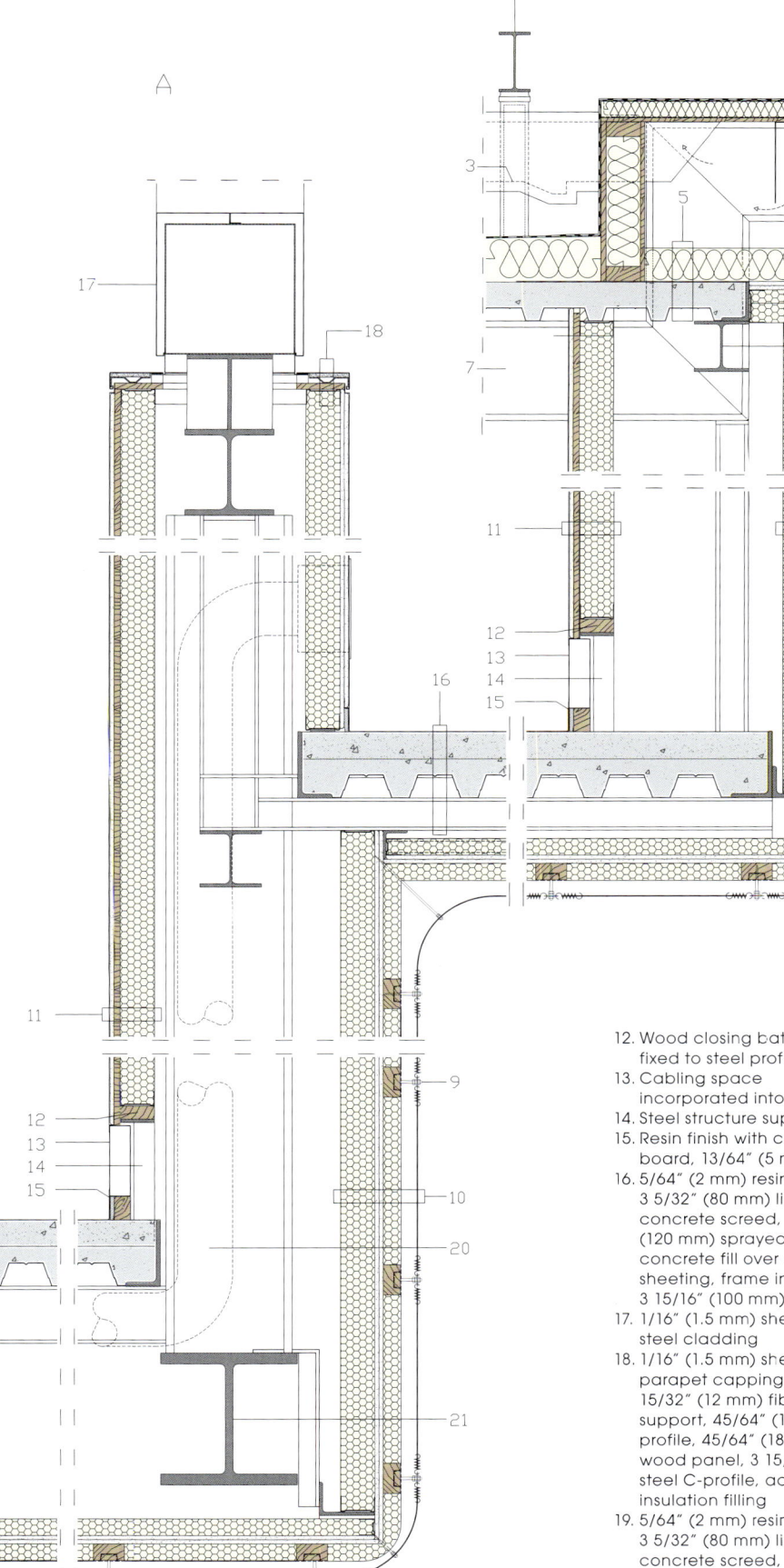

DETAIL B – NORTH FAÇADE
VERTICAL SECTION – SCALE 1:20

1. Motorized glazed steel frame with 25/64 – 25/64 – 25/64" (10 – 10 – 10 mm) safety glass and sun filter for evacuation of fumes and smoke
2. Fixed steel double-glazed skylight with 25/64 – 25/64 – 25/64" (10 – 10 – 10 mm) safety glass and sun filter
3. Steel guttering, 15/64" (6 mm) waterproofing panel, 1 49/64" (45 mm) insulation filling, 1 37/64 x 1 37/64" (40 x 40 mm) box-shaped metal profiles, 1/8" (3 mm) sheet steel interior finish
4. HEA 300 beam supporting glazed roof
5. 3 15/16 x 3 15/16" (100 x 100 mm) steel L-profile for fixing skylight opening mechanisms
6. IPE 180 tracks for roof and façade cleaning system on supporting system of box-shaped structural work
7. Double waterproofing bituminous sheath, 1 37/64" (40 mm) insulation layer, 4 23/32" (120 mm) sprayed lightweight concrete fill over corrugated sheeting, 5 29/32 x 3 15/16" (150 x 100 mm) double steel L-profile, 1/8" (3 mm) galvanized steel cladding
8. Pre-painted steel flashing, waterproofing panel on L-profile 1 37/64 x 1 37/64" (40 x 40 mm), 1 3/8" (35 mm) insulation layer
9. Pre-painted steel capping
10. 9 27/32 x 11 13/16" (250 x 300 mm) box beam constructed of metal structural work supporting double-skin façade
11. 4 23/32" (120 mm) C-profile joists coupled and welded to box beam
12. Steel finishing plate, window frame anchoring joint, heat insulating steel window frame
13. 15/64 – 15/32 – 5/32" (6 – 12 – 4 mm) insulating double glazing with silicone vertical joints
14. 6 19/64 x 3 5/32" (160 x 80 mm) steel box-shaped profile supporting glazing
15. Threaded adjustment element
16. 4 23/32 x 3 5/32" (120 x 80 mm) steel box-shaped profile bracing
17. Steel frame with 47 1/4 x 63" (1200 x 1600 mm) glazing treated with coloured ceramic paste applied in relief
18. 15/16" (24 mm) Ø steel tie rods providing bracing
19. 1/8" (3 mm) galvanized steel cladding, vapour barrier, 2 11/64" (55 mm) thermal insulation board, 31/64" (12.5 mm) plasterboard, 3 15/16" (100 mm) acoustic insulation foam filling, 19/32" (15 mm) fibrocement panel on frame of 1 49/64 x 3 15/16" (45 x 100 mm) wood battens, 5/64" (2 mm) resin finish
20. Running track for blinds
21. Janssen insulated steel double-glazing assemblies with 5/16 – 15/32 – 15/64" (8 – 12 – 6 mm) safety glass
22. Floor in 25/32" (20 mm) natural stone tiles, 2 11/64" (55 mm) concrete bedding layer, 13 25/32" (350 mm) reinforced concrete slab
23. 19/32" (15 mm) spacer joint
24. Floor in 25/32" (20 mm) natural stone tiles, waterproofing bituminous sheath, 3 5/32" (80 mm) pre-cast concrete slab, 2 61/64" (75 mm) cellular glass panel, reinforced concrete slab

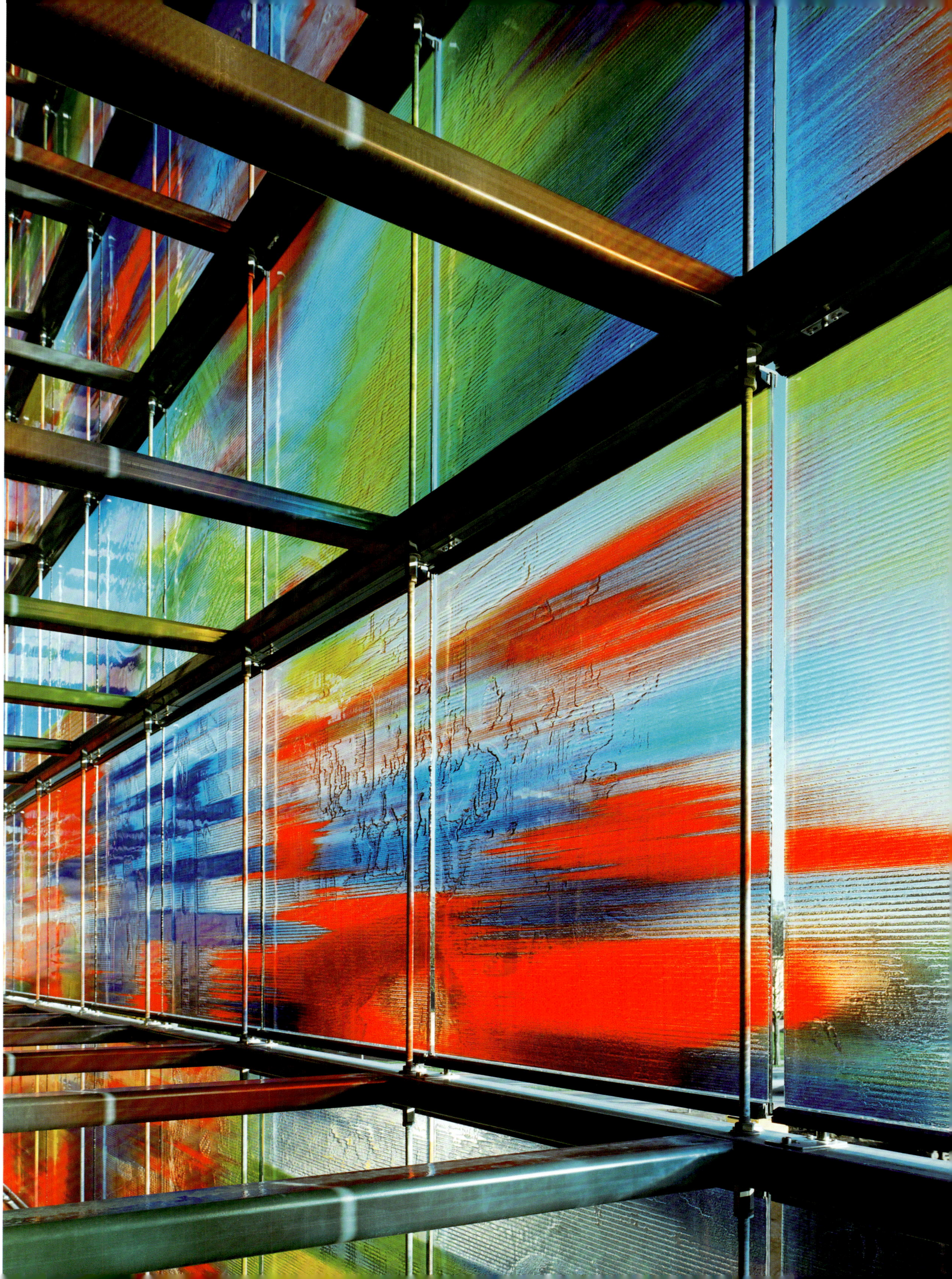

YY Section – Not to scale

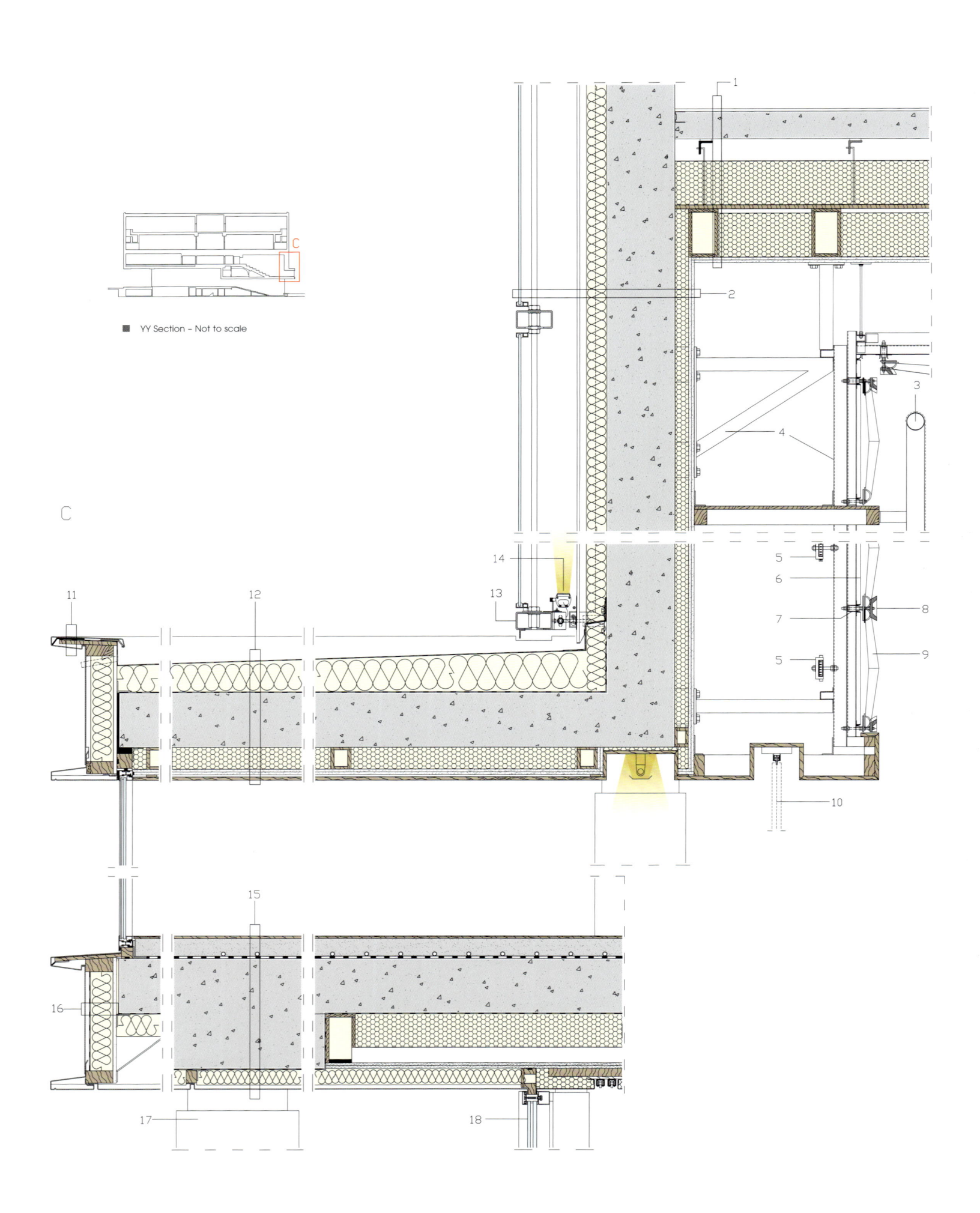

C

104 / Netherlands Institute

DETAIL C – AUDITORIUM
VERTICAL SECTION – SCALE 1:20

1. 15/32" (12 mm) moveable smoke-tight panels, 27 9/16" (700 mm) inverted T reinforced concrete beam (parallel to plane of section), 2 23/64 x 2 23/64" (60 x 60 mm) steel L-profiles, tie rods supporting suspended acoustic panel, 7 7/8" (200 mm) mineral wool acoustic insulation, 45/64" (18 mm) acoustic insulation panel, 8 21/32 x 6 11/16" (220 x 170 mm) acoustically insulating wood beam and 7 7/8" (200 mm) mineral wool acoustic insulation, double 63/64" (25 mm) acoustic panel
2. Double 63/64" (25 mm) acoustic panel, 2 23/64" (60 mm) acoustic insulation foam filling, 11 13/16" (300 mm) reinforced concrete structure, 3 35/64" (90 mm) thermal insulation board, 15/32" (12 mm) shade panel, 15/16" (24 mm) Ø tie rods providing bracing, steel frame with 47 1/4 x 63" (1200 x 1600 mm) glazing treated with coloured ceramic paste applied in relief
3. Projection screen
4. Acoustically insulated frame in steel omega profiles fixed to wall and suspended ceiling
5. Lighting with coloured LEDs
6. Blue polyester Barrisol fabric finish with aluminium fasteners
7. Omega profile welded to spacer profile
8. 3 5/32 x 3 5/32 x 1 3/16" (80 x 80 x 30 mm) brass terminal anchor and finishing piece on M8 spacer bolt, 3 35/64 x 3 35/64 x 13/64" (90 x 90 x 5 mm) stainless steel plate
9. Three-dimensional star-shaped decorative element in laminated wood for sound diffusion
10. Velvet curtain with polyester lining
11. Galvanized steel flashing, 19/32" (15 mm) supporting panel in insulating material
12. Double bituminous sheath, insulation filling forming slope, vapour barrier, 9 27/32" (250 mm) reinforced concrete slab, 3 15/16" (100 mm) acoustic insulation foam filling, double 63/64" (25 mm) gypsum board panel, blue polyester fabric, suspended ceiling in 19/32" (15 mm) micro-perforated acoustically insulating wood panels
13. 3 5/32 x 6 19/64" (80 x 160 mm) steel box-shaped profile supporting façade anchored to wall by adjusting rods
14. Façade backlighting system with lighting fixed to supporting structure
15. Floor in 7/16" (11 mm) parquetry, 3 5/32" (80 mm) reinforced concrete slab, 25/64" (10 mm) Ø radiant panels, high performance board insulation, projecting 19 11/16" (500 mm) reinforced concrete slab, vapour barrier, 2 3/4" (70 mm) thermal insulation board, 1/16" (1.5 mm) galvanized steel finishing panels
16. 1/16" (1.5 mm) sheet steel cladding, vapour barrier, 3 15/16" (100 mm) insulation filling, 19/32" (15 mm) thermal insulation board
17. V-shaped columns in reinforced concrete finished with galvanized steel (parallel to plane of section)
18. 3 5/32 x 6 19/64" (80 x 160 mm) Janssen insulated steel double-glazing assemblies with 15/32 – 15/32 – 5/8" (12 – 12 – 16 mm) layered safety glass

THEATRE AND MUSIC CENTRE – NÍJAR, SPAIN
MGM – MORALES GILES MARISCAL

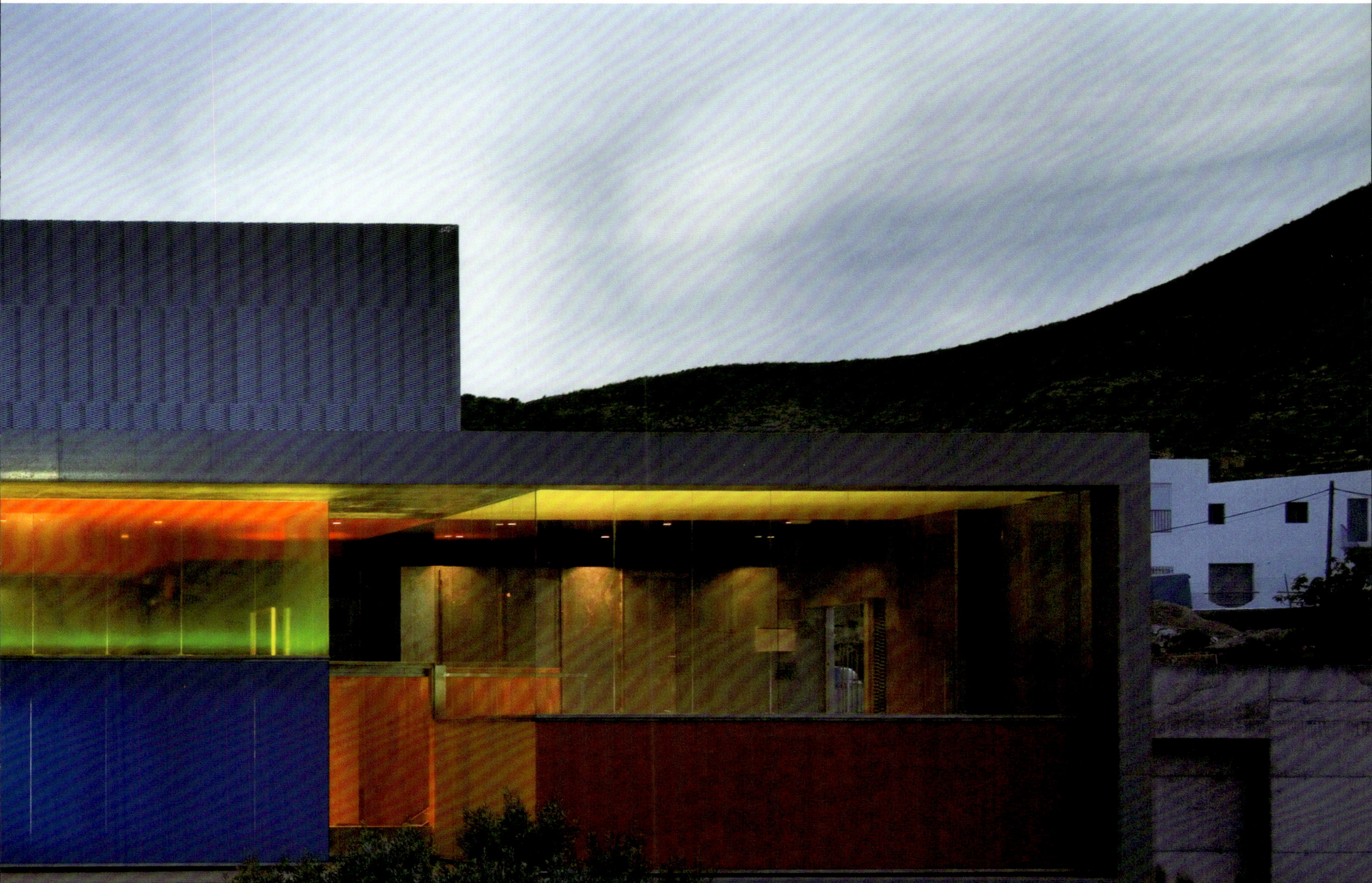

The Theatre and Music Centre, designed by José Morales, Sara de Giles and Juan G. Mariscal at Níjar in Andalusia, is set in an urban and natural landscape with a pronounced character of its own. The daunting desert backdrop, the line of the horizon and various neighbourhood features influenced and suggested certain design choices.

The Centre is devoted to theatrical expression and theatre in the broadest sense. It stands in a plot once terraced with allotments, a place defined by its soft colour tones. The complex is made up of two units, starkly simple in outline, transforming the landscape and creating an interplay of architecture and the natural features picked up in the volumes themselves. One example of this is the overhang that offers shade and protection from the Almería sun.

The site wraps round the bottom of the complex, anchoring it to various levels of terracing and unifying the whole. From this levelled base the architecture soars up in two separate bodies which face the main thoroughfare.

The outer shell is designed as one continuous system linking curtain walls and roofs by using the same cladding in pierced stretched aluminium sheeting. The supporting structure is a light metal shell. The shape and consistency of the cladding gives a uniform perception of the whole complex and a sense of great lightness to the compact clear-cut architectural volumes, while the technical purpose is to filter the glare and give varying daylight effects inside the Centre.

The interior is conceived as a continuous empty space filling with glass-clad features in the form of "colour boxes". The design also links firmly to the outer landscape by crosswise "cuts" which divide up the volumes and give a new balance to the interplay of design features and space.

The brightly coloured "boxes" create a markedly dynamic effect when glimpsed from the outside as well. Activities within can be seen through the protective outer sheath, especially at night through the glass walls that slice through the façade. These wide apertures, which the architects refer to as "mouths", give the building character and embrace the landscape.

The jutting overhang creates a covered courtyard outside, a protected area extending and highlighting the interior layout.

The plinth-like base houses dressing and changing rooms, as well as plant rooms, while the two volumes serve separate functions: on the one side a cinema, theatre or ballroom; on the other, rehearsal rooms, laboratories and an exhibition hall.

■ Site Plan - Scale 1:3500

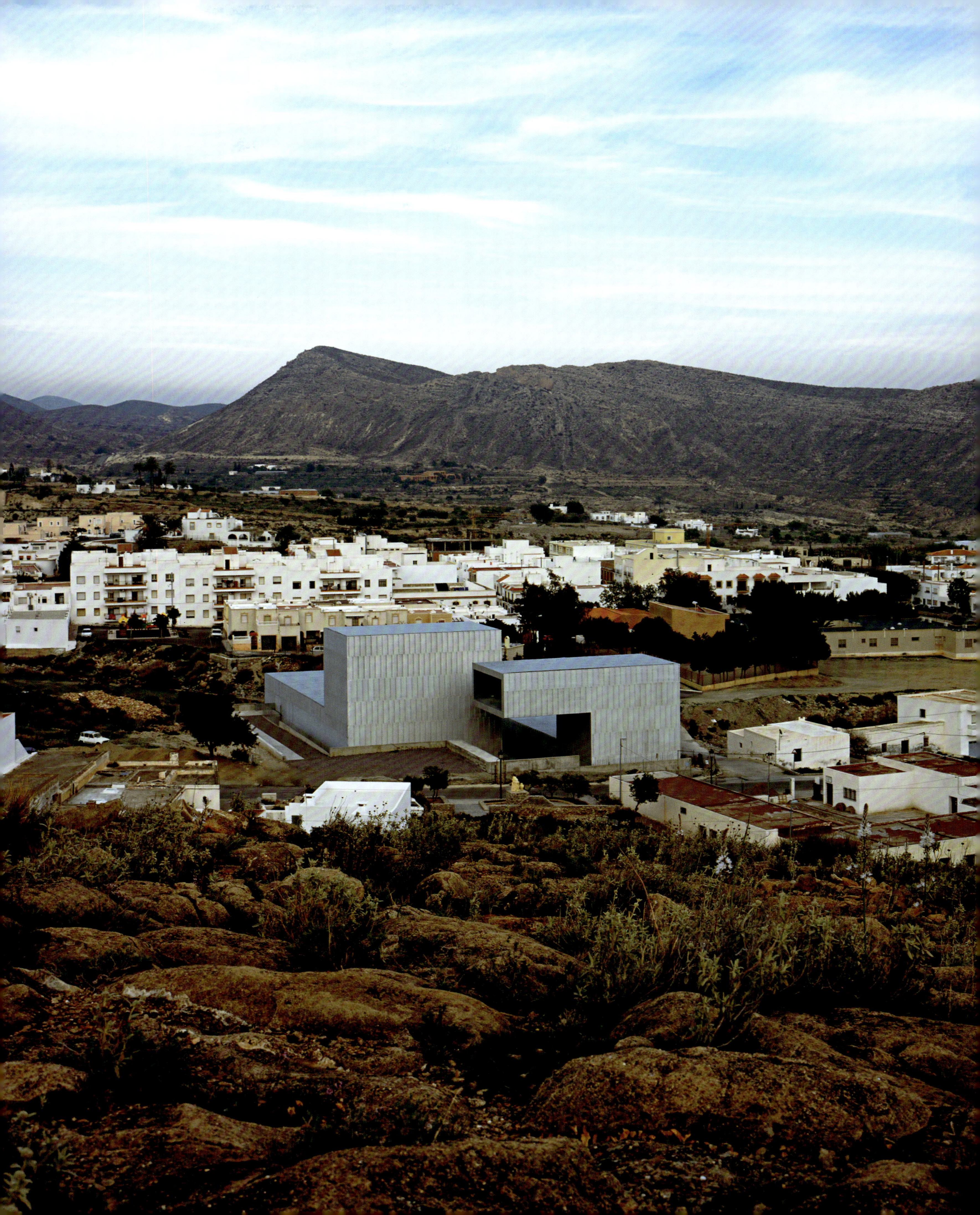

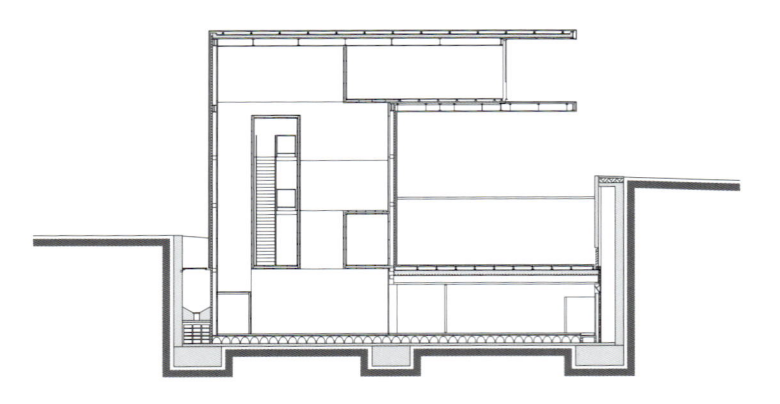

■ KK Section – Scale 1:400

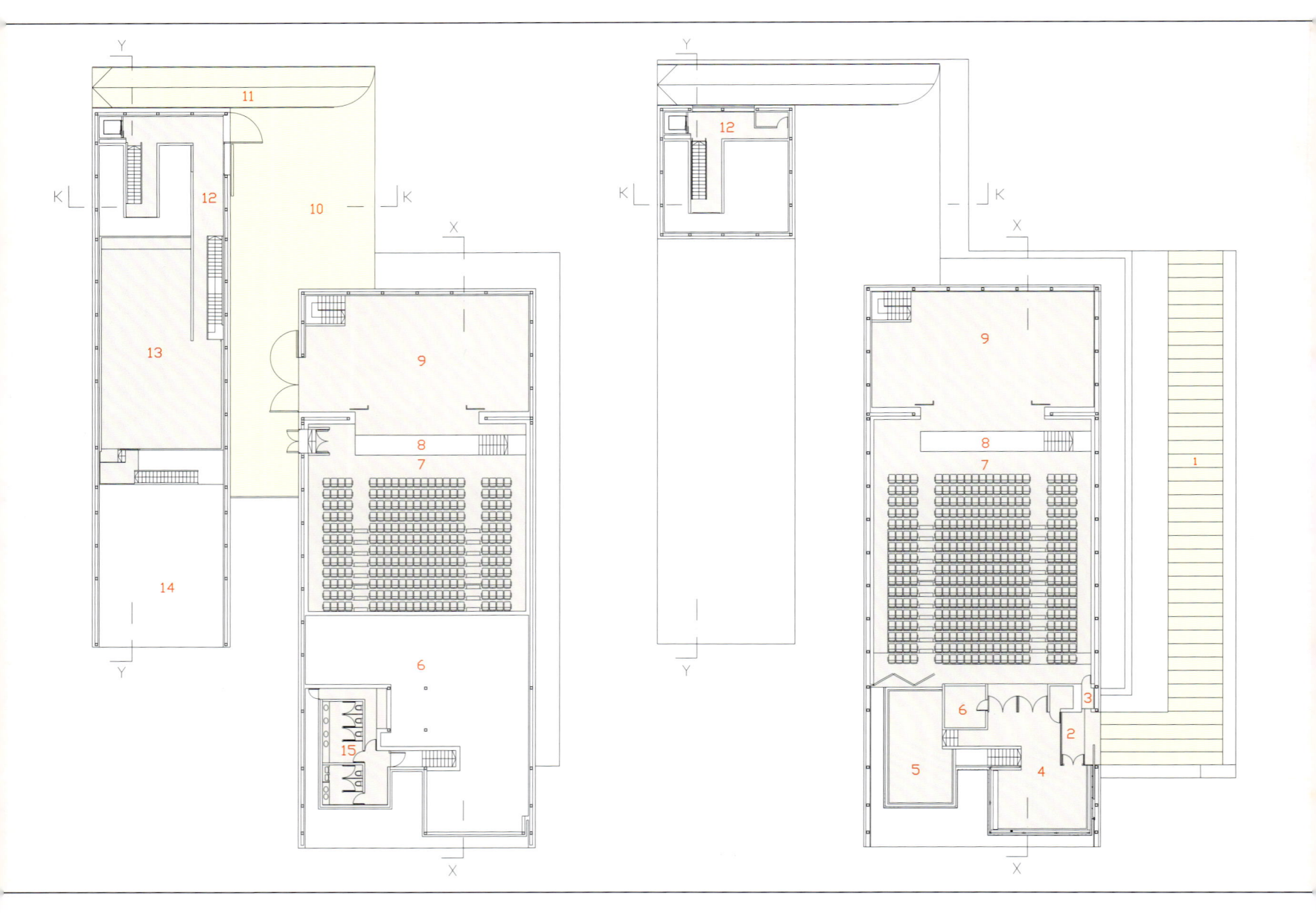

■ First Floor Plan – Scale 1:400

■ Second Floor Plan – Scale 1:400

1. Access Route to Auditorium
2. Public Entrance
3. Ticket Office
4. Foyer
5. Bar
6. Plant Room
7. Stalls
8. Orchestra Pit
9. Stage
10. Patio
11. Access Ramp to Laboratories
12. Entrance Hall
13. Music Laboratory
14. Terrace (no access)
15. Bathrooms

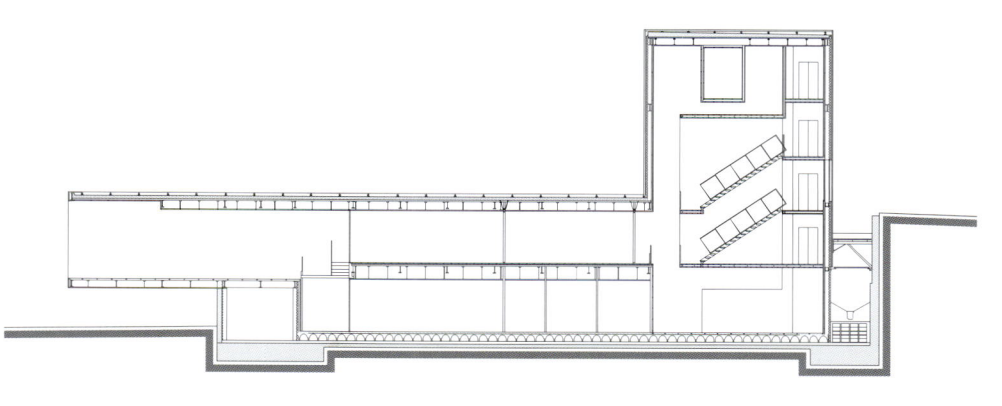

■ YY Section – Scale 1:400

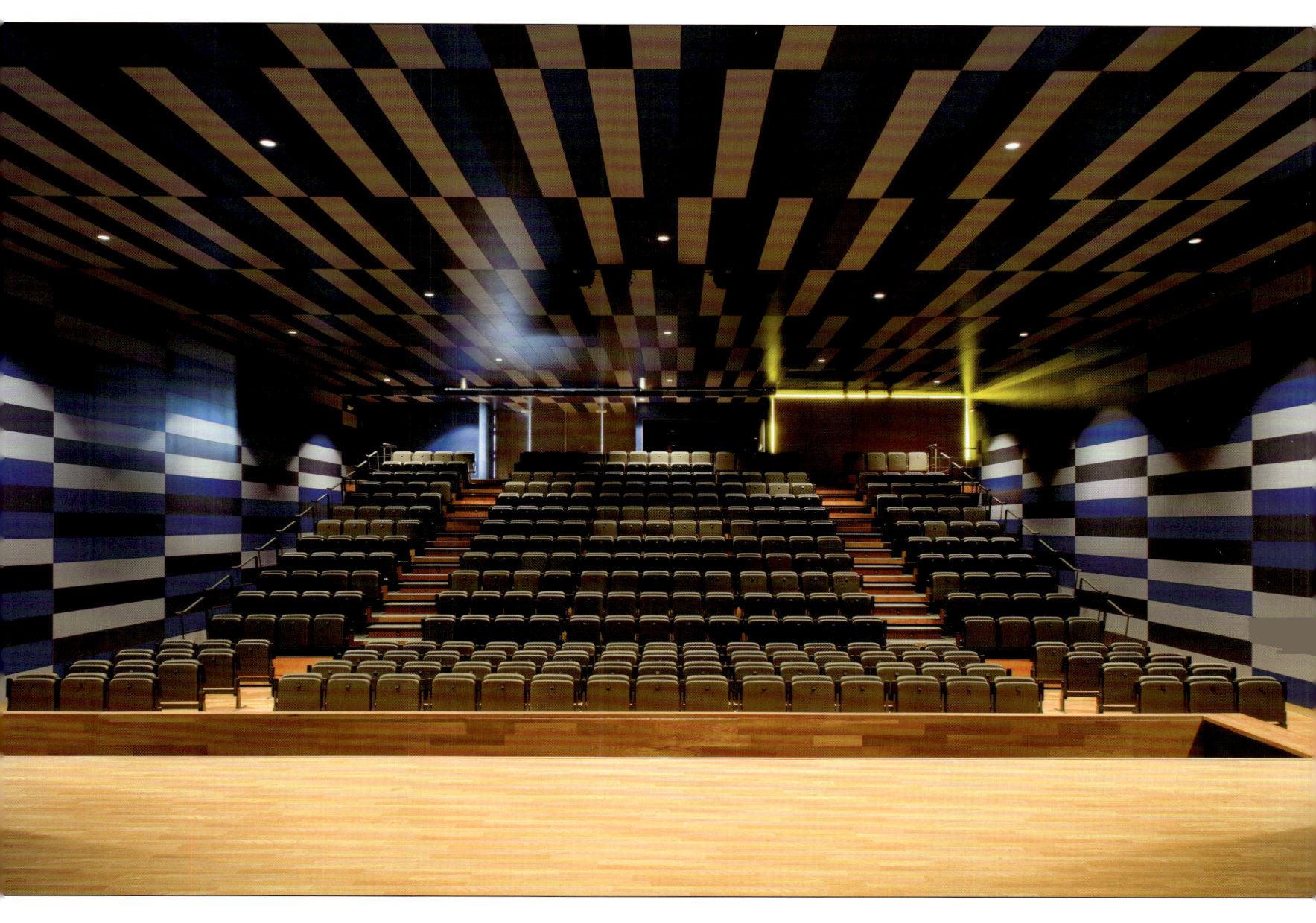

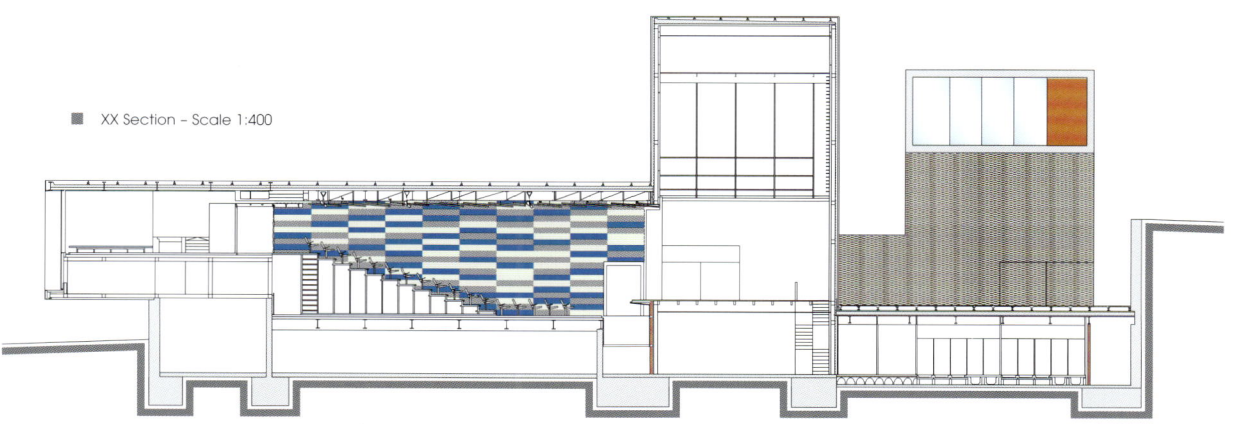

■ XX Section – Scale 1:400

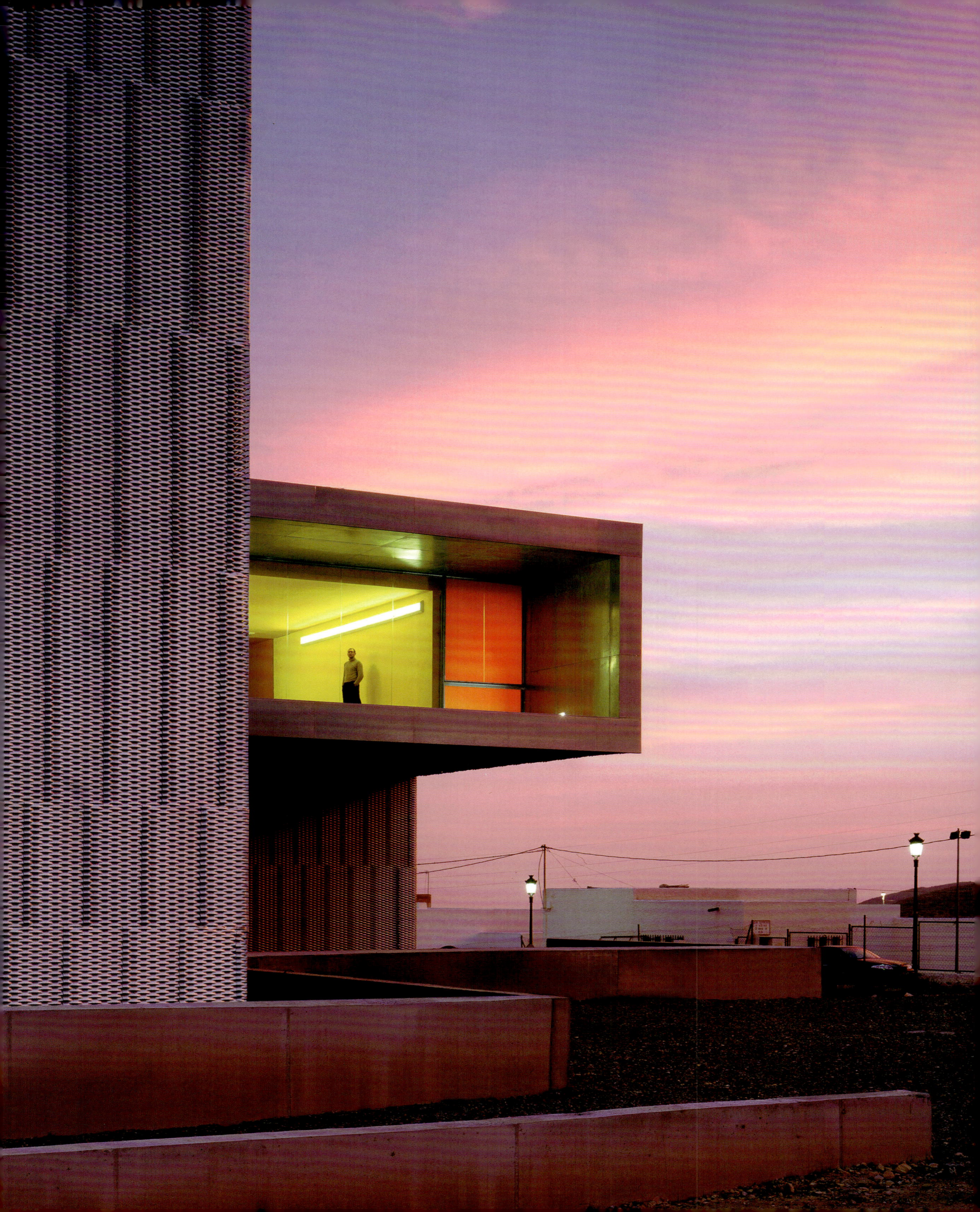

■ South-East Elevation – Scale 1:300

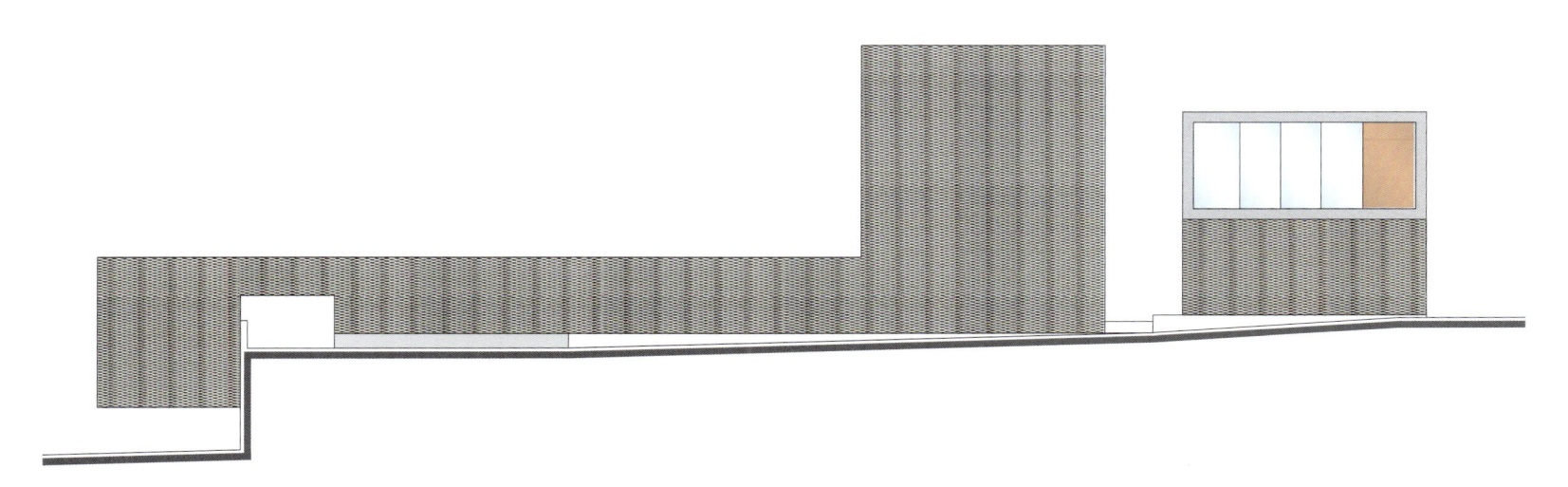

■ North-West Elevation – Scale 1:300

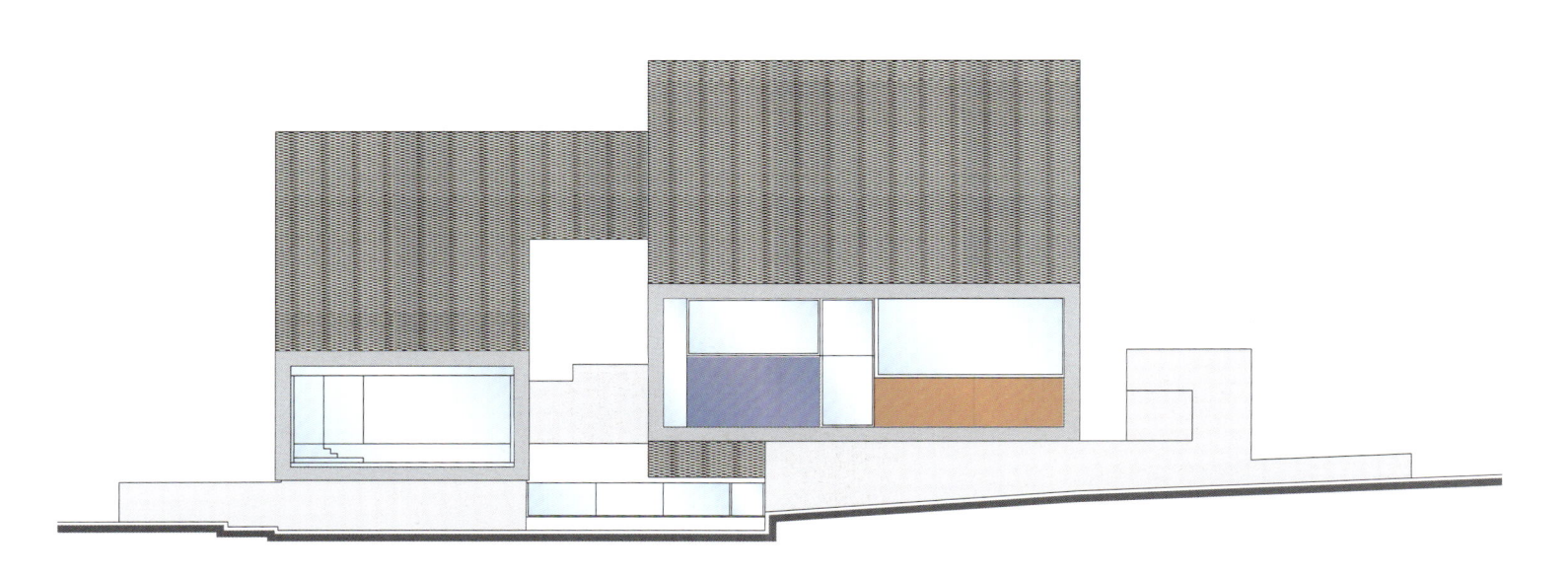

■ North-East Elevation – Scale 1:300

DETAIL A: LABORATORIES
VERTICAL SECTION – SCALE 1:30

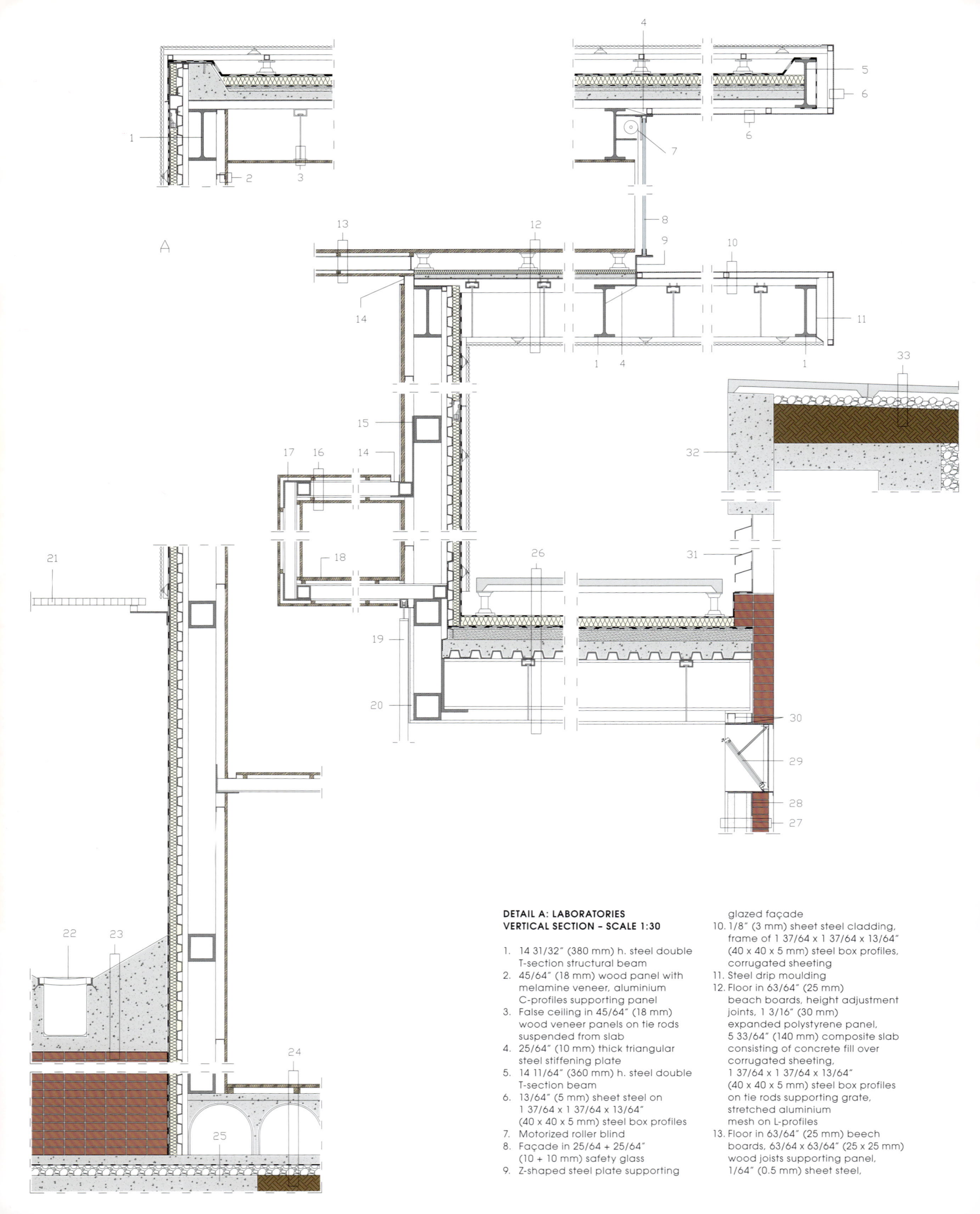

1. 14 31/32" (380 mm) h. steel double T-section structural beam
2. 45/64" (18 mm) wood panel with melamine veneer, aluminium C-profiles supporting panel
3. False ceiling in 45/64" (18 mm) wood veneer panels on tie rods suspended from slab
4. 25/64" (10 mm) thick triangular steel stiffening plate
5. 14 11/64" (360 mm) h. steel double T-section beam
6. 13/64" (5 mm) sheet steel on 1 37/64" x 1 37/64 x 13/64" (40 x 40 x 5 mm) steel box profiles
7. Motorized roller blind
8. Façade in 25/64 + 25/64" (10 + 10 mm) safety glass
9. Z-shaped steel plate supporting glazed façade
10. 1/8" (3 mm) sheet steel cladding, frame of 1 37/64 x 1 37/64 x 13/64" (40 x 40 x 5 mm) steel box profiles, corrugated sheeting
11. Steel drip moulding
12. Floor in 63/64" (25 mm) beach boards, height adjustment joints, 1 3/16" (30 mm) expanded polystyrene panel, 5 33/64" (140 mm) composite slab consisting of concrete fill over corrugated sheeting, 1 37/64 x 1 37/64 x 13/64" (40 x 40 x 5 mm) steel box profiles on tie rods supporting grate, stretched aluminium mesh on L-profiles
13. Floor in 63/64" (25 mm) beech boards, 63/64 x 63/64" (25 x 25 mm) wood joists supporting panel, 1/64" (0.5 mm) sheet steel,

3 15/16 x 3 15/16 x 25/64"
(100 x 100 x 10 mm) steel box
profiles, 1/64" (0.5 mm) sheet steel,
63/64 x 63/64" (25 x 25 mm)
wood joists supporting panel,
45/64" (18 mm) wood veneer panel
14. Steel C-profile trim
15. Steel L-profile securing projecting
volume to box profile
16. 45/64" (18 mm) wood veneer
panel, 63/64 x 63/64" (25 x 25 mm)
wood joists supporting panel,
15/32" (12 mm) corrugated
sheeting, frame of 3 15/16"
(100 mm) steel box profiles, 15/32"
(12 mm) corrugated sheeting,
63/64 x 63/64" (25 x 25 mm) wood
joists supporting panel,
45/64" (18 mm) wood veneer
17. 7 7/8 x 7 7/8" (200 x 200 mm)
steel L-profile closing off and
anchoring structure
18. Floor in 63/64" (25 mm)
beech boards
19. Sliding steel door
20. Gypsum board panel
21. Protective steel grating on steel
profiles
22. Rainwater drainage system
23. Concrete guttering on perforated
brick base
24. Floor in 63/64" (25 mm) oak
boards, wood joists, 1 31/32"
(50 mm) concrete screed,
ventilation space with plastic
elements, 2 61/64" (75 mm)
concrete screed,
waterproofing membrane,
ballast layer, earth
25. Reinforced concrete foundation
26. External floating floor in concrete
tiles on adjustable joints, PVC
waterproofing membrane, 2 3/4"
(70 mm) extruded polystyrene
insulation, double waterproofing
membrane, 25/64" (10 mm)
levelling mortar, foamed concrete
screed forming 2% slope,
5 33/64" (140 mm) composite slab
consisting of concrete fill over
corrugated sheeting, 14 31/32"
(380 mm) h. steel double T-section
structural beam (parallel to plane
of section), false ceiling in
gypsum board panels
suspended from tie rods
27. 4 23/32" (120 mm) bricks,
1 3/16" (30 mm) gypsum
board and fibreglass panel,
space for sewage pipes,
1 31/32" (50 mm)
gypsum board and
fibreglass panel
28. Steel L-profile securing
window frame
29. Aluminium double-glazed transom
window for ventilation
30. Steel profiles forming lintel
31. Aluminium ventilation grate
32. Reinforced concrete structure
33. Floor in concrete tiles, ballast

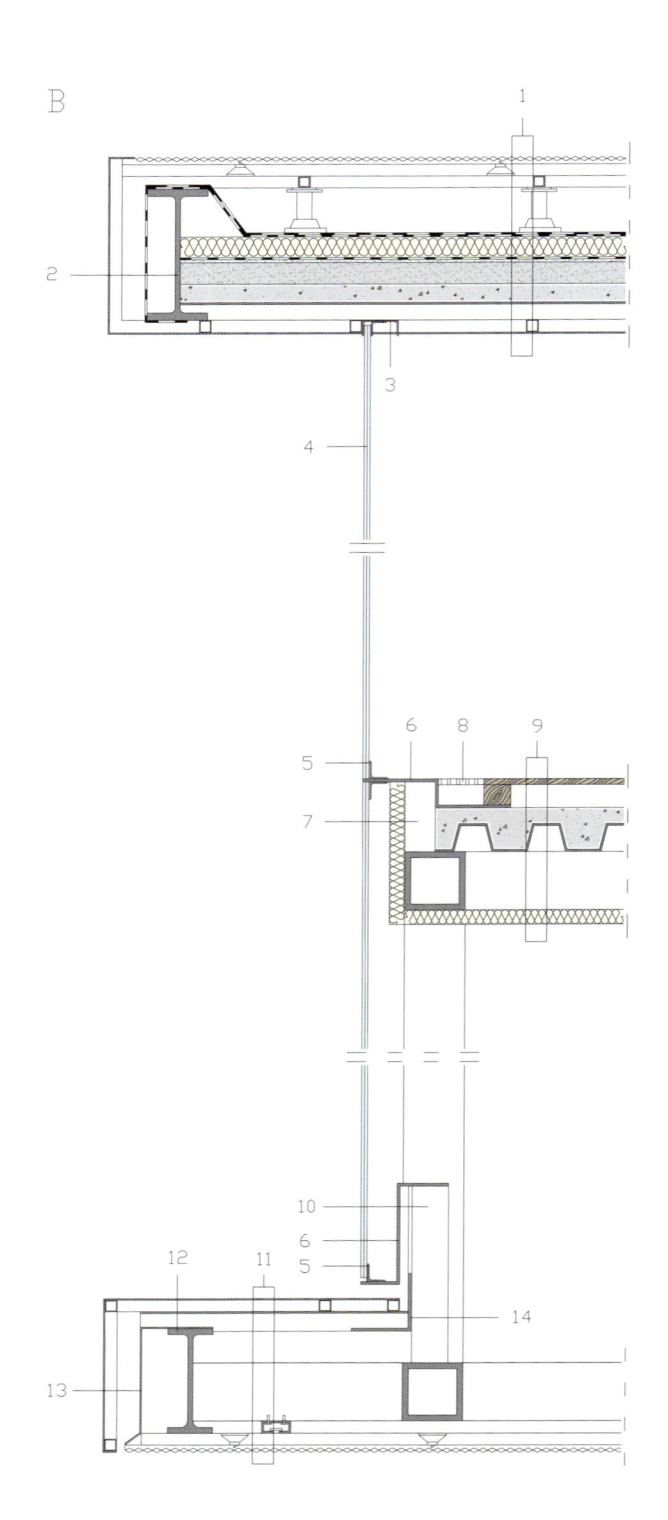

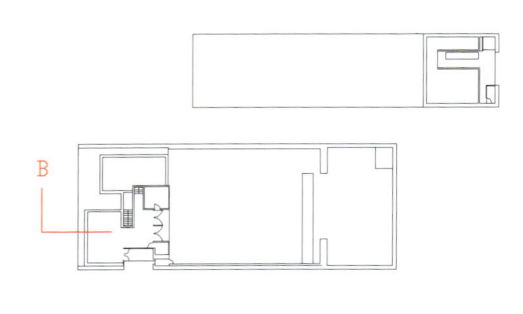

DETAIL B: THEATRE
VERTICAL SECTION – SCALE 1:25

1. 19/32" (15 mm) thick stretched aluminium mesh with 2 3/4 x 15/16" (70 x 24 mm) cells, L-profile supporting grille on frame of 1 37/64 x 1 37/64 x 13/64" (40 x 40 x 5 mm) steel box profiles, height adjustment joints, double PVC waterproofing membrane, 2 3/4" (70 mm) extruded polystyrene board insulation, bituminous waterproofing membrane, 25/64" (10 mm) mortar levelling, foamed concrete screed forming 2% slope, 4 23/32" (120 mm) composite slab consisting of concrete fill over corrugated sheeting, 1 37/64 x 1 37/64 x 13/64" (40 x 40 x 5 mm) steel box profiles, 13/64" (5 mm) sheet steel cladding
2. IPE 450 steel structural beam
3. 4 23/32 x 1 31/32" (120 x 50 mm) steel C-profile supporting glass
4. 25/64 + 25/64" (10 + 10 mm) coloured safety glass with polyvinyl butyral film
5. 1 31/32 x 1 31/32" (50 x 50 mm) steel L-profile
6. 1/8" (3 mm) profiled steel plate anchoring façade system
7. HEB 100 steel beam
8. Grating over installation space
9. Timber floor in 3 15/16 x 63/64" (100 x 25 mm) beech boards on wood joists, 5 29/32" (150 mm) composite slab consisting of concrete fill over corrugated sheeting, frame in 7 7/8" (200 mm) steel box profiles, 1 31/32" (50 mm) fibreglass board insulation
10. HEA 120 steel beam
11. 7/64" (3 mm) sheet steel, frame of 1 37/64 x 1 37/64 x 13/64" (40 x 40 x 5 mm) steel box profiles, corrugated sheeting, frame of 7 7/8" (200 mm) steel box profiles, system for attaching cladding form by C-profiles, 1 37/64 x 1 37/64 x 13/64" (40 x 40 x 5 mm) steel box profile, stretched aluminium mesh fixed with L-profiles
12. IPE 360 steel joist
13. Steel drip moulding
14. Steel L-profile

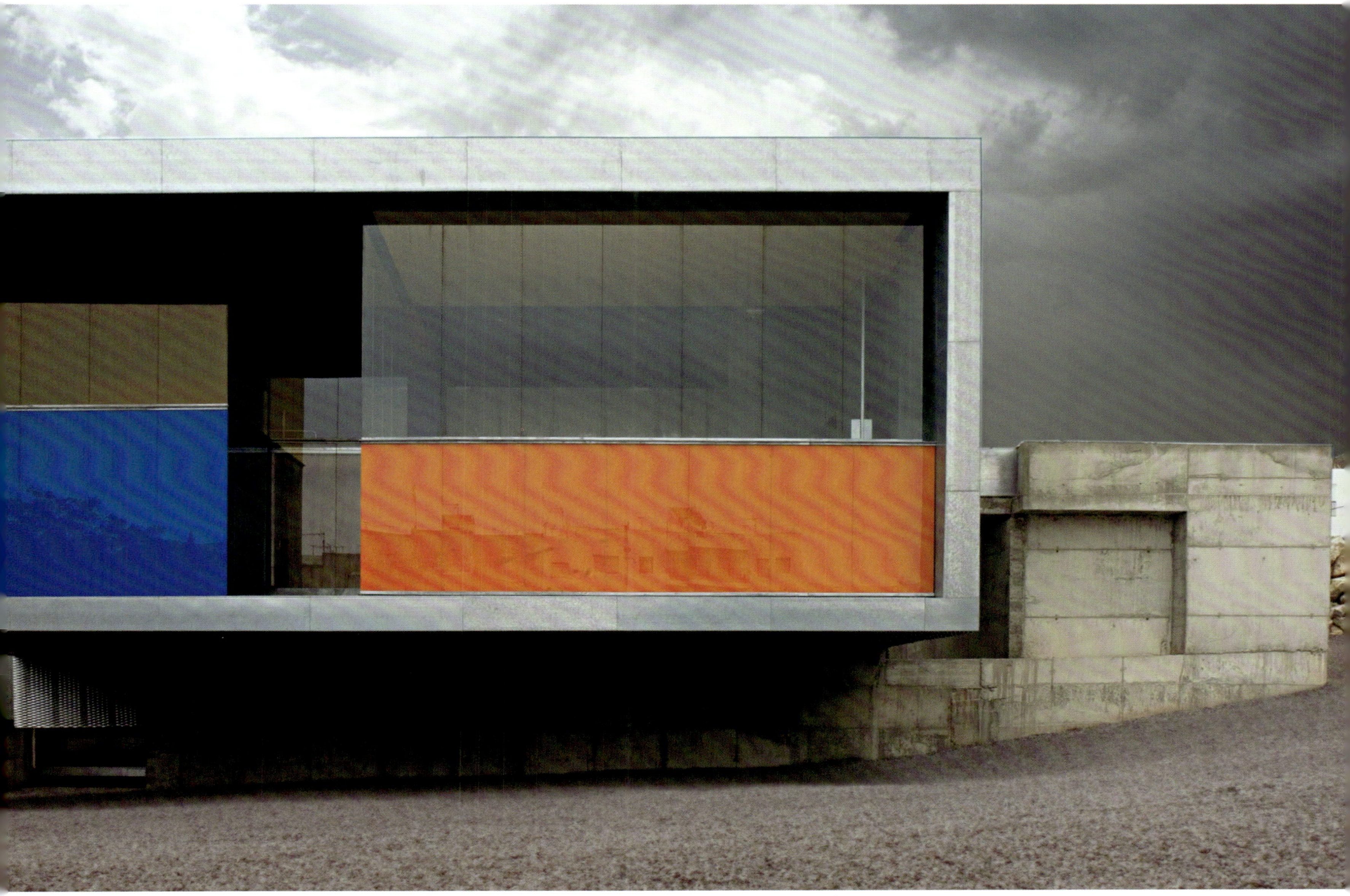

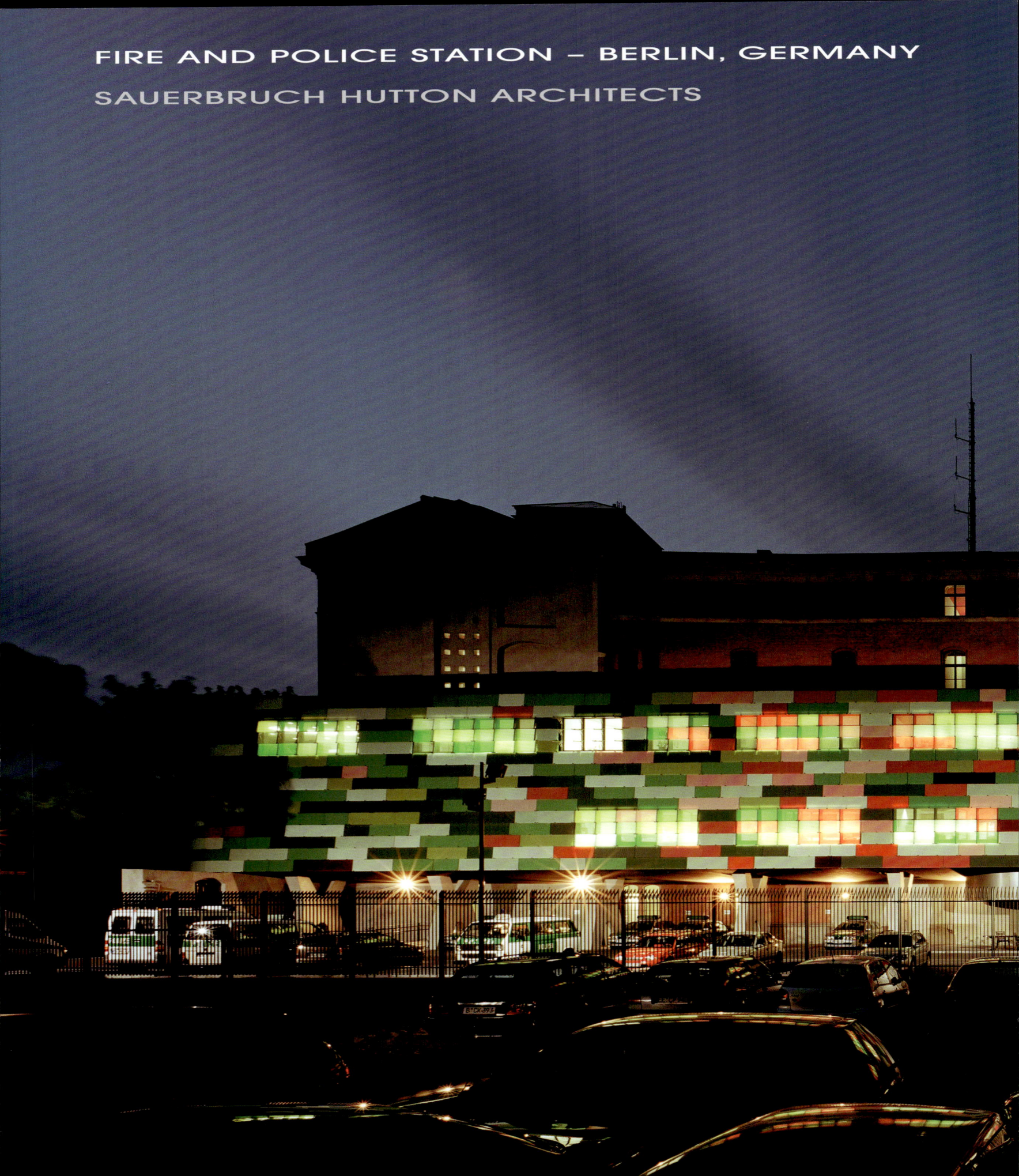

FIRE AND POLICE STATION – BERLIN, GERMANY
SAUERBRUCH HUTTON ARCHITECTS

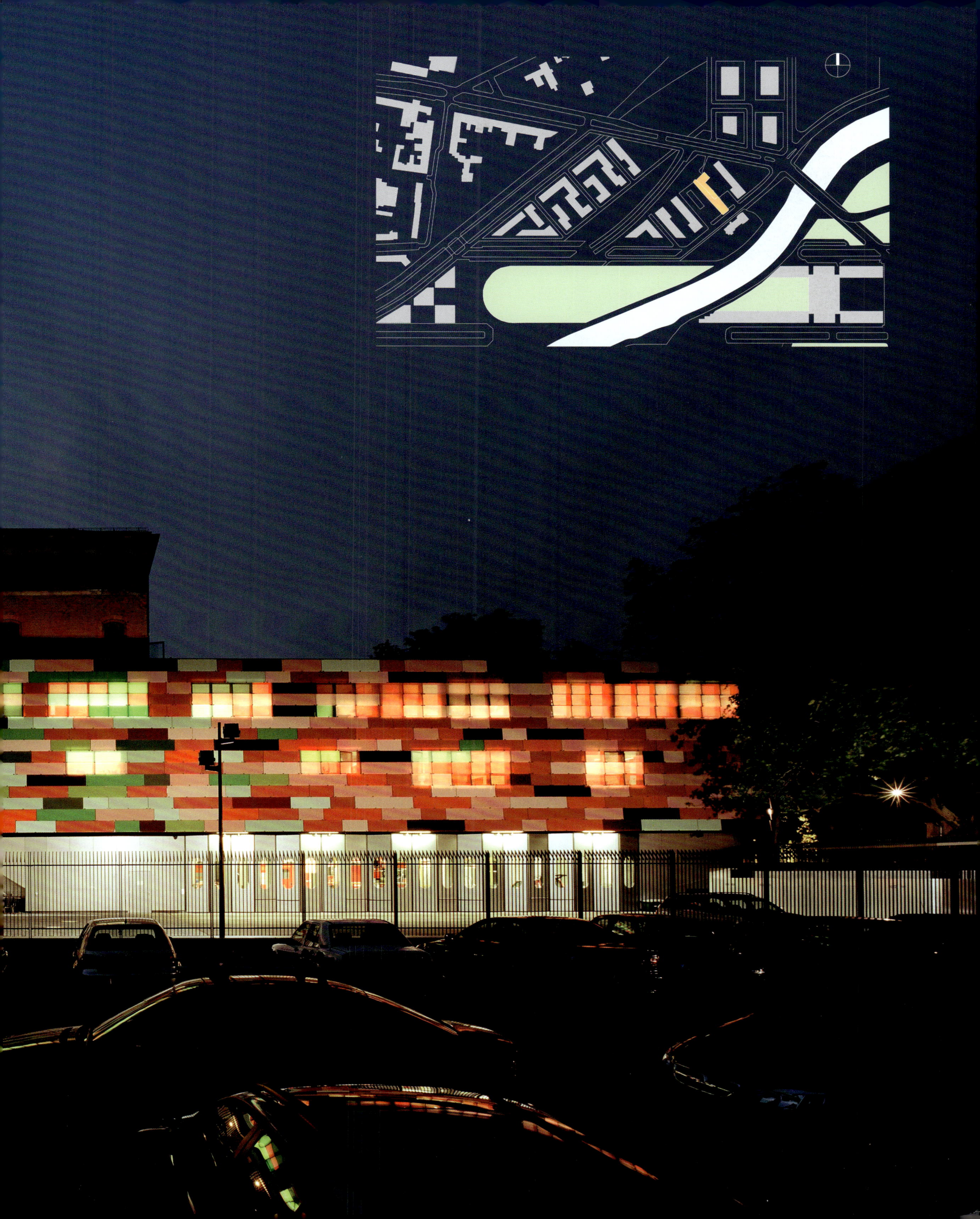

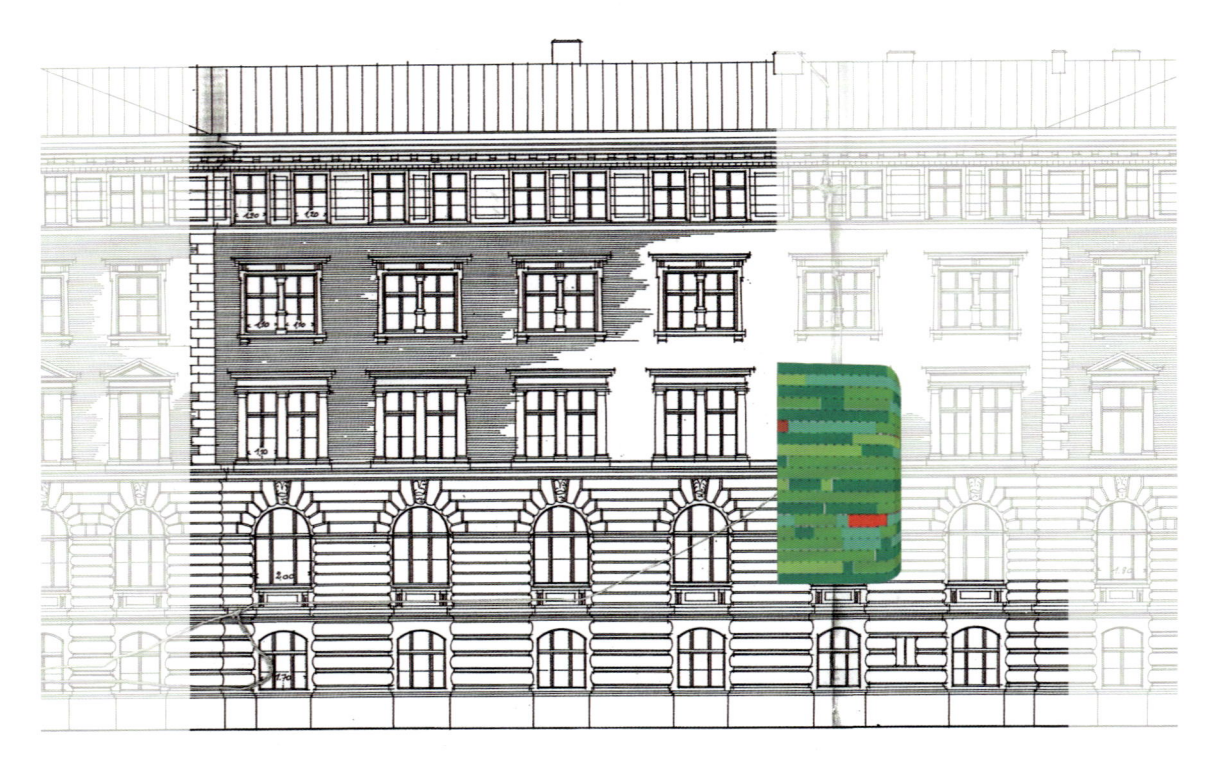

■ How the Project Fits Into the Original Complex "in Grey, the Sections Destroyed During World War Ii" – Scale 1:250

In March 1999, a competition was launched to design a new station for the fire and police departments in Berlin. The winning project had to preserve the old disused building on the proposed site, extend the existing structure and create open spaces. Sauerbruch Hutton was awarded the commission for its compact solution that delivers maximum economic and environmental efficiency by extending the connection corridor of the old building, and adding just one new building: an elongated, two-storey structure on the south side that projects out towards the river.

The existing five-storey building, erected in 1907 as a tax office, and bombed during the Second World War, has a solid sandstone and brick neo-Renaissance façade. The new building makes no attempt at compromise or dialogue with its older counterpart. It stands alongside, a demure two storeys, projecting a few metres on the west front. Here, the two buildings are linked by an almost fully glazed façade that provides views of the old building from inside the new construction.

The public entrance to the Fire and Police Station has been created from a former window of the old building. The pedestrian ramp leading up to the new entrance from Alt Moabit Strasse lends an almost surreal touch to this traditional façade. Bright colours – a signature feature of Sauerbruch Hutton – give the façade new life. Here, the glass panels are the familiar red and green of the German police force and fire department. The 65 cm (25 1/2") high, 2.5 m (8 ft) long panels curve around the sides of the building, overlapping slightly like shingles and acting as both façade cladding and sun shading for the internal windows. They automatically adapt to outside weather conditions via a system that in turn can be adjusted by the building's occupants.

The new two-storey body is raised from the ground to make way for ground-level garages for police cars and fire engines. On the side closest to the old structure, the building rests on X-shaped struts, providing a structural frame that does not impinge on the old building or damage its foundations. Pillars form the other structural supports, allowing flexible space utilization. The building is supported by a transversal structural wall positioned at the stair column. A roof garden compensates for the extensive macadam courtyards required to accommodate large service vehicles.

Although very different, the new building does connect with the older structure to create a natural complex with a human dimension that fits comfortably into the surrounding park and the banks of the river Spree.

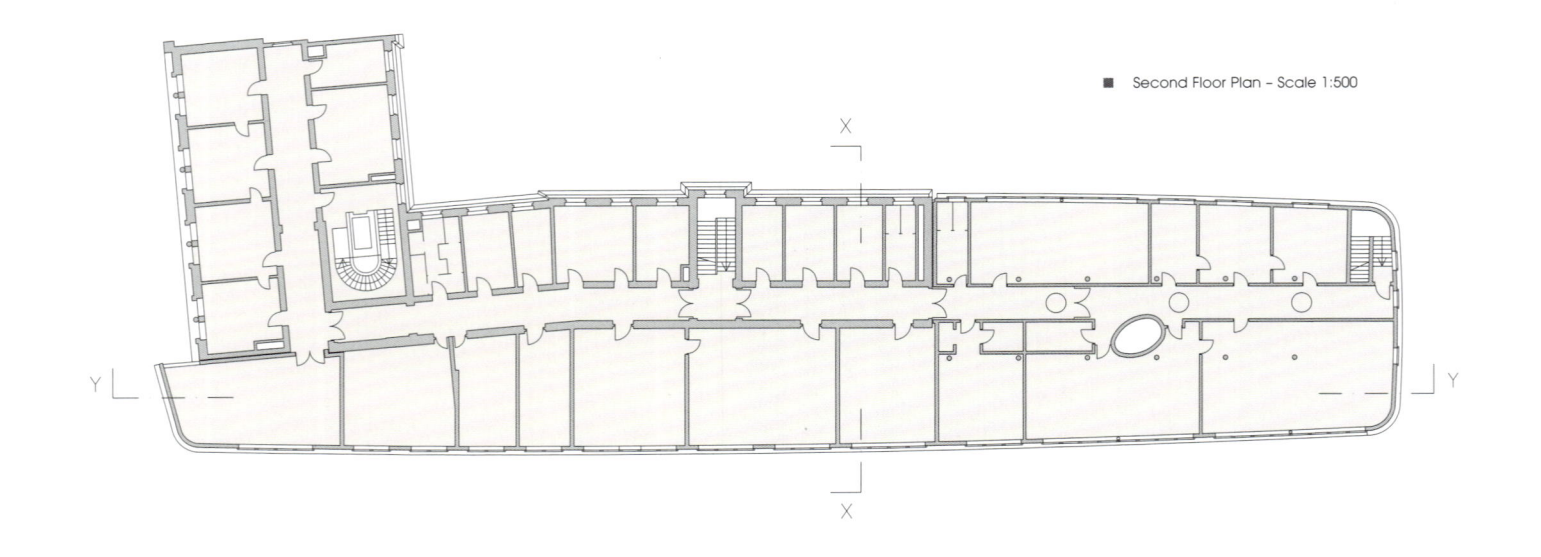

■ Second Floor Plan – Scale 1:500

Ground Floor Plan - Scale 1:500

■ South-West Elevation's Chromatic Range

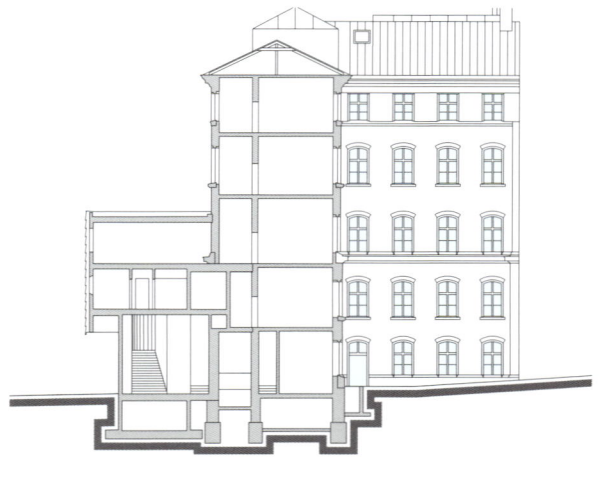

■ XX Section – Scale 1:500

YY Section – Scale 1:500

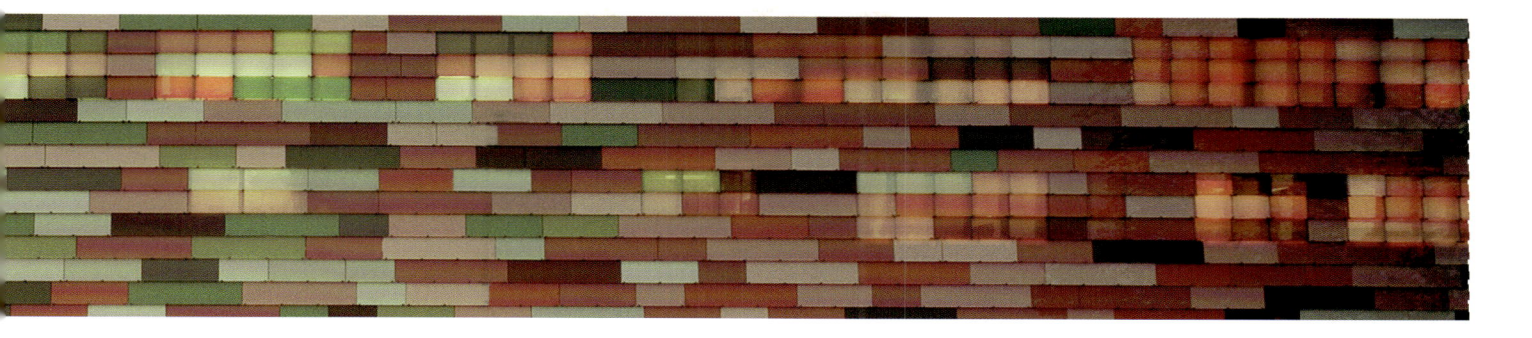

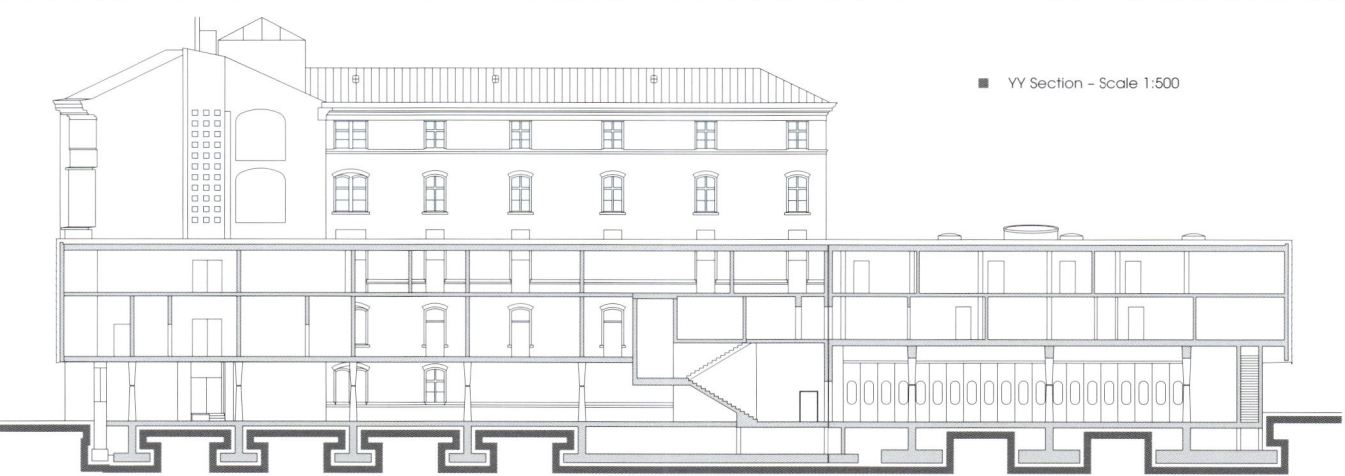

123 / Sauerbruch Hutton

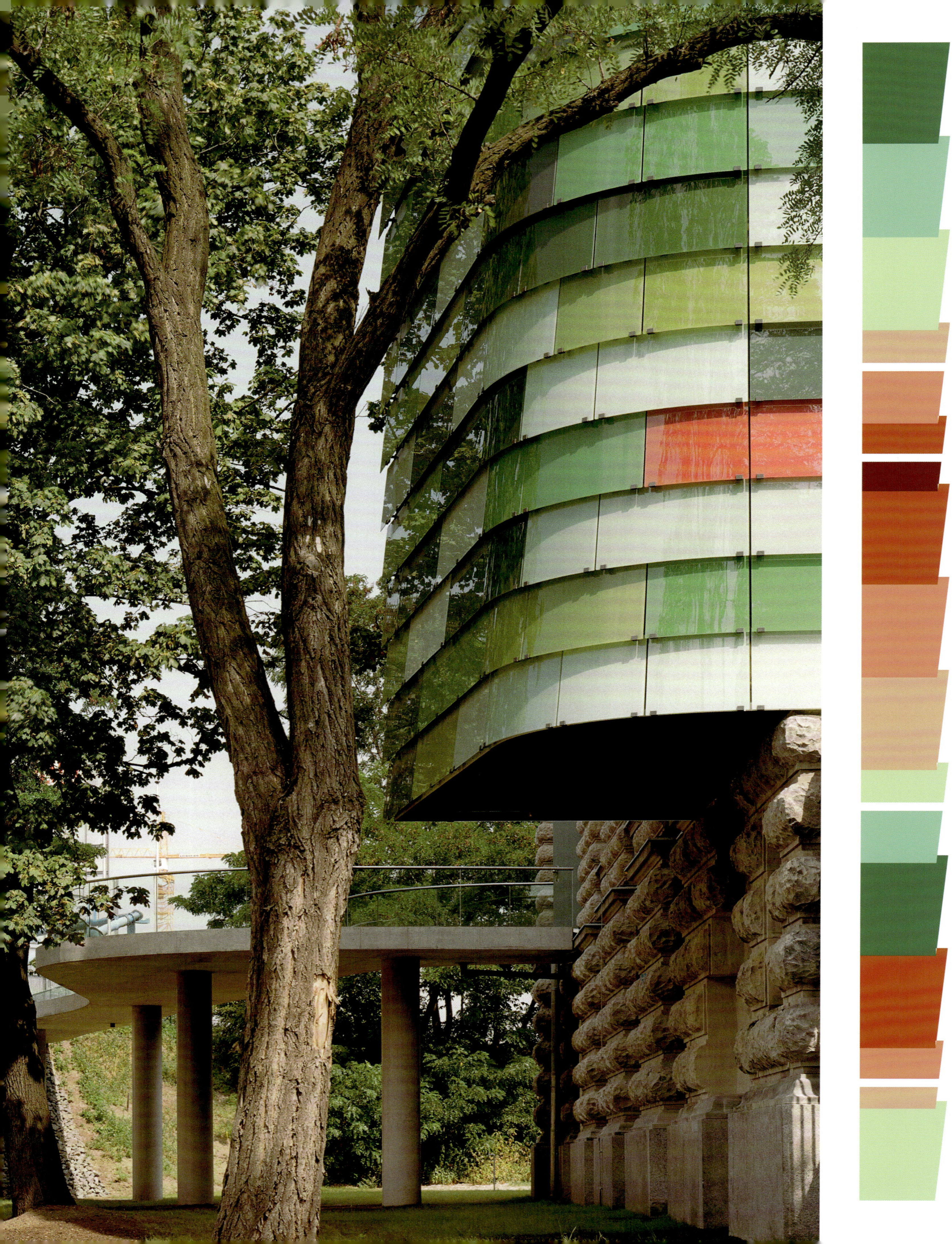

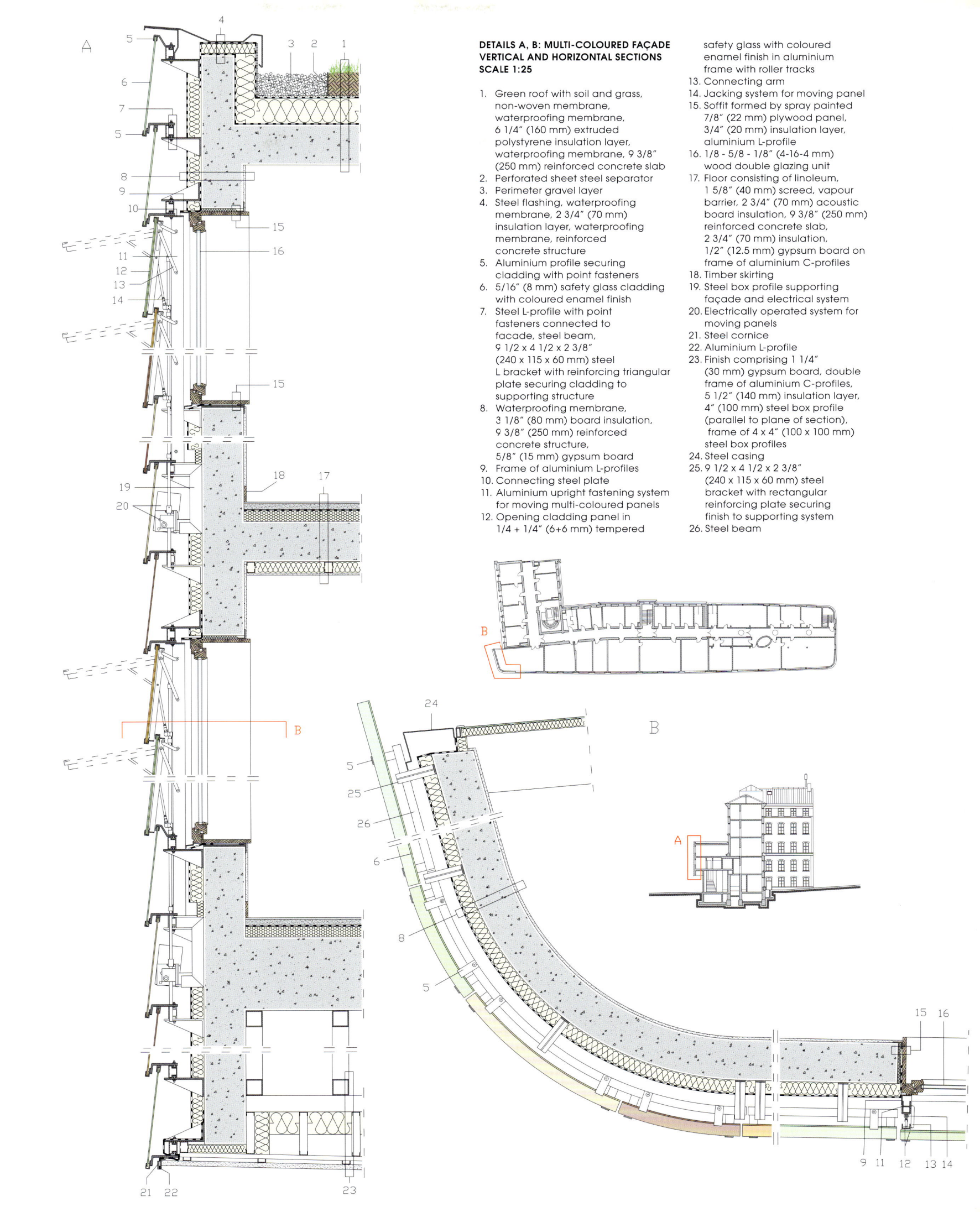

DETAILS A, B: MULTI-COLOURED FAÇADE VERTICAL AND HORIZONTAL SECTIONS SCALE 1:25

1. Green roof with soil and grass, non-woven membrane, waterproofing membrane, 6 1/4" (160 mm) extruded polystyrene insulation layer, waterproofing membrane, 9 3/8" (250 mm) reinforced concrete slab
2. Perforated sheet steel separator
3. Perimeter gravel layer
4. Steel flashing, waterproofing membrane, 2 3/4" (70 mm) insulation layer, waterproofing membrane, reinforced concrete structure
5. Aluminium profile securing cladding with point fasteners
6. 5/16" (8 mm) safety glass cladding with coloured enamel finish
7. Steel L-profile with point fasteners connected to facade, steel beam, 9 1/2 x 4 1/2 x 2 3/8" (240 x 115 x 60 mm) steel L bracket with reinforcing triangular plate securing cladding to supporting structure
8. Waterproofing membrane, 3 1/8" (80 mm) board insulation, 9 3/8" (250 mm) reinforced concrete structure, 5/8" (15 mm) gypsum board
9. Frame of aluminium L-profiles
10. Connecting steel plate
11. Aluminium upright fastening system for moving multi-coloured panels
12. Opening cladding panel in 1/4 + 1/4" (6+6 mm) tempered safety glass with coloured enamel finish in aluminium frame with roller tracks
13. Connecting arm
14. Jacking system for moving panel
15. Soffit formed by spray painted 7/8" (22 mm) plywood panel, 3/4" (20 mm) insulation layer, aluminium L-profile
16. 1/8 - 5/8 - 1/8" (4-16-4 mm) wood double glazing unit
17. Floor consisting of linoleum, 1 5/8" (40 mm) screed, vapour barrier, 2 3/4" (70 mm) acoustic board insulation, 9 3/8" (250 mm) reinforced concrete slab, 2 3/4" (70 mm) insulation, 1/2" (12.5 mm) gypsum board on frame of aluminium C-profiles
18. Timber skirting
19. Steel box profile supporting façade and electrical system
20. Electrically operated system for moving panels
21. Steel cornice
22. Aluminium L-profile
23. Finish comprising 1 1/4" (30 mm) gypsum board, double frame of aluminium C-profiles, 5 1/2" (140 mm) insulation layer, 4" (100 mm) steel box profile (parallel to plane of section), frame of 4 x 4" (100 x 100 mm) steel box profiles
24. Steel casing
25. 9 1/2 x 4 1/2 x 2 3/8" (240 x 115 x 60 mm) steel bracket with rectangular reinforcing plate securing finish to supporting system
26. Steel beam

DIAGNOSTIC AND THERAPEUTIC CENTRE, CEDT
DAIMIEL, SPAIN

ESTUDIO.ENTRESITIO

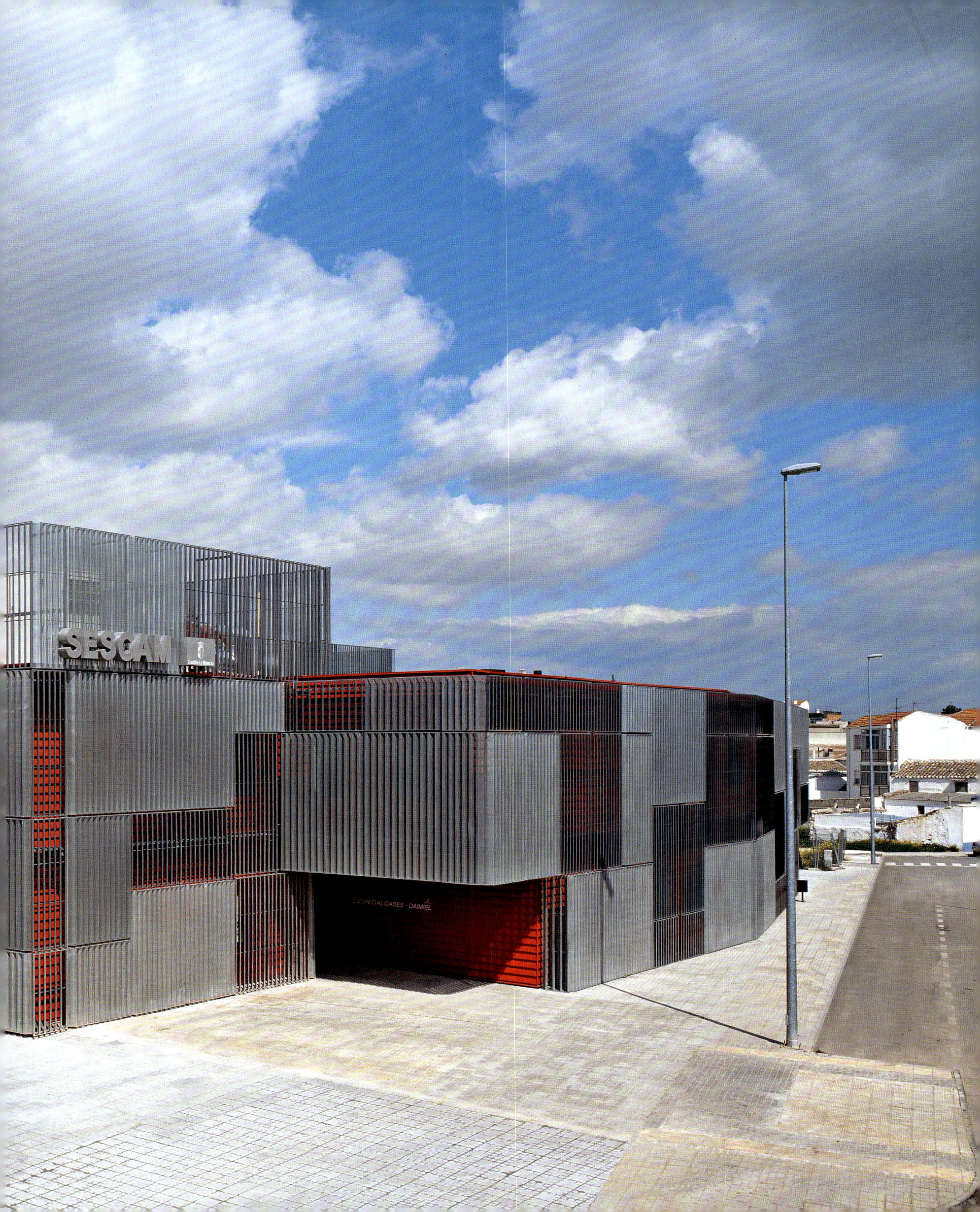
SESCAM
ESPECIALIDADES - DAIMIEL

■ South Elevation – Scale 1:400

In recent years, Spanish practice Entresitio has tackled the architectural issues posed by building for social services, healthcare and diagnostics provision. Its architects have developed a deep understanding of the complex layout requirements of healthcare constructions: the key nodes and communication circuits, and the need to avoid inappropriate intersections and overlapping to ensure maximum rationality for patients and practitioners.

The two-storey diagnostic and therapeutic centre, CEDT, in Daimiel in Spain's Castilla-La Mancha region is organized according to a logical breakdown of the functions carried on inside. The easy-to-access ground floor houses the public reception area, emergency ward and general medicine bay, with doctors' surgeries and diagnostics stations. The upper floor is reserved for specialist medicine: operating theatres (on the north side of the building), intensive care wards, doctors' surgeries, a conference room, medical personnel rest room, services and equipment rooms. The polygonal plan is sectioned by distribution corridors that branch off at right angles to diagnostics and general medicine areas, ensuring secluded environments for more serious specialist treatment. The layout is characterized by five rectangular inner courts lying parallel to each other. Essential as a means of bringing light and ventilation into the building, the courts have wide glazed lights and external cladding in corrugated sheet steel panels, placed so as to create an alternating pattern of horizontal and vertical grooves to break up the reverberation of the light. The doctors' surgeries look out over the courts, as do the central connection corridors and public waiting areas. The materials, colours and finishes give a physical sense of the precision and cleanliness befitting a hospital setting. The clean geometry is echoed in the stark wall cladding; the shades of white are enhanced by light streaming in from the inner courts.

Likewise the finishes – gres tiles, phenolic panels and plaster – fit seamlessly with the building's function. Providing maximum environmental comfort for patient and practitioner also meant paying great care to noise abatement. Accordingly, floor slabs are acoustically insulated while the flooring is made from natural rubber.

The new diagnostic and therapeutic centre is located in an extensive low-rise residential area. The building's striking form makes it an easily identifiable landmark, as its public function requires. Similar to other healthcare programmes developed by Entresitio, the Daimiel centre presents as a relatively complex volume, in apparent contrast to the rigorously linear layout. Set in ample grounds with extensive pedestrian areas, the building looks like a stack of separate volumes. The empty volume of the upper floor terrace breaks up the solid mass. The louvres shielding the rooftop air conditioning plant create a series of virtual, semi-transparent volumes. The slightly recessed volumes around the entrance help lighten the overall structure and at the same time create intermediate covered areas around the main access.

The building's architectural hallmark is its outer envelope. Bright red folded sheet steel panels are sheathed in a series of galvanized, perforated and folded sheet steel louvres. The result is a softly textured exterior, dynamic elevations and veiled perception of the volumes behind. This effect is enhanced by the different orientation of the various louvre sections.

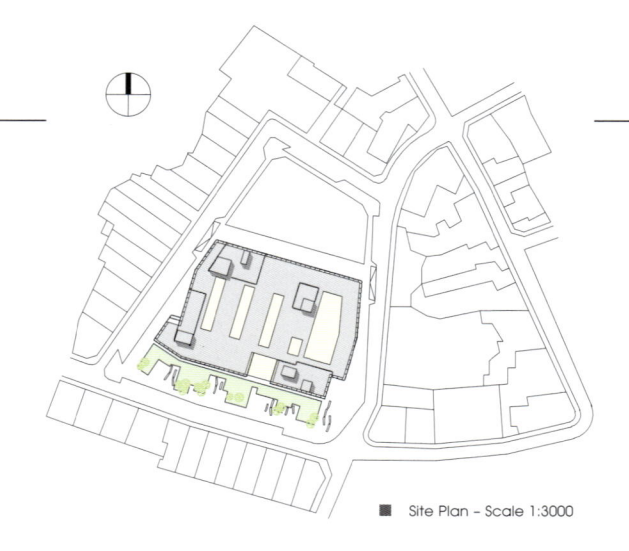

■ Site Plan – Scale 1:3000

■ North Elevation - Scale 1:400

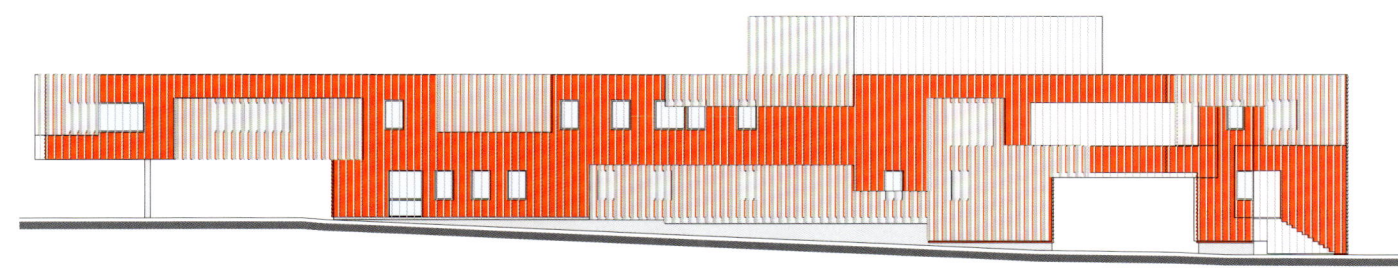

■ Ground Floor Plan – Scale 1:400

1. Main Entrance
2. Information
3. Emergency
4. Radiology
5. Warehouse
6. Physiotherapy
7. Waiting Area
8. Doctors' Office
9. Nurses' Office
10. Treatment Room
11. Courtyard
12. Doctors' Changing Room
13. Doctors' Residence
14. Surgery
15. Plant Room
16. Conference Room
17. IT Area
18. Terrace

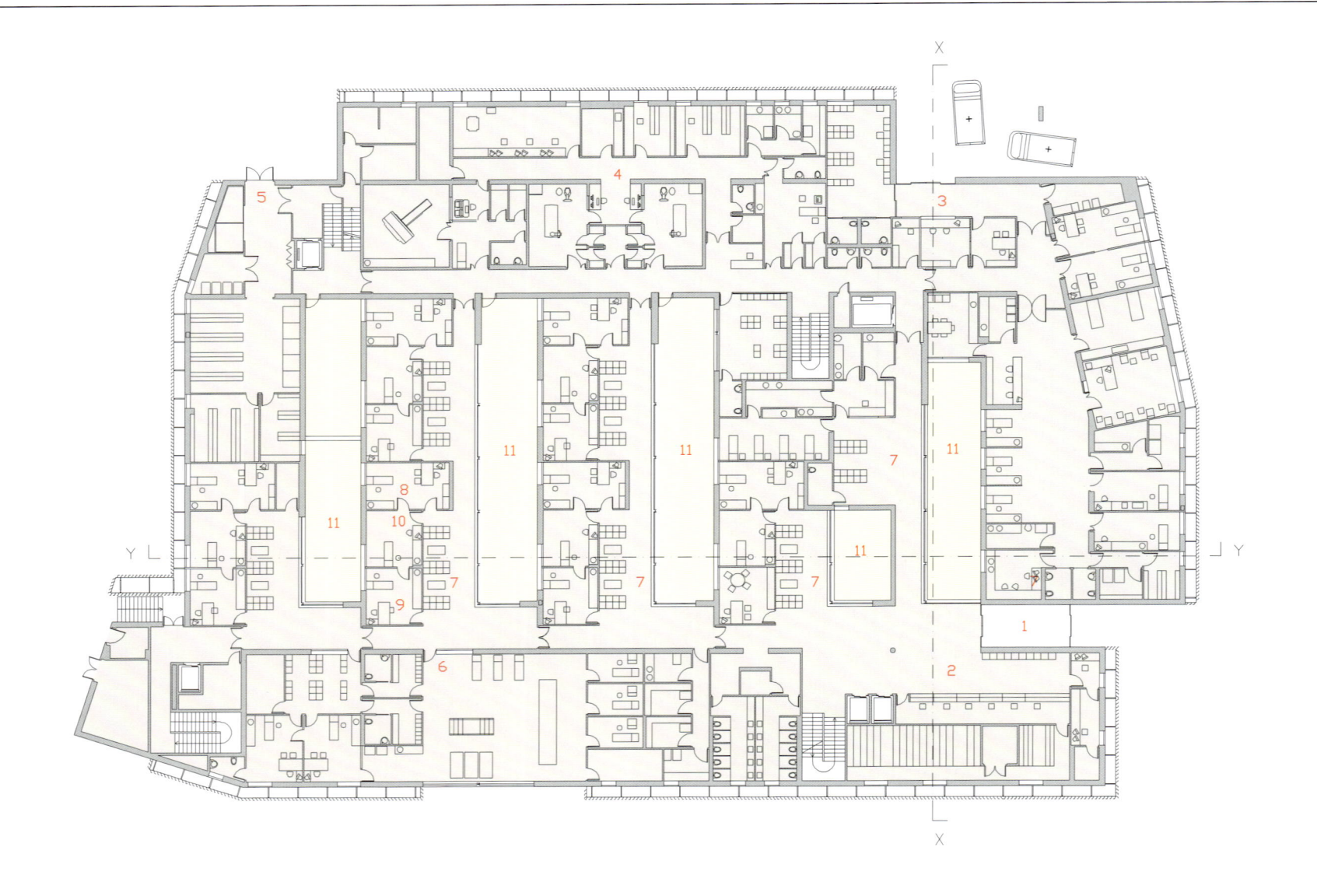

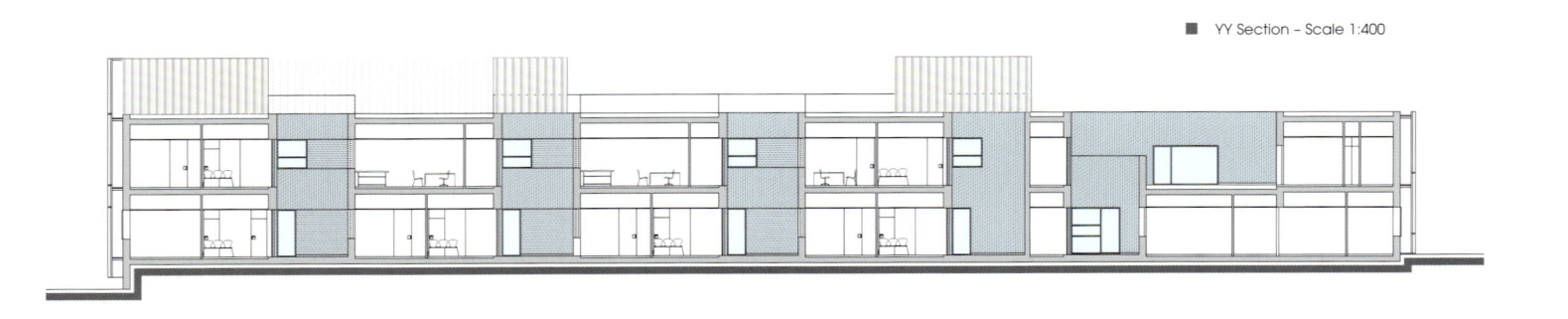

■ YY Section – Scale 1:400

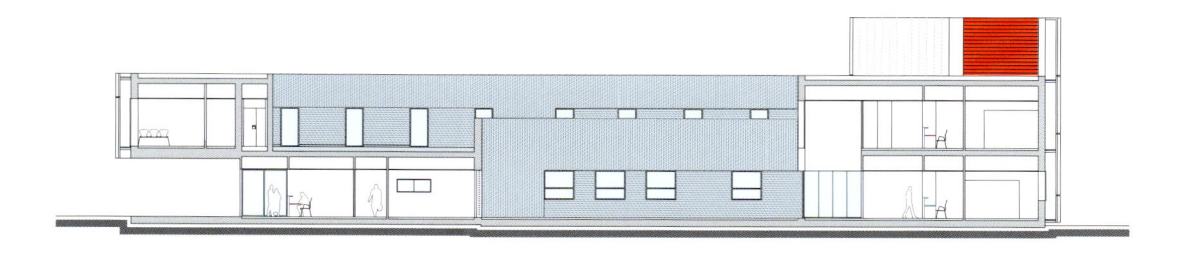

■ XX Section – Scale 1:400

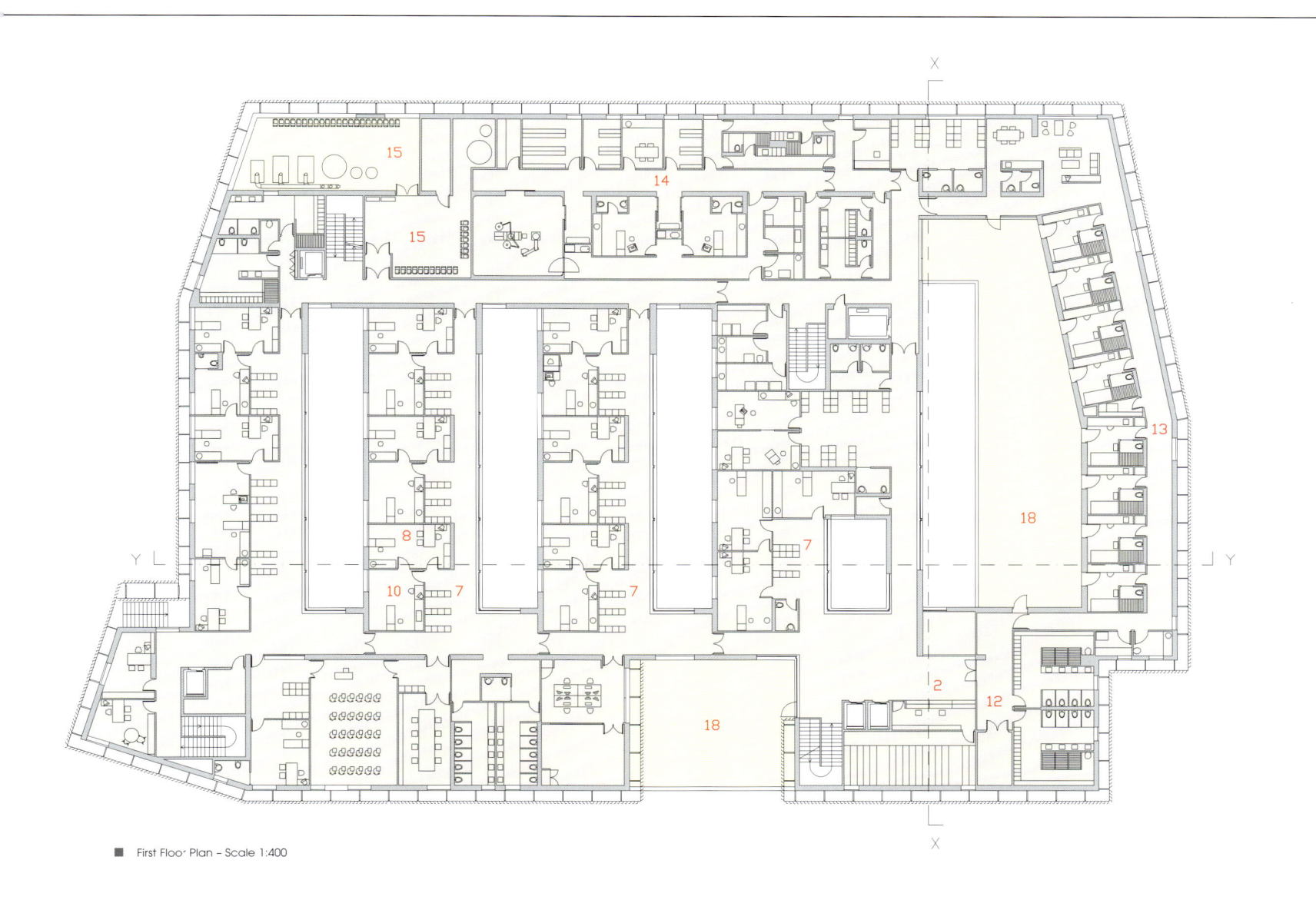

■ First Floor Plan – Scale 1:400

131 / estudio.entresitio

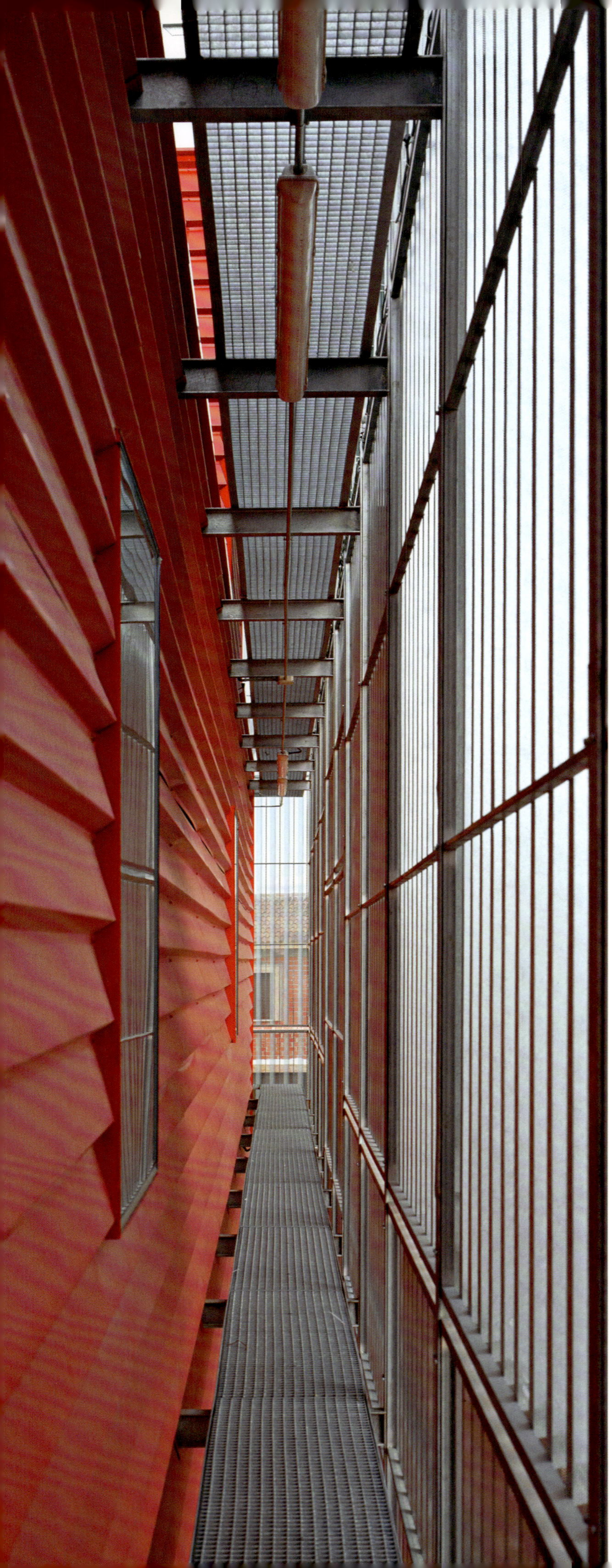

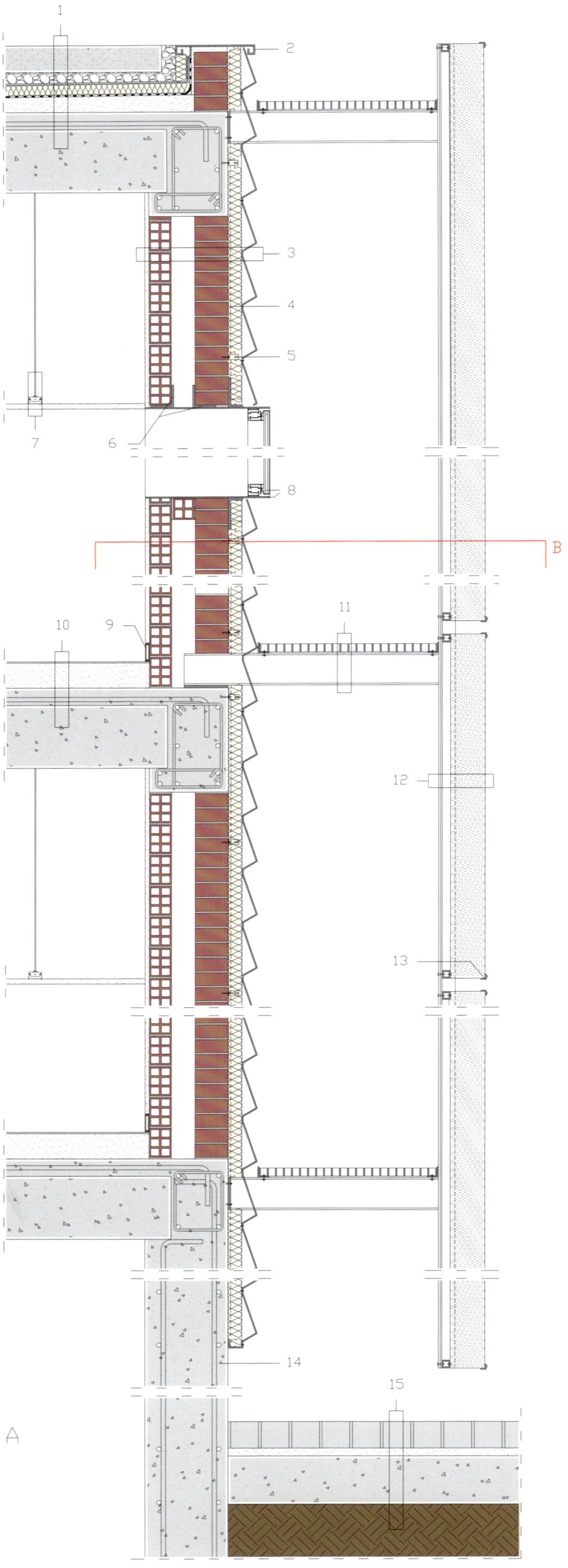

1
2
3
4
5
6
7
8
B
9
10
11
12
13
14
15
A

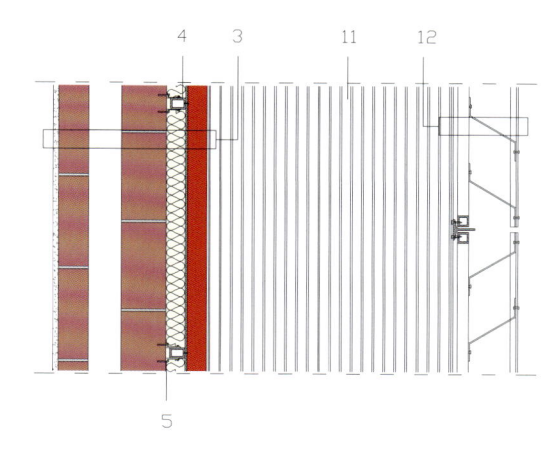

**DETAILS A, B: FACADE
VERTICAL AND HORIZONTAL SECTIONS
SCALE 1:20**

1. Roof pavement in 3 15/16" (100 mm) grey draining concrete, 1 37/64 – 3 5/32" (40 – 80 mm) ballast levelling layer, protective geotextile felt, 1 37/64" (40 mm) polystyrene board insulation, waterproofing membrane, screed forming slope, 11 13/16" (300 mm) reinforced concrete slab with pre-cast elements
2. Galvanized steel flashing
3. Facade cladding in folded steel painted red, 1 31/32" (50 mm) polyurethane foam board insulation, masonry wall of 1 31/32 x 4 23/32 x 9 29/64" (50 x 120 x 240 mm) solid bricks, airspace, supporting wall of 3 5/32 x 4 21/64 x 9 27/32" (80 x 110 x 250 mm) perforated bricks, 19/32" (15 mm) polished plaster interior finish
4. 1 3/16 x 1 37/64" (30 x 40 mm) steel box-shaped upright supporting cladding
5. Galvanized steel profiles anchoring upright to wall
6. 3 11/32 x 3 11/32" (85 x 85 mm) and 5/16" (8 mm) thick steel L-profiles containing wall and supporting wall
7. False ceiling of 25/32" (20 mm) gypsum board panels, frame of aluminium C-profiles and tie rods suspended from slab
8. Window with anodized aluminium frame and 5/32 – 15/32 – 5/32" (4 – 12 – 4 mm) double glazing with prefabricated galvanized sheet steel counter frame painted red
9. Skirting of interlocking 3 15/16 x 19/32" (100 x 15 mm) and 3 35/64 x 25/64" (90 x 10 mm) anodized aluminium C-profiles
10. Natural rubber flooring, 3 47/64" (95 mm) screed, 11 13/16" (300 mm) reinforced concrete slab with pre-cast elements
11. 1 3/16" (30 mm) walkable steel grille fixed to beam by 1 37/64 x 1 37/64" (40 x 40 mm) steel L-profiles and screws, projecting bracket in IPE 120 steel supporting cladding structure
12. Facade cladding structure formed by 2 9/32 x 2 23/64" (58 x 60 mm) T-section uprights connected to supporting beams, frame of 1 3/16 x 1 3/16" (30 x 30 mm) box-shaped aluminium profiles, Z-shaped micro-perforated galvanized steel slats
13. Steel L-profile trim fastening slats
14. 11 13/16" (300 mm) thick reinforced concrete foundation
15. 3 15/16 x 3 15/16" (100 x 100 mm) concrete block paving, 1 3/16" (30 mm) screed, 7 3/32" (180 mm) concrete levelling layer, earth

estudio.entresitio

C

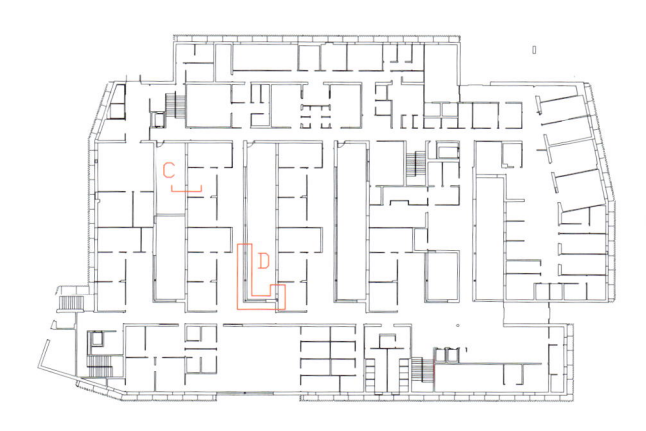

**DETAILS C, D: FACADE ON INNER PATIO
VERTICAL AND HORIZONTAL SECTIONS
SCALE 1:20**

1. Parapet formed by 1 3/8 x 1 3/8" (35 x 35 mm) box-shaped steel uprights and crosspieces
2. Facade cladding in corrugated galvanized sheet steel fitted vertically, 1 31/32" (50 mm) polyurethane foam board insulation, masonry wall of 1 31/32 x 4 23/32 x 9 29/64" (50 x 120 x 240 mm) solid bricks, airspace, supporting wall of 3 5/32 x 4 21/64 x 9 27/32" (80 x 110 x 250 mm) perforated bricks, 19/32" (15 mm) polished plaster interior finish
3. 1 3/16 x 1 37/64" (30 x 40 mm) steel box-shaped upright supporting cladding
4. Galvanized steel profiles anchoring upright to wall
5. 3 11/32 x 3 11/32" (85 x 85 mm) and 5/16" (8 mm) thick steel L-profiles containing wall and supporting wall
6. 1 3/16" (30 mm) thick wood closure with fireproof paint
7. Sunblind with adjustable louvres with supporting frame of 2 23/64 x 2 23/64" (60 x 60 mm) box-shaped profiles
8. Casing in folded 13/64" (5 mm) thick sheet steel
9. Operable transom window with anodized aluminium frame and galvanized steel counter frame with 5/32 – 15/32 – 5/32" (4 – 12 – 4 mm) double glazing
10. Window sill finished in galvanized sheet steel
11. Facade cladding in corrugated galvanized sheet steel fitted horizontally
12. 1 3/16 x 1 37/64" (30 x 40 mm) box-shaped steel crosspiece supporting cladding fixed to brick structure by L-profiles and screws
13. Internal patio formed by gravel layer of varying thicknesses, protective geotextile felt, earth
14. 9 27/32 x 13 25/32" (250 x 350 mm) reinforced concrete column
15. Interior finish in folded sheet steel, 25/32" (20 mm) extruded polystyrene board insulation, 5 33/64 x 5 33/64" (140 x 140 mm) painted steel column formed by two coupled UPN 140 beams, fireproof polyurethane foam filling
16. Glazed wall with anodized aluminium frame and 5/32 – 15/32 – 5/32 + 5/32" (4 – 12 – 4 + 4 mm) double glazing with solar protection
17. Interior finish in 13/64" (5 mm) folded sheet steel, 25/32" (20 mm) polystyrene board insulation, painted HEB 140 steel column

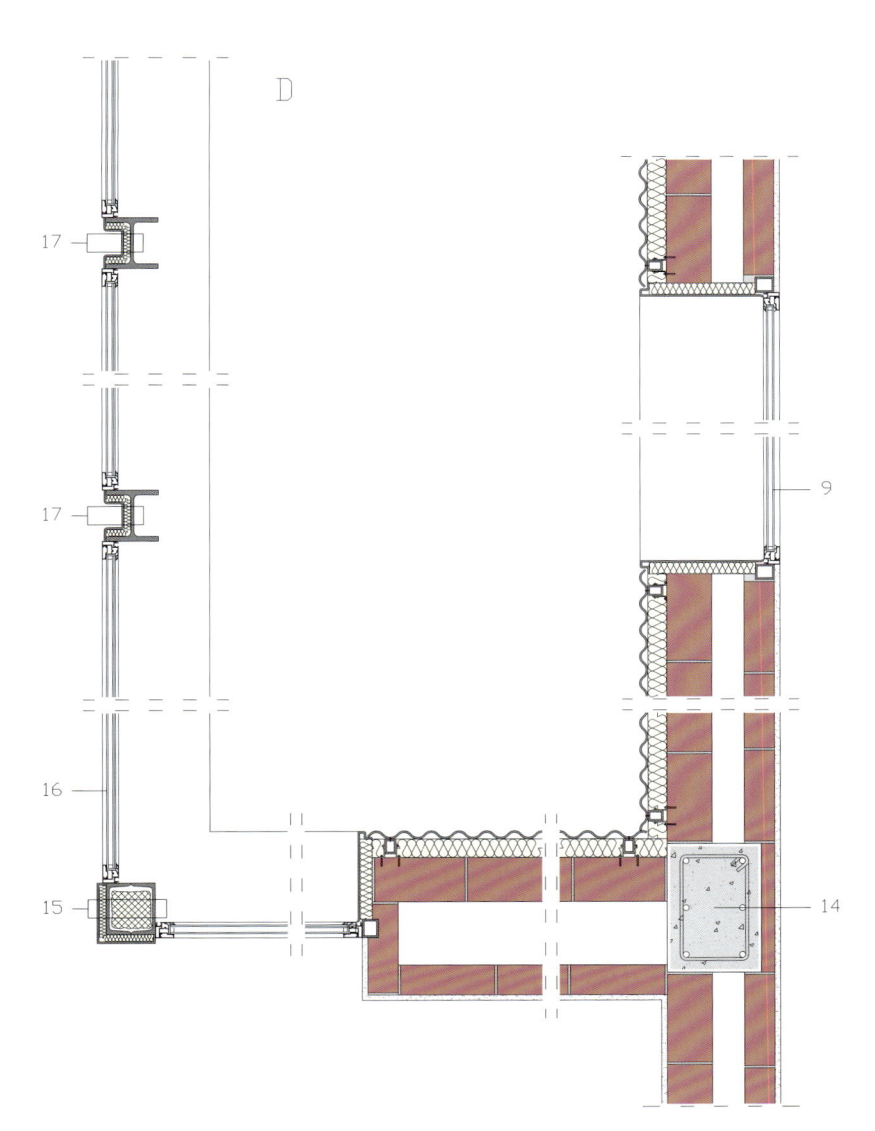

THE PUBLIC – WEST BROMWICH, UK
ALSOP ARCHITECTS

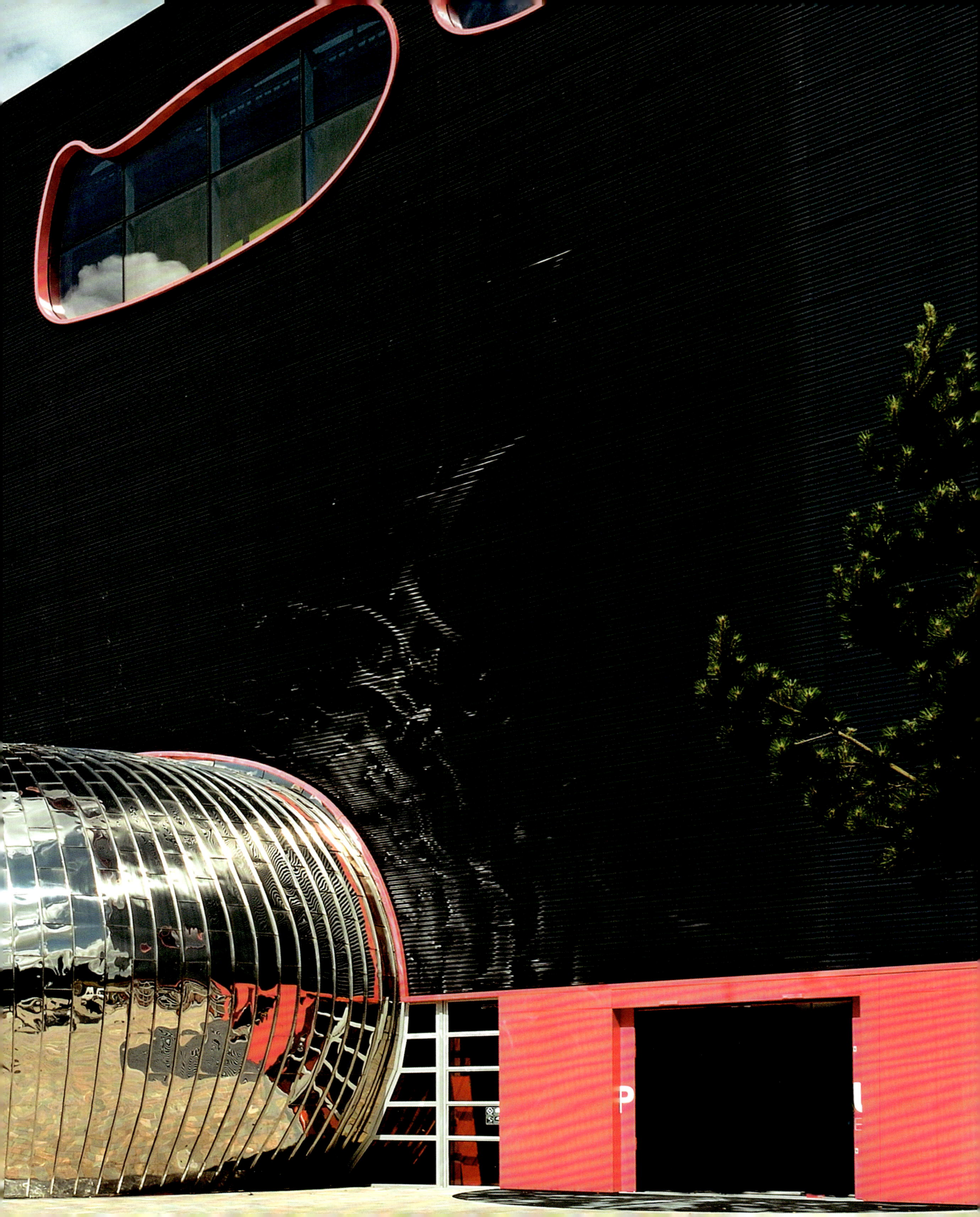

The Fun Palace was a project by Cedric Price. Although never built, it remains a seminal concept for an extremely innovative type of multi-purpose cultural building whose key feature was its lack of formal design. The aim of the project was to make available a single, hands-on space whose diverse functions were interconnected episodes. It was to be a place where people would go not for any particular purpose but simply for the fun of the unexpected or the simple pleasure of a human experience. "The activities designed for the site should be experimental, the place itself expendable and changeable. The organization of space and the objects occupying it should, on the one hand, challenge the participants' mental and physical dexterity and, on the other, allow for a flow of space and time, in which passive and active pleasure is provoked". (1*) Will Alsop's The Public building, inaugurated in June 2008 in West Bromwich, brings Price's Fun Palace immediately to mind.

The Public is a complex building, totally innovative and ahead of its time. It is the outcome of a long and intricate development process that produced a broad range of sketches and models, perhaps the most Will has ever produced for one single brief. The building was transformed as time and drawings went by however; the many ideas generated often went into other projects by Alsop's practice. Like Price's unrealized Fun Palace, The Public can be considered Will Alsop's seminal building. West Bromwich in the West Midlands of England is a depressed, former industrial area with no cultural activities of note yet today the focus of a wide-reaching regeneration plan costing a total of around 700 million pounds. The Public stands as the symbol of the whole scheme. The idea of a new-concept arts venue was the brainchild of Sylvia King, who in 1974 set up the Jubilee Arts Trust, a community arts organization headquartered initially in a double-decker bus that did the rounds of the local neighbourhoods. Later the Trust was housed in a modest building in West Bromwich until 1994 when Sylvia King met Will Alsop and suggested he devise a truly innovative site. It should not so much be a place for exhibiting works of art but one where art would be produced. In 1998 a competition was held. Unlike other architects, Will Alsop did not present drawings or a model because it was not clear what the project's aim was. Rather he suggested the approach to adopt: interacting with the client and local population through workshops and public meetings so that the requirements of client, place and end users could be appropriately met. The result, he claimed, would be a hub of energy and arts, a place that would receive as well as irradiate, where art would not just be conserved but lived and regenerated continuously. Sylvia King was enthralled with the proposal and the process got underway with the help too of Will Alsop's longstanding friend, artist Bruce McLean. McLean worked on several installations to raise awareness and encourage local inhabitants to imagine an arts-led venue of their dreams that would allow them to express and increment those dreams. It was to be a building they should be proud to feel ownership for and not, as often happens, an imposition from above with no connection to the cultural life of the city.

Originally the project was called CPlex. In 2000, a 5-metre model of it was exhibited at the British Pavilion of the "Less Aesthetics More Ethics" Venice Biennale directed by Massimiliano Fuksas. After that, other institutions like the Arts Council, Advantage West Midlands, the European Regional Development Fund and the Lottery became players, and the project's name was changed to The Public. The outward appearance is clear and simple: a 112 x 21 x 22 metres (367 x 69 x 72 ft) black box. The envelope is completely independent of the interior elements. The amoeba-shaped openings on the black box are framed with fuxia. It is a mysterious secret box visible from the motorway, which is also why the roof housing the plant and equipment has been designed to stand out as a landmark. Although its function is not necessarily obvious, the building's singular appearance sets it apart from its surrounds. All its complexity is kept within. The interior is a single space, a technologically sophisticated avant-garde arena populated and animated by elements with names like "Pod", "Rock", "Pebble", "Lily-Pad" and "Sock". They float like separate structures but although autonomous, they never break the spatial continuity of the whole.

Even if iconic, The Public was designed with energy efficiency in mind. The interior is a "bio-climatic" environment: the pods ensure energy-efficient power supplies into spaces where people gather, and natural ventilation is employed wherever possible. This is especially apparent on mild days when the wide groundfloor apertures are thrown open to allow natural circulation of air.

(1*) Cedric Price - "A Laboratory of Fun" - *New Scientist*, 14th May 1964)

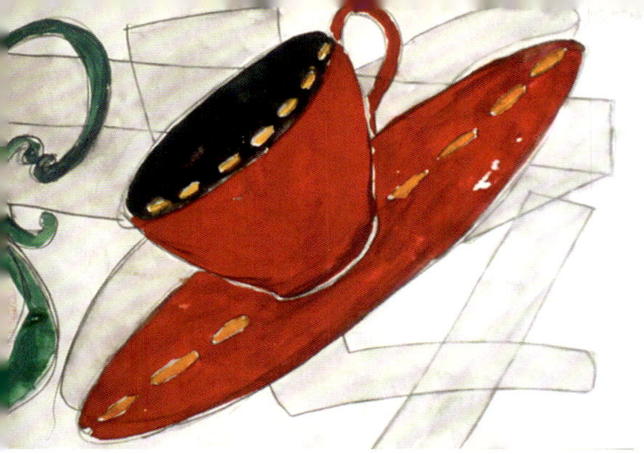

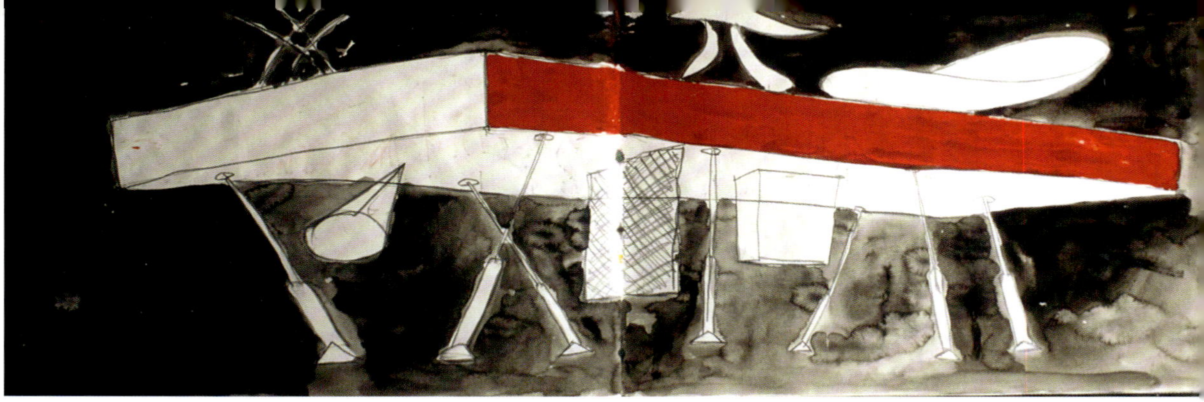

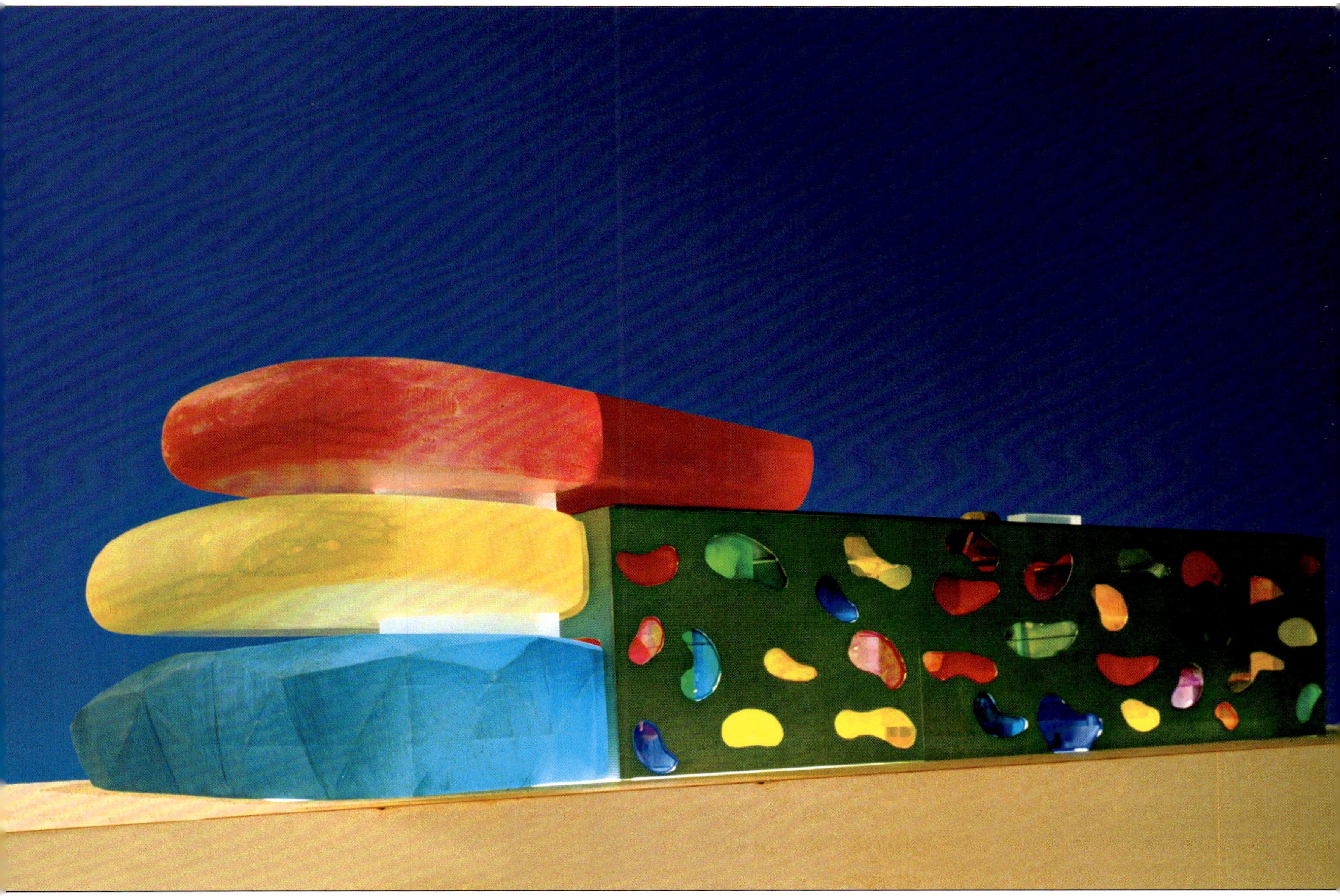

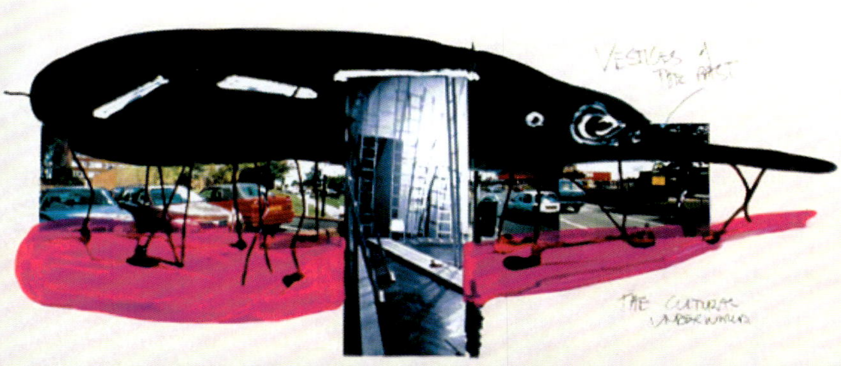
THE CULTURAL

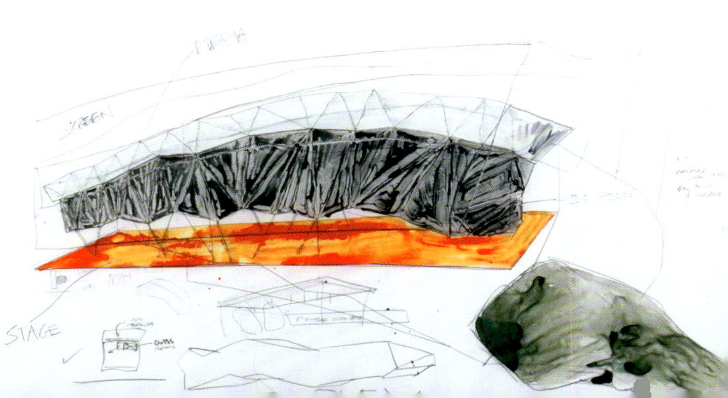
STAGE

■ Ground Floor Plan - Scale 1:600

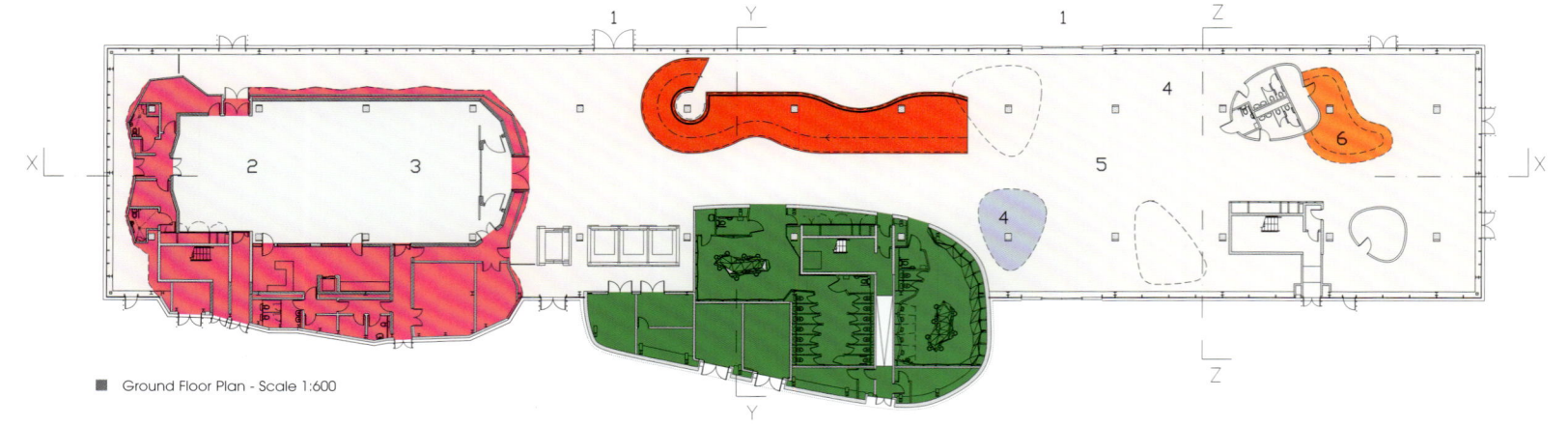

1. Main Entrance
2. Stage
3. Theatre
4. Retail
5. Lobby
6. Café
7. Ramp
8. Production Suite
9. Family learning Centre
10. Gallery
11. Flexible Workspace
12. Art/Dance Studio
13. Void
14. Digital Art Workshop
15. Resource Room
16. Presentation room
17. Training Room
18. Seminar
19. Meeting Pod
20. Offices

140 / The Public

■ 1ST Floor Plan - Scale 1:600

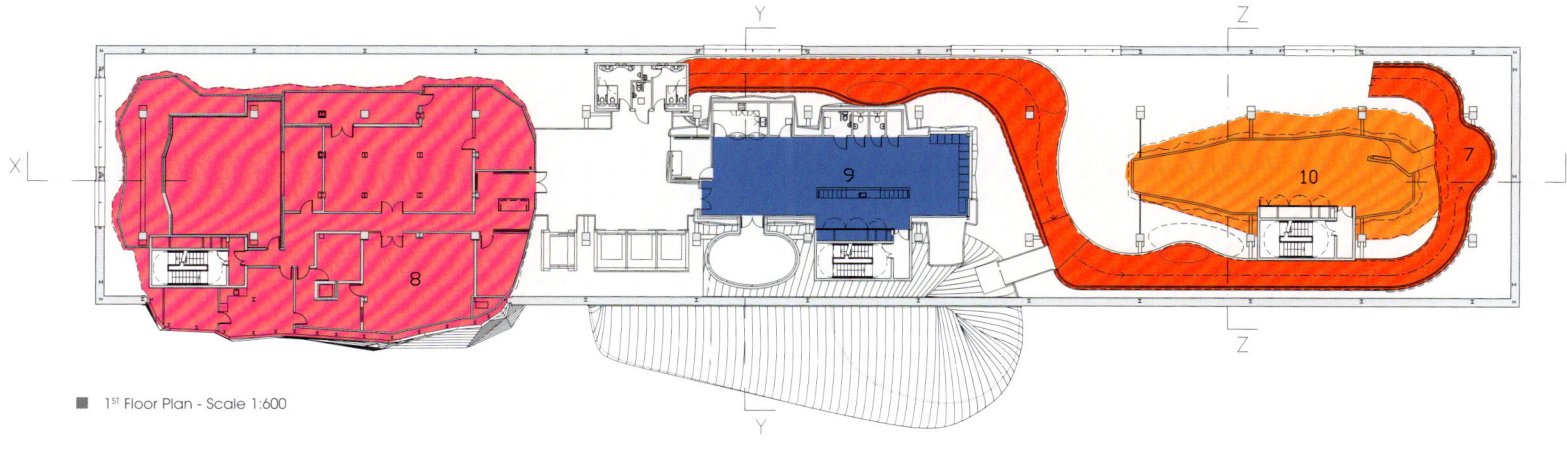

141 / Alsop Architects

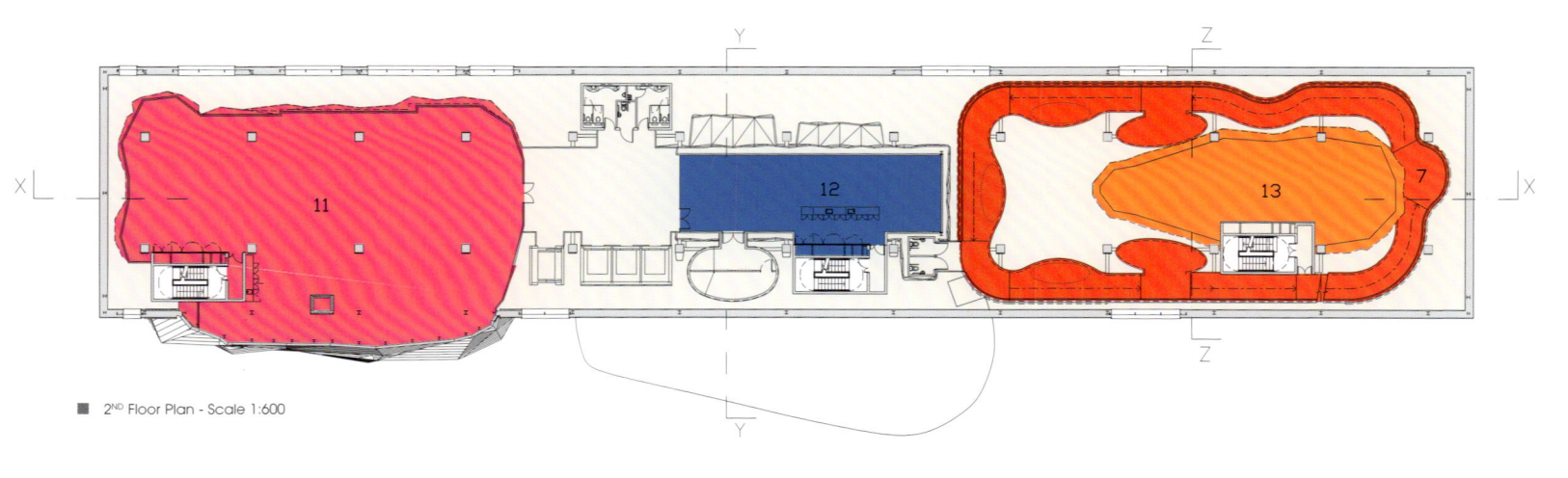

142 / The Public

2ND Floor Plan - Scale 1:600

■ 4ᵀᴴ Floor Plan - Scale 1:600

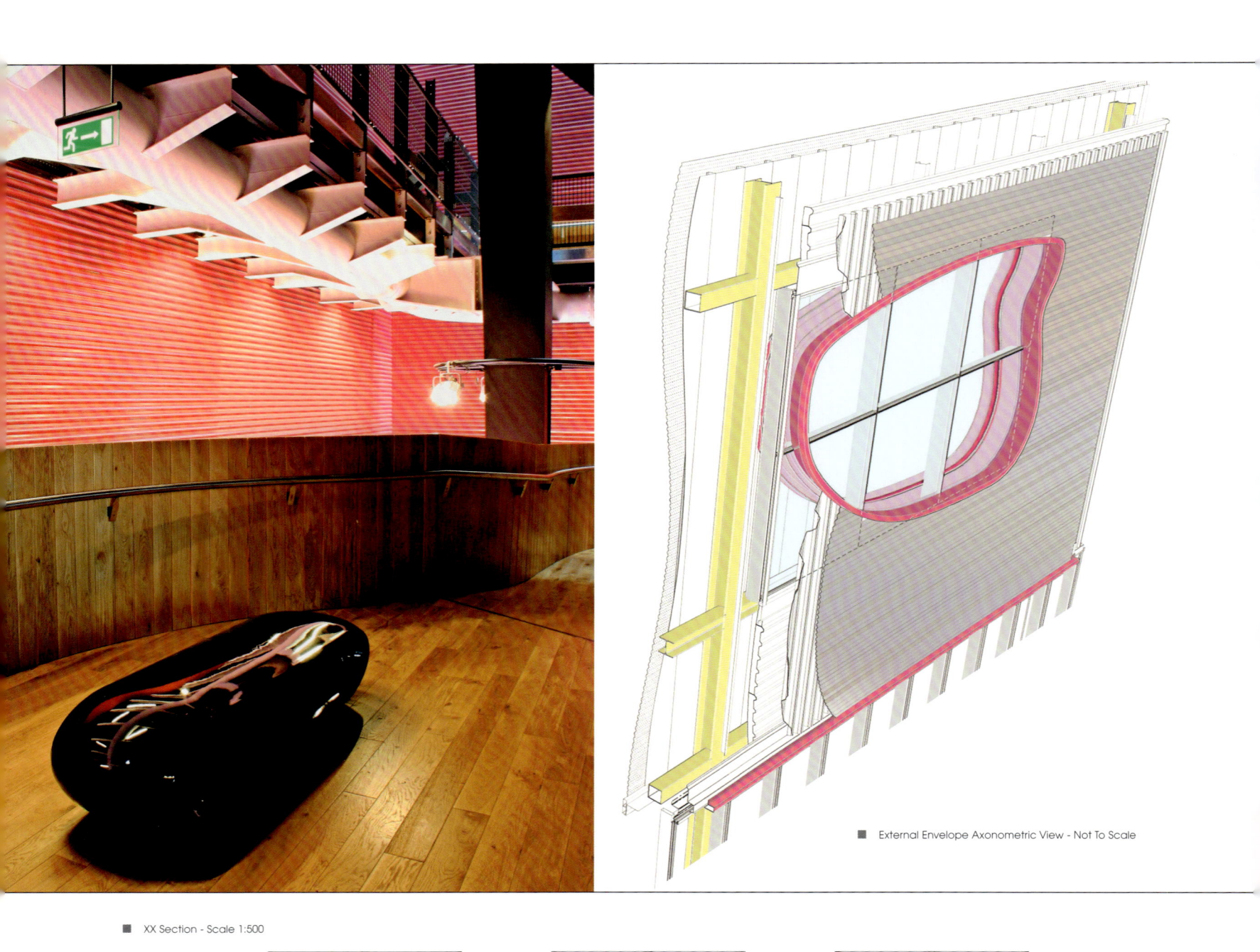

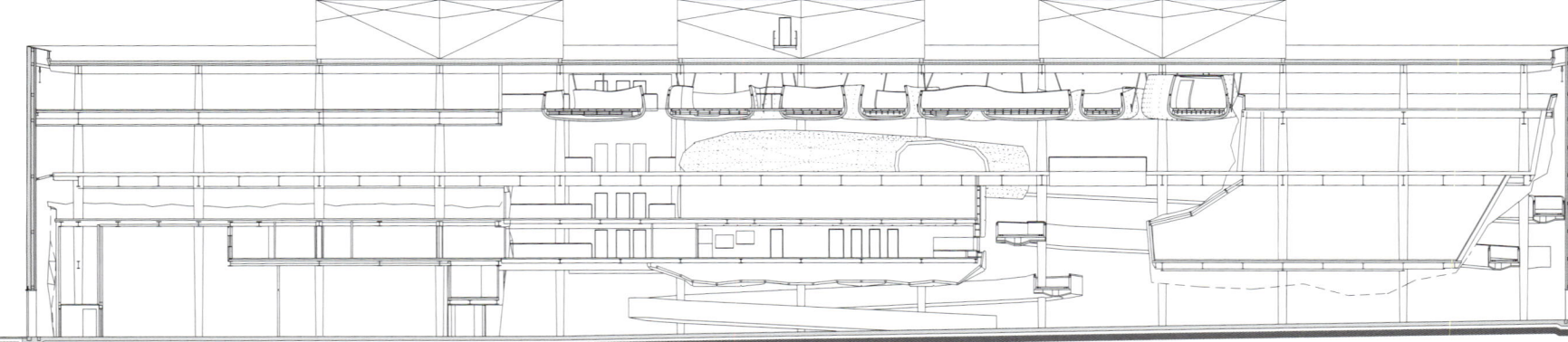

■ External Envelope Axonometric View - Not To Scale

■ XX Section - Scale 1:500

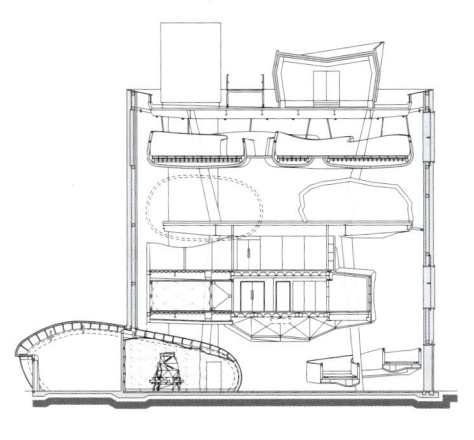

■ YY Section - Scale 1:500

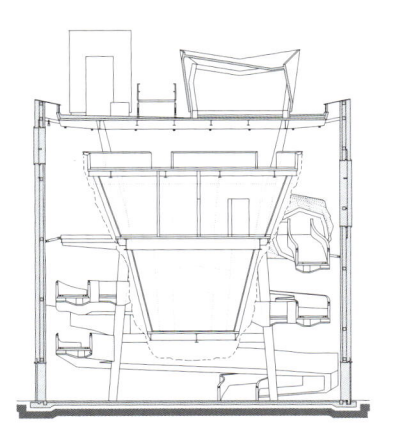

■ ZZ Section - Scale 1:500

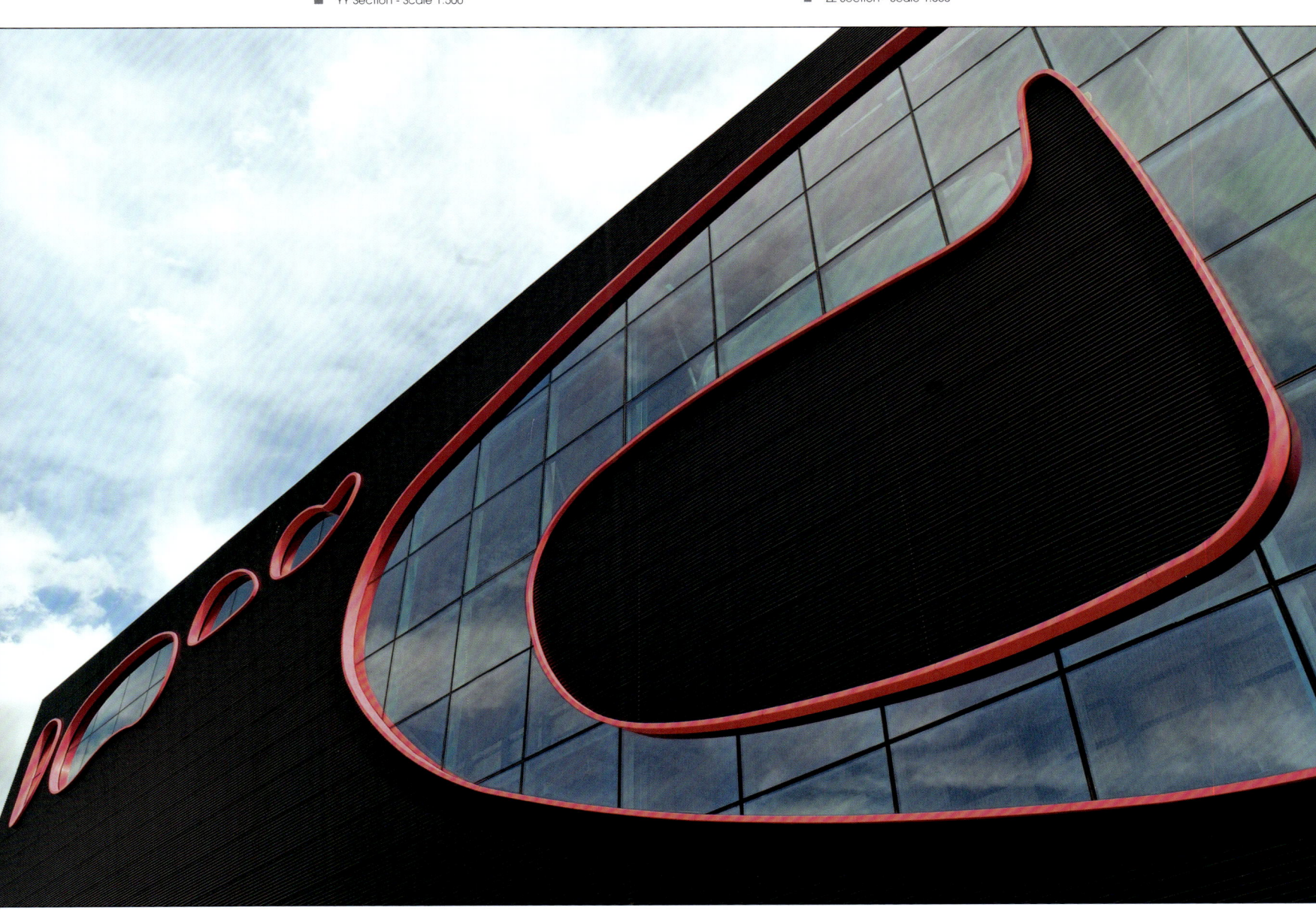

145 / Alsop Architects

146 / The Public

DETAIL A: FAÇADE
VERTICAL SECTION - SCALE 1:20

1. Perimeter walkway constructed from 1/4" (6 mm) thick steel grille on adjustable piers formed by steel profiles on 2" (50 mm) waterproofed concrete screed
2. 1/16" (2 mm) steel casing, 4 3/4 x 2" (120 x 50 mm) wood joists, double 2" (50 mm) board insulation between joists, waterproofing membrane, 11 7/8" (300 mm) reinforced concrete slab
3. Installation space housing perimeter heating formed by 3/8" (10 mm) thick aluminium grille, 1/16" (1 mm) thick steel profile containment with feet
4. Floor with 1/16" (5 mm) NONSLIP-VINYL finish, 2 3/4" (70 mm) screed, 1 1/4" (30 mm) board insulation
5. Glazed façade with frame formed by 3 1/2 x 2" (90 x 50 mm) and 7 1/8 x 2" (180 x 50 mm) aluminium box-shaped profiles with 3/8 - 5/8 - 1/8 + 1/8" (10/16/4.4+4.4) double glazing
6. Structural upright formed by 12 x 12" (305 x 305 mm) steel I-beam (parallel to plane of section)
7. 3 1/8 x 2 3/4" (80 x 70 mm) recess for cold cathode tube lighting system formed by 3/4 x 3 1/8" (18 x 80 mm) and 5/16 x 4 1/8" (8 x 105 mm) MDF battens
8. Interior wall covering formed by 16 1/2 x 1/16" (420 x 2 mm) pink aluminium profile fastened by 6 1/2 x 1 3/8" (165 x 35 mm) galvanized steel angle
9. Interior perimeter lighting system (parallel to plane of section)
10. Pink 1/16" (2 mm) thick aluminium profile trim
11. 1/16" (0.8 mm) sheet steel joint between glazed wall and façade cladding
12. Exterior wall with 1/16" (0.9 mm) blue aluminium sinusoidal cladding, 4" (100 mm) 1/16" (0.9 mm) thick corrugated steel, sandwich panel formed by 5 1/2 x 3 1/2" (140 x 90 mm) 1/16" (0.9 mm) thick corrugated steel with 3 1/8" (80 mm) internal board insulation, 5 1/2" (140 mm) steel C-profile bracing (parallel to plane of section) bolted to steel I-beams via 7 1/8 x 4 1/8" (180 x 105 mm) C-profiles
13. 8 x8" (203 x 203 mm) steel I-beam supporting façade
14. Interior wall formed by 1/16" (0.7 mm) pink perforated steel sinusoidal gladding, black geotextile membrane shading, 1 1/4" (30 mm) board insulation, 2 3/8" (60 mm) acoustic panel, 12 x 12" (305 x 305 mm) steel I-beam (parallel to plane of section)
15. 4 x 6 3/4" (100 x 170 mm) steel L-profile with screws securing internal leaf of wall
16. Interior covering of circular window formed by 6 1/8 x 5/16" (155 x 8 mm) MDF panel attached to 1 3/8 x 4 3/4" (35 x 120 mm) wood joist
17. Closed window with 4 x 2 3/8" (100 x 60 mm) aluminium box profile frame and 3/8 - 7/8 - 1/8 + 1/8" (10/21/4.4+4.4 mm) double glazing
18. Cleaning cradle support (parallel to plane of section)
19. 7 7/8 x 7 7/8" (200 x 200 mm) steel box beam bracing
20. 1/16" (1.6 mm) steel angle profile fastener
21. 1/16" (0.7 mm) steel flashing
22. Aluminium bar (parallel to plane of section) securing glass, 1/16" (0.7 mm) Corten steel sheeting exterior finish, double 3 1/8" (80 mm) board insulation, 1/16" (0.7 mm) shaped steel sheeting
23. Skylight in 3/8 - 5/8 - 1/8 + 1/8" (10/16/4.4+4.4) double glazing
24. Frame of 2 x 2 1/16" (50 x 50 x 5 mm) steel box profiles supporting transom window with connecting steel plates
25. Transom window with 1/4 - 3/4 - 1/4" (6/20/6 mm) aluminium double glazing unit
26. 7 7/8 x 4 x 1/16" (200 x 100 x 5 mm) steel plate fixing frame to concrete edging by anchors
27. Roof formed by waterproofing membrane, double 5 1/2" (140 mm) board insulation, vapour barrier, 5 1/8" (130 mm) composite slab formed by concrete fill over corrugated sheeting, 24 x 5 1/2" (610 x 140 mm) tapered structural I-beam
28. 7 7/8 x 4" (200 x 100 mm) steel I-beam supporting cleaning cradle connected via steel plate to 8 x 5 1/4" (203 x 133 mm) steel I-beam supporting roof
29. False ceiling formed by painted 1/2" (12 mm) gypsum board on 2 3/8 x 1" (60 x 25 mm) wood battens

147 / Alsop Architects

SANTA CATERINA MARKET
BARCELONA, SPAIN
MIRALLES TAGLIABUE ARQUITECTOS

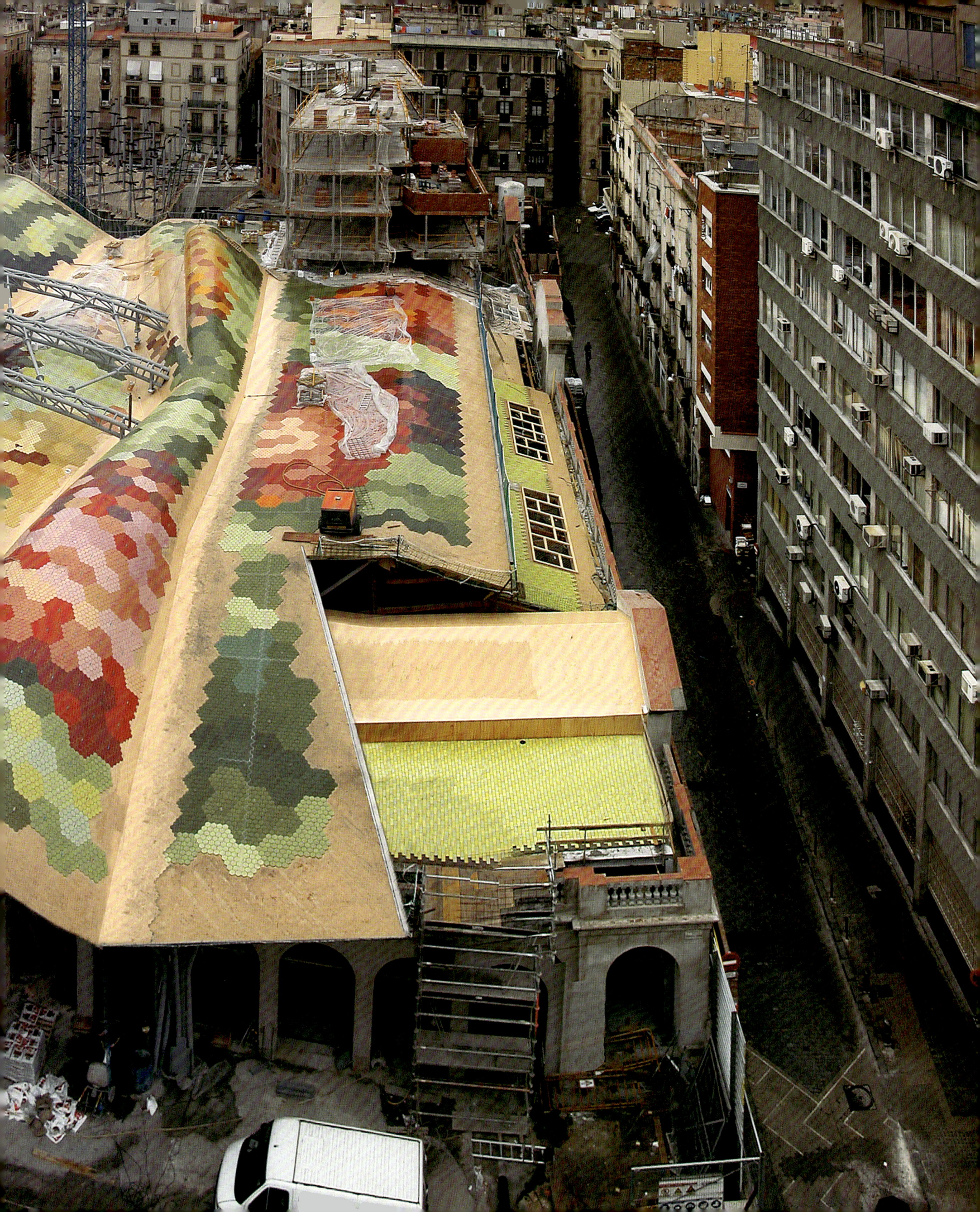

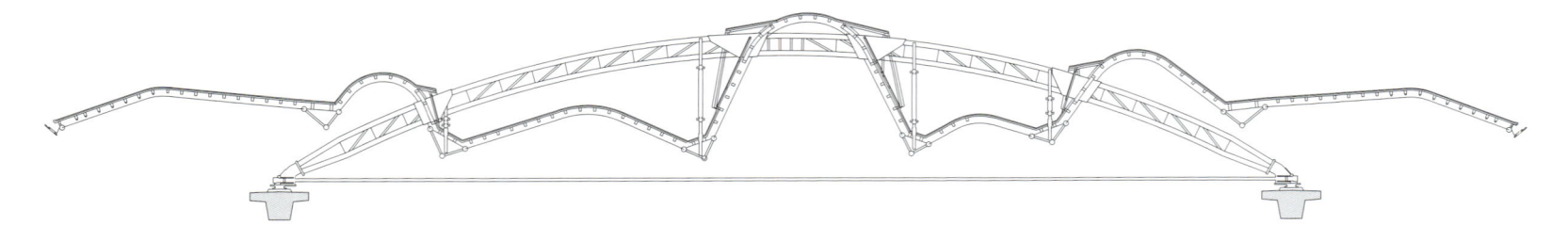

■ XX Roof Cross Section – Scale 1:300

The restoration of the Santa Caterina Market in the old centre of Barcelona is underpinned by strong commitments: to reconstitute a failing urban fabric, with its mix of residential and business functions, and mediate between old and new by developing architectural elements that reflect the aesthetic and symbolic values of an historic site but also accommodate modern technology.

The covered market with its stalls and shops abuts onto a series of apartments for the elderly. Three underground levels house services for the whole neighbourhood, namely a solid waste collection unit level 3; 1,008 sqm (10,850 sq ft) a two-storey car park, storage space for the market above and an area displaying the Gothic remains of the church of Santa Caterina level -2; 4,498 sqm (48,418 sq ft); level -1; 4,197 sqm (45,178 sq ft). The ground level accommodates the market stalls 2,068 sqm (22,260 sq ft), other commercial areas and the entrance to the apse. The 5-storey residential building covers a surface area of 3,749 sqm (40,355 sq ft). The major feature and symbol of the whole area is, however, the 5,500 sqm (59,203 sq ft), three-barrelled roof covered with a mosaic of 325,000 ceramic pieces in some 67 colours resting on a wooden under-structure and protected by transparent insulating and waterproofed over-layers.

The perimeter wall has been preserved on three sides and in part reconstructed (at the points marked out by upside down banisters.) The impressive structure is supported by metal pillars, two large longitudinal reinforced concrete beams 43 and 72 m (141 and 236 ft), three transverse metal arches, longitudinal V-shaped metal beams, and parabolic arches in steel and laminated wood. Wooden trusses salvaged from the old roof have been restored and replaced.

■ Colour Range for Roof Cladding

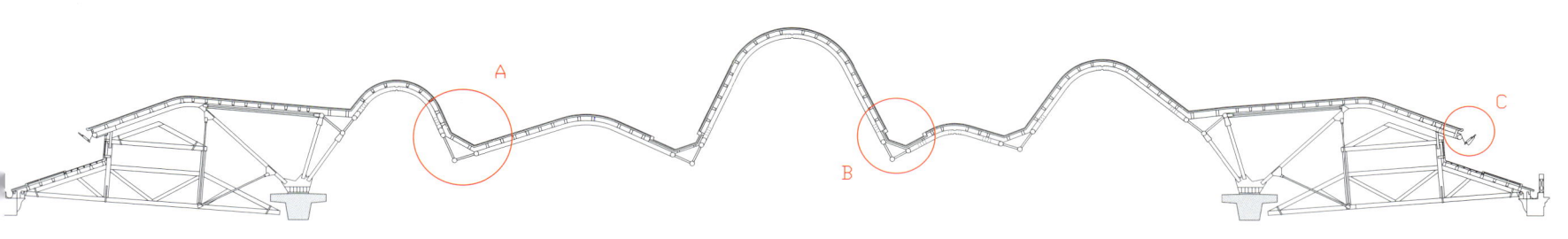

■ YY Roof Cross Section – Scale 1:300

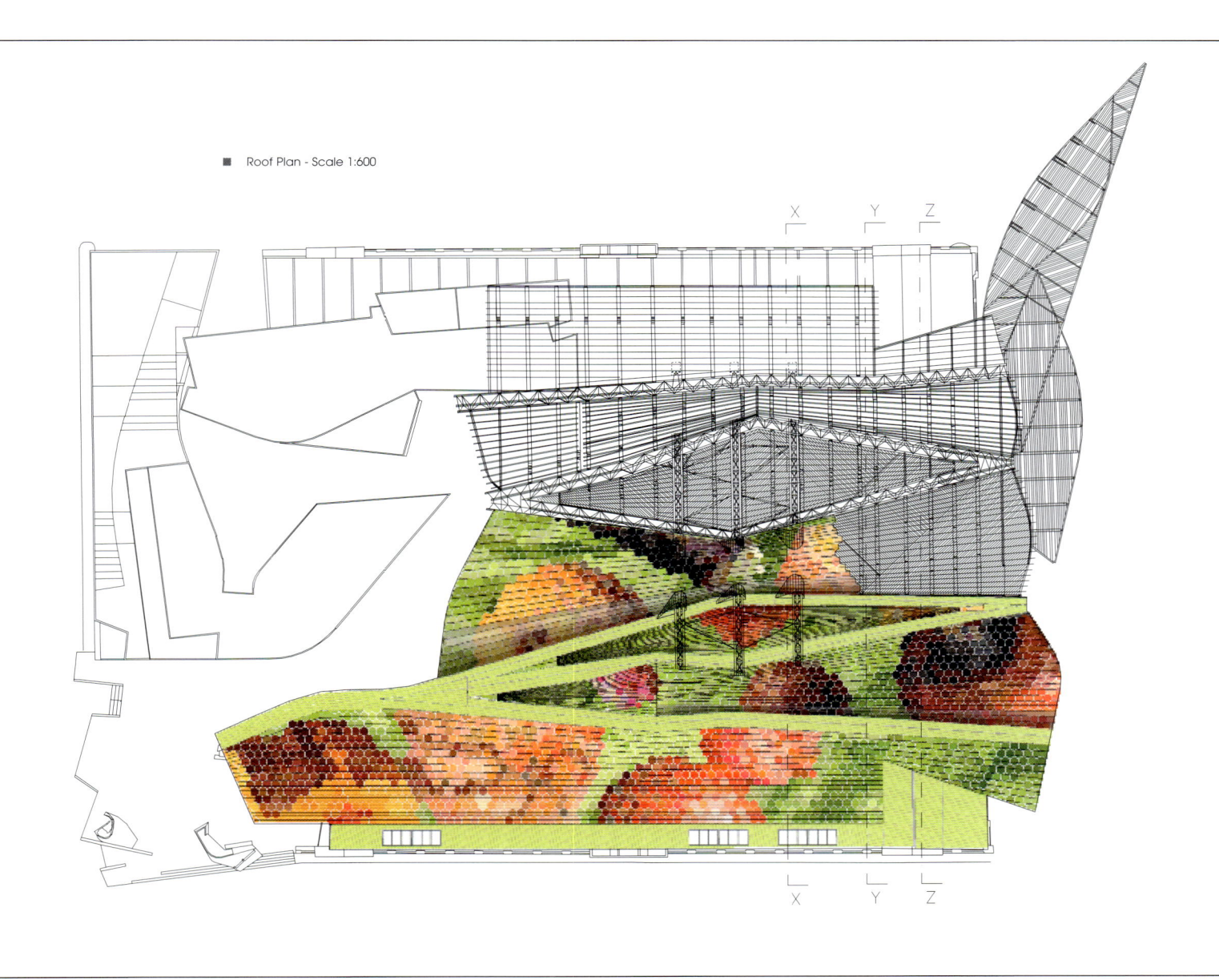

■ Roof Plan – Scale 1:600

■ ZZ Roof Cross Section – Scale 1:300

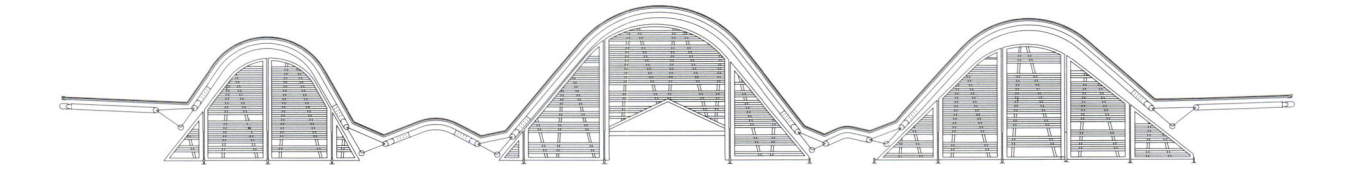

151 / Miralles Tagliabue

152 / Market

**DETAILS A, B, C: MOSAIC ROOF
VERTICAL SECTIONS – SCALE 1:25**

1. Roof formed by mosaic of multicoloured 3/8" (10 mm) ceramic tiles, layer of glue, polyester waterproofing membrane, double shaped 3/4" (20 mm) spruce fir boards, 1 5/8 x 1 5/8" (40 x 40 mm) timber beams sandwiching rockwool insulation, double shaped 3/4" (20 mm) spruce fir boards, 5 7/8 x 3/8" (150 x 10 mm) timber beam, timber spacer, double 5 1/8 x 2 3/4" (130 x 70 mm) steel L-profiles, structural arch formed by 7 7/8" (200 mm) spruce fir glulam beam (parallel to plane of section)
2. Steel plate connecting bracket
3. Structural lattice formed by Ø 8 5/8" (220 mm) pipe profiles, Ø 3 1/8" (80 mm) steel bars and steel plates
4. 6 3/4 x 4" (170 x 100 mm) steel U-profile
5. Steel profile trim
6. EPDM waterproofing joint
7. Connecting structure of steel plates
8. Sealant joint
9. Steel L-profile trim
10. Steel L-profile connecting beam to lattice
11. Steel flashing
12. Ø 8 5/8" (220 mm) steel pipe profile edge
13. Frame of shaped corrugated sheet steel, 3/4" (20 mm) steel plate, 4 3/4 x 1 1/4" (120 x 30 mm) steel C-profile, shaped sheet steel rain gutter

154 / Market

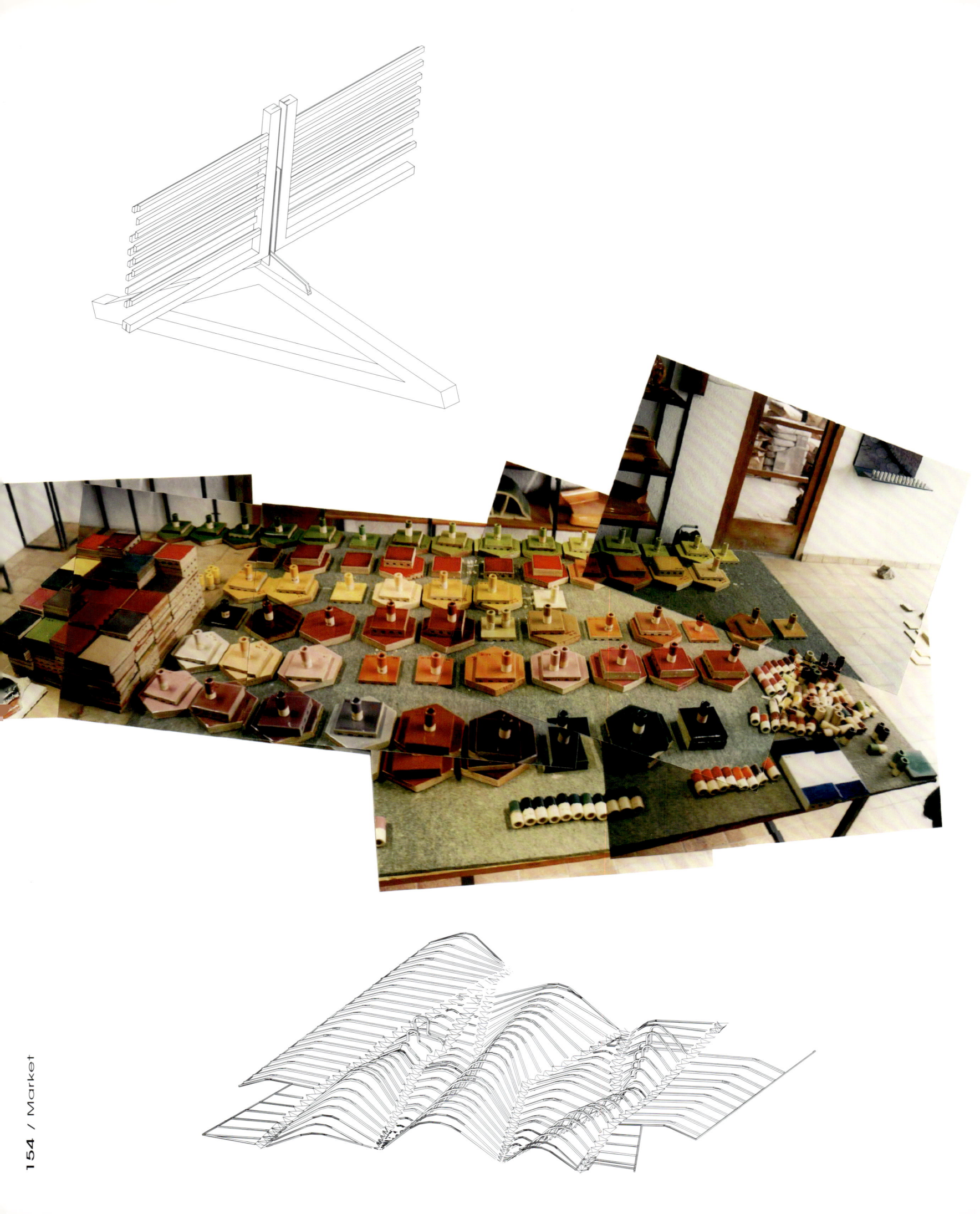

■ Colour Shading On Roof

155 / Miralles Tagliabue

156 / Market

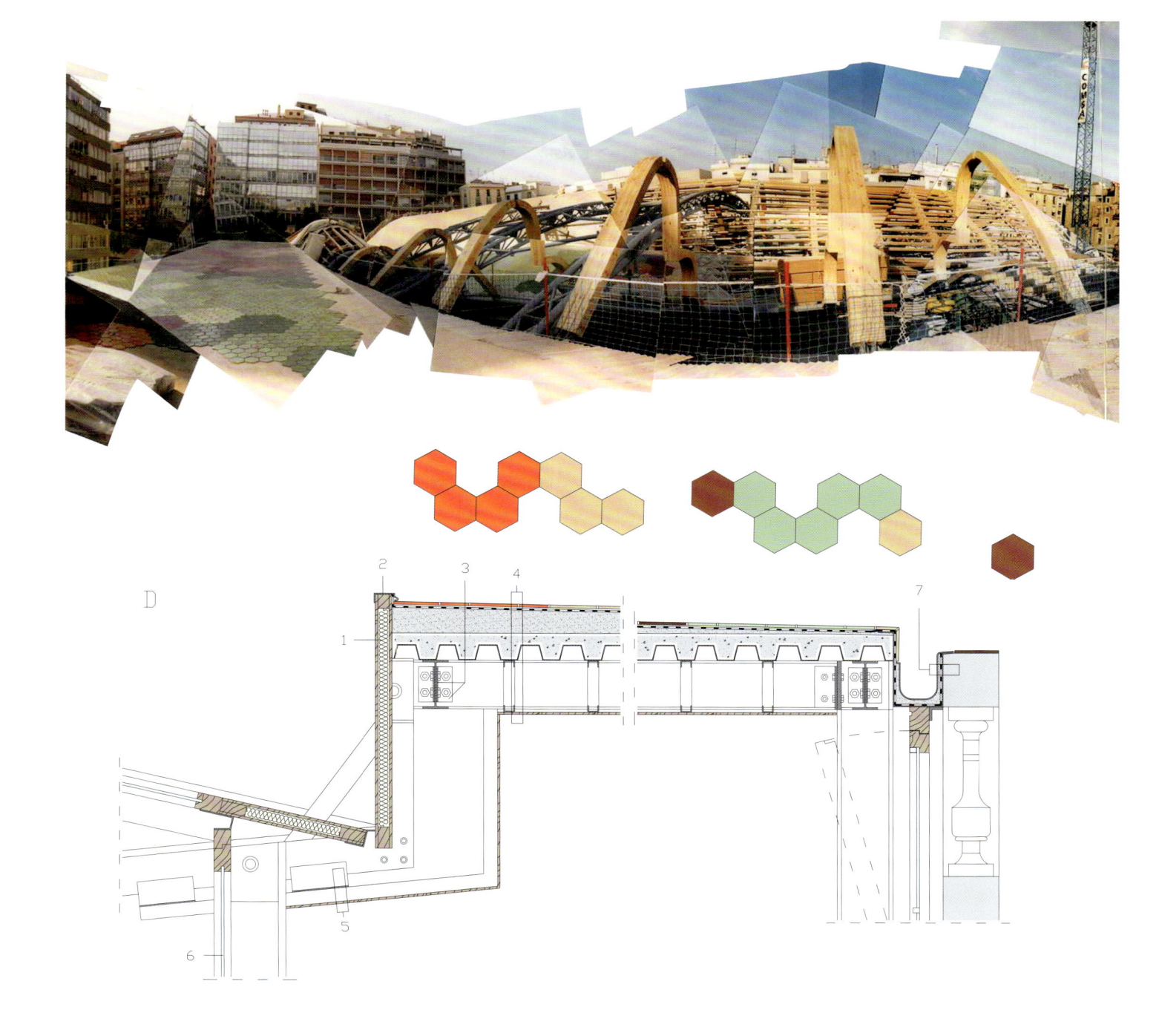

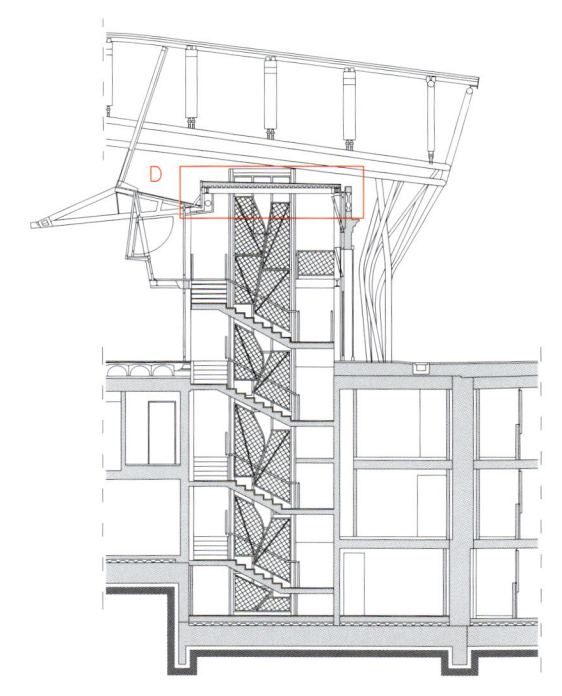

DETAIL D: ROOF OVER STAIRS
VERTICAL SECTION – SCALE 1:20

1. 2 3/8" (60 mm) insulated sandwich panel infill
2. Steel flashing
3. Steel plates connecting to structure formed by frame of 7 1/8" (180 mm) h. I-beams
4. Roof formed by mosaic of multi-coloured 3/8" (10 mm) ceramic tiles, layer of glue, waterproofing membrane, lightweight concrete screed forming 2% slope, 4" (100 mm) slab consisting of concrete fill over corrugated sheeting, 7 1/8" (180 mm) steel I-beam (parallel to plane of section), false ceiling in 5/16" (8 mm) timber panels on frame of C-profiles
5. 5/16" (8 mm) timber panel, 2" (50 mm) steel box profile (parallel to plane of section), connecting steel L-profile
6. Timber framed window
7. Sheet steel rain gutter, concrete screed forming slope, waterproofing membrane, sheet steel, concrete cornice

■ Partial Section – Scale 1:250

FLOWER MARKET
BARCELONA, SPAIN

WILLY MÜLLER ARCHITECTS

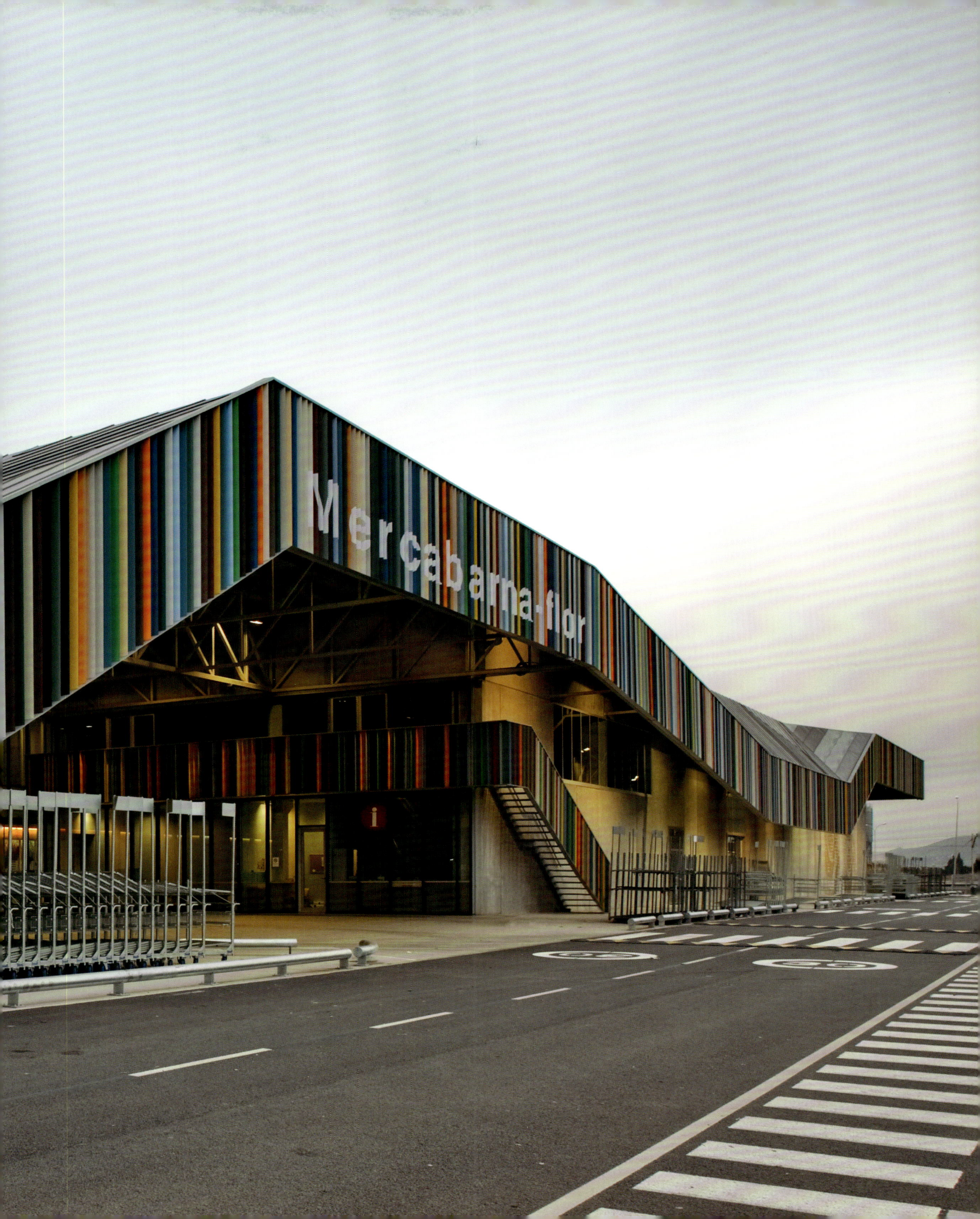
Mercabarna-flor

■ YY Section – Scale 1:400

160 / Flower Market

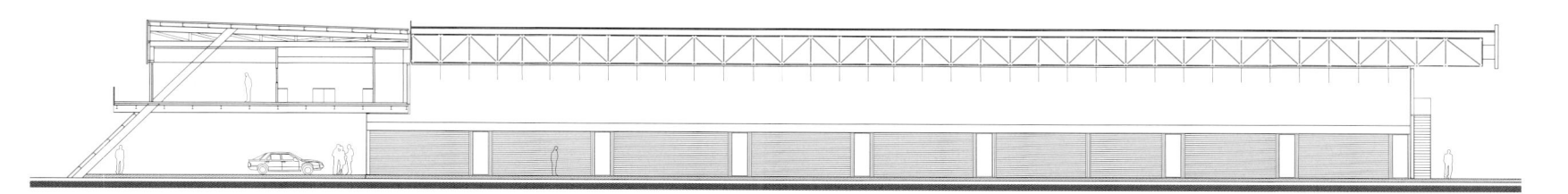

■ XX Section – Scale 1:400

Barcelona's new flower market lies to the south west of the Catalan capital in a well-served industrial district situated on a flat stretch of land near the sea. The site covers a total surface area of 40 thousand square metres, which includes a large road-level parking space for 500 vehicles, and runs alongside a fast through-road near the city's cargo airport terminal.

The 16,000 sqm (172,200 sq ft), two-storey building was designed by Willy Müller Architects. The rectangular floor plan echoes traditional covered market formats while meeting the rational spatial organization and equipment standards required of a modern flower and nursery products storage and distribution centre. The Mercabarna-Flor brand comprises three different commercial sectors: cut flowers, which have a turn-over time of three days; indoor plants, whose wholesale and retail timeframe is around 15 days and where the allocated space serves as both storage and showroom; and finally, the dried flowers and accessories sector. The facility is accordingly divided into three functional areas. In the centre of the building, the dried flowers and accessories section is equipped with fire prevention and security devices. The cut flowers and house plants sectors require different equipment to meet the different ambient requirements: industrial cooling plant to keep the cut flowers section at 2–15°C and radiant floor heating to maintain 15–26°C in the indoor plant section. All the environments are high ceilinged and the distribution corridors wide to facilitate product handling. Alongside the showroom and sales areas are a quality restaurant, offices and a multi-purpose area catering for a variety of activities including vocational training, making the Mercabarna-Flor a self-sufficient facility.

The metal roof juts out over the pedestrian approach to provide a protective canopy. It extends over adjacent access areas and a drive-through drop off point, enveloping these separate outside areas as it slopes right down to the ground.

The striking geometry and use of colour building hark back to the innovative covered markets of the 19th century that proudly displayed their engineering prowess in the use of iron and steel. The complex folds of the roof and the walls of the Mercabarna-Flor market are in galvanized steel and zinc. The different finishes lend a variegated appearance. The folds and intersections of the shell-like roof reach to the ground, altering the aspect of the elevations. The huge stretches of roof are broken by an irregular pattern of darker grey lines and different finishes. The complex colour array on the vertical metal sections echo the 24 colours of the floral world. The overall impression is of a coloured island rooted to the ground.

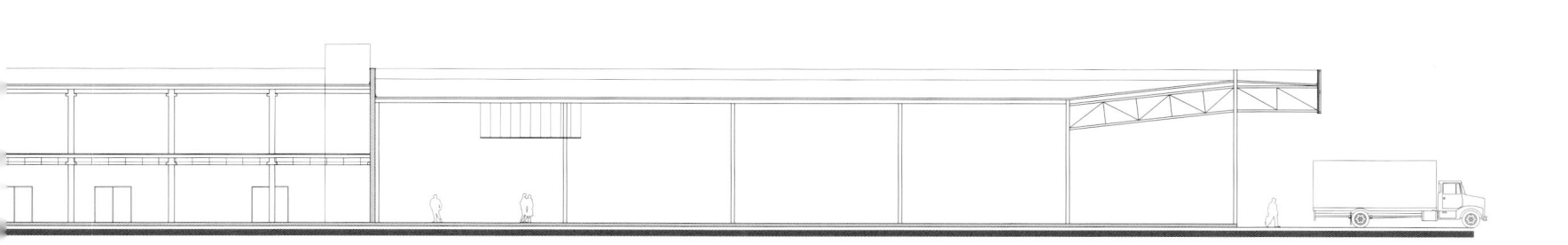

■ West Elevation – Scale 1:400

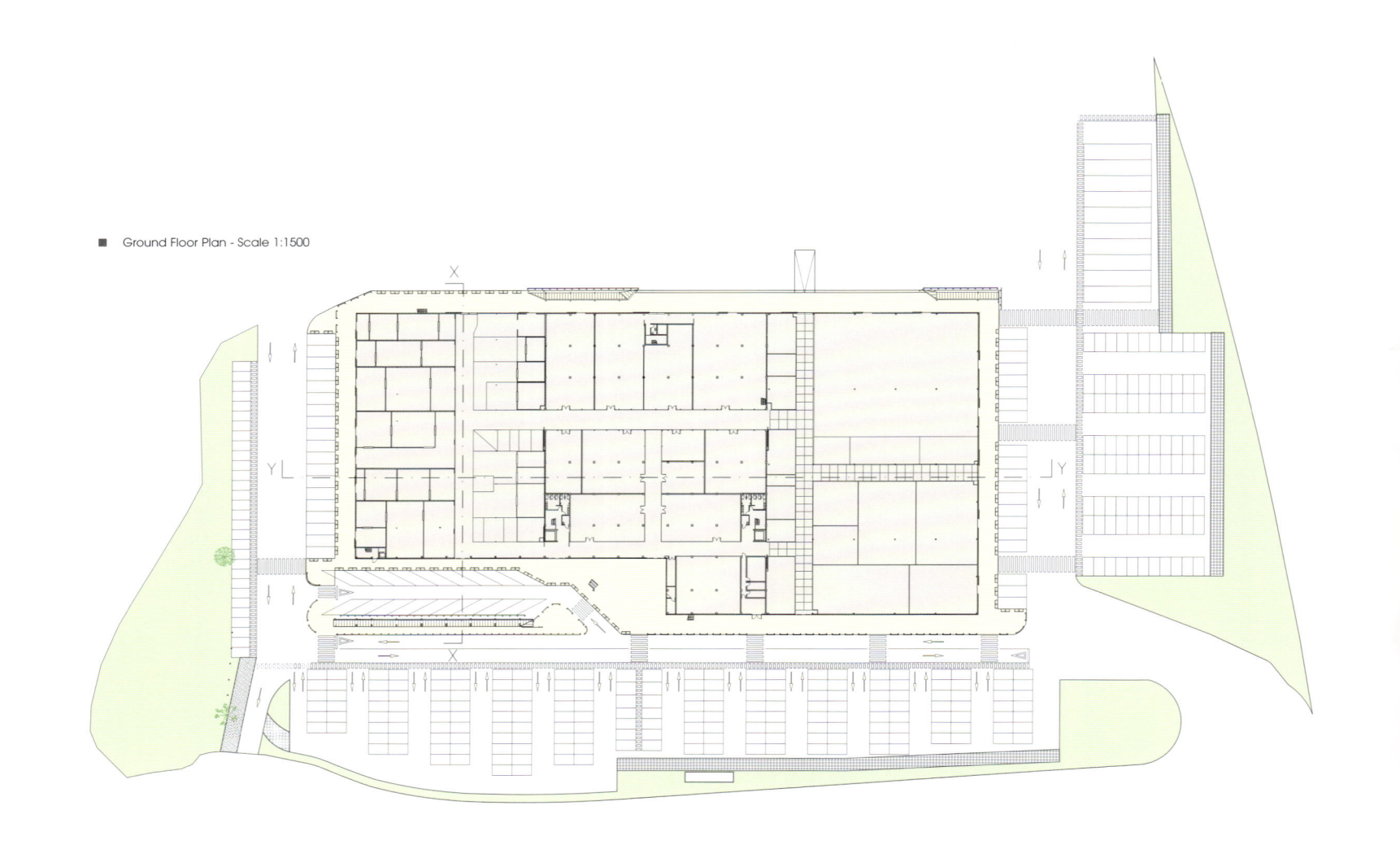

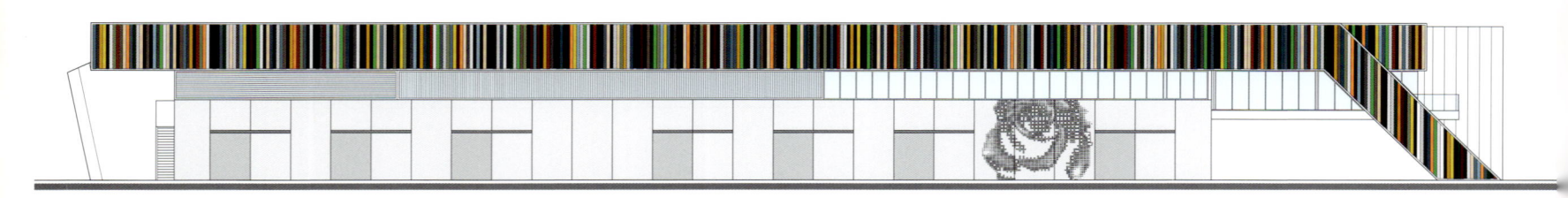

■ Ground Floor Plan – Scale 1:1500

■ East Elevation – Scale 1:400

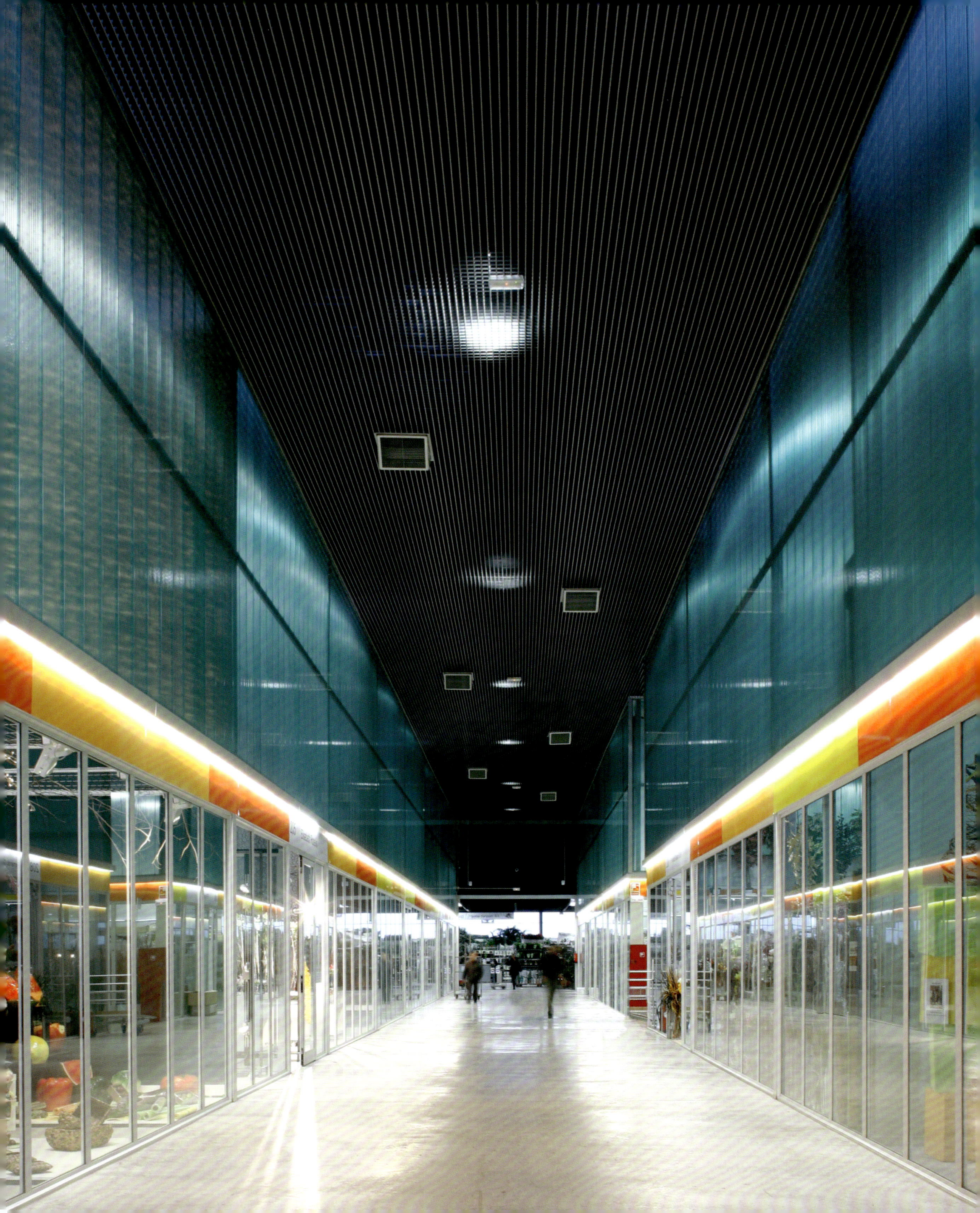

■ North Elevation – Scale 1:400

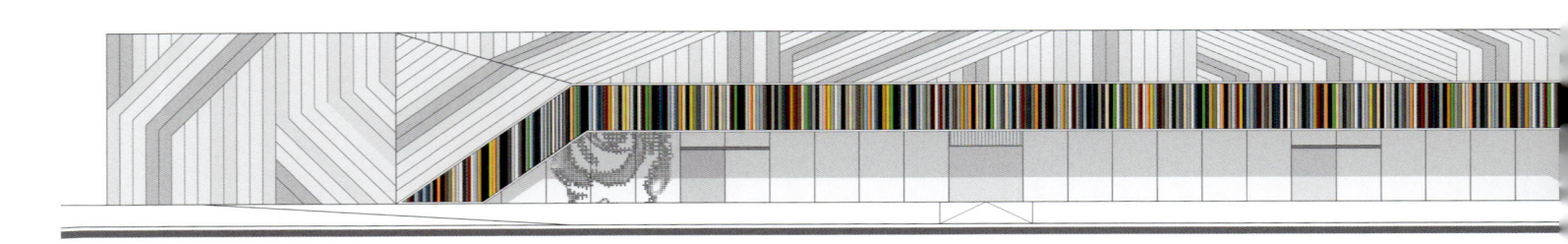

164 / Flower Market

■ South Elevation – Scale 1:400

165 / Willy Müller

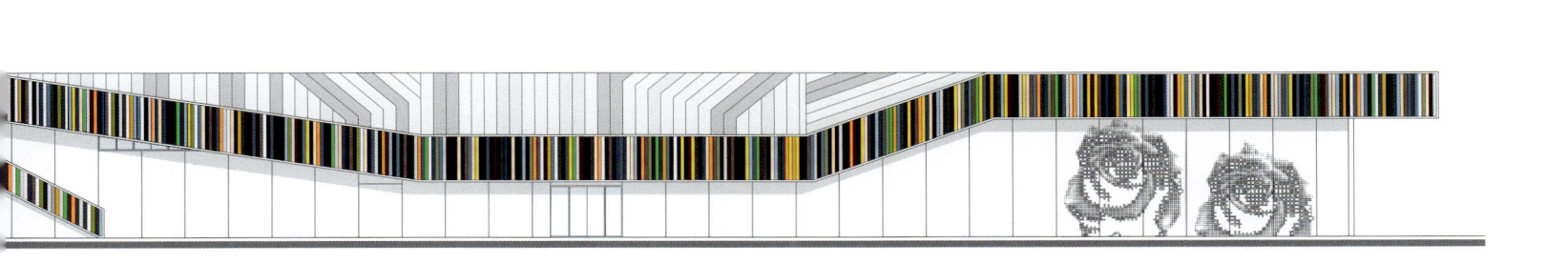

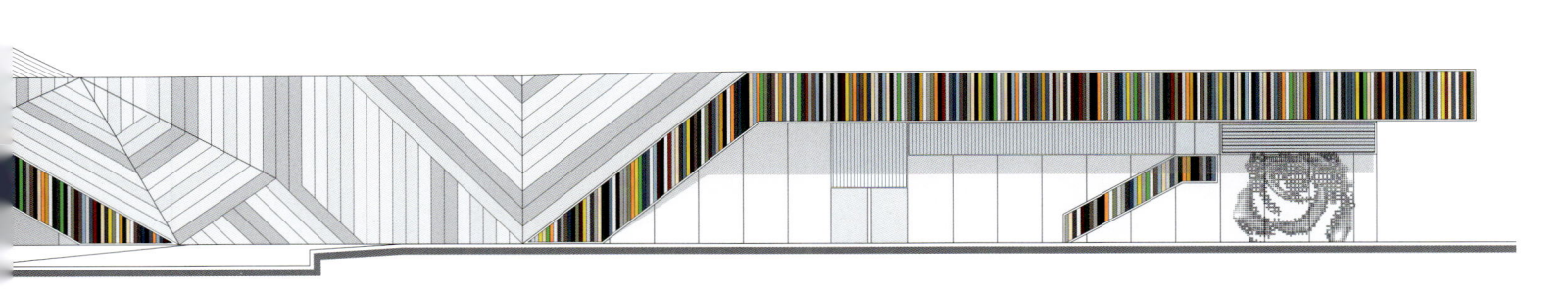

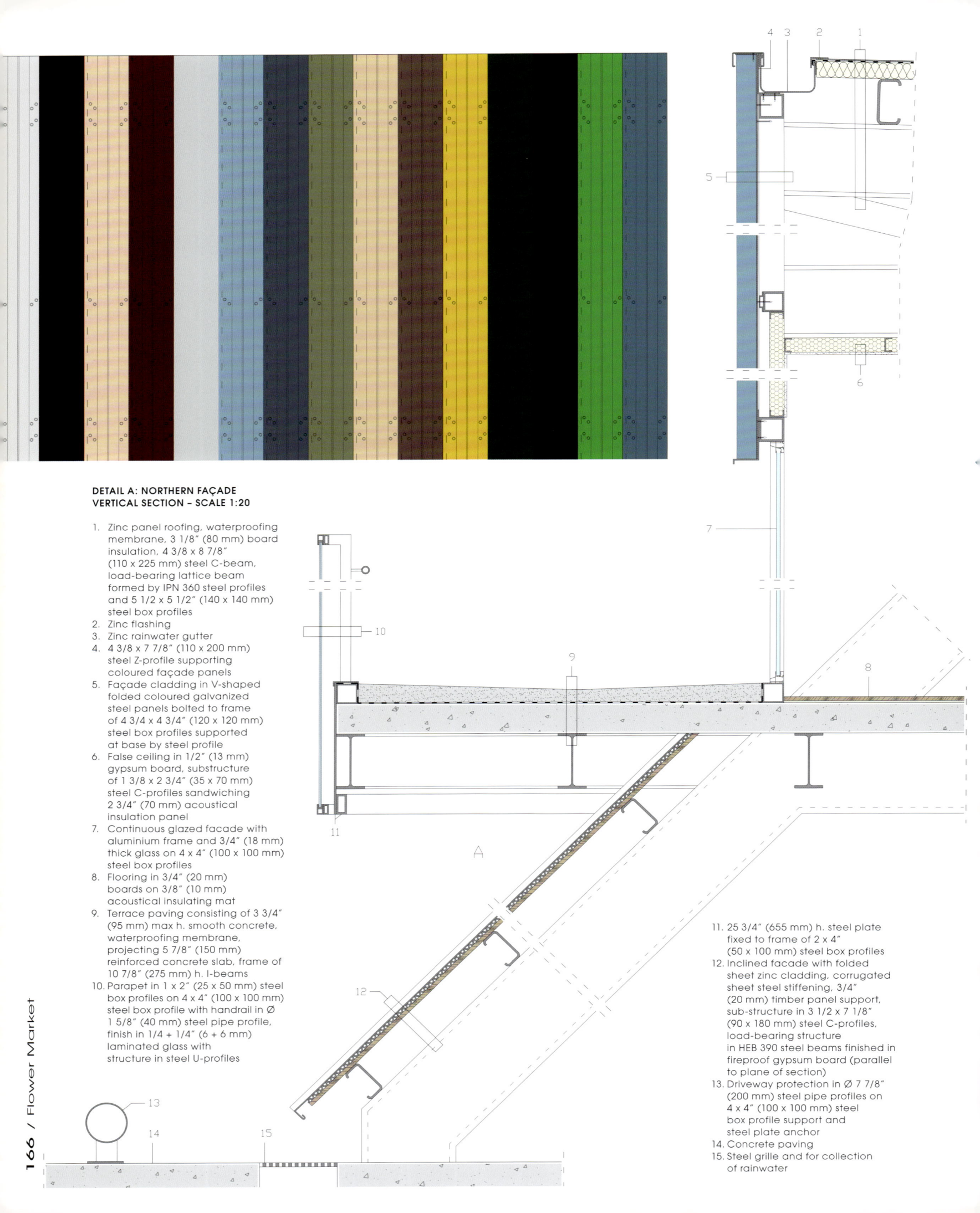

DETAIL A: NORTHERN FAÇADE
VERTICAL SECTION – SCALE 1:20

1. Zinc panel roofing, waterproofing membrane, 3 1/8" (80 mm) board insulation, 4 3/8 x 8 7/8" (110 x 225 mm) steel C-beam, load-bearing lattice beam formed by IPN 360 steel profiles and 5 1/2 x 5 1/2" (140 x 140 mm) steel box profiles
2. Zinc flashing
3. Zinc rainwater gutter
4. 4 3/8 x 7 7/8" (110 x 200 mm) steel Z-profile supporting coloured façade panels
5. Façade cladding in V-shaped folded coloured galvanized steel panels bolted to frame of 4 3/4 x 4 3/4" (120 x 120 mm) steel box profiles supported at base by steel profile
6. False ceiling in 1/2" (13 mm) gypsum board, substructure of 1 3/8 x 2 3/4" (35 x 70 mm) steel C-profiles sandwiching 2 3/4" (70 mm) acoustical insulation panel
7. Continuous glazed facade with aluminium frame and 3/4" (18 mm) thick glass on 4 x 4" (100 x 100 mm) steel box profiles
8. Flooring in 3/4" (20 mm) boards on 3/8" (10 mm) acoustical insulating mat
9. Terrace paving consisting of 3 3/4" (95 mm) max h. smooth concrete, waterproofing membrane, projecting 5 7/8" (150 mm) reinforced concrete slab, frame of 10 7/8" (275 mm) h. I-beams
10. Parapet in 1 x 2" (25 x 50 mm) steel box profiles on 4 x 4" (100 x 100 mm) steel box profile with handrail in Ø 1 5/8" (40 mm) steel pipe profile, finish in 1/4 + 1/4" (6 + 6 mm) laminated glass with structure in steel U-profiles
11. 25 3/4" (655 mm) h. steel plate fixed to frame of 2 x 4" (50 x 100 mm) steel box profiles
12. Inclined facade with folded sheet zinc cladding, corrugated sheet steel stiffening, 3/4" (20 mm) timber panel support, sub-structure in 3 1/2 x 7 1/8" (90 x 180 mm) steel C-profiles, load-bearing structure in HEB 390 steel beams finished in fireproof gypsum board (parallel to plane of section)
13. Driveway protection in Ø 7 7/8" (200 mm) steel pipe profiles on 4 x 4" (100 x 100 mm) steel box profile support and steel plate anchor
14. Concrete paving
15. Steel grille and for collection of rainwater

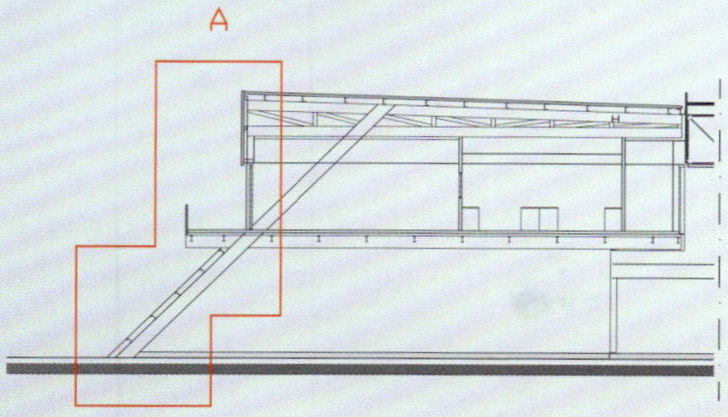
A

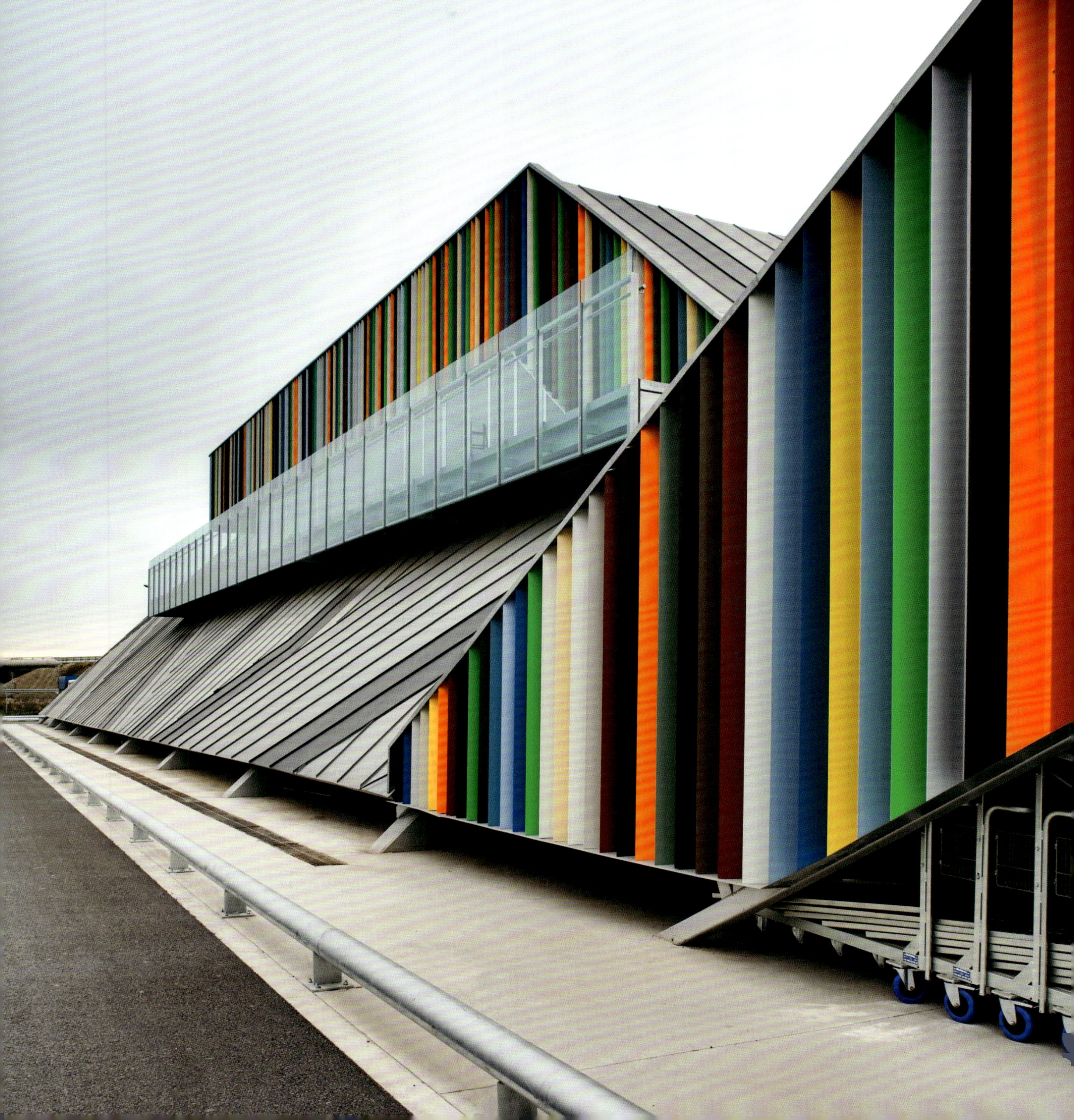

ST GILES COURT DEVELOPMENT
LONDON, UK

RENZO PIANO BUILDING WORKSHOP

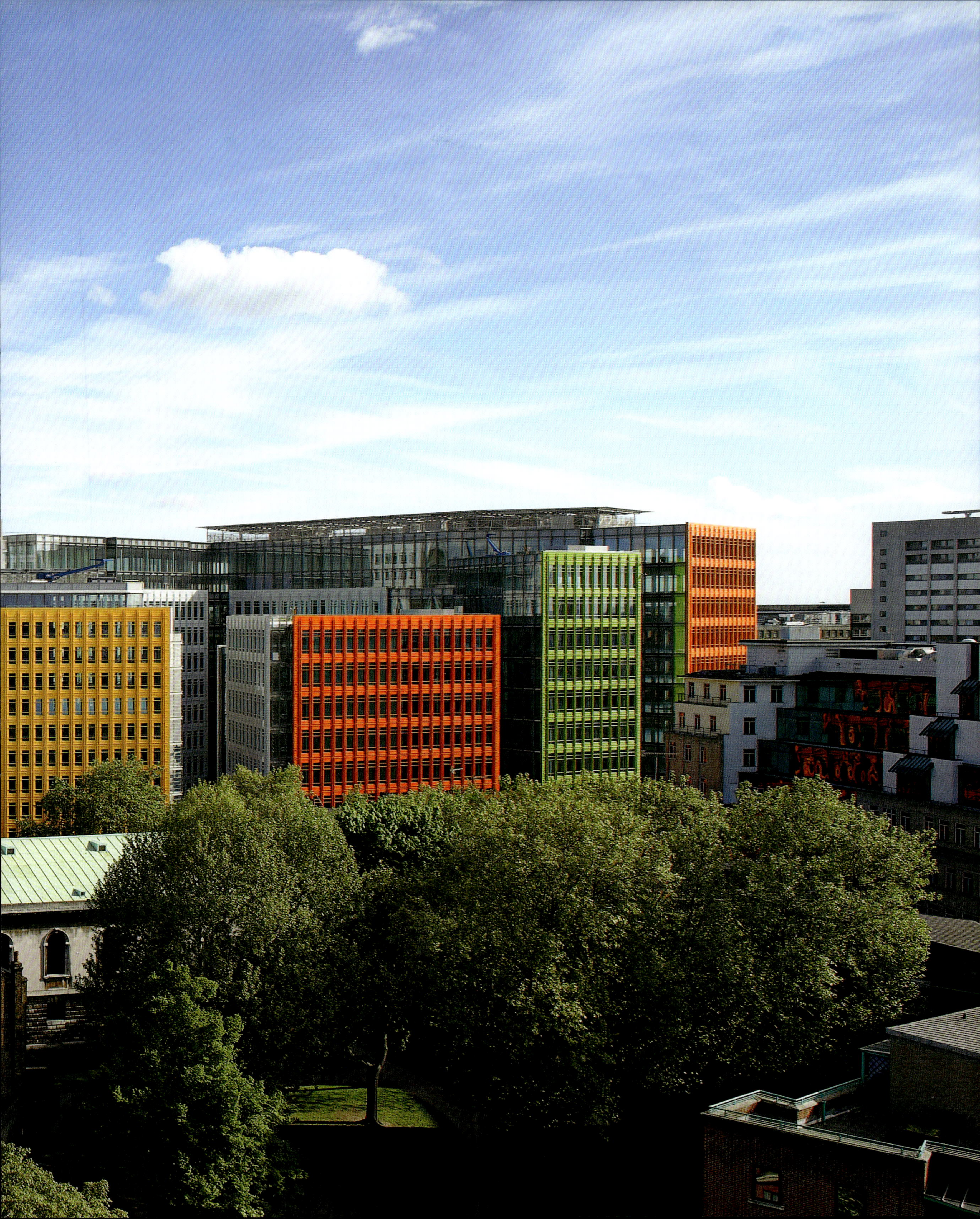

170 / St Giles Court

In 2001 RPBW was invited by Stanhope, the developers, to propose a masterplan for the Central St Giles site in Central London overlooked by Centrepoint, the striking landmark building by Richard Seifert dominating the district since 1966. Foster and Partners had also previously been invited to provide initial thoughts, but RPBW won the job because Stanhope wanted to do something different with the site, and Piano was thought to be the best person to achieve this. Behind Centrepoint towards Covent Garden lurked an anonymous grey Ministry of Defence building, incongruous in this now creative part of central London. The hermetic, and congested 0.7 ha site intersecting Covent Garden, Bloomsbury and Soho needed a scheme to unlock and connect it.

Pension fund managers Legal & General, the site's owners (now together with Mitsubishi Estate Company) and developers Stanhope, wanted a mixed use development. Tongues have been wagging. Some feel it is over-scaled for its context, others find in the façade of the ten-floor building a too great similarity with the texture and vivid colours of LEGO bricks. Sceptics worry that other developers will use a related formula to get planning permission for "copy-cat" central London schemes. Central St Giles' vibrancy was never going to please everyone, but amidst this bout of Anglo-Saxon architectural angst, it has won the full support of the Commission for Architecture and the Built Environment. CABE's Chief Executive, Paul Finch, describes it as "one of London's great commercial buildings", one that "sets the standards by which office architecture should be judged." An incongruous mix of Mr Freedom's Pop Art furniture shop, a pub favoured by Goths and a church and garden has populated the street past and present. The nearby building site of the Crossrail station and Denmark Street's musical instrument shops spell cultural flux and expression. Local community organizations and English Heritage were consulted, and the team struggled to deal with some awkward physical conditions, with public housing on adjacent streets physically marooned up until now at the edge of a closed site.

Piano's arrangement of 40,000 sqm (430,000 sq ft) of office space apartments (56 retail and 53 affordable) around a public courtyard has five public routes cutting through it. This makes the space memorable yet physically connected to surrounding streets. He also raises the blocks 7 metres (23 ft) above ground level, giving permeability to an extensively glazed multicultural mix of upmarket restaurant brands and retailers and to the public routes between them. All face onto the street, and internally a public courtyard with two trees, sculpture and furniture chosen by Piano. Colour is lacking in London buildings, as anyone riding the London Eye will observe. You cannot discuss Piano's colours without referring to the composition of his "zingy", "vibrant" "cheeky" and "very London" façades of glazed ceramic tiles (14 street, 8 inner). They do not match up, being set at slightly different angles in order to be parallel to the district's medieval street pattern. Crenellated mullions (which Piano is also using in the Shard of Glass at London Bridge) in the window structure keep the structure light, break up the massing and bring light into office spaces via low iron glazing so panoramic views can be fully enjoyed.

The hand of the architect is omnipresent in practical and elegant bespoke detailing throughout, on floor grilles, on hand-finished polished plaster walls, pendant light fittings, spotlights (I-Guzzini), glazed fin panels, slender columns and orange digital floor numbers in the elevator. The office doors are the only feature that appears a little straightlaced. Considered right down to the last detail: this is far from the norm of spec office buildings in London, which may be serviceable but do not use bespoke design enough (even Piano's solutions for the ceilings are neat). The west facing, beautifully landscaped 1,850 sqm (20,000 sq ft) roof terrace on the eighth floor and south-facing winter garden adds exclusivity. The ideal tenant for the top floors of Piano's offices would be an advertising agency or other creative firm that can take full advantage of the ambience offered by the individualistic architecture, views out and location.

Piano's scheme remakes a formerly confused area, infusing it with a strong architectural identity that has authenticity and connects districts. The building ticks all the sustainability boxes with its double skin façade, sedum roof, 60% reuse of rainwater, biomass boiler generating 80% of heat, and 90% recyclable materials. Huge, bold Gothic cathedrals felt civically enriching when they were unveiled in centuries past, and Central St Giles' open character and invigorating presence adds to, rather than subtracts from, the city's porous and plural cultural life.

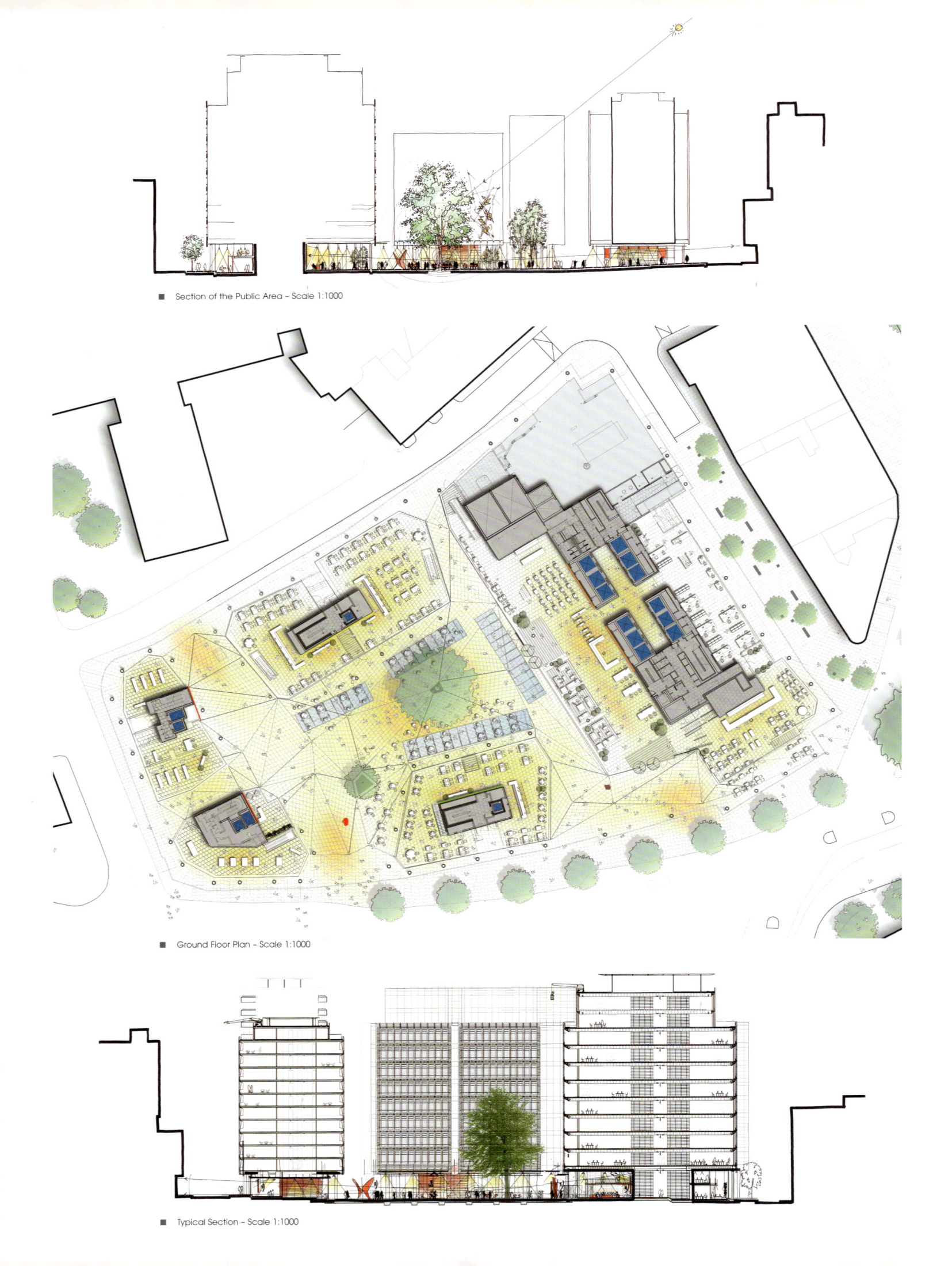

■ Section of the Public Area – Scale 1:1000

■ Ground Floor Plan – Scale 1:1000

■ Typical Section – Scale 1:1000

172 / St Giles Court

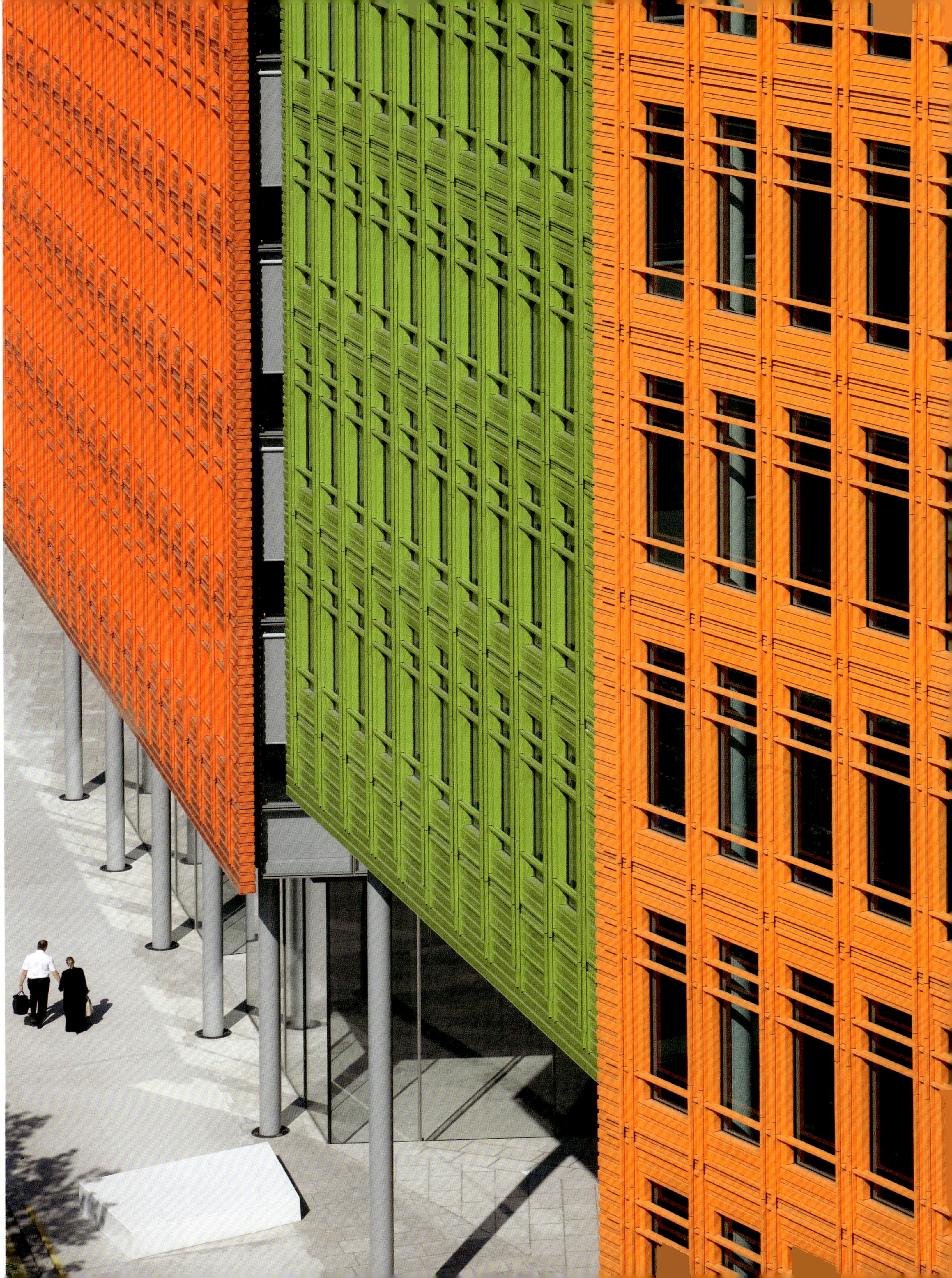

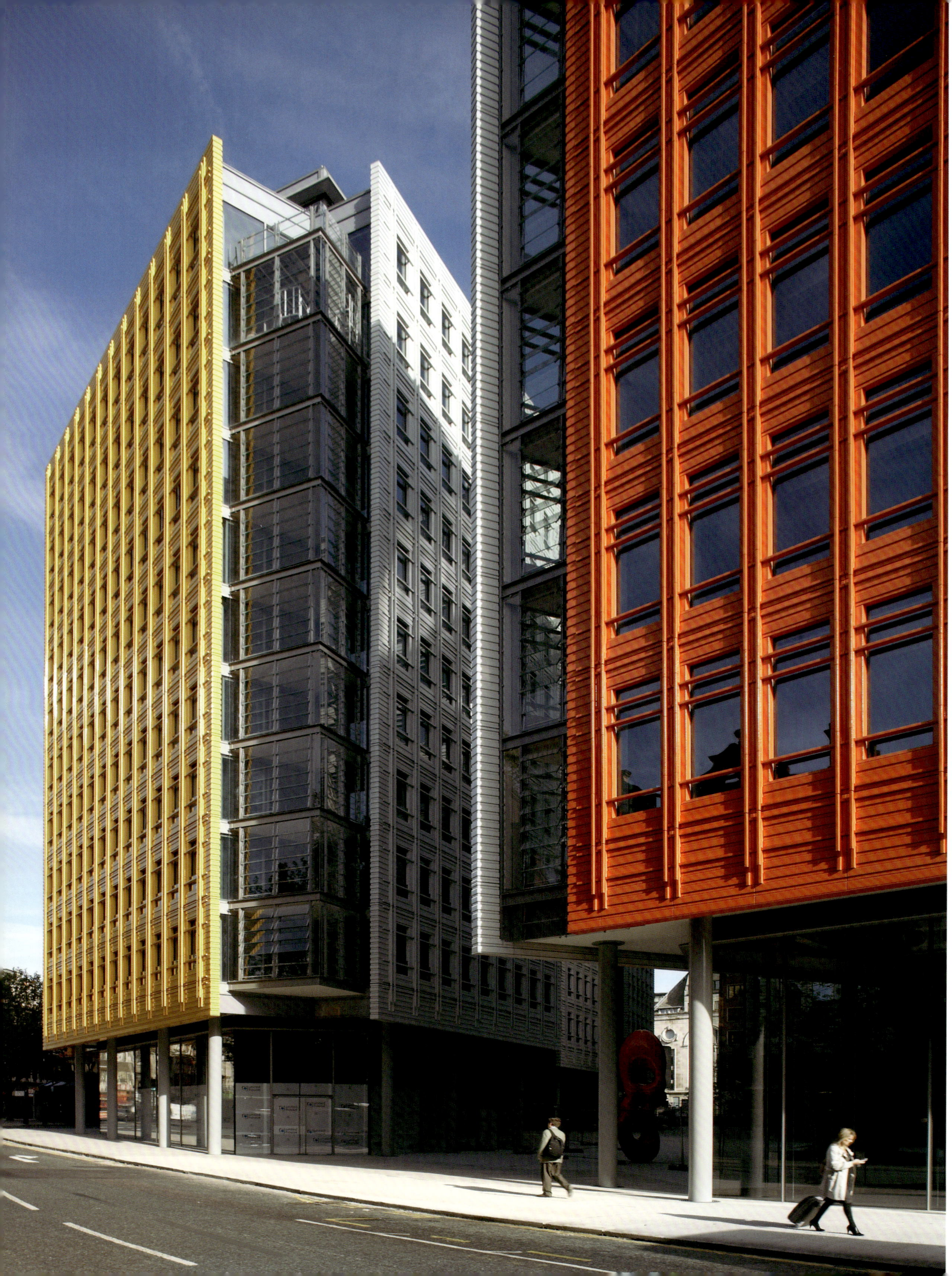

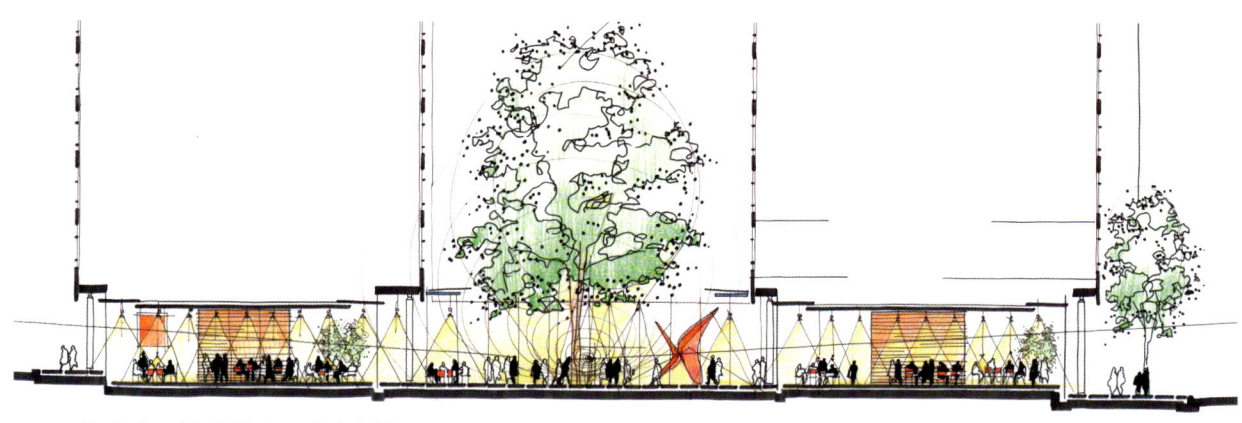

■ Section of the Public Area – Scale 1:600

■ Floor Plan with Facades' Colour Range – Scale 1:600

■ Facades' Colour Range

| Red |
| Orange |
| Yellow |
| Green |
| Grey |
| Light Grey |

175 / RPBW

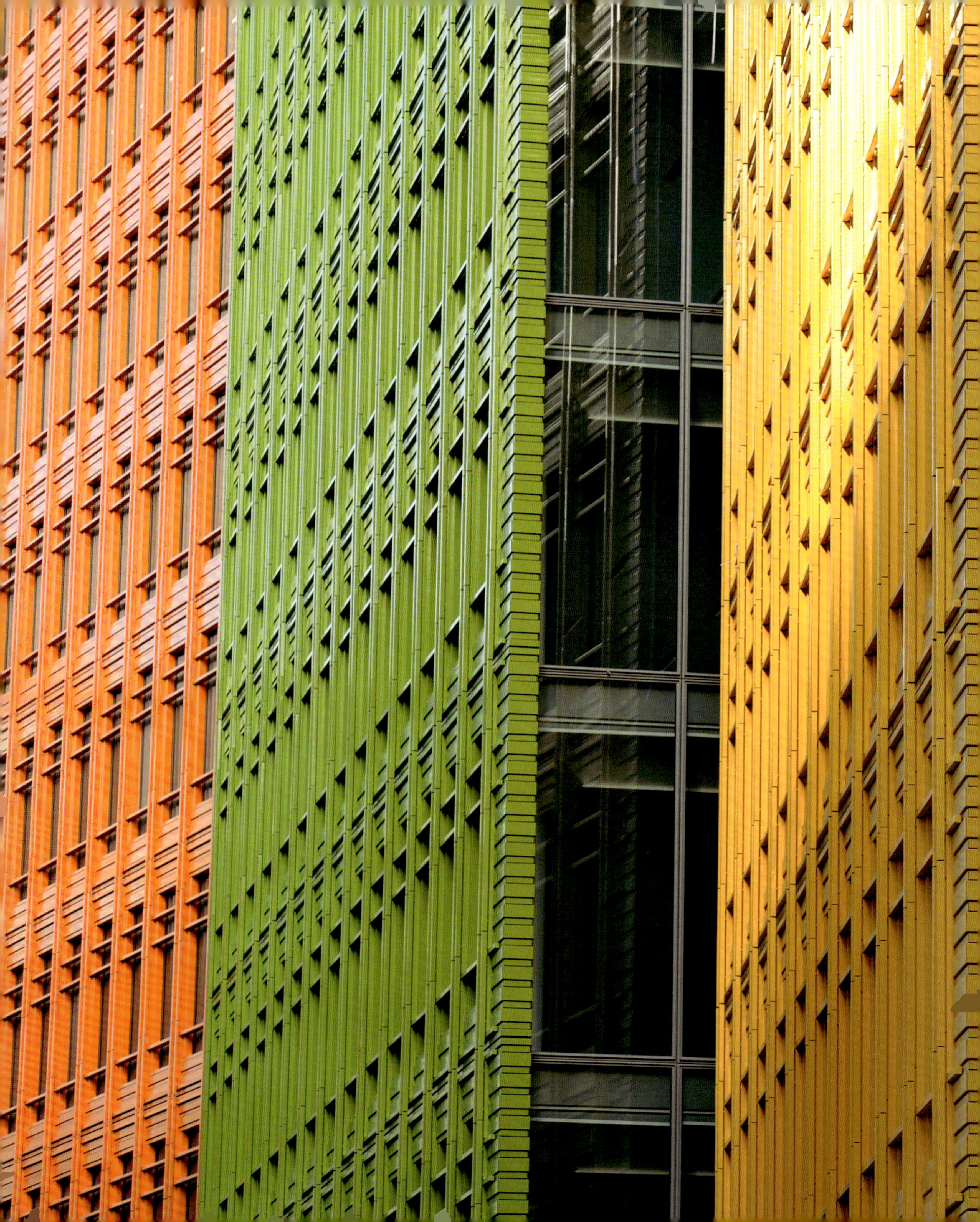

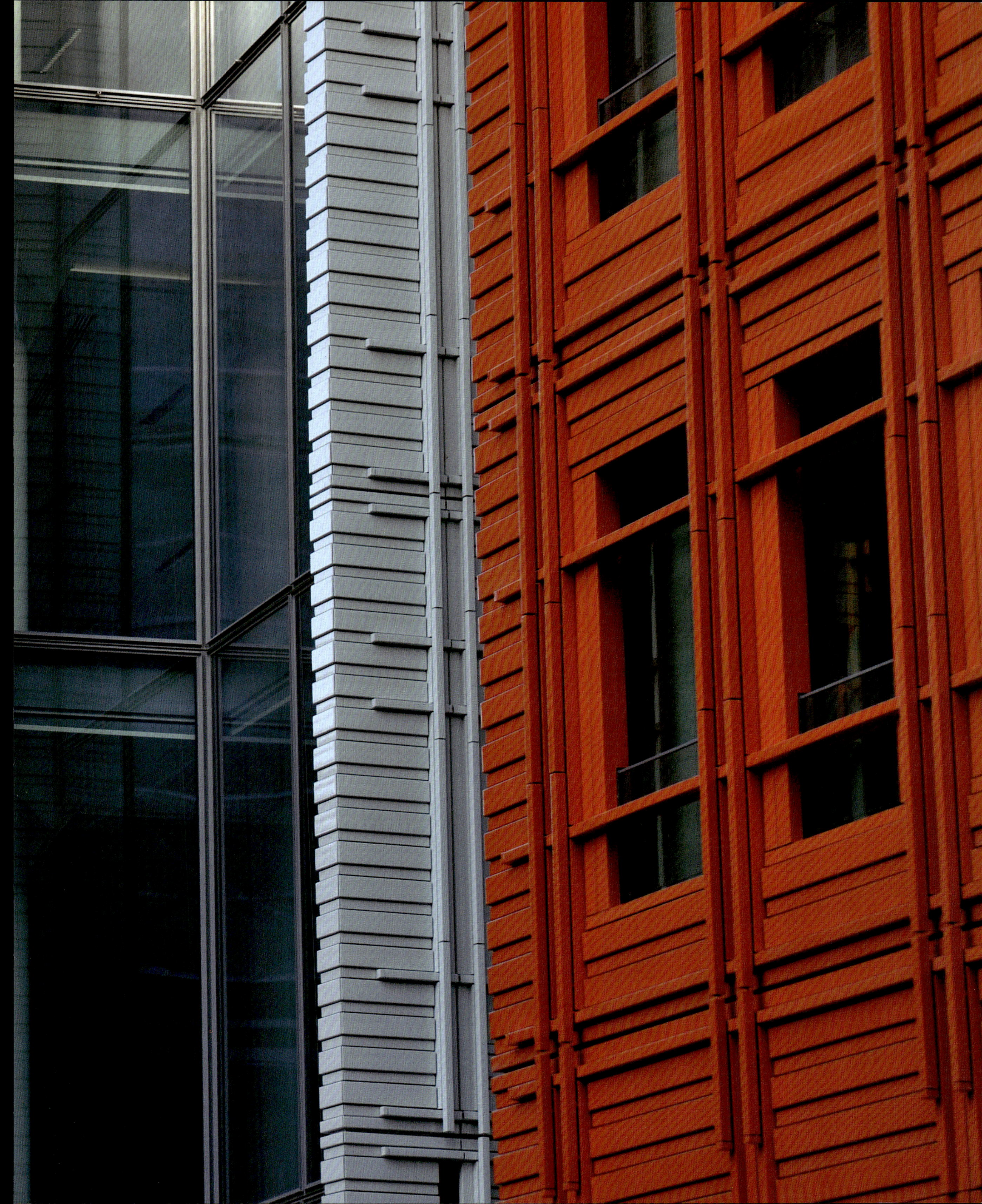

178 / St Giles Court

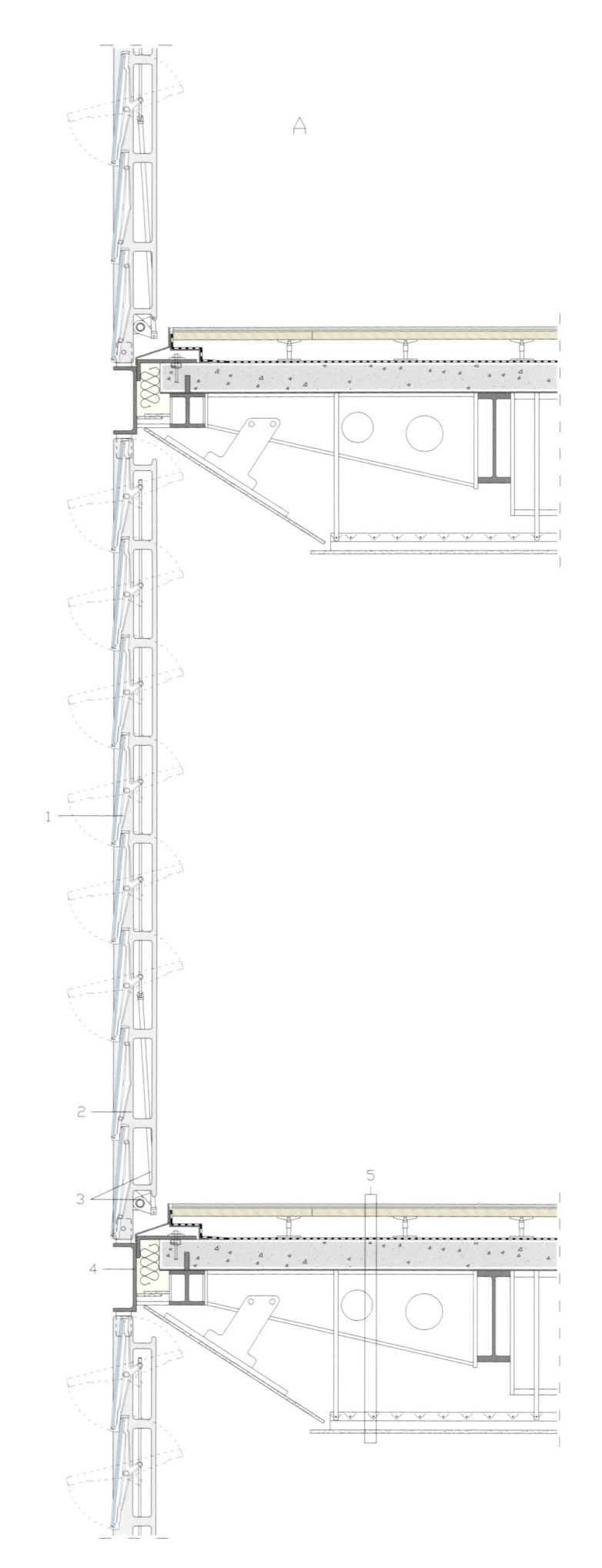

**DETAIL A: FAÇADE WITH SUN SHADING
VERTICAL SECTION – SCALE 1:25**

1. Façade with electrically operated sun shading louvres in 1/4 + 1/4" (6+6 mm) glass for directing sunlight onto aluminium structure
2. Aluminium frame
3. Structure of steel tie rods and connectors for regulating louvres
4. Stringcourse supporting façade structure formed by 11 7/8 x 4" (300 x 100 mm) steel C-profiles
5. Raised floor consisting of 3/8" (10 mm) ceramic tiles, layer of glue, 1 3/8" (35 mm) sodium sulphate panel, adjustable piers, vapour barrier, 5 1/8" (130 mm) composite slab of concrete fill over corrugated sheeting, structure of I-beams of various sizes with tapered edge beam, false ceiling comprising 5/8" (15 mm) gypsum board on frame of aluminium C-profiles and tie rods suspended from slab

DETAIL B:
FAÇADE WITH CERAMIC CLADDING
VERTICAL SECTION – SCALE 1:25

1. Façade in coloured vitrified ceramic tiles of various shapes with aluminium fastening system, 4 3/4" (120 mm) sheet aluminium and insulation sandwich panel
2. 5/16 - 1/2 - 1/4 + 1/4" (8/14/6+6 mm) aluminium double-glazing unit
3. Ø 15 3/4" (400 mm) steel column
4. Structure of steel profiles securing façade to slab
5. Gypsum board secured to tapered beam by steel plates and flange
6. False ceiling formed by micro-perforated aluminium sheeting on frame of aluminium C-profiles and tie rods suspended from beam
7. Reinforcing steel disc
8. Ventilation grille, 2 3/8" (60 mm) sheet aluminium and insulation sandwich panel, steel I-beam (parallel to plane of section) supporting glass abutment
9. Abutment formed by triple layer of 1/2" (12 mm) safety glass
10. Continuous glazed façade formed by 5/16 + 5/16 - 1/2 - 1/2" (8+8/14/12 mm) double glazing with aluminium frame
11. Aluminium trim on entrance lintel

B

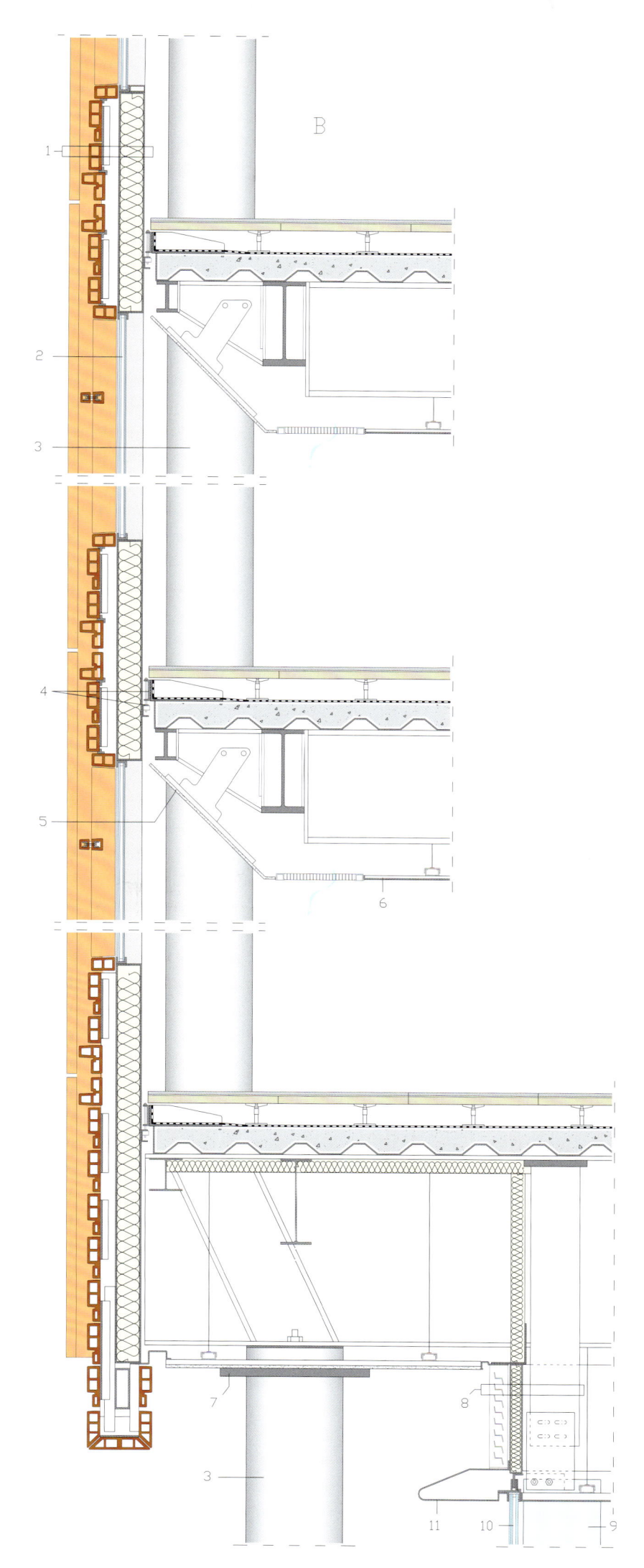

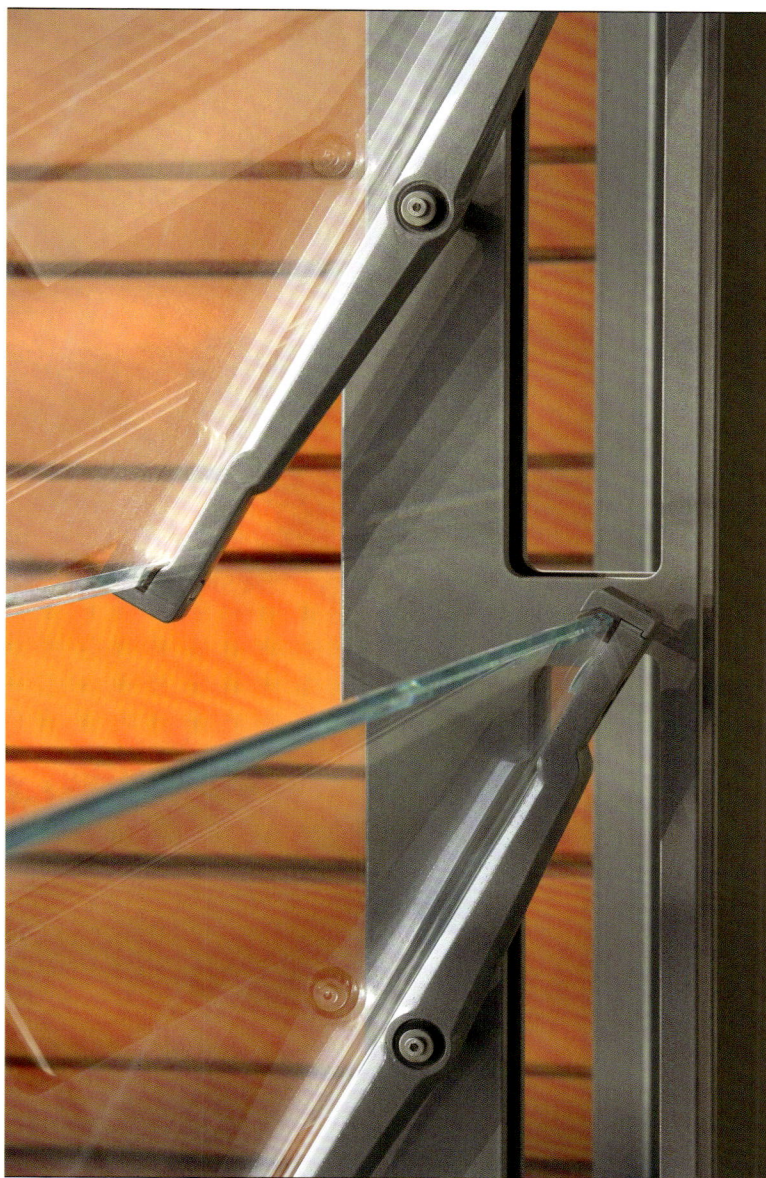

NEW TERMINAL T4 BARAJAS AIRPORT
MADRID, SPAIN

RICHARD ROGERS PARTNERSHIP
ESTUDIO LAMELA

Gates
Puertas K83 K89

Gates
Puertas K83 K89

Gates
Puertas K83 K89

If airports have become machines for processing people and baggage, then architecture should be the art of humanizing that process. Airport traffic is growing at the rate of 8-10% annually, a doubling in numbers over the last 7-8 years. Airport terminals are forced to process far more people than ever before, and, with two specific commercial forces driving the industry – the booming traffic in low-cost travel and the increasing consolidation of airlines into international airlines (which may result in the operation of just 4-5 major airlines in a decade's time) – change is the only constant. Changes at every conceivable level – physical, infrastructural, technical, technological, commercial – have meant that airports are in enormous flux as urban places. This makes them a "fascinating" field for architects to operate in, says Simon Smithson, who runs the Madrid office of Richard Rogers Partnership, and oversaw as project architect the design and realization of the 1,000 million euro NAT (New Terminal Area) at Madrid's Barajas Airport (to the north west of the existing Terminal complex dating from 1933), commissioned by AENA (Spanish Airports and Air Navigation) which was formally opened at a private reception of 500 guests by Spanish Prime Minister José Luis Rodriguez Zapatero on February 4 this year. At this event it became clear that the airport will have a huge impact on Madrid's position in Europe. The only task the Spanish need to complete is the Metro connection to the city centre. They have made the new Metro station and hope to complete the track system that will make the building reachable from Madrid's city centre in 15 minutes in the near future.

The project is the largest RRP has undertaken to date, 1 million square metres of buildings that make up the Terminal and the satellite (for international flights), and serve three new runways. Approaching the building by road, its undulating linear ribbed metal roof stretches out in front of you, seemingly for a vast distance, on the flat sierra landscape. However jaunty the external image of a terminal seems, air travellers usually brace themselves to negotiate the chaos that customarily defines the assemblage of airport functions. Once inside the new Terminal building, the design never loses its sense of place. With what must be one of the clearest diagrams ever created for an airport building, the experience of getting through the four major steps is a pleasantly smooth process. At Foster's Chek Lap Kok terminal the traveller also proceeds in virtually a straight line to check in, immigration, shopping and boarding. At Barajas, four linear strips describe this process – entry, check-in spine, processing spine, and pier – each interspersed with a light "canyon" (three in total), with skylights that filter natural light from above right through the two floors of the Terminal. The architects designed the layout to have minimal dependency on signage, and no corridors. The spacious, streamlined plan also means that significant amounts of retail are accommodated into the building without compromising the transparency of the environment.

The Terminal is part of a long-term Spanish government expansion programme for transport infrastructure. Along with Italy and Portugal, the country now invests more in relation to GDP on transport infrastructure than the other EU member states. Its entry into the field has come relatively recently, with the first motorway built at the time of the Barcelona Olympics, and the first high speed rail link for the Seville Expo, while Spain's most important airports have reached saturation point over the last decade. The government was determined that the new Barajas Terminal would have the greatest potential for growth, up to 35 million passengers a year, and offer serious competition to Schiphol, Heathrow, Paris' Charles de Gaulle and Frankfurt hubs, as well as new generation airports such as Kuala Lumpur, Kansai, Denver and others. "The client had the vision and the courage to build big. The impact of the French Grand Projets led a lot of politicians in Spain became interested in big (scale) projects", says Smithson. RRP won the Terminal competition in 1997 in consortium with Estudio Lamela (and engineers Initec and TPS). Their 50 strong multidisciplinary team of architects, engineers, service engineers and airport planners completed the executive design in two bursts, each six months long. The working ethos was one of close collaboration: at the Madrid site office, the core team of 30 architects, contractor and client sat at desks two metres apart from each other. The fast-track construction was completed in just six years. RRP brought their experience of working on Heathrow's rather more slow-track Terminal 5, along with their determination to create a credible, socially-oriented response to industry change. All the elements had to be very simple, robust, and flexible – explains Smithson, as the content was likely to change constantly in the future. The architects looked at a range of spatial options. Foster's Stansted is a single-level terminal, but they knew that would not work here. Through their search for ways of introducing daylight in all passenger areas and down into the lower baggage collection level, the architects came up with the "canyon" idea: full-height empty spaces running horizontally between the four blocks making up the terminal, linked by walkways secured to the roof supports. The phasing of the "canyons" is not only critical to the easy navigation of the space, but also allows passengers experiential respite, and a high degree of visual access (children especially enjoy watching the baggage carousels from above). Above the "canyons" a sequence of 95 12-metre wide oval skylights contribute to the overall sense of an airy calm atmosphere free of ceilings that press down on you (elsewhere there are other 458 circular skylights). The friendly appearance of 12,300 Wok-type ceiling lamps add a small touch of character. The architects wanted to introduce welcome drama into the space akin to that of the 19th-century railway station, and the result is an abiding sense of being in a church. That is reinforced by the 212,000 sqm (2,282,000 sq ft) soffit ceiling clad in laminated strips of Chinese bamboo, a cheap renewable material rarely if ever previously used in this context. Along with the natural "Perlato" limestone floors they give the entire space a tactility and warmth rarely experienced in a terminal building. At the same time, the sheer glazed facade offers a visual transparency between interior and exterior landscape, and a personal sense that at any point in one's trajectory, one is not enclosed. The combined impact of these elements, on top of the space being so simple to use, makes the quality of the experience of the weary jetlagged individual a top priority, rather than a secondary factor to the processing efficiency of the building. Beneath the sine waves of the bamboo-clad steel roof's continuous surface, the linear concourses are given rhythm and movement by their inclined support pillars, painted to create a kilometre-long vista of graduated, rainbow colour (at the south end, from red to orange, at the north, from blue to green) that gives zing to the tired senses. It is a rhythm set up in tandem with the undulations of the roof, one that seems to offer a visual metaphor of breathing architecture. The low energy consumption policy of the design backs up that perception. The working of airport systems and procedures has been modernized and improved, with high-speed belt conveyor systems (topped by expressive air conditioning ducts reminiscent of fog horns, an example of RRP's typically exposed structural design). The architects made sure that all the secondary elements – including 172 check in desks, 88 boarding gates, 26 security controls and 58 passport controls – that serve these were designed in as neutral a way as possible. The structure is a three-storey concrete frame above ground, with a 20-metre (66 ft) basement. "Tree trunks" hold up the steelwork of the roof, stabilized in both directions. The roof extends beyond the cladding line, tipping the emphasis to it rather than to the facade. An exterior curtain wall is supported by cables rather than vertical mullions, with shading capable of reducing solar gain hung from the roof overhang, which is propped up by a row of Y-shaped columns. This facade structure is a tensile truss, which in section looks like a kipper fish. Their graduation of painted colour (yellow, turning to red) adds definition to the buoyant flair of the structure's design, and a conspicuous yet not overwhelming appearance from the approach roads.

The facilities, including a satellite building 2 km away connected by an Automatic People Mover (APM) which caters for all the international, non-Schengen flights (and includes its own spa), and adjacent parking buildings with 9000 spaces, are very straightforward industrial structures clearly expressing their use. An intelligent parking system, with a sensor above each bay so the computer system can relay the geographical position of free spaces on screen as you take your ticket, is designed to minimize parking time.

The new Terminal, which has already won a number of awards, harmonizes the many valuable forces at work in its design. It is a jewel produced by Spain's long running building boom that a wide public can enjoy. Its quality underlines the country's exemplary political commitment to the highest standards in design and the capacity of architecture as a conduit for cultural change. It demonstrates that functional architecture can coexist with beautiful, vibrant places, and that airports as a typology can still represent a brave new world, in the hands of the right patrons and architects.

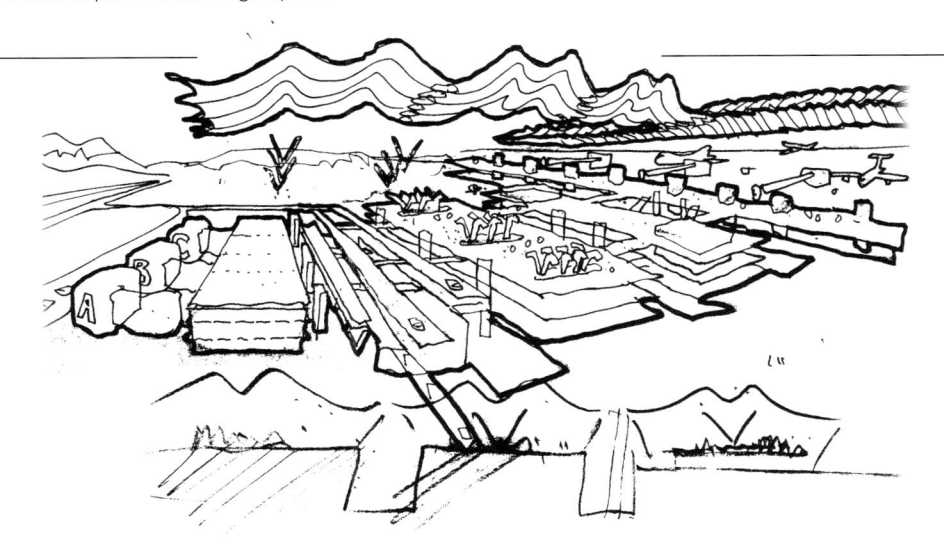

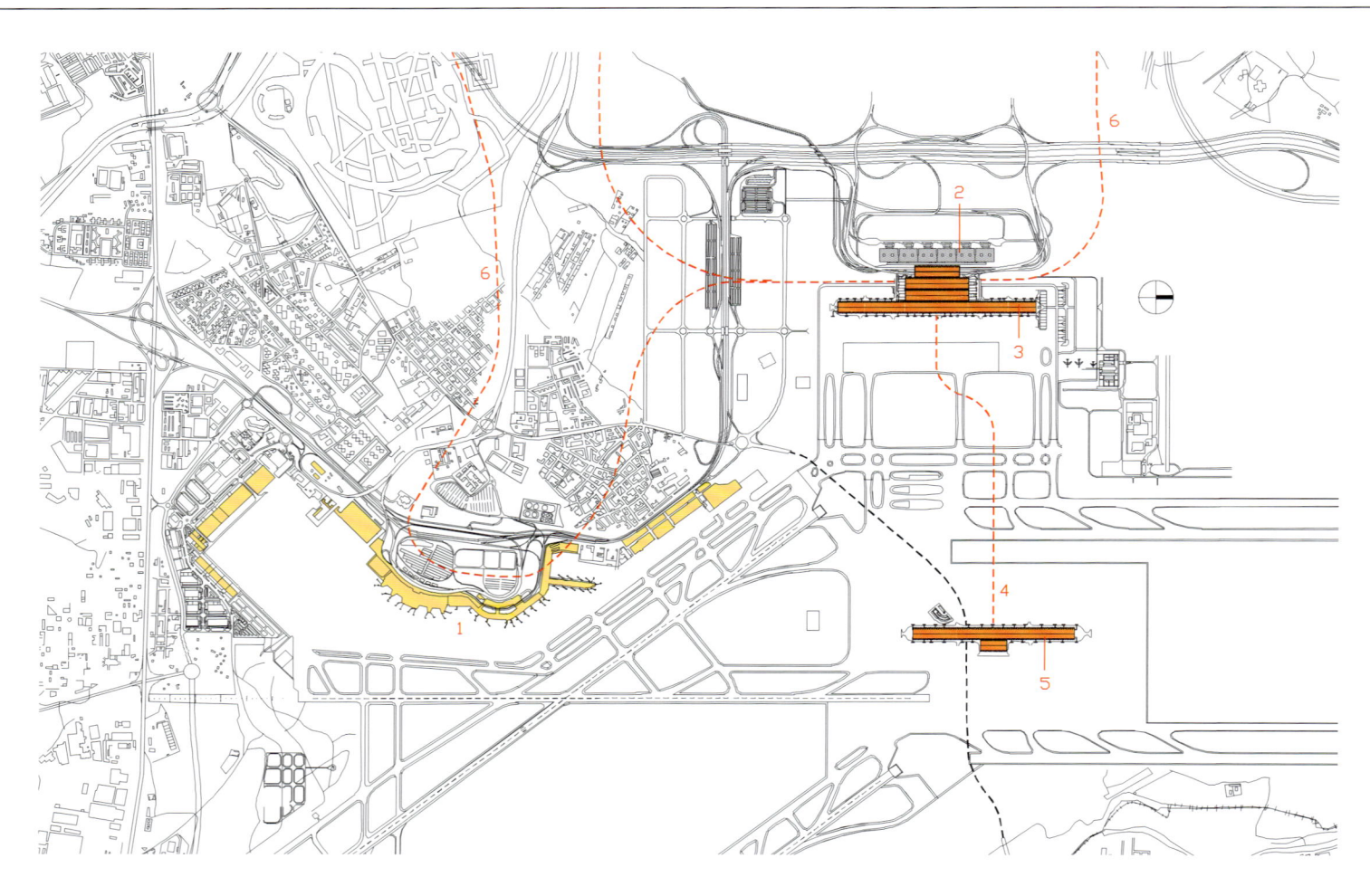

■ Site Plan – Scale 1:40000

1. Existing Terminals
2. Car Park
3. New Terminal Building T4
4. Connection Tunnel
5. New Satellite Building T4-S
6. Subway

Terminal
Ground Floor Plan – Scale 1:5000

- Retail
- Luggage Handling
- Airside Passengers
- Vertical Circulations

Satellite
Ground Floor Plan – Scale 1:5000

- Car Park Building
- Airport Services

187 / Richard Rogers

■ **Terminal**
　XX Section – Scale 1:1000

🚶 Arrivals

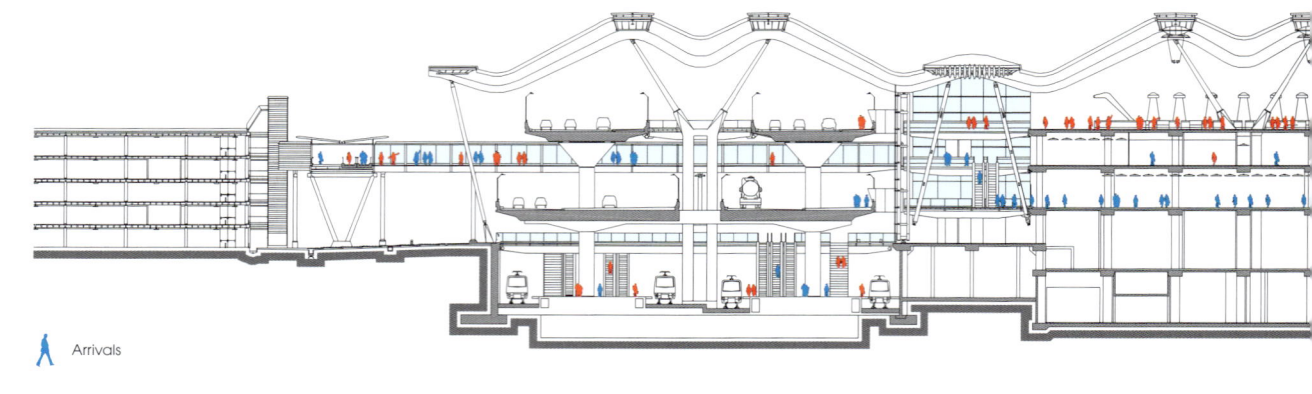

🚶 Departures

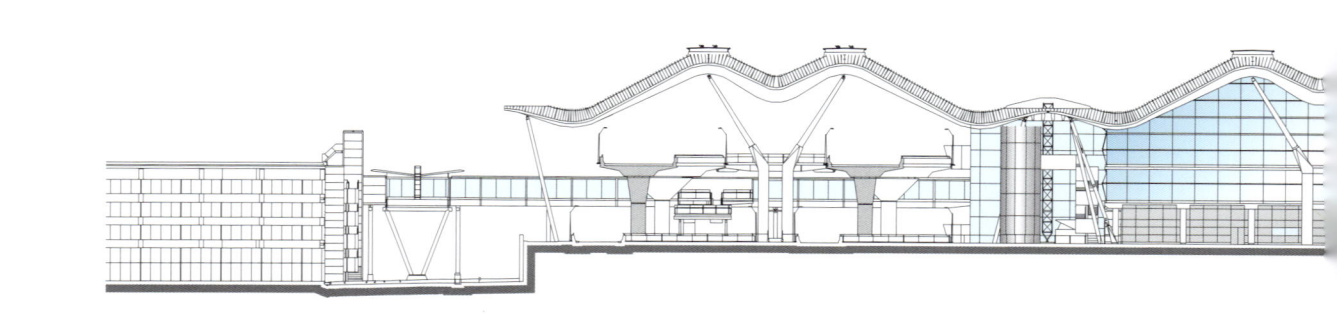

■ **Terminal**
　YY Section – Scale 1:1000

188 / Terminal T4

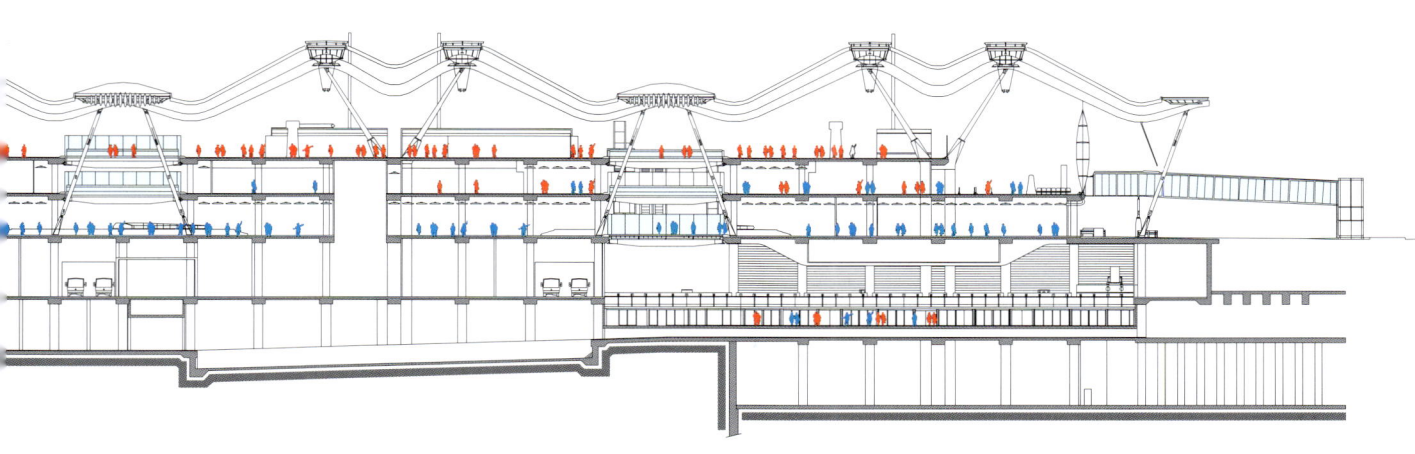

189 / Richard Rogers

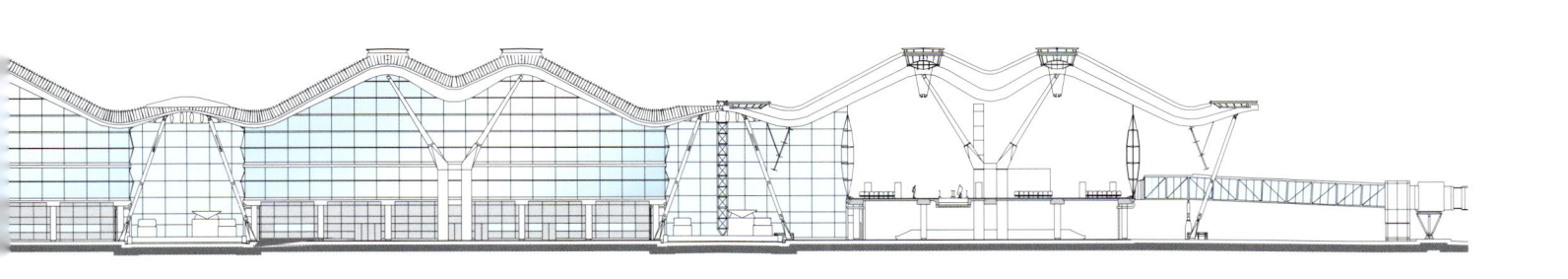

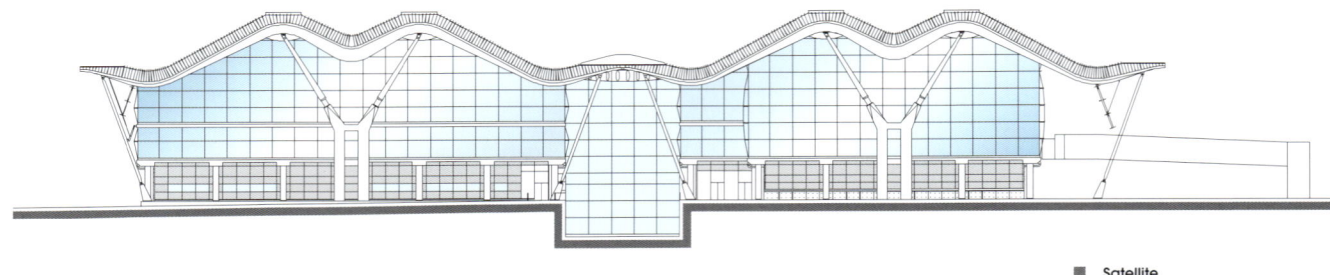

■ **Satellite**
South Elevation – Scale 1:1000

■ **Satellite**
ZZ Section – Scale 1:1000

🚶 Arrivals

🚶 Departures

191 / Richard Rogers

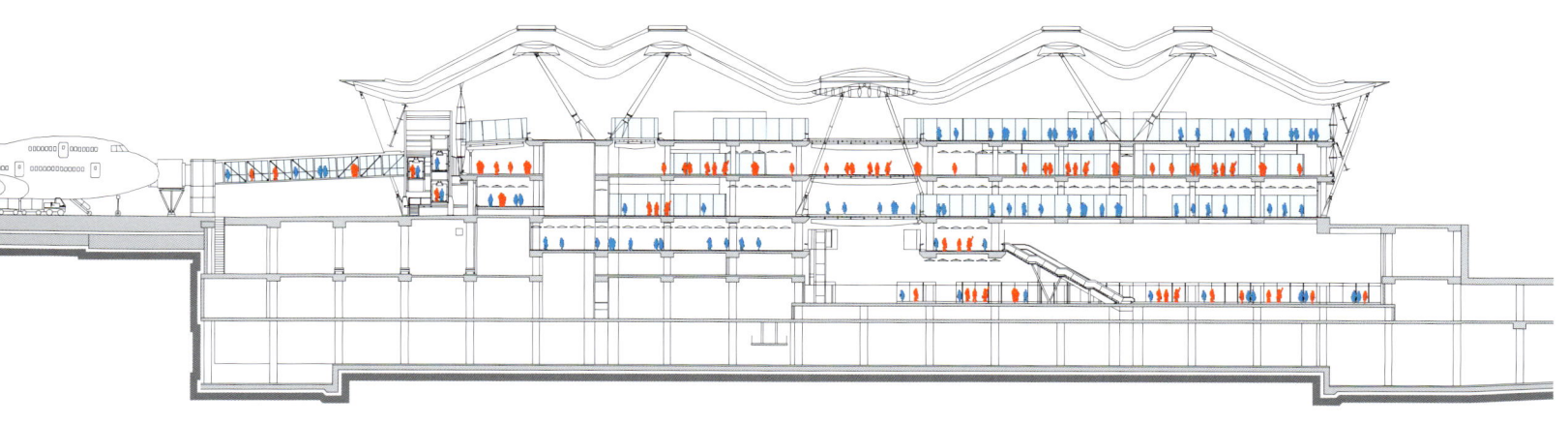

192 / Terminal T4

**STRUCTURE SUPPORTING
GLAZED FACADE OF TERMINAL
EAST AND WEST SIDES
DETAILS A, C: VERTICAL SECTIONS
SCALE 1:15
DETAIL B: AXONOMETRIC VIEW
SCALE 1:20
DETAIL D: HORIZONTAL SECTION
SCALE 1:15**

1. Exterior
2. Interior
3. Fin for anchoring upper fork to the roof beam
4. Polished stainless steel sheet stop
5. Forged and electro-polished stainless steel upper fork
6. Stainless steel U-profile
7. Silicone seal
8. Climalit double-glazing assembly: external 15/32" (12 mm) Cool-Lite KN tempered solar control glass, 15/32" (12 mm) airspace, internal 15/64"+15/64" (6+6 mm) Stadip Silence acoustic laminated safety glass with PVB film interlayer
9. Stainless steel Macalloy traction bar
10. Anodized aluminium sheet in natural colour
11. Insulation
12. Forged and electro-polished stainless steel upper double connecting rod with spherical bolt and joint
13. Steel beam formed by two 2 63/64" (76 mm) Ø tubular profiles with 25/64" (10 mm) thick connecting plate

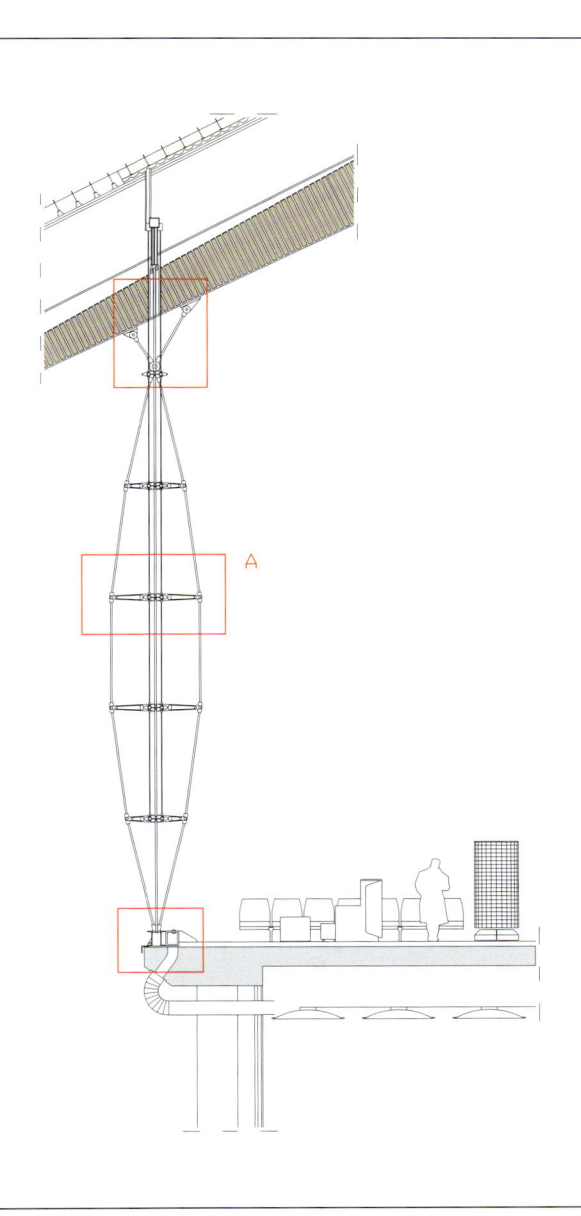

14. Anodized aluminium profile in natural colour
15. Lacquered aluminium profile
16. Layer of injected polyurethane foam
17. EPDM coupling
18. Forged and electro-polished stainless steel connector
19. Forged and electro-polished stainless steel connecting rod
20. Forged and electro-polished stainless steel lower fork
21. Painted steel box for anchoring and housing facade support structure (open on external side for inspecting fasteners)
22. Housing profile for pane
23. Spherical bolt and joint
24. Air duct in rolled steel with anodized aluminium upper cover in natural colour
25. Flooring and skirting in "Perlato" natural stone, 25/32" (20 mm) bedding mortar layer, 1 37/64" (40 mm) light concrete slab with added polypropylene fibre, 31 1/2" (800 mm) h. post-tensioned reinforced concrete beam supporting precast reinforced concrete slabs
26. 15/32" (mm) Ø stainless steel tie rod
27. Stainless steel tie rod connector
28. Bellows joint between glass panes

193 / Richard Rogers

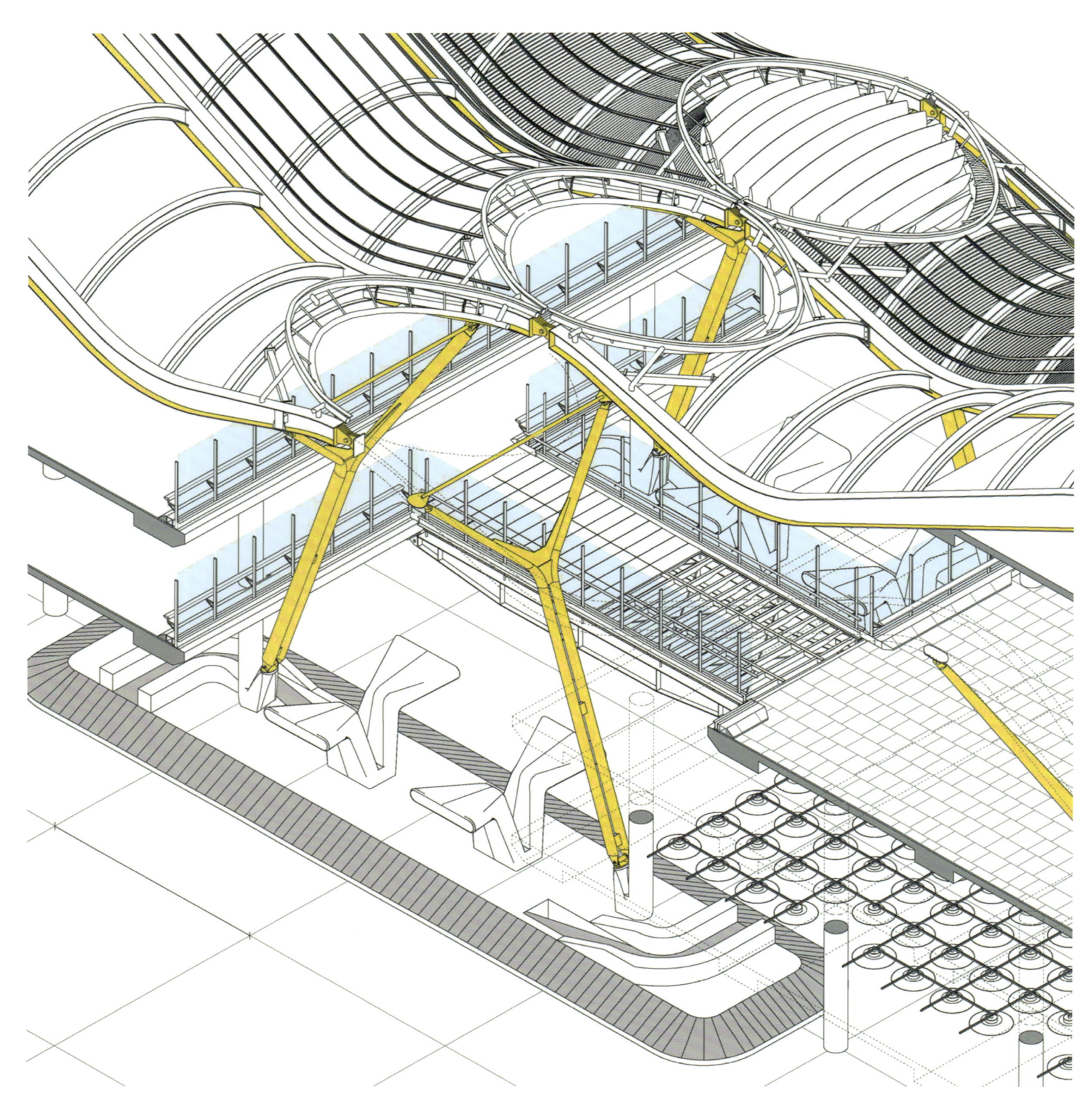

Axonometric View of "Canyon" – Not to Scale

194 / Terminal T4

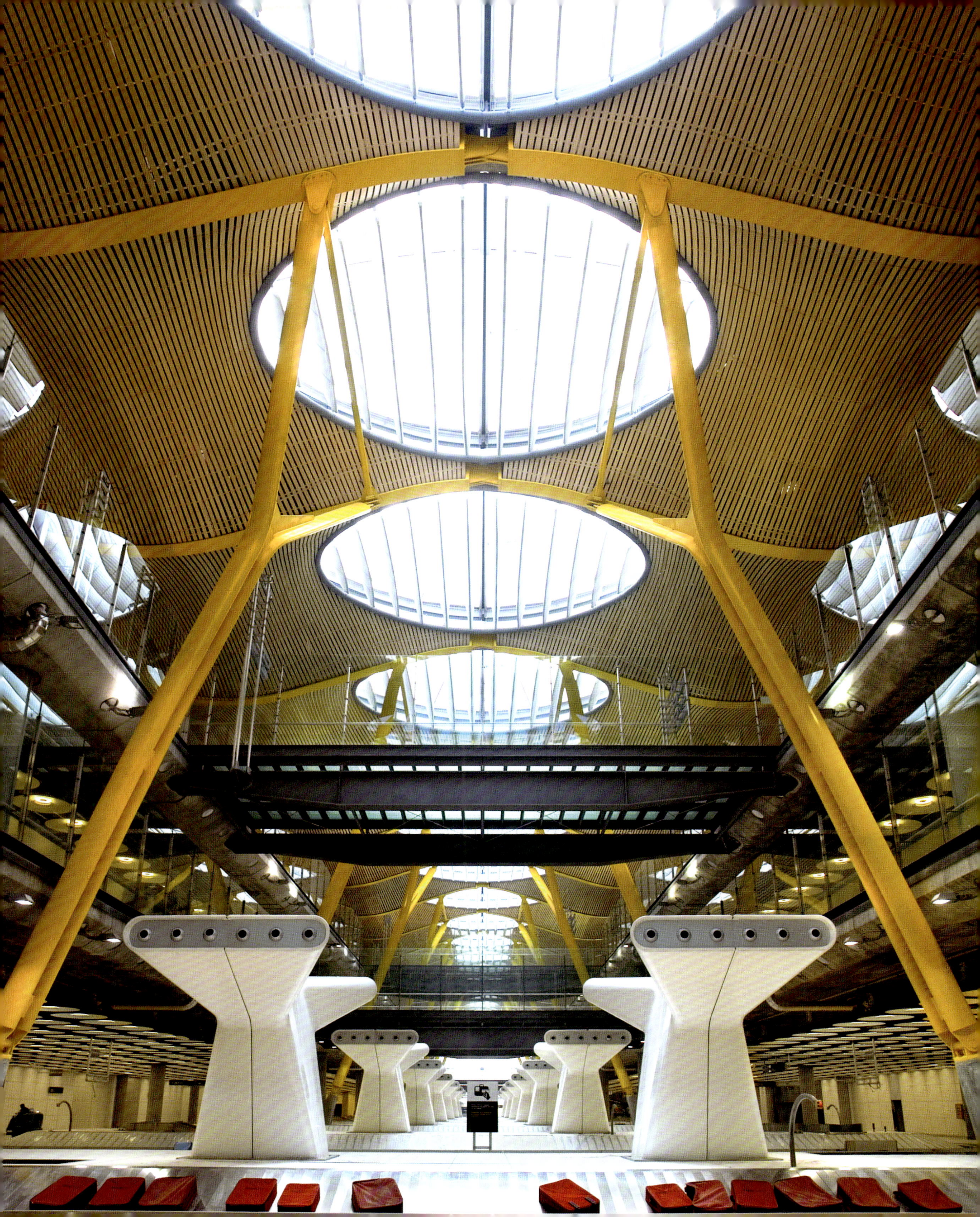

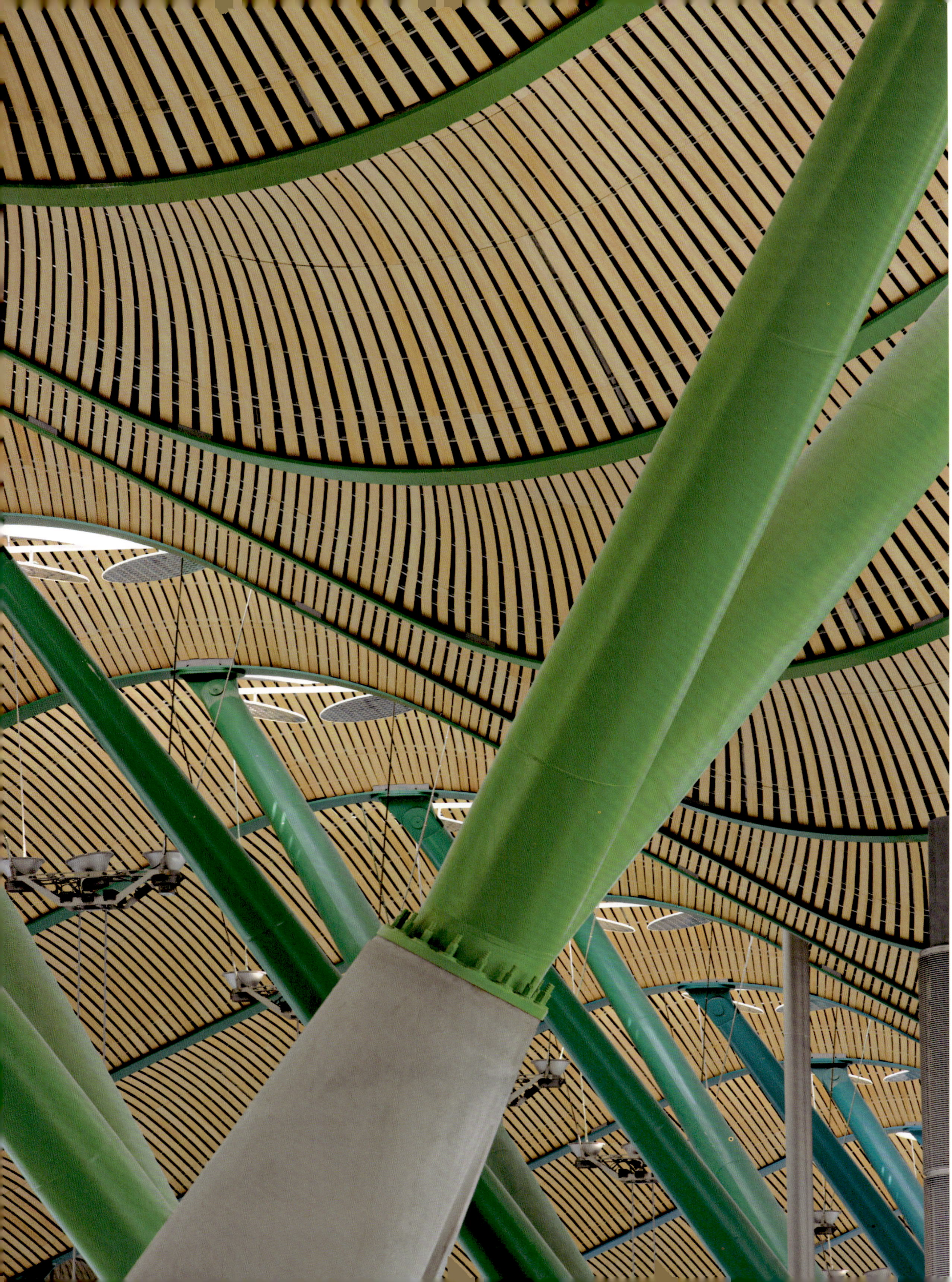

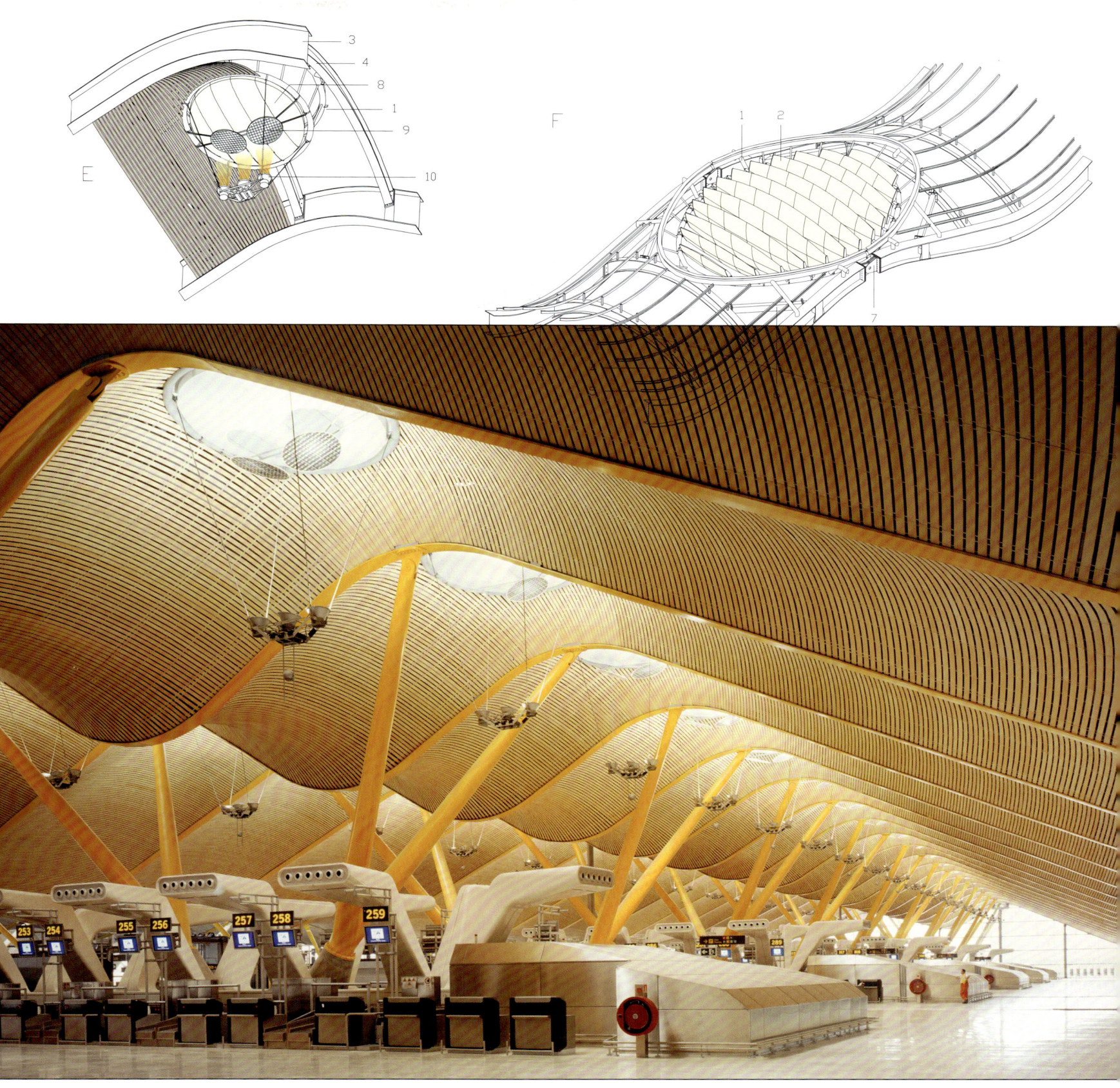

TERMINAL AND SATELLITE BUILDING
DETAIL E: CIRCULAR SKYLIGHT
DETAIL F: OVAL SKYLIGHT
AXONOMETRIC VIEWS – NOT TO SCALE

1. Structure supporting skylight formed by circular section tubular profiles in rolled steel
2. Translucent elements for diffusing natural light: internal framework of fibreglass and polyester resin bars and plates, fibreglass and silicone covering with anti-mould surface treatment, dirt-prevention polymeric film and light extruded aluminium supporting frame
3. Rolled steel main beam (variable height) spaced at 29′6″ (900 cm) with 19/32″ (15 mm) core
4. Rolled steel secondary beam positioned every 11′6″ (350 mm), formed by IPE 500, HEB 500 or HEB 700 profiles, depending on zone
5. UPN 100 profiles
6. Reinforcing metal profile
7. Connecting point between modules of precast structure supporting roof
8. Translucent cloth formed by fibreglass fabric and aluminium frame
9. Mirror reflectors for diffusing light symmetrically: circular section aluminium frame with honeycomb internal plate
10. Projectors suspended by steel cable fixed to skylight structure

197 / Richard Rogers

SOCCER CITY STADIUM
JOHANNESBURG, SOUTH AFRICA

BOOGERTMAN + PARTNERS ARCHITECTS

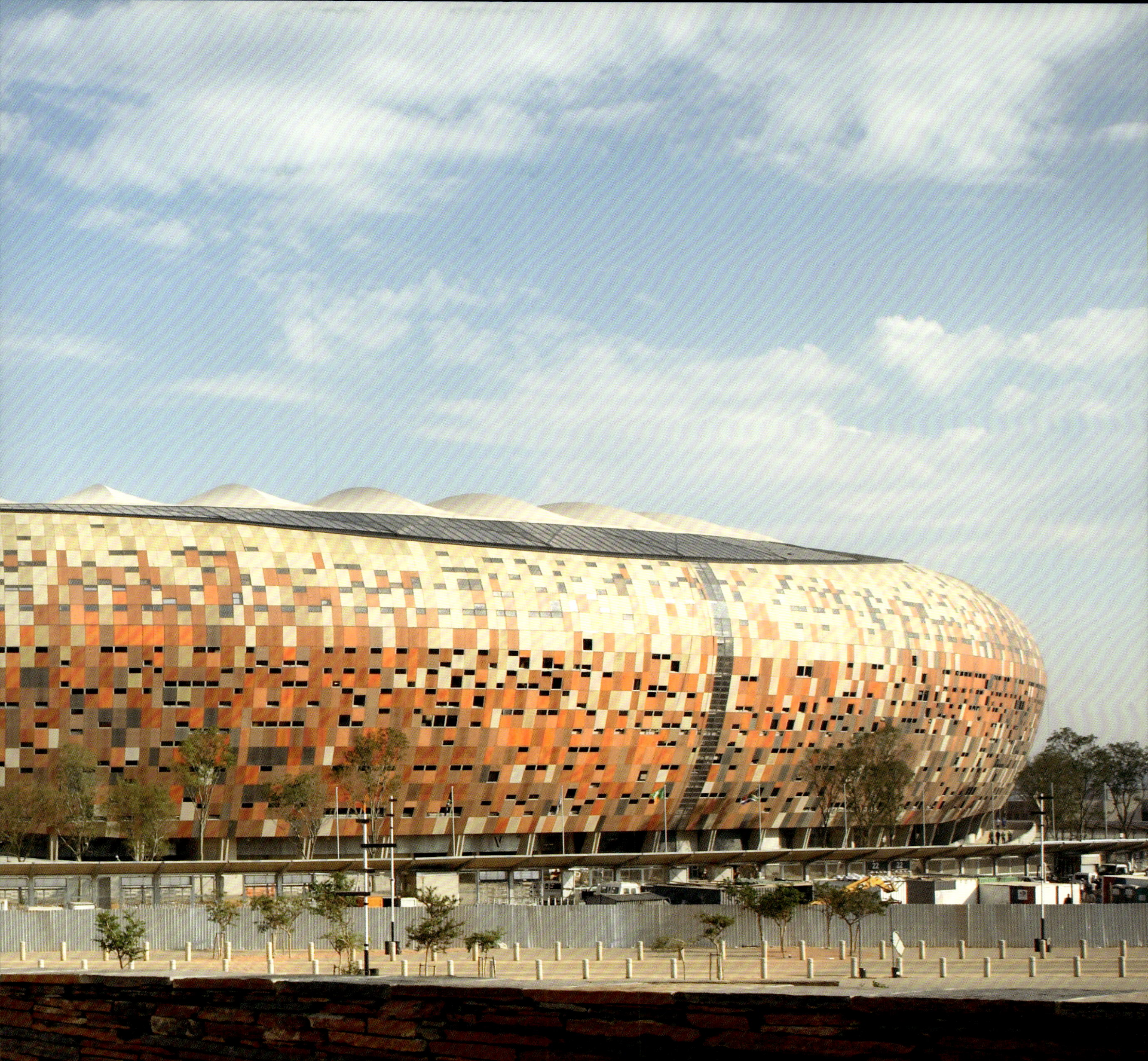

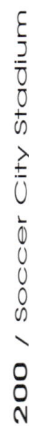

On being assigned the 2010 Soccer World Cup, South Africa has embarked on a sweeping modernization and upgrading programme of her sports facilities to meet international regulations.

Located in Johannesburg, a city founded on mineral wealth and today also a financial hub, Soccer City Stadium lies in the district of Soweto, the black township that significantly became world famous during the civil rights struggle against apartheid. The stadium will host the opening ceremony of the championship, intermediary-round games and the final.

The architectural upgrade is the work of South African practice Boogertman Urban Edge + Partners in partnership with Populous and entailed partial demolition of some structures and the building of new facilities to ensure requisite international standards.

Seating capacity has been increased to 88,853. All spectators are ensured unimpeded views with regulation distances from the pitch guaranteed even for those in the highest tiers. The stadium is surrounded by ample parking areas. Access routes are disposed like spokes around a hub, making the renovated stadium a pivotal centrepiece.

The envelope encircling the entire structure takes its cue from the calabash, or African pot, a widely used natural container. Clayey, earthy colours give it the appearance of traditional pottery, a reference to the melting pot of African cultures this continent represents.

Reinforced concrete sections supporting the two tier levels and gallery are set at regular intervals around the bowl. The vertical circulation ramps are concealed behind the outer calabash, a sinuous mosaic of cement with reinforced glass fibre panels (FibreC by Rieder) in a range of eight different shades and two different textures. These are interspersed at irregular intervals by glass cut outs. A truss-supported roof surrounds the whole stadium.

The covered stand has also undergone upgrading. New offices and changing rooms have been added along with new electronic equipment.

Inside, facilities include a 300-place restaurant, four television studies for live broadcasts and a Football Museum: after the World Cup, the scores will be immortalized and put on display.

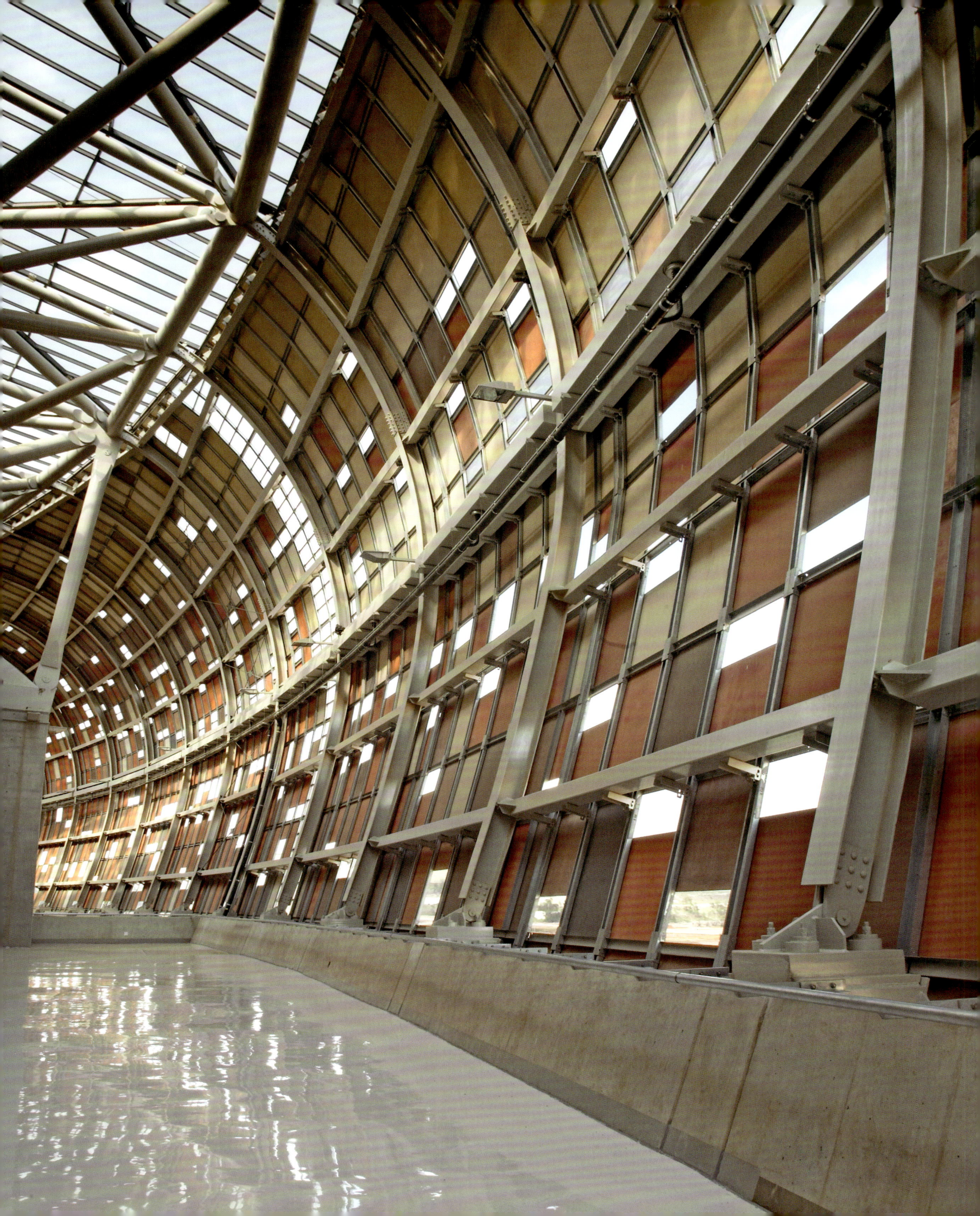

■ XX Section - Scale 1:1000

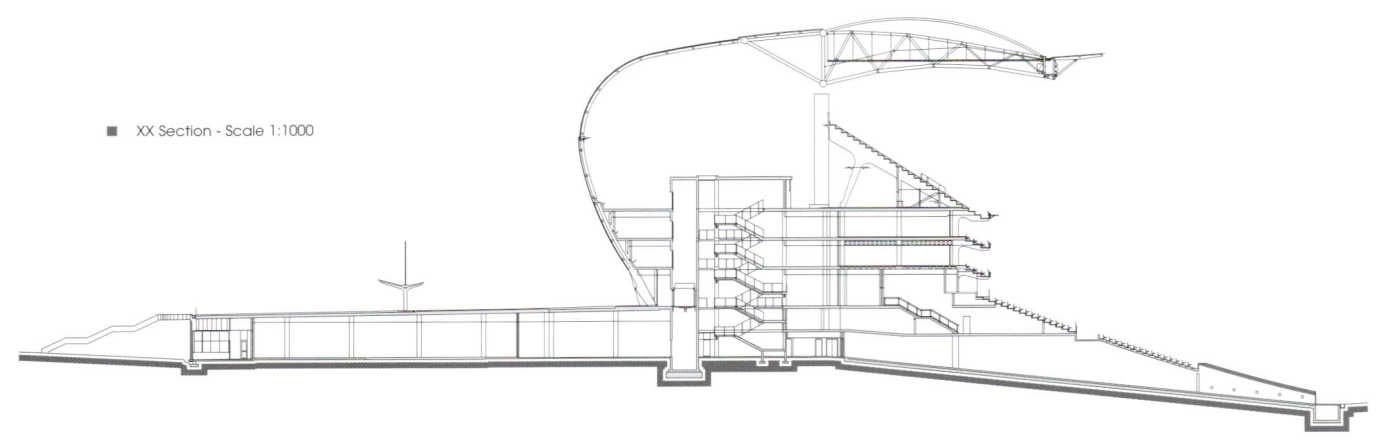

■ YY Section - Scale 1:1000

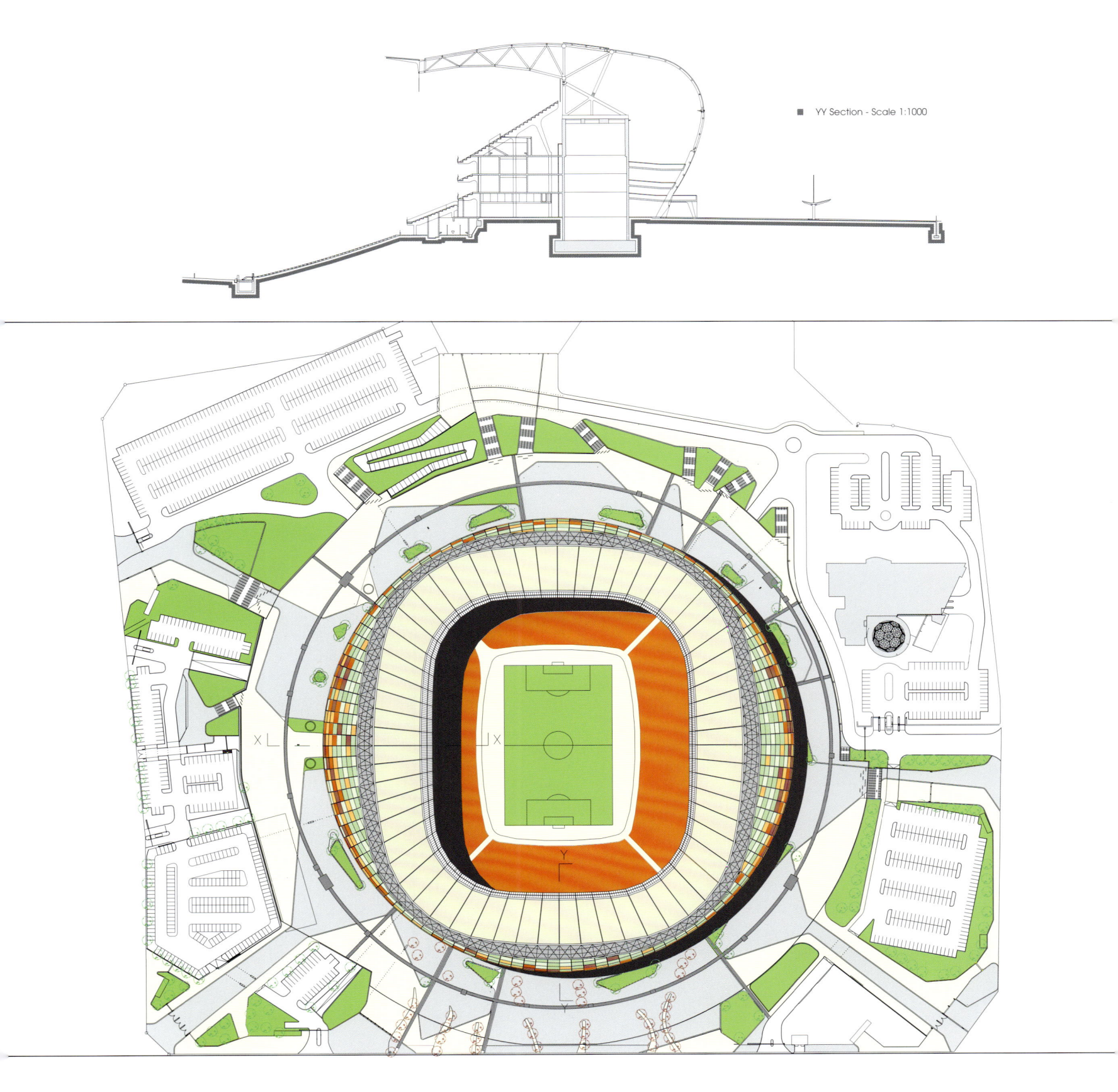

■ Site Plan - Scale 1:3000

203 / Boogertman

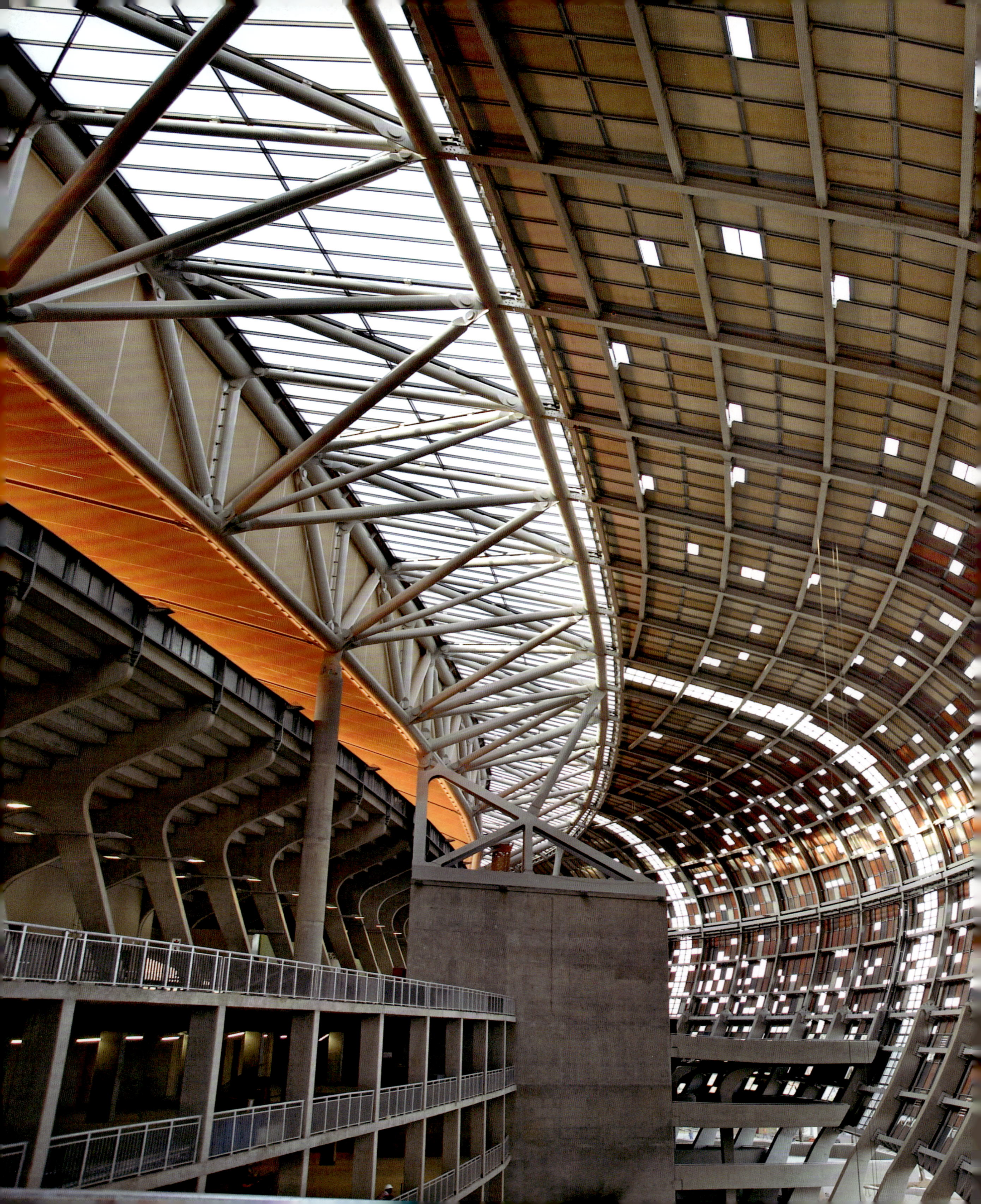

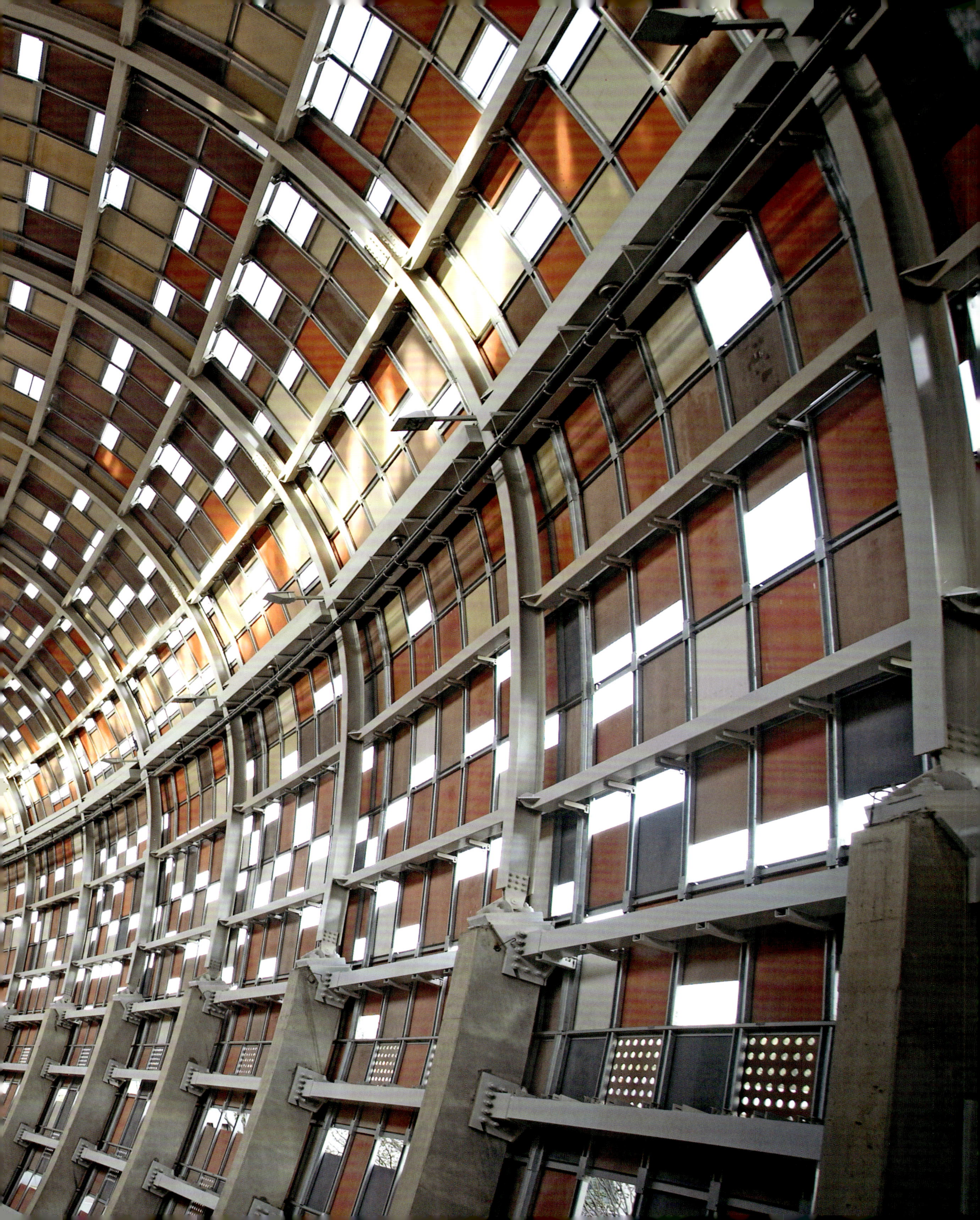

206 / Soccer City Stadium

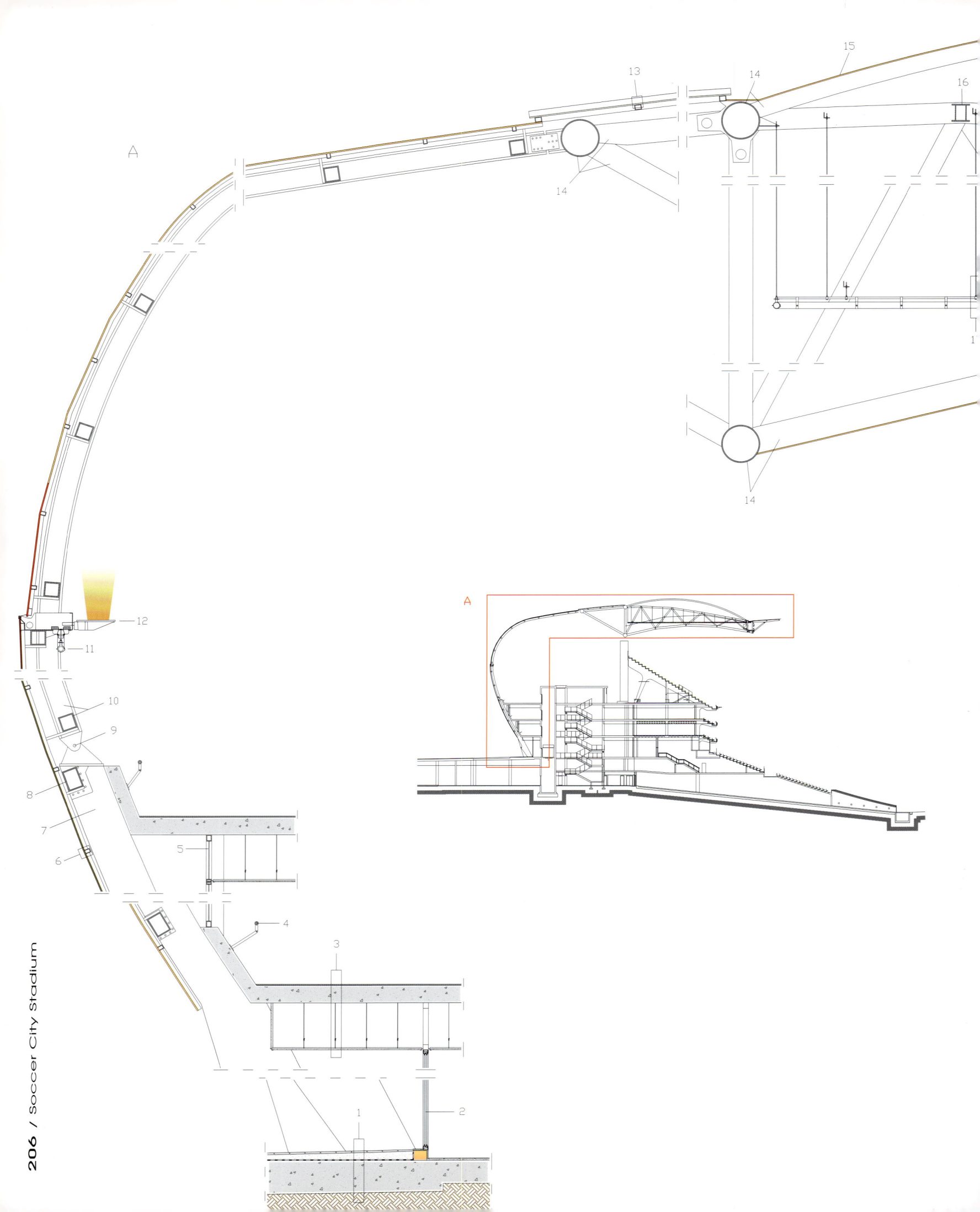

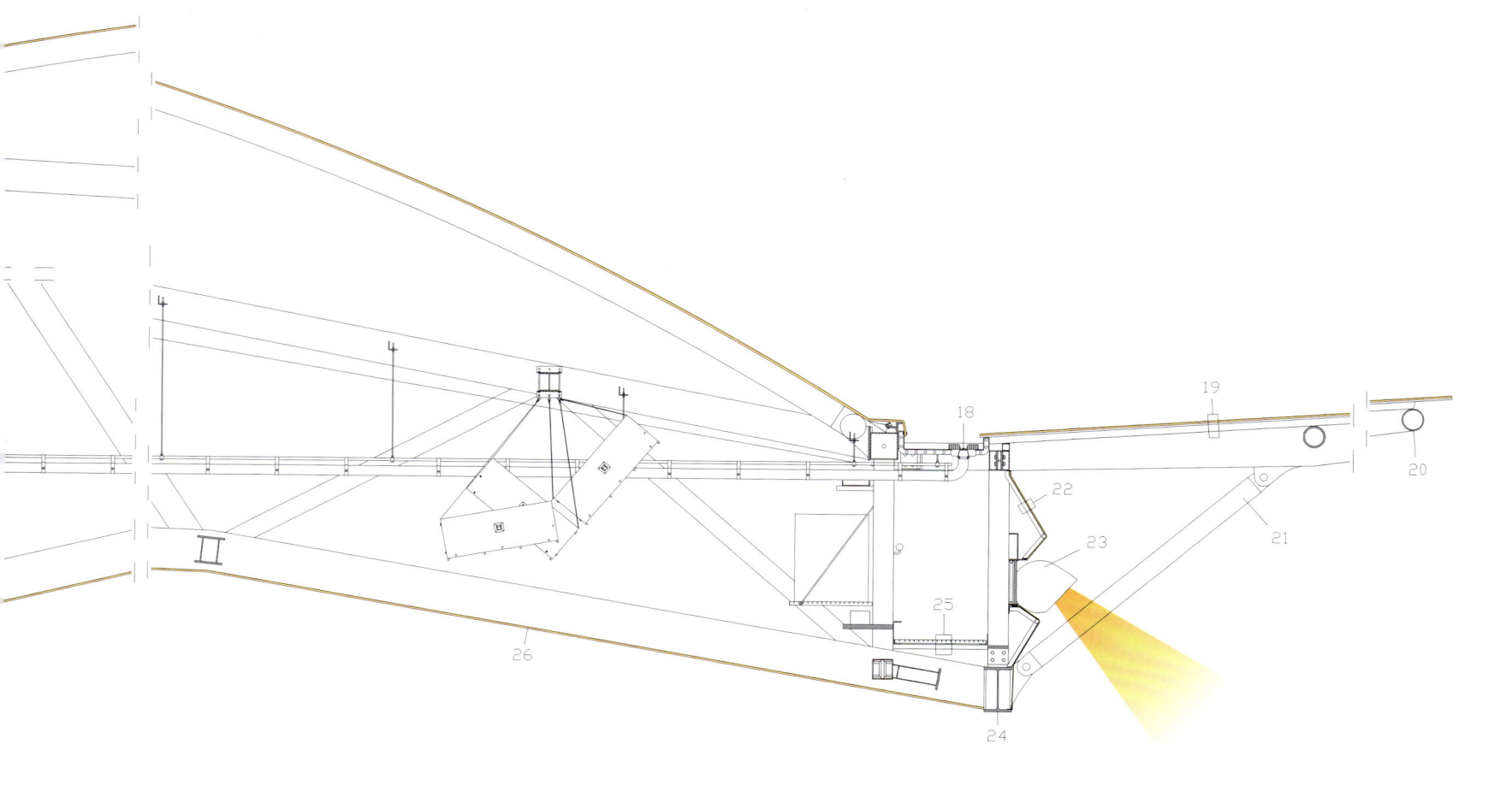

DETAIL A:
ROOF AND CONSTRUCTION SYSTEM
VERTICAL SECTION - SCALE 1:70

1. 2 3/8" (60 mm) concrete block pavers at 2 % slope, 1 1/4" (30 mm) screed, waterproofing membrane, 22 3/4" (580 mm) reinforced concrete slab, earth
2. Glazed curtain wall with aluminium frame and 1/4 - 3/4 - 1/4" (7.5/20/7.5 mm) double glazing
3. Ramp constructed from 1/16" (5 mm) epoxy resin finish, 11 7/8" (300 mm) reinforced concrete slab, false ceiling formed by frame of 3/4 x 3/4" (20 x 20 mm) steel C-profiles and 5/8" (15 mm) gypsum board on steel tie rods suspended from slab
4. Handrail in Ø 2 3/8" (60 mm) steel pipe profiles
5. Aluminium framed window with 3/8" (10 mm) glass
6. Shell formed by 1/2" (13 mm) Rieder Fibre C concrete and fibreglass panels on frame of 2 x 2 3/8" (50 x 60 mm) steel box profiles anchored by 1 3/8 x 1 3/8" (35 x 35 mm) steel box profiles
7. Curved concrete column with horizontal eccentricity of 255 7/8" (6.5 m) relative to base
8. 11 7/8 x 3/4" (300 x 200 mm) steel box beam anchoring and bracing cladding and bolted to plates
9. Steel hinged joint connecting two structural elements
10. 14 3/4 x 7 1/4" (375 x 185 mm) curved steel I-beam with interposed 11 x11" (245 x 245 mm) box profiles anchoring and bracing cladding
11. Rainwater gutter
12. Halogen spotlights
13. Skylight constructed from 3/8" (10 mm) polycarbonate panels on frame of 10 1/4 x 1 1/4" (260 x 260 mm) steel box profiles
14. Trussed structure formed by tie rods and Ø 35 1/2" (900 mm) framework steel pipe profiles
15. ptfe finish on trussed structure
16. Coupled 11 7/8 x 11 7/8" (300 x 300 mm) steel I-beam bracing
17. Syphonic dewatering system formed by pipes on steel tie rods suspended from structure
18. Rainwater gutter
19. Canopy constructed from 3/8" (10 mm) polycarbonate panels, frame of 3 1/8 x 3 1/8" (80 x 80 mm) steel box profiles, tapered steel beam (parallel to plane of section)
20. 4 7/8" (125 mm) pipe beam providing bracing
21. Steel beam supporting roof beam
22. Screening constructed from 1/16" (2 mm) perforated sheet steel and frame of 2 x 2" (50 x 50 mm) steel box profiles
23. Halogen spotlights lighting field
24. 11 7/8 x 19 3/4" (300 x 500 mm) steel I-beam
25. Maintenance walkway constructed from steel grilles on 1 3/4 x 1 3/4" (45 x 45 mm) steel box profiles
26. Perforated PTFE mesh ceiling finish on trussed structure

AGBAR TOWER – BARCELONA, SPAIN
ATELIERS JEAN NOUVEL AND B720 ARQUITECTOS

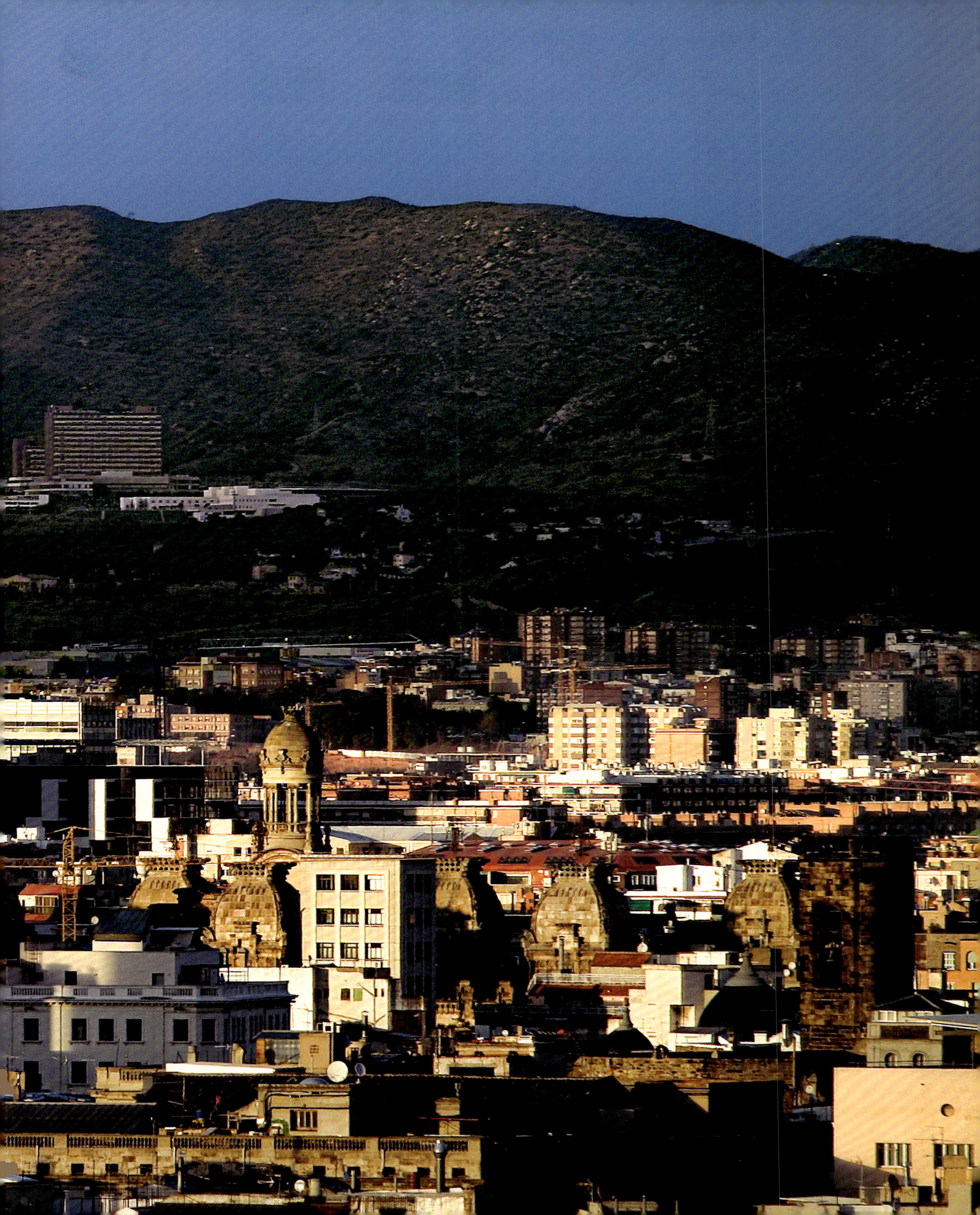

Located on Plaça de les Glòries Catalanes, the 142 m, 35-storey Agbar tower is a "small skyscraper" that fits perfectly into the acute angle formed by the Avenida Diagonal and Carrer Badajoz.

Its shape emulates a fountain at constant, stable pressure – a very suitable image for the headquarters of a water utility. To reinforce this imagery, the building does not stand at ground level but springs from a sheet of water at the bottom of a crater-like dip.

Four basement floors fill the whole plot, housing support functions and parking areas. The auditorium in the first basement rises from the ground to blend with the undulated landscaped space around the tower.

The building's interior core and exterior perimeter are both load-bearing, a design that frees the intervening space of structural columns. Two concrete oval cylinders support a system of metallic beams which in turn supports composite metal/concrete decks.

The floor plan is determined by the building's eccentric core. A compact area around the lift lobbies gradually broadens out to become unencumbered space for offices and other functions.

The outer wall is composed of an irregular mesh of square modules, giving the impression of a "pixelated" surface. Windows irregularly punctuate the exterior surface, based on calculations of the surface's exposure to direct sunlight. This, together with the point-support grid and flexible office space configuration, give the building its very distinctive appearance. As if by osmosis the external mesh array is repeated internally. The fractal geometry of the outer wall, developed by designers together with Tecno, employs industrial processes that were also used to produce the component elements that fit neatly into the horizontal and vertical curves of the building – a sort of spatial imprinting.

The corrugated aluminium plate cladding – backed by a rockwool layer lying against the outer wall – follows this mesh structure. The outer skin is lacquered in 25 graded colours. From earthy reds at the base, the tower gradually becomes a shimmering blue on the upper storeys, as if seeking to blend with the sky.

The outer cylinder rises straight from the ground up to the 18th floor where it starts to curve gently and gradually inward until the 26th floor. At this point, concrete is no longer used, and the building is topped by a metal and glass dome.

On the last 6 storeys, the different-thickness, post-tensioned, concrete structural floor slabs cantilever out from the central core to occupy the large space under the dome. These areas are earmarked for senior management offices.

The whole building has an outer skin of laminated glass slats of differing degrees of transparency. The result is an intriguing veil blurring the graduated colours of the tower behind. The incline of each specially treated panel is a function of the solar irradiation falling on each wall section.

■ Typical Floor Plan – Scale 1:400

1. Lifts
2. Service Elevator
3. Waiting Room
4. Meeting Room
5. Offices
6. Copy Machine Room
7. Cafeteria

■ Cafeteria Floor Plan – Scale 1:400

■ Typical Floor Plan – Scale 1:400

211 / Jean Nouvel / b720

Neither tower nor American-type skyscraper, the building rises up like an apparition in the midst of a peaceful city. Unlike the slender spires and bell towers that typically pierce our skylines, this fluid mass bursts from the ground like a geyser under permanent pressure.

The building's surface recalls water. Materials are smooth, flowing, shimmering and transparent, nuanced in colour and light. It is an architecture of the earth without the heaviness of stone, a form that echoes the intriguing ancient shapes of Catalonia, carried down from the highlands of Montserrat by some mysterious wind.

The Agbar tower resonates against Barcelona's skyline: an ambiguity of materiality and light, it stands like a distant mirage, marking the point of entry onto the Avenida Diagonal that courses from the Plaça de les Glòries Catalanes.

This singular object will become the new symbol of the international city of Barcelona, and one of its best ambassadors.

Jean Nouvel

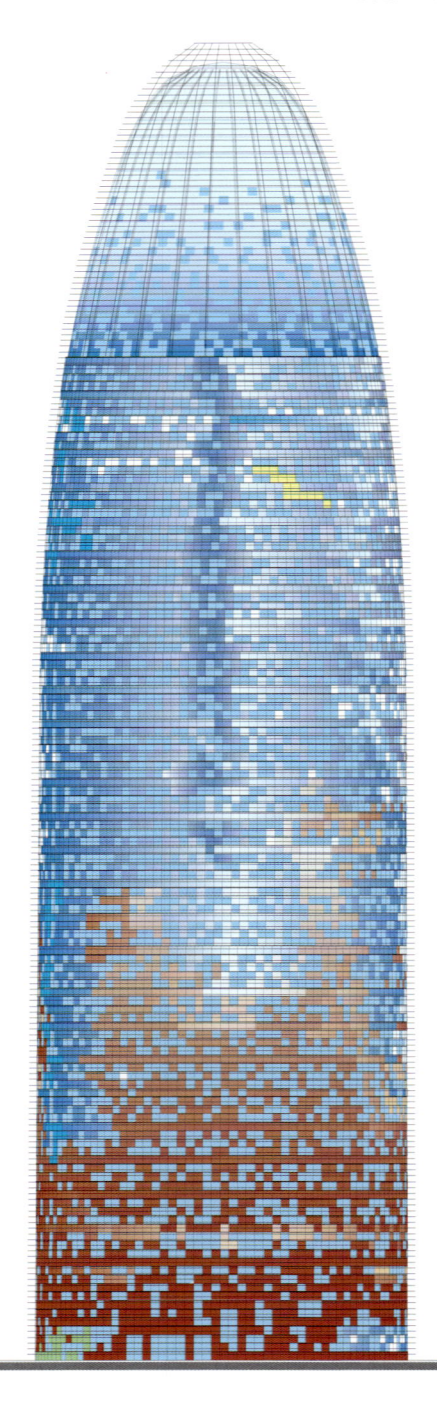

■ North Elevation – Scale 1:800

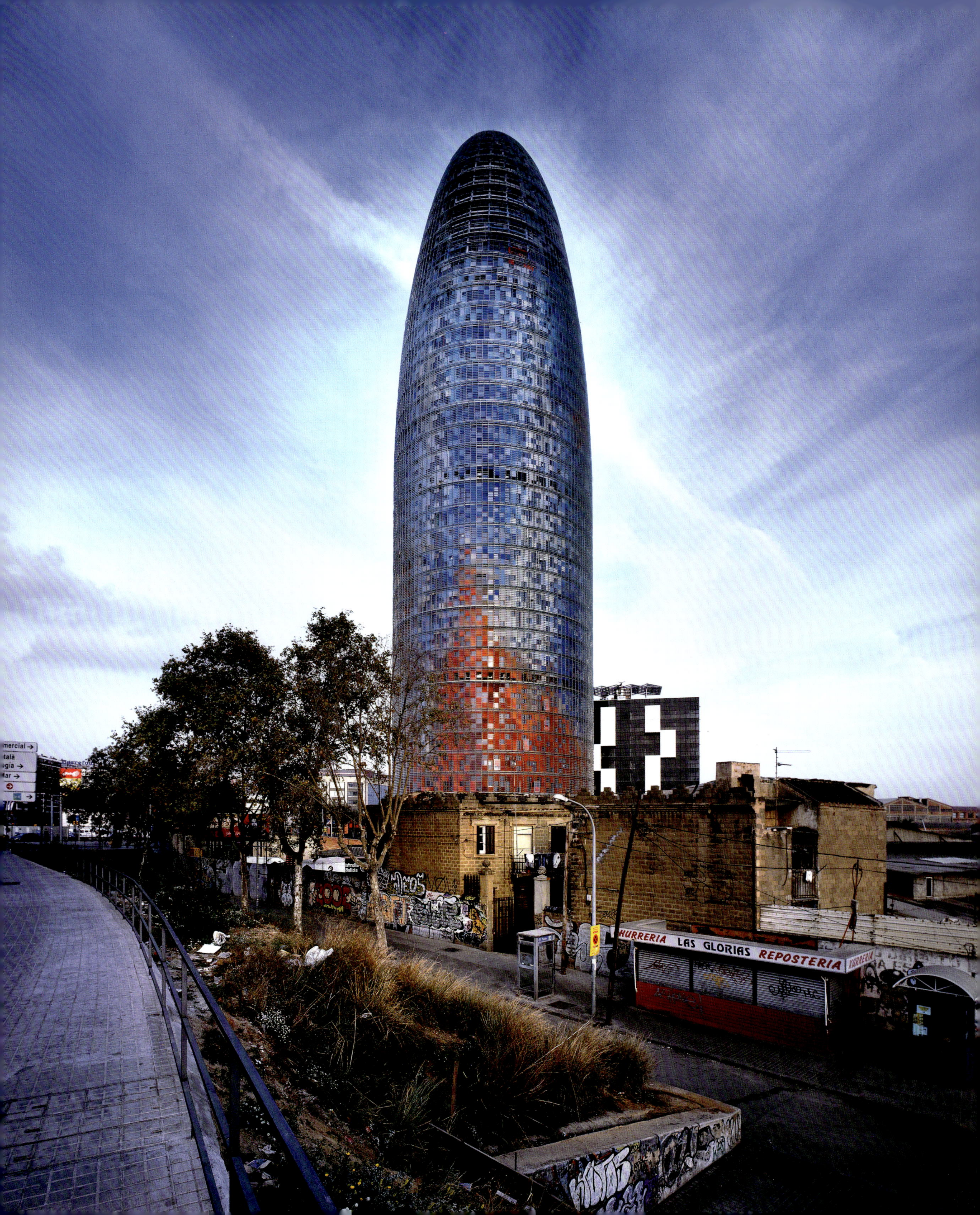
HURRERIA LAS GLORIAS REPOSTERIA

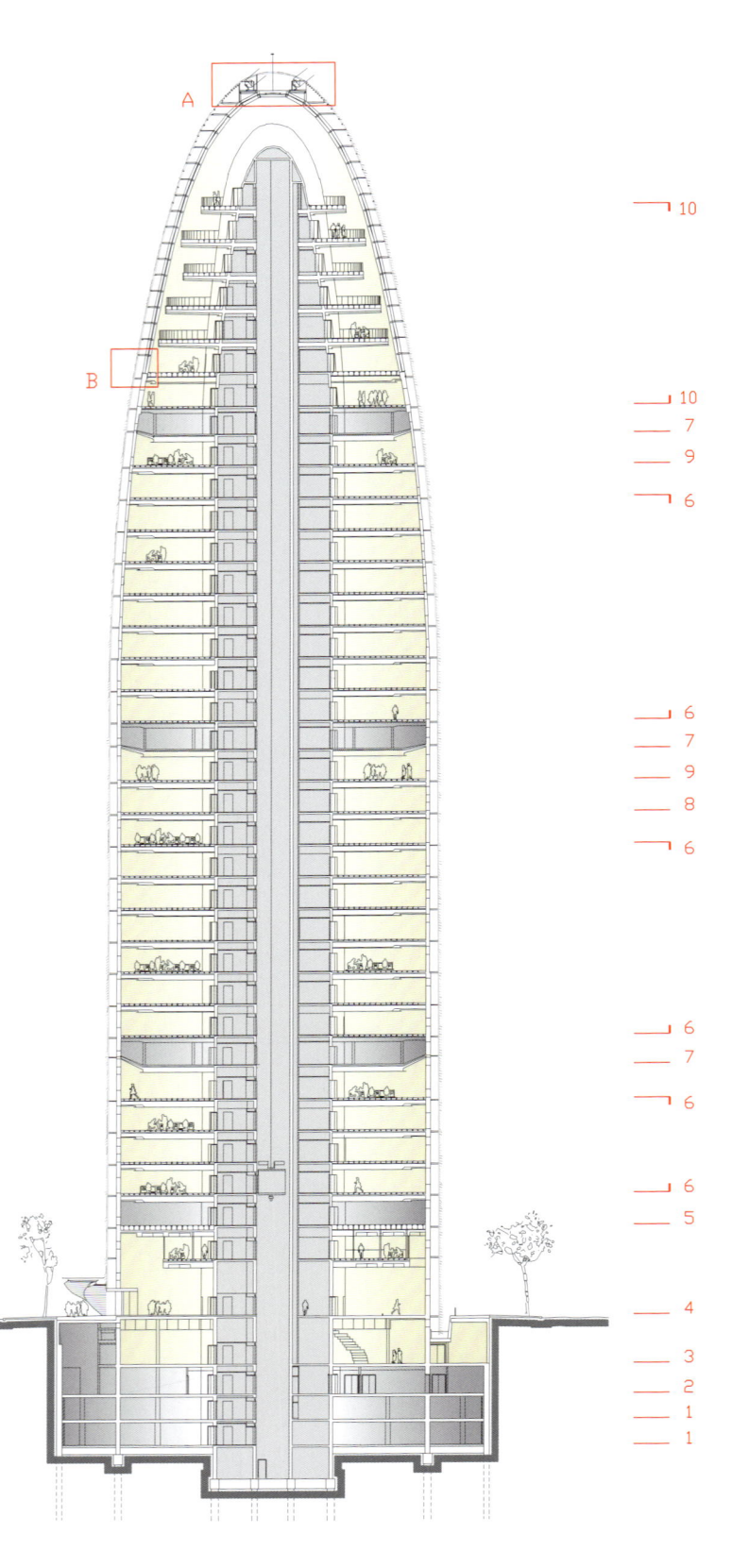

■ XX Section – Scale 1:800

1. Car Park
2. Utilities
3. Auditorium
4. Hall
5. Medical Utilities
6. Offices
7. Services Level
8. Multifunctional Rooms
9. Cafeteria
10. Management Offices

- Dome – Angle of Silk-Screened Glass Louvres

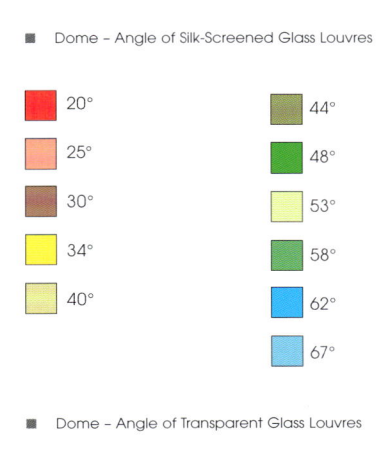

  - 20°
  - 25°
  - 30°
  - 34°
  - 40°
  - 44°
  - 48°
  - 53°
  - 58°
  - 62°
  - 67°

- Dome – Angle of Transparent Glass Louvres

  - 72°
  - 76°
  - 20°
  - 25°
  - 48°
  - 53°
  - 58°
  - 62°
  - 67°
  - 72°
  - 76°

1. East
2. North-East
3. North
4. North-West
5. West
6. South-West
7. South
8. South-East

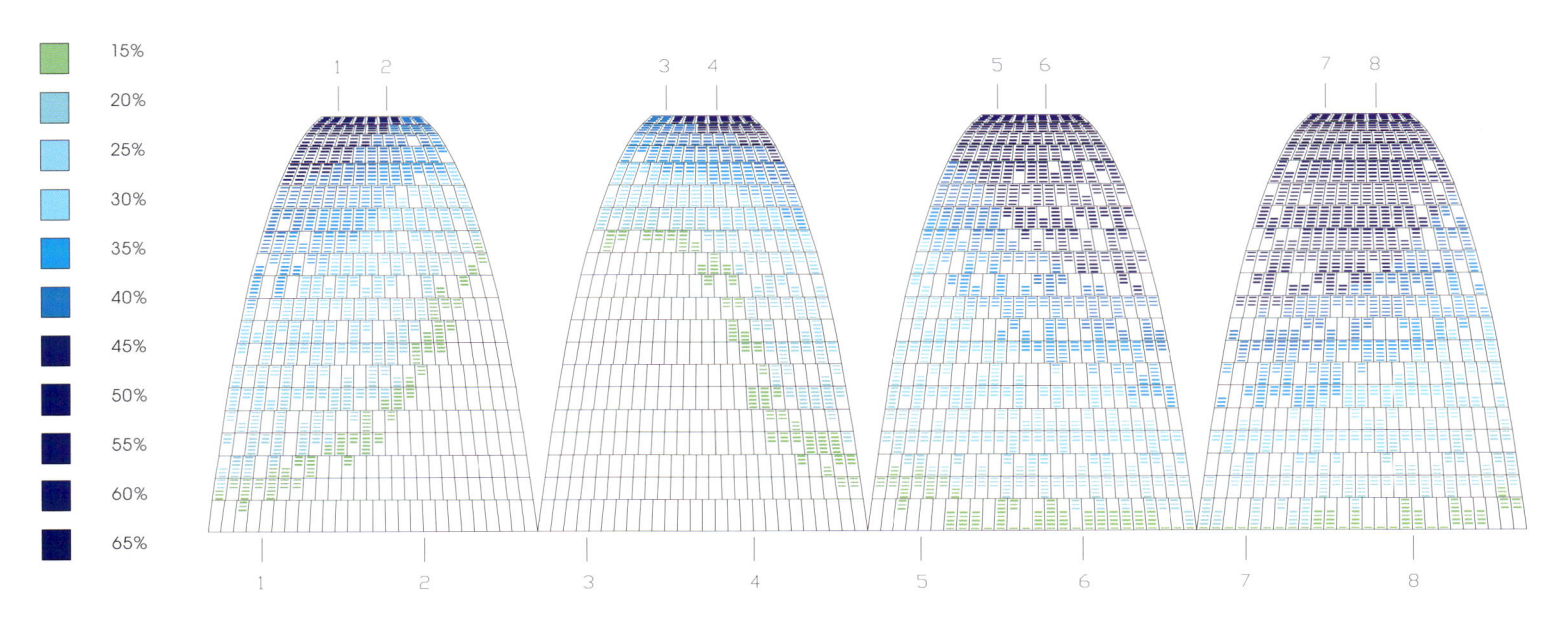

- Dome – Silk-Screening of Glass Louvres

  - 15%
  - 20%
  - 25%
  - 30%
  - 35%
  - 40%
  - 45%
  - 50%
  - 55%
  - 60%
  - 65%

215 / Jean Nouvel / b720

DETAIL A: DOME
VERTICAL SECTION – SCALE 1:50

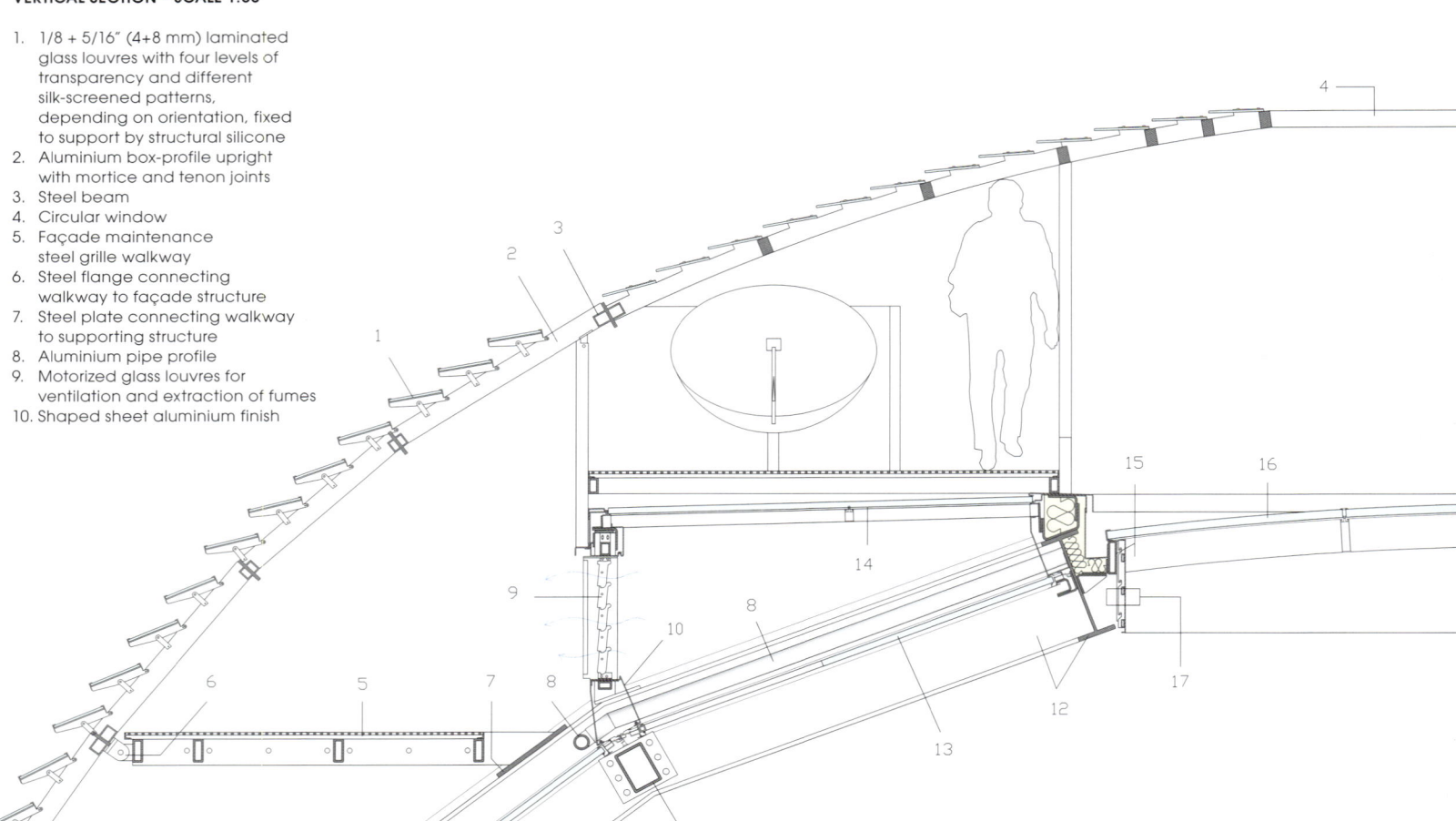

1. 1/8 + 5/16" (4+8 mm) laminated glass louvres with four levels of transparency and different silk-screened patterns, depending on orientation, fixed to support by structural silicone
2. Aluminium box-profile upright with mortice and tenon joints
3. Steel beam
4. Circular window
5. Façade maintenance steel grille walkway
6. Steel flange connecting walkway to façade structure
7. Steel plate connecting walkway to supporting structure
8. Aluminium pipe profile
9. Motorized glass louvres for ventilation and extraction of fumes
10. Shaped sheet aluminium finish

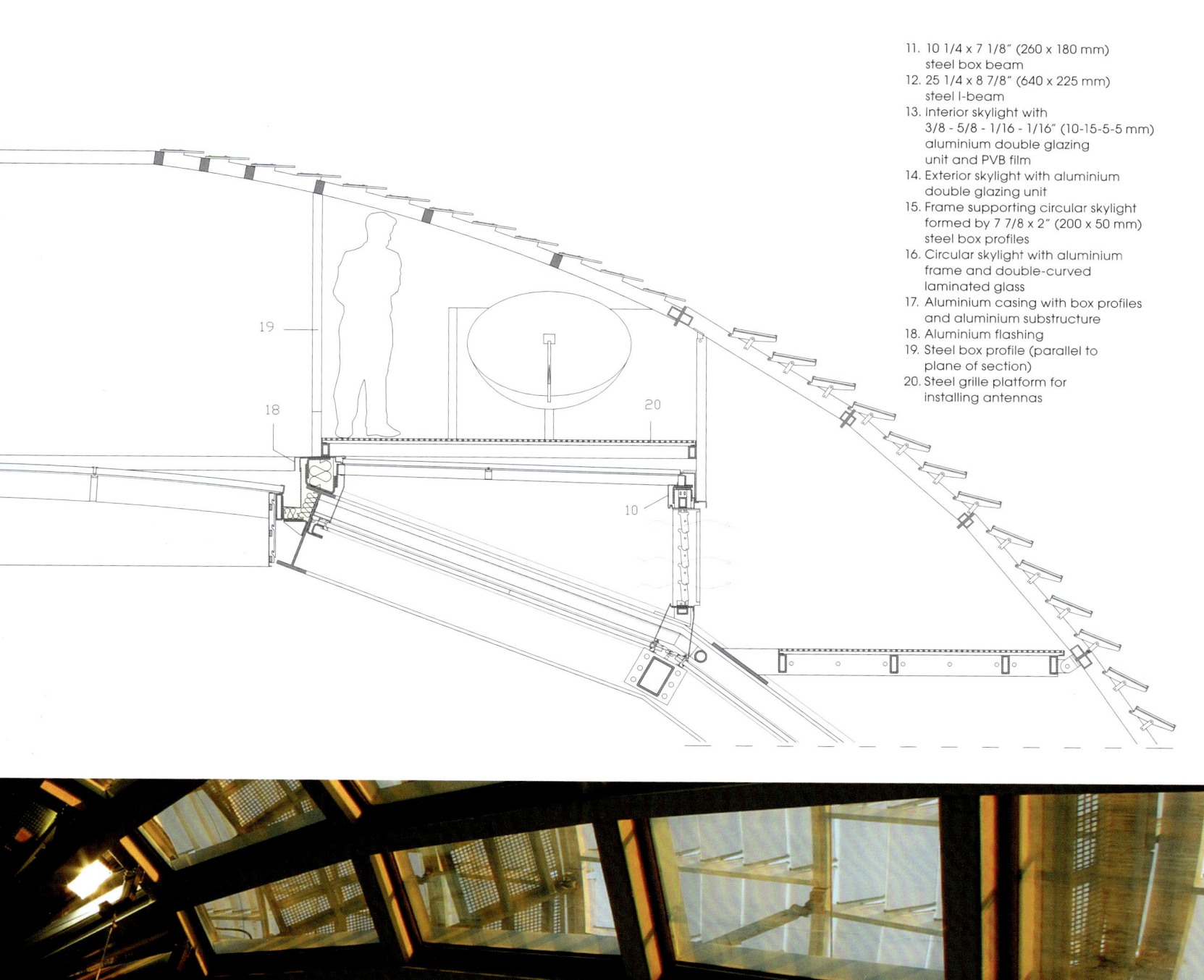

11. 10 1/4 x 7 1/8" (260 x 180 mm) steel box beam
12. 25 1/4 x 8 7/8" (640 x 225 mm) steel I-beam
13. Interior skylight with 3/8 - 5/8 - 1/16 - 1/16" (10-15-5-5 mm) aluminium double glazing unit and PVB film
14. Exterior skylight with aluminium double glazing unit
15. Frame supporting circular skylight formed by 7 7/8 x 2" (200 x 50 mm) steel box profiles
16. Circular skylight with aluminium frame and double-curved laminated glass
17. Aluminium casing with box profiles and aluminium substructure
18. Aluminium flashing
19. Steel box profile (parallel to plane of section)
20. Steel grille platform for installing antennas

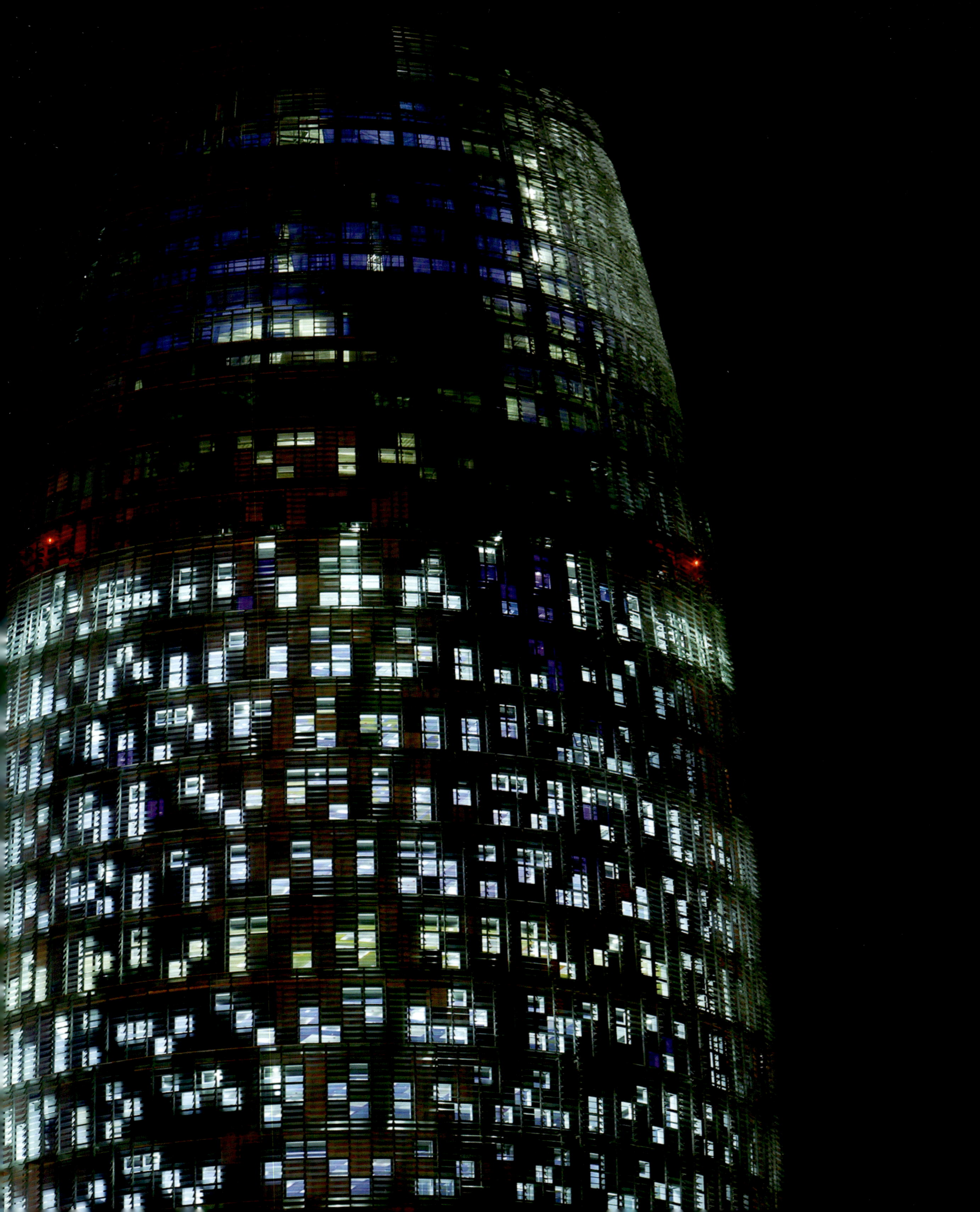

DETAIL B: DOME SUPPORT
VERTICAL SECTION – SCALE 1:20

1. 1/8 + 5/16" (4+8 mm) laminated glass louvres with four transparency levels and different silk-screened patterns, depending on orientation, fixed to support by structural silicone
2. Aluminium box-profile upright with mortice and tenon joints
3. Steel beam
4. Steel flange and plates connecting walkway to façade
5. Façade maintenance steel grille walkway, waterproofing membrane, steel plate, 5 1/2 x 2 3/8" (140 x 60 mm) steel box beam, steel box profile (parallel to plane of section)
6. 2 x 2" (50 x 50 mm) steel L-profile supporting grille
7. Façade maintenance ladder running track
8. Aluminium profile
9. Glazed façade formed by 3/8 - 5/8 - 1/16 - 1/16" (10-15-5-5 mm) modular aluminium double-glazing units with PVB film
10. 10 1/4 x 7 1/8" (260 x 180 mm) steel box beam supporting façade
11. Connecting steel plate
12. 25 1/4 x 8 7/8" (640 x 225 mm) steel I-beam (parallel to plane of section)
13. Steel grille for collection and filtering of rainwater
14. Aluminium profile supporting corrugated sheeting
15. Rainwater gutter formed by lacquered corrugated sheet aluminium and aluminium profiles
16. Aluminium L-profile
17. Waterproofing layer
18. Aluminium profiles supporting cladding
19. 1 5/8" (40 mm) rockwool board insulation, steel plate connecting walkway to structure, reinforced concrete beam
20. Modular window with lacquered aluminium frame with EPDM membrane around edges and 1/4 - 5/8 - 1/8" (6-15-4 mm) low-emissivity double glazing
21. Connecting steel plate (parallel to plane of section), screed, aluminium profile supporting sill
22. Steel ventilation grille, frame of 1 5/8 x 1 5/8" (40 x 40 mm) box profiles, reinforcing plate
23. Aluminium cladding, waterproof 1 1/4" (30 mm) plywood panel
24. Steel reinforcing bar
25. Floating floor in concrete panels with Thassos marble finish, height adjustable joints, 4 3/8" (110 mm) composite slab consisting of concrete fill over corrugated sheeting, 14 1/8" (360 mm) steel I-beam

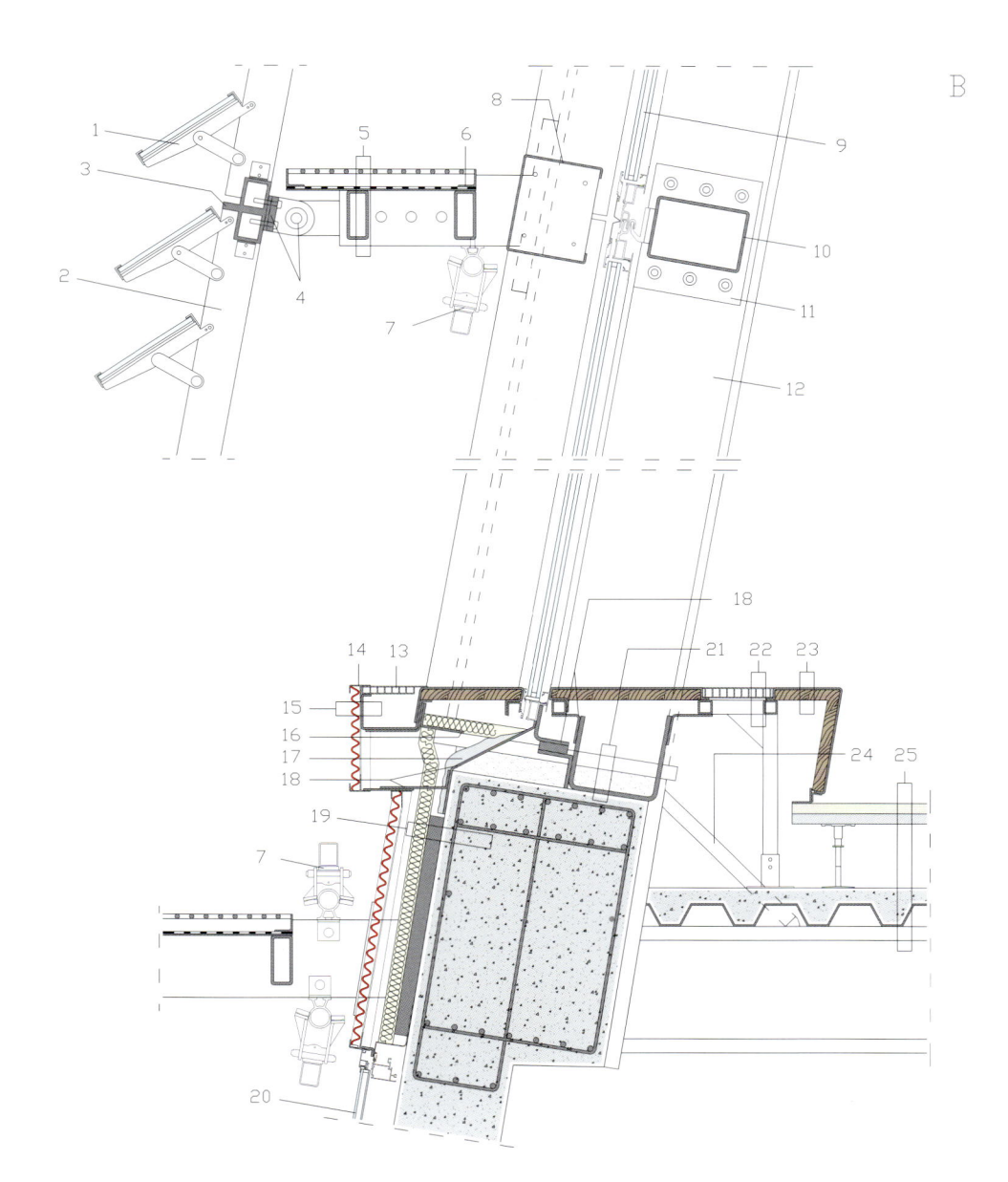

**DETAIL C: FAÇADE MODULAR WINDOW
VERTICAL SECTION – SCALE 1:10**

1. Modular window with lacquered aluminium frame with EPDM membrane around edges and 1/4 - 5/8 - 1/8" (6-15-4 mm) low-emissivity double glazing
2. Lacquered aluminium frame
3. EPDM joint
4. Transparent silicone joint
5. Steel L-profile securing façade to supporting structure
6. Satin finish aluminium profile
7. Polyethylene foam insulation layer
8. Light well cladding formed by folded sheet aluminium with super mirror polish finish
9. Lacquered aluminium profile trim
10. Lacquered corrugated sheet aluminium on frame of aluminium profiles, 1 5/8" (40 mm) rockwool board insulation, EPDM membrane, waterproofing membrane, steel L-profile fastening façade to supporting structure, reinforced concrete structure
11. Fastening clip

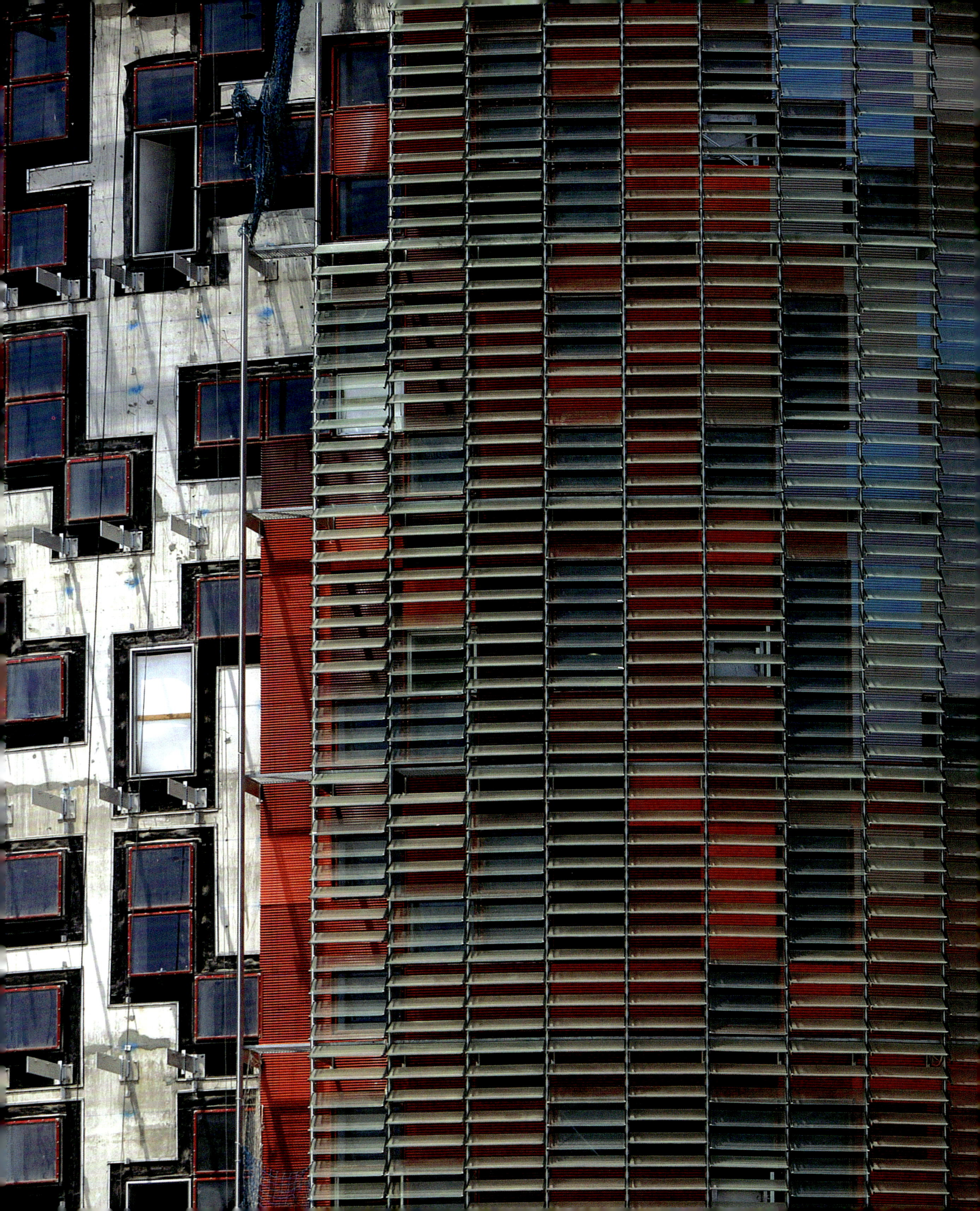

BRANDHORST MUSEUM – MUNICH, GERMANY
SAUERBRUCH HUTTON ARCHITECTS

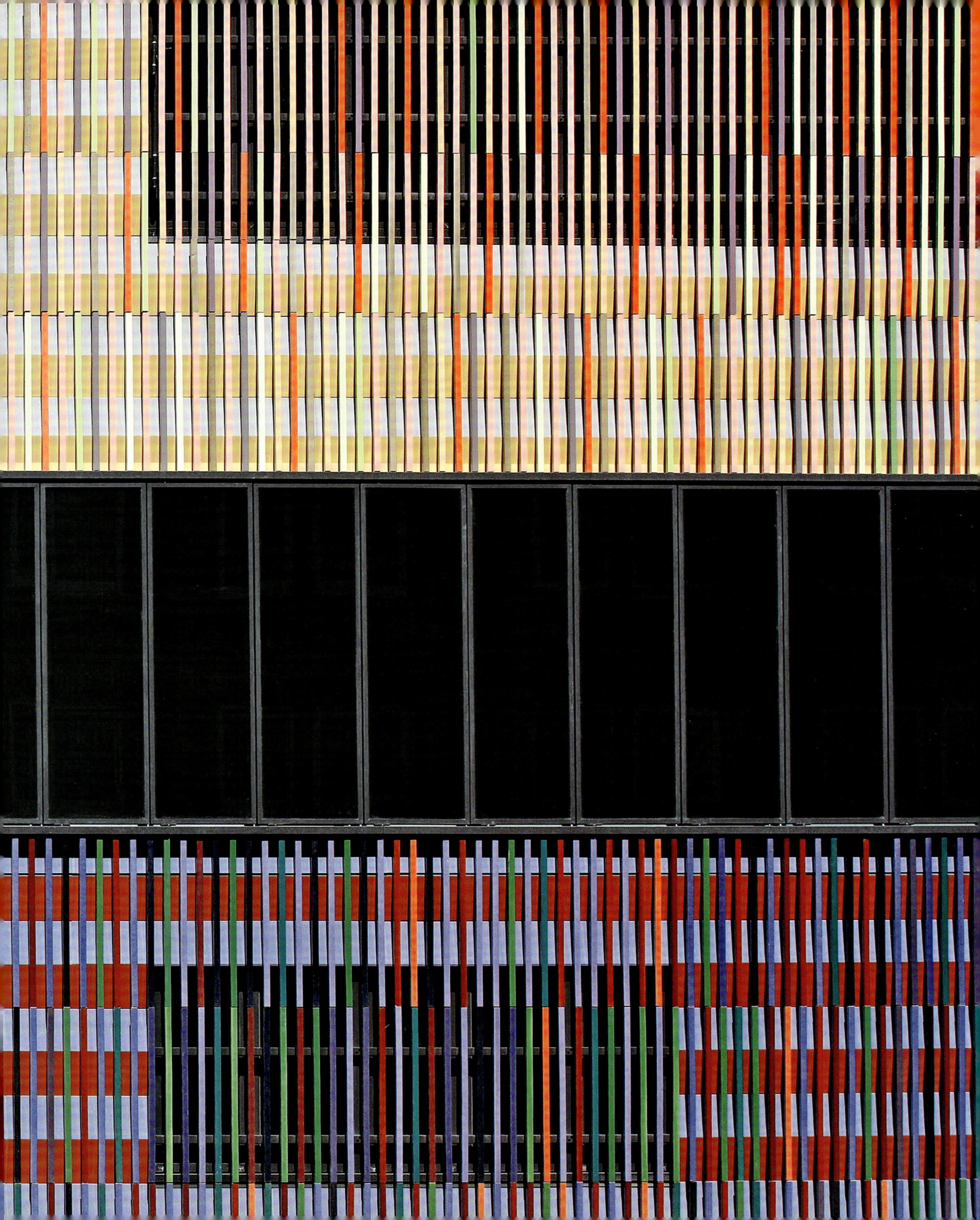

■ Noise Absorption

■ Zenith Light with Day Light Use

■ Cooling

■ Heating

■ High Thermal Insulation

■ Exhaust Water of Surrounding Buildings 28°C
   Ground Water at 18°C

224 / Brandhorst Museum

YY Section - Scale 1:500

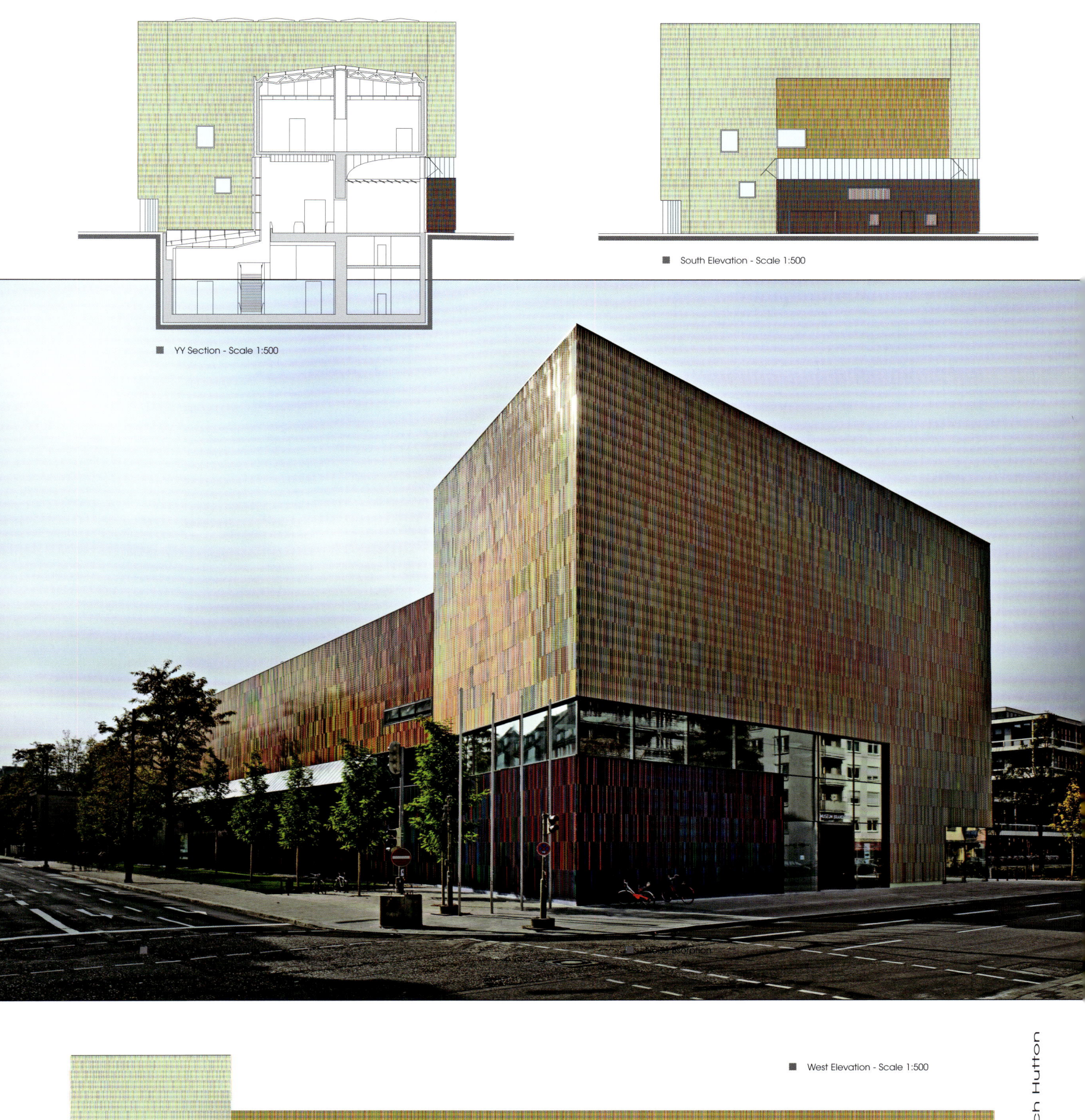

South Elevation - Scale 1:500

West Elevation - Scale 1:500

225 / Sauerbruch Hutton

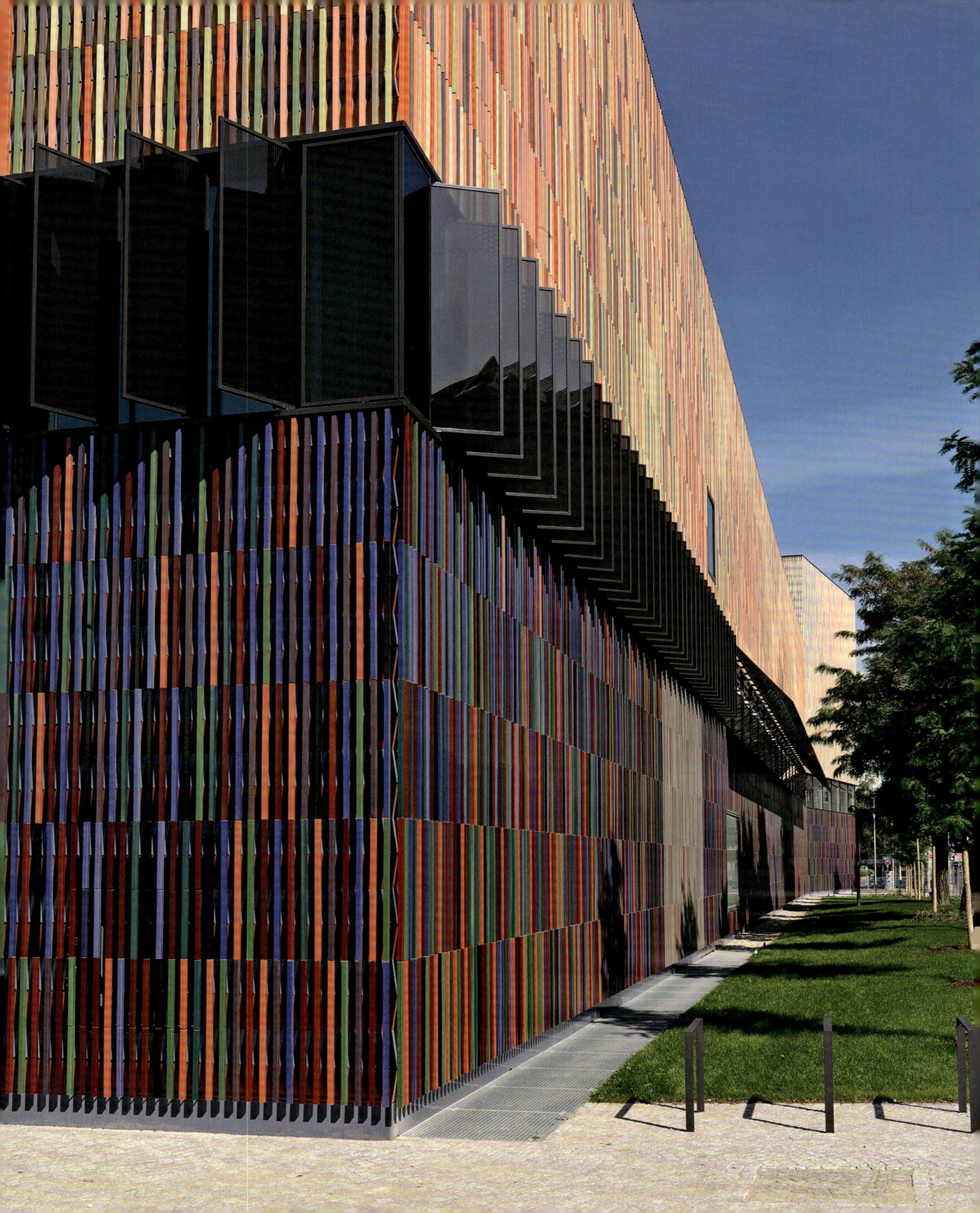

Ground Floor Plan - Scale 1:500

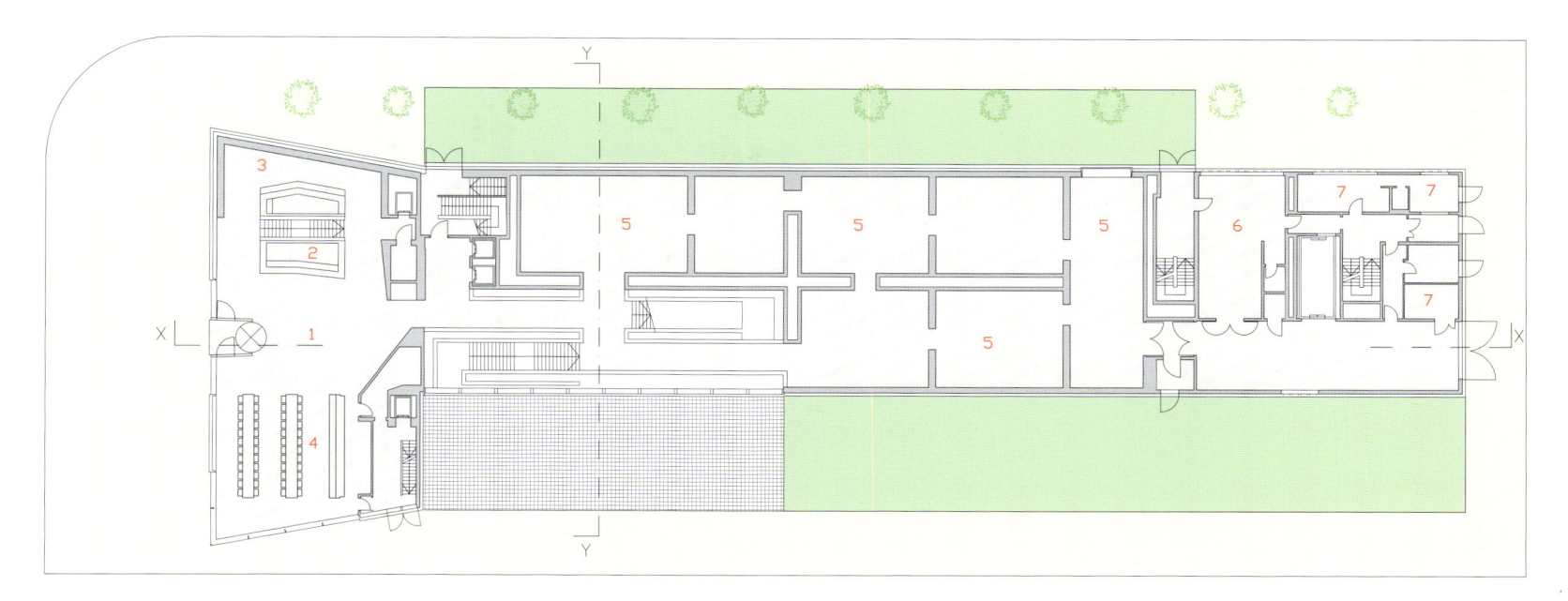

The new Brandhorst Museum is a signal in the urban and institutional matrix of Munich. This svelte, immaculately-assembled object gathers together many pertinent themes in contemporary architectural and museological thinking. Yet one's first impression of the building designed by Matthias Sauerbruch and Louisa Hutton is, simply, to register its presence as a spirited, multicoloured neighbour to neo-Classical museums and bourgeois apartment houses. "Impression" may in fact describe the exterior essence, the way it communicates through colour and its comprehensibility as a tectonic phenomenon. "Impression" also of course recalls early Modernist paintings: the agency of colour, the deconstruction of light, and the integration of modern life.

The Brandhorst Museum is a box. If mention of such a fundamental spatial container triggers association with the writings of Robert Venturi, with that American's polemics regarding the significance of surface, one might consider the Brandhorst as an exquisite box, as a literal treasure chest. Yet the Brandhorst's boxiness also results from the particularity of its site. It is the latest and perhaps the final instalment in a glorious set-piece, the family of museums instigated by Leo von Klenze's Alte Pinakothek in the early nineteenth century, poetically reconstituted by Hans Döllgast after World War II, and extended in recent years by the adjacent Pinakothek der Moderne. As such, Sauerbruch Hutton's Brandhorst Museum is not merely an object; it is a fragment in this compound of museums and museum buildings. The freestanding building rises two tall storeys above an extensive basement. As it must accommodate the practical needs of an independent museum (storage, service rooms, loading bays), much of the exterior is blank. Or, we might say, opaque. This is also due to the remarkable system of interior illumination. Lower galleries draw light from a strip of clerestory window; upper galleries are illuminated directly through a filigreed ceiling. The external surface is then treated as a fabricated colour field – already something of a Sauerbruch Hutton specialty – with a myriad ceramic bars, held forward of an envelope of perforated metal, that shift in hue or spectrum one to the next.

There are in toto 23 different glazes and three major groupings that help suggest a tripartite massing for the building. Like Op Art sculpture, the Brandhorst is animated by human movement. Entry is from the farthest corner, into a genial café and bookstore and thence to a linear, side-lit volume that houses an open staircase connecting galleries in the expansive basement, clerestory-lit chambers at ground level, and the splendid exhibition spaces on the top floor. The walls are white, the floors oak. The comparative intimacy of the lower galleries, with their meandering path, dissipates above where the broad exhibition halls reach up to ceilings of translucent fabric. A few flush "picture windows" allow for re-orientation back to the city and museum precinct.

The Brandhorst is not orthogonal but somewhat hammer-headed, cranking back from the street corner. This is no affectation. Above the entry, the slightly swollen upper gallery is tailored precisely to a dozen large canvases by the contemporary American master, Cy Twombly. There one is left almost entirely alone with art. The architecture almost disappears, the exterior ceramics almost forgotten in the presence of art.

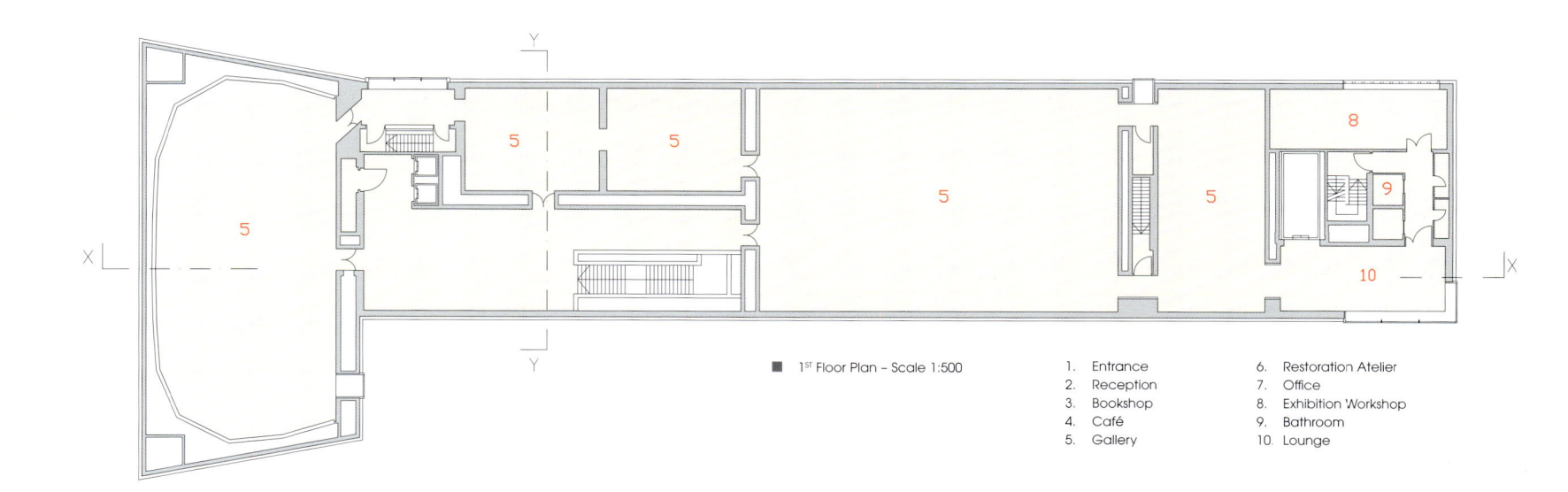

1st Floor Plan - Scale 1:500

1. Entrance
2. Reception
3. Bookshop
4. Café
5. Gallery
6. Restoration Atelier
7. Office
8. Exhibition Workshop
9. Bathroom
10. Lounge

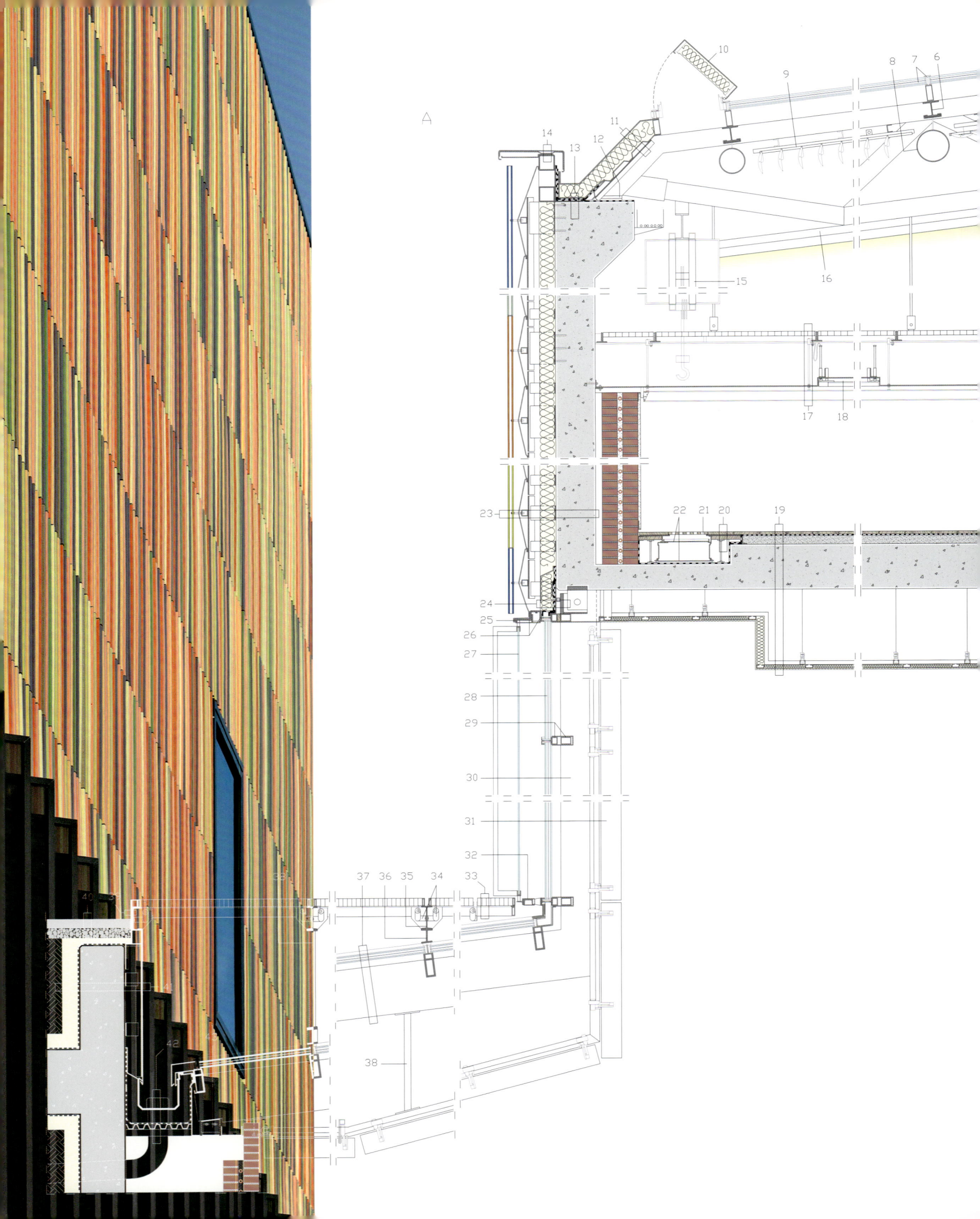

A

229 / Sauerbruch Hutton

**DETAIL A: CONSTRUCTION SYSTEM
VERTICAL SECTION - SCALE 1:30**

1. Roof ridge formed by 1/2 - 1 3/8 - 5/16" (12/35/8 mm) Okalux opaque glass sheets sandwiching board insulation, 6 1/4" (160 mm) insulation, 7 7/8" (200 mm) reinforced concrete slab
2. 10 5/8" (270 mm) reinforced concrete structure
3. 4 1/2 + 4 1/2" (115+115 mm) double brick wall, embedded radiant heating with 1 5/8" (40 mm) mortar fill, render
4. Structure of HEB 140 beams supporting roof
5. Steel plate connected to structure
6. HEB 120 beam
7. Okalux translucent skylight with 1/2 - 1/2- 1/8 -1/2 - 5/16 + 5/16" (12/12/4/12/8+8 mm) aluminium double-glazed assembly with insulating membranes on frame of 4 3/4 x 2" (120 x 50 mm) steel box profiles
8. Ø 9 1/8" (230 mm) aluminium pipe profile housing installations suspended from load-bearing structure
9. Motorized sun screen with adjustable aluminium louvres
10. Motorized ventilation hatch in sheet aluminium with insulation
11. Aluminium flashing, 4 3/8" (110 mm) insulation layer, corrugated sheeting, steel L-profile support
12. Steel plates anchoring beams to load-bearing structure
13. Aluminium flashing, double waterproofing membrane, steel angle profile connector, reinforced concrete beam
14. Shaped sheet aluminium flashing, frame of 4 3/4 x 4 3/4" (120 x 120 mm) steel box profiles
15. Mobile maintenance system
16. Diffused lighting system
17. False ceiling formed by double Barrisol translucent cloth on aluminium frame, steel plate bracing, steel tie rod, frame of inverted T-profiles suspended by tie rods from structural beams, walkable steel grille
18. Track for Erco spotlights
19. 7/8" (22 mm) Dinesen oak floorboards, vapour barrier, 2 3/4" (70 mm) screed, 13 3/4" (350 mm) reinforced concrete

slab, frame of 2 3/8 x 1 1/4" (60 x 30 mm) aluminium C-profiles suspended from slab, 1 1/4" (30 mm) insulation layer, false ceiling in 3/8" (10 mm) sound-absorbent gypsum board
20. 7/8" (22 mm) oak board, steel plate, 1 1/4" (30 mm) wood board, height-adjustable pier
21. Oak grille
22. Installation space with perforated aluminium hatch
23. 1 5/8 x 1 5/8 x 43 3/8" (40 x 40 x 1100 mm) NBK coloured hollow ceramic cladding tiles, anchor pin, sheet aluminium bracing, 2 x 2" (50 x 50 mm) steel box profile, 2" (50 mm) steel T-profile upright, connecting steel L-profile, 4 3/4" (120 mm) board insulation, 11 7/8" (300 mm) reinforced concrete structure, 2" (50 mm) air space
24. Sheet aluminium, insulation layer, double waterproofing membrane, shaped sheet aluminium, 1 1/4 x 1 1/4" (30 x 30 mm) steel box profile, steel L-profiles connecting to load-bearing structure
25. Aluminium flashing
26. Supporting structure of steel L-profiles
27. Adjustable sun shading with aluminium frame and 1/4 + 1/4" (6+6 mm) safety glass
28. Glazed curtain wall with aluminium frame and 1/4 + 1/4 - 1/2 - 1/8 - 1/2 - 1/4" (6+6-12/4/12/6 mm) double glazing
29. 2 3/8 x 1 3/4" (60 x 45 mm) and 2 3/8 x 3 1/8" (60 x 80 mm) steel profiles supporting facade finished in sheet aluminium
30. Steel I-beam upright finished in sheet aluminium
31. Interior sun shading formed by adjustable aluminium louvres on supporting steel tie rods and pins
32. Structure of steel C-, T- and box profiles supporting façade
33. Walkable steel grille on frame of 2 3/4 x 1" (70 x 25 mm) steel box profiles
34. Connecting structure of steel plates and profiles
35. 7 1/8 x 3 1/8" (180 x 80 mm) steel I-profile supporting grille
36. Connecting steel I-profile

37. Skylight with aluminium frame and 1/4 + 1/4 - 1/2 - 1/8 - 1/2 - 1/4 + 1/4" (6+6/12/4/12/6+6 mm) double glazing, supporting 12 5/8 x 6 3/4" (320 x 170 mm) steel I-beam finished in sheet aluminium
38. 2 x 2" (50 x 50 mm) box profile spacer
39. Aluminium flashing, steel angle profile, supporting 7 1/8 x 2 3/4" (180 x 70 mm) steel C-profile
40. 2 3/4" (70 mm) stone block paving, gravel layer, board insulation
41. Aluminium flashing, supporting steel L-profile, connecting steel L-profile, 13 3/4" (350 mm) reinforced concrete structure, waterproofing membrane, 4 3/4" (120 mm) board insulation, earth
42. Sheet aluminium gutter for collecting and filtering rain water, waterproofing membrane, double corrugated sheeting
43. Steel L-profiles supporting skylight on wall below
44. Roller blind
45. Interior sun shading with adjustable louvres
46. Strip window with aluminium frame and 1/4 - 3/8 - 1/8 - 5/16 - 1/4 + 1/4" (6/10/4/8/6+6 mm) double glazing
47. Connecting steel profile
48. Exterior sun shading with aluminium frame and 1/8 - 3/8 - 1/8 + 1/8" (4/10/4+4 mm) safety glass with acrylic resin
49. Steel shaft support
50. C-shaped aluminium gutter for collecting condensation
51. Aluminium sheeting, steel L-profile, steel C-profile, air space, steel box profile supporting false ceiling, wood base
52. Steel casing
53. Fixed louvres formed by translucent Barrisol membrane on aluminium and polycarbonate substructure
54. 7/8" (22 mm) Dinesen floorboards, 2 5/8" (65 mm) screed, 2" (50 mm) screed with radiant heating, 12 1/4" (310 mm) reinforced concrete slab
55. Gravel layer, double non-woven membrane, aluminium sheeting, waterproofing membrane, 5 7/8" (150 mm) board insulation
56. Continuous steel plate edging

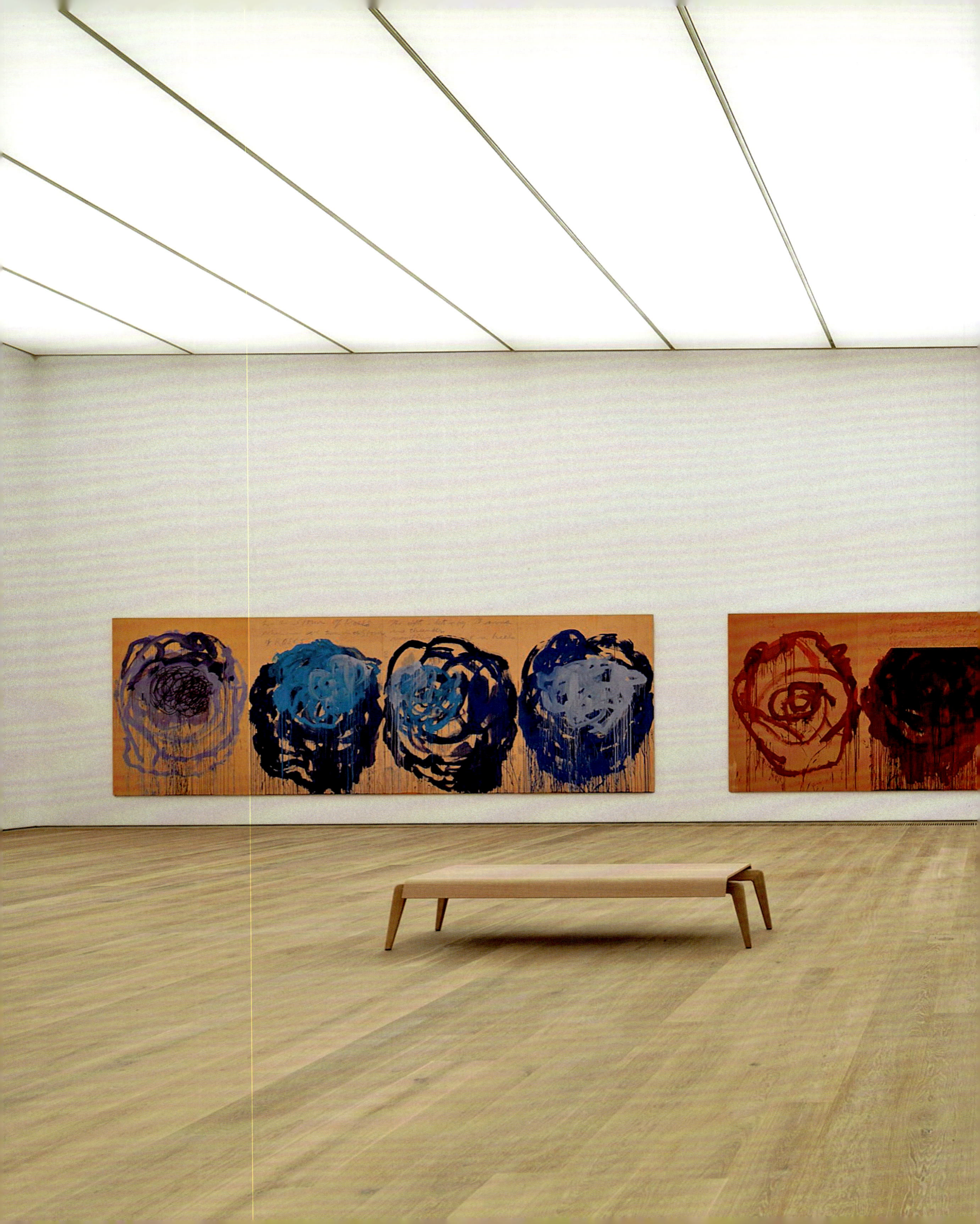

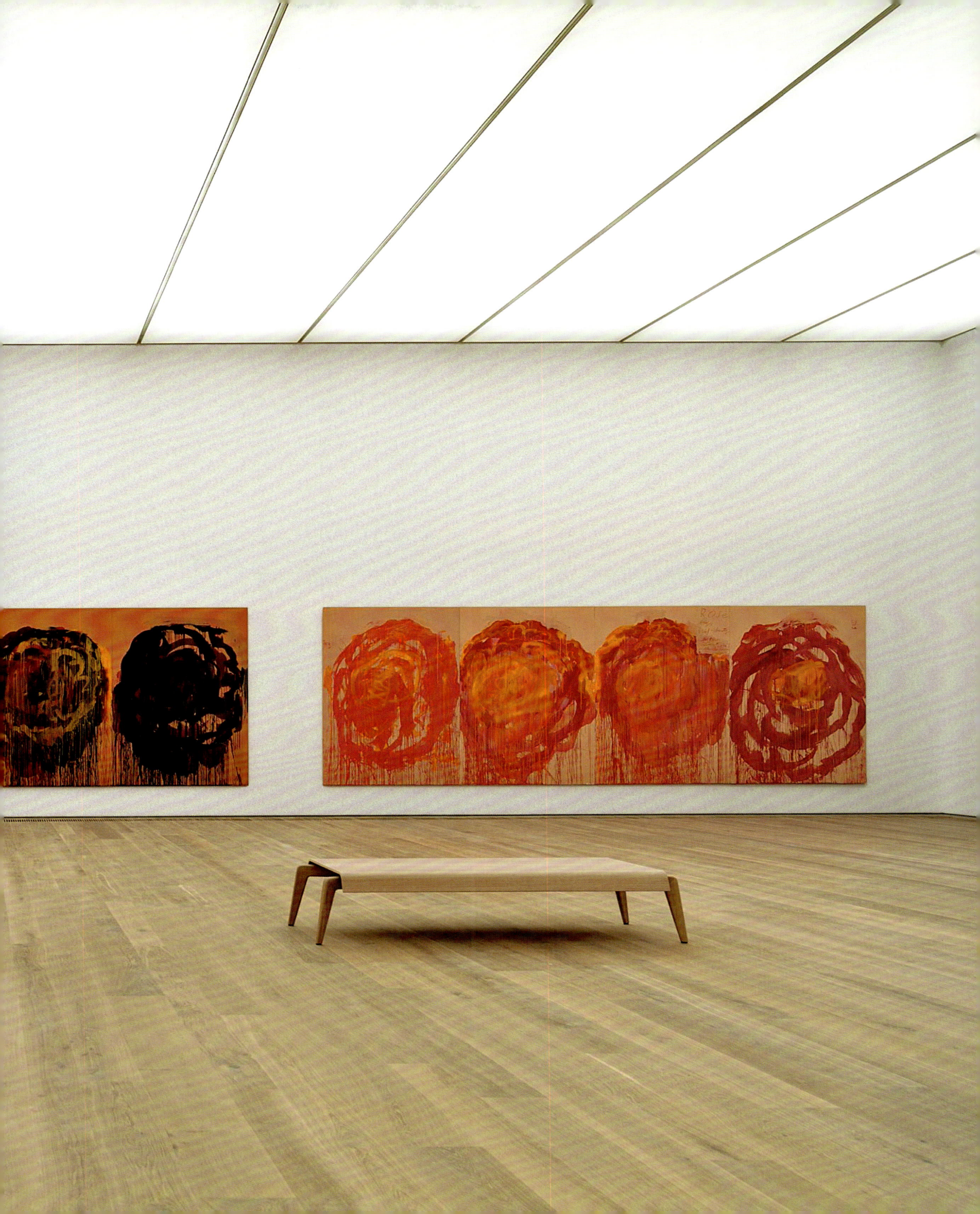

PROJECT CREDITS

TAMSA OFFICES – VERACRUZ, MEXICO
CARUSO E TORRICELLA ARCHITETTI

Location: Veracruz, Mexico / **Client:** TAMSA, Tubos de Acero de Mexico, Tenaris Group / **Completion:** 2001 / **Gross Floor Area:** 10,000 m² **Architect:** Caruso-Torricella Architetti / **Design Team:** Giulia Migiarra, Giuliana Barilli, Andrea Bracchetti, Lea Campioli, Filippo Fantini, Simone Fumagalli, Elena Gelmetti, Massimiliano Molteni, Roberto Pigorini, Silvia Refaldi, Pablo Rosenberg, Alessandro Valenti / **Structural Consultant:** SPS (Arturo Donadio), Garcia Jarque Ingenieros / **Services Consultant:** Serin (Lodovico Osio), TRIPLE I / **Project Manager:** TAMSA (Andres Medrano) **Sign Design:** Landor (Robert Matza) / **Colour Consulant:** Juan José Cambre / **Main Contractor:** Techint Mexico / **Sheet Metal Contractor:** K.S. Metals / **Heat-Mirror Glass:** Southwall Technologies / **Roof and Metal Façade:** Rheinzink

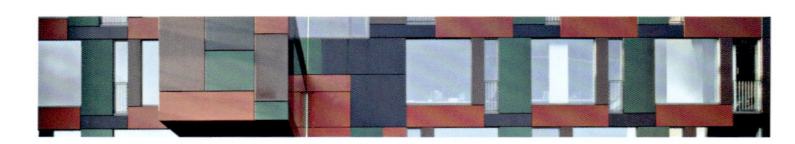

2 HARBOUR BUILDINGS – MÜNSTER, GERMANY
BOLLES+WILSON

Location: Münster, Germany / **Client:** LVM Versicherungen (Nr. 12-14), Julia Bolles-Wilson, Peter L. Wilson (Nr. 16) / **Design:** 2003 / **Completion:** 2005 **Gross Floor Area:** 11,037 m² / **Construction Costs:** 9,100,000 Euros / **Architect:** Bolles+Wilson, Julia Bolles-Wilson, Peter L. Wilson / **Design Team:** Axel Kempers, Susanne Asmuth, Anne Elshoff, Kirsten Hollmann, Valentina Ikstadt, Cornelia Kober, Hanspeter Müller, André Pannenbäcker, Andreas Polzer, Cäcilia Reppenhorst, Thomas Refflinghaus, Klaus Kuchenbuch, Manuel Kortenjan, Christoph Lammers / **Structural Consultant:** ahw Ingenieure / **Service Consultant:** Ingenieurbüro Nordhorn / **Fire Protection:** Dipl.-Ing. Richard Wolejszo / **Anodized Aluminium Façade Panels:** HD Wahl, Aluteca / **Windows:** Alco Systeme Fassadensysteme / **Solar Protection:** Warema Renkhoff / **Needle Felt Floor:** DLW Armstrong **Wooden Doors:** Herholz / **Elevators:** Osma

CONDOMINIUM TRNOVSKI PRISTAN – LJUBLJANA, SLOVENIA
SADAR VUGA ARHITEKTI

Location: Trnovski Pristan, Ljubljana, Slovenia / **Client:** Begrad / **Design:** 2002 / **Completion:** 2004 / **Gross Floor Area:** 4,010 m² / **Architect:** Sadar Vuga Arhitekti / **Design Team:** Jurij Sadar, Boštjan Vuga, Tina Hocevar, Miha Pesec, Tadej Zaucer, Mojca Kocbek / **Structural Consultant:** Elea **Mechanical and Electrical Consultant:** Te Biro / **Traffic - Site Consultant:** Gasper Blejec / **Landscape Design:** Andrej Strgar / **Lighting:** Arcadia **Window Frames, Glazed Façade and Roof:** Schüco

"ELS COLORS" NURSERY SCHOOL – BARCELONA, SPAIN
RCR ARANDA PIGEM VILALTA ARQUITECTES

Location: Manlleu, Barcelona, Spain / **Design:** 2002 / **Completion:** 2004 / **Gross Floor Area:** 930 m² / **Construction Costs:** 811,000 Euros
Architect: RCR Aranda Pigem Vilalta Arquitectes / **Design Team:** M. Tàpies, M. Subiràs, G. Rodriguez, M. Braga, F. Spratley, M. Linares. J. Torrents
Structural Consultant: Blázquez-Guanter Arquitectes / **Furniture Design:** RCR Aranda Pigem Vilalta Arquitectes / **Service Consultant:** Grau-Del Pozo Enginyers / **Contractor:** Construccions Ferrer, Metàl.liques / **Metal Work:** Fusteria Planella / **Finishes:** PT Polimer Tècnic / **Flooring:** MCD (Pavimentos Sintéticos) / **Glass:** Cristalleries

CLAPHAM MANOR SCHOOL – LONDON, UK
DRMM ARCHITECTS

Location: Southwest London, UK / **Completion Date:** July 2009 / **Gross Floor Area:** 927 m² / **Site Area:** 3,665 m² / **Client:** London Borough of Lambeth
Architects: dRMM (de Rijke, Marsh, Morgan Architects) / **Architects Team:** Philip Marsh (Project Director), Michael Spooner, Junko Yanagisawa, Mirko Immendoerfer, Satoshi Isono, Jonas Lencer, Russ Edwards / **Project Manager:** Sprunt / **Structural:** Michael Hadi Associates / **Acoustics:** Fleming & Barron
Main Contractor: The Construction Partnership / **Curtain Walls:** Schüco / **Coloured Glass:** Lisburn Glass Group / **Acoustic Ceiling:** Knauf
Ironmongery: Izé / **Glazing:** Birchdale Glass / **Rubber Flooring:** Pulastic

ØRESTAD COLLEGE – COPENHAGEN, DENMARK
3XN

Location: Copenhagen, Denmark / **Client:** Copenhagen City Hall / **Design:** 2003 / **Completion:** 2007 / **Gross Floor Area:** 12,000 m² / **Architect:** 3XN, Kim Herforth Nielsen, Bo Boje Larsen, Kim Christiansen / **Design Team:** Kim Herforth Nielsen, Michael Kruse, Tommy Bruun, Per Damgaard-Sørensen, Trine Berthold, Kristjan Eggertsson, Jørgen Søndermark, Rikke Zachariasen, Pia Hallstrup, Maj Quist, Rasmus Kruse, Lars Ketil Carlsen, Anders Barslund Christensen, Morten Mygind, Nicolaj Borgwardt Schmidt, Trine Dalgaard, Britt Hansen, Ritha Jørgensen, Flemming Vind Christiansen, Holger Mouritzen, Klaus Mikkelsen, Robin Vind Christiansen, Klaus Petersen, Allan Brinch, Mogens Jepsen / **Structural Consultant:** Søren Jensen / **Educational Consultant:** Helle Mathiasen / **Acoustics Consultant:** Frederik Wiuff / **Contractors:** Hoffmann, Jakon, Bravida, Marius Hansen Facader, G4S Group 4 Securicor / **Paint Work:** C. Møllmann & Co / **Inner Glass Walls:** Lafuco / **Sunscreening, Glass Lamellas:** Colt
Natural Ventilation, Control: Window Master / **Inner Guards and Handrail:** Galten Stål & Glas / **School Fittings and Fixtures:** PO-Inventar, Deto
Indoor Shades: Fischer Mørklægning / **Sports Equipment:** Virklund Sport / **Kitchen Equipment:** Bent Brandt

UNIVERSITY LIBRARY – UTRECHT, THE NETHERLANDS
WIEL ARETS ARCHITECTS

Location: Utrecht, The Netherlands / **Client:** Utrecht University / **Design:** 1997 / **Completion:** 2004 / **Gross Floor Area:** 36,250 m² / **Architect:** Wiel Arets Architect & Associates / **Design Team:** Wiel Arets, Harold Aspers, Dominic Papa, René Thijssen, Frederik Vaes, Henrik Vuust / **With:** Pauline Bremmer, Nick Ceulemans, Lars Dreessen, Jacques van Eyck, Harold Hermans, Guido Neijnens, Michael Pedersen, Vincent Piroux, JanVanweert, Michiel Vrehen, Richard Welten / **Interior Design:** Wiel Arets Architect & Associates / **Landscape Architect:** West 8 / **Façade Print:** Kim Zwarts **Consultants:** ABT Adviseurs in Bouwtechniek, Huygen Installatieadviseurs, Cauberg - Huygen Raadgevende Ingenieurs, Adviesbureau Peutz & Associates, Wilimas Bouwadviseurs, Adapt 3D / **Contractor:** Heijmans-IBC Bouw, GTI Utiliteit Midden, Permasteelisa Central Europe / **Custom Furniture and Desks:** Quinze & Milan / **Chairs and Tables:** Vitra

NETHERLANDS INSTITUTE FOR SOUND AND VISION – HILVERSUM, THE NETHERLANDS
NEUTELINGS RIEDIJK ARCHITECTS

Location: Hilversum, The Netherlands / **Client:** Netherlands Institute for Sound and Vision, Hilversum / **Design:** 1999 / **Completion:** 2006 **Gross Floor Area:** Offices, Museum, Archives, Audiovisual Library 30,000 m², Parking Garage 5,000 m² / **Construction Costs:** 40,000,000 Euros **Architect:** Neutelings Riedijk Architecten / **Design Team:** Willem Jan Neutelings, Michiel Riedijk, Frank Beelen, Joost Mulders, Tania Ally, Wessel Vreugdenhil, Lennaart Sirag, Bas Suijkerbuijk, Julia Söffing, Willem Bruijn, Stan Vandriessche, Wonne Ickx, Patricia Lopes Simóes / **Technical Design and Building Consultancy:** Bureau Bouwkunde / **Structural Consultant:** Aronsohn Raadgevende Ingenieurs / **Mechanical Consultant:** Royal Haskoning / **Building Physics Consultant:** Cauberg-Huygen Raadgevende Ingenieurs / **Contractor:** Heijmans Bouw Best / **Architectural Design and Concept Facade:** Neutelings Riedijk Architecten in cooperation with Bureau Bouwkunde / **Graphic Design Facade:** Studio Jaap Drupsteen **Development Glass Panels:** Neutelings Riedijk Architecten in Cooperation with TNO Eindhoven, Studio Drupsteen and Saint-Gobain / **Metal/ Glass Curtain Wall:** Sorba Projects / **Roof:** Daktechno / **Glass:** Saint-Gobain Glass Solutions / **Interior Finishes:** Keijsers Interior / **Walls/Flooring:** Kolen / **Carpet Manufacturer:** Eliëns / **Elevators/Escalators:** Thyssen Krupp

THEATRE AND MUSIC CENTRE – NÍJAR, SPAIN
MGM – MORALES GILES MARISCAL

Location: Níjar, Almería, Spain / **Client:** Junta de Andalucía,Empresa Pública de Gestíon de Bienes Culturales, Diputación Provincial de Almería, Ayuntamiento de Níjar / **Design:** 1998 / **Completion:** 2006 / **Gross Floor Area:** 2,550 m² / **Construction Costs:** 2,360,000 Euros / **Architect:** MGM - José Morales Sánchez, Sara de Giles Dubois, Juan González Mariscal / **Structural Consultant:** Francisco Duarte Jimenéz, Acuili, Amoenitas **Technical Architects:** Reyes López Martín, Gabriel Flores / **Stage Equipment:** Chemtrol / **Contractor:** Garasa-Esñeco / **Structural Steelwork:** Metacrisa / **Exterior Mesh:** Italfilm / **Exterior Façade Installation:** Carpintería Metálica Fenoy / **Steel Structure Installation:** Rampemar **Waterproofing:** Intemper / **Insulation:** Texsa, Pladur, Aislamientos Peláez / **Aluminium Metalwork System:** Laminex / **Sliding Doors:** Carpintería Metálica Fenoy / **Flooring:** Juan Carlos Garcia Amezcua / **Interior Finishes:** Jai-Juan Antonio Ibáñez, Decofloor / **Painting:** Barnices Valentine **Glass:** La Veneciana Bética / **Steel Structure:** ArcelorMittal

FIRE AND POLICE STATION – BERLIN, GERMANY
SAUERBRUCH HUTTON ARCHITECTS

Location: Berlino, Germany / **Client:** Government District, Berlin / **Design:** 1999 / **Completion:** 2004 / **Gross Floor Area:** 6,850 m² / **Construction Costs:** 12,400,000 Euros / **Architect:** Sauerbruch Hutton Architects, Matthias Sauerbruch, Louisa Hutton, Jens Ludloff, Juan Lucas Young / **Design Team:** Sven Holzgreve, Jürgen Bartenschlag / **With:** Lara Eichwede, Daniela Mccarthy, Nicole Winge, Matthias Fuchs, Marcus Hsu, Konrad Opitz, Stefan Bömelburg, Jochen Felten, Benita Hermann, Miriam Ellerbrock, Florian Völker, Helmuth Hanle / **Structural Consultant:** Arup / **Environmental Consultant:** PBR Planungsbüro Rohling / **Landscape Consultant:** Weidinger Landschaftsarchitektur / **Glass:** BGT Glas / **Windows:** ESTO Türen- u. Fensterbau / **Flooring:** Forbo-Krommenie

DIAGNOSTIC AND THERAPEUTIC CENTRE, CEDT – DAIMIEL, SPAIN
ESTUDIO.ENTRESITIO

Location: Daimiel, Ciudad Real, Spain / **Client:** Sescam, Castilla-La Mancha Health Service / **Design:** 2002 / **Completion:** 2007 / **Gross Floor Area:** 5,565 m² / **Construction Costs:** 6,248,000 Euros / **Architects:** María Hurtado de Mendoza Wahrolén, César Jiménez de Tejada Benavides, José María Hurtado de Mendoza Wahrolén / **Design Team:** Carolina Leveroni, Jorge Martínez Martín, Verena Ruhm, Raquel Fernández Antoñanzas, Vidal Fernández Díez, Cristina Fidalgo García, Vincent Rodriguez, Fabrice Quemeneur, Filipe Minderico, Laura Sánchez, Carrasco, Irene de la Cruz García / **Structural Consultant:** Geasyt / **Technical Architect:** Juan Carlos Corona Ruiz / **Quantity Surveyor:** Santiago Hernán Martín **Main Contractor:** Arción Construcciones / **Red Steel Sheet:** Hiansa / **Exterior Shades:** José Prado Cerrajería / **Roof Sealing:** Giscosa **Glass:** Saint-Gobain Glass, Cristalería El Cid / **Climate Installation:** Enermes / **Electrical Installation:** Jesús Bárcenas / **Inner Walls:** Abet Laminati **Bathroom Equipment:** Duravit / **Windows:** Alcoa

THE PUBLIC – WEST BROMWICH, UK
ALSOP ARCHITECTS

Location: West Bromwich, UK / **Client:** CPlex 1998-2003, The Public Building Limited 2003-2006, Sandwell Metropolitan Borough Council 2006-2008 **Design and Construction Years:** 1998-2008 / **Completion Date:** 2008 / **Gross Floor Area:** 9,274 m² / **Architects:** Alsop Architects (1998-2004), Flannery & de la Pole (2004-2008) / **Project Direction:** DCA Consultancy (2006-2008) / **Construction Manager:** ISG Interior Exterior / **Project Manager:** Davis Langdon, Sandwell MBC / **Exhibition Designer:** Ben Kelly Design / **Structural Engineer:** Adams Kara Taylor / **Lighting Designer:** Kevan Shaw / **Acoustic:** Sandy Brown Associates / **Theatre:** Paul Covell (concept by Charcoalblue) / **Security:** Arup Security / **Interactive Designers:** Digit, AllofUs / **RFID Technology:** Avonwood Development / **Envelope:** Richardson Roofing / **M&E Services:** Bailey / **Balustrading, Trees:** Structural Stairways / **Joinery & Exhibition Fit Out:** Mivan / **Partition & Ceilings:** McDermott / **Soft Flooring & Screed Repairs:** Tynedale Carpets **Decorating:** Midland Decorators / **IT Exhibition Installation:** Electrosonic / **IT Data & Voice Infrastructure:** Cable & Wireless / **Theatre Fit Out:** Fagan Electrical / **Theatre Seating:** Hussey Seatway / **Aluminium Sinusoidal Cladding:** Rautaruukki Corporation

SANTA CATERINA MARKET – BARCELONA, SPAIN
MIRALLES TAGLIABUE ARQUITECTOS

Location: Barcelona, Spain / **Client:** IMMB / **Architect:** EMBT - Enric Miralles, Benedetta Tagliabue Arquitectos / **Project Manager:** Igor Peraza
Design Team: Hirotaka Koizuni, Josep Miàs, Tomoko Sakamoto, Marta Cases, Constanza Chara, Joan Poca, Alejandra Vazquez, Marco Dario Chirdel, Josep Belles / **Model:** Fabián Asunción, Ignacio Quintana, Christian Molina, Stefan Geenen, Maarten Vermeiren, Torsten Schmid / **Special Assistants:** Ricardo Flores, Eva Prat / **Structural Consultant:** Robert Brufau / **Contractors:** Universal de Obras y Contratas, Placo P.T.T. LLeida, Construcciones Guamora / **Carpentry:** Frapont / **Climatization:** Servi Confort / **Structures:** Esmycsa - Estructuras Metalicas, Tecno Cal / **Waterproofing:** Tecnicas Dry
Ceramic Tiles: Cerámica Cumella

FLOWER MARKET – BARCELONA, SPAIN
WILLY MÜLLER ARCHITECTS

Location: Barcelona, Spain / **Client:** Mercabarna / **Completion Date:** 2008 / **Site Area:** 15,000 m^2 / **Construction Cost:** 9,200,000 Euros / **Architect:** WMA - Willy Müller Architects / **Design Team:** Frédéric Guillaud, Caterina Morna, Rupert Maurus, Isabella Pintani, Valeria Santoni, Bruno Louzada, Francisco Villeda, Iris Cantante, Marco Loperfido, Mara Cascais, Sabine Bruinink, Mario Perez Botero / **Structures:** Area 5 / **Installations and Urbanism:** Greccat / **Structures:** Monesmet / **Roof:** Gadama / **Photovoltaic Roof:** Master Renovables / **Natural Ventilation System:** Breezair

ST GILES COURT DEVELOPMENT – LONDON, UK
RENZO PIANO BUILDING WORKSHOP

Location: London, UK / **Client:** Legal & General with Mitsubishi Estate Corporation, Stanhope / **Completion:** 2010 / **Architect:** Renzo Piano Building Workshop in collaboration with Fletcher Priest Architects / **Design Team:** J.Moolhuijzen, M.van der Staay (partner and associate in charge), N.Mecattaf (associate) with L.Battaglia, S.Becchi, A.Belvedere, G.Carravieri, E.Chen, D.Colas, P.Colonna, W.Matthews, G.Mezzanotte, S.Mikou, Ph.Molter, Y.Pagès, M.Pare, L.Piazza, M.Reale, J.Rousseau, S.Singer Bayrle, R.Stampton and M.Aloisini, R.Biavati, M.Pierce, L.Voiland; O.Auber, C.Colson, Y.Kyrkos (models) / **Services and Structural Consultant:** Ove Arup & Partners / **Cost Consultant:** Davis Langdon / **Pre-Construction Advice:** Bovis Lend Lease / **Landscape Consultant:** Charles Funke Associates / **Façade Consultant:** Emmer Pfenninger & Partners / **Lighting:** P. Castiglioni / **G.Bianchi** / **Fit-Out for Affordable Residential:** PRP / **Sub & Superstructure Concrete:** Byrne Bros. / **Steel Frame:** Hares / **Brick & Blockwork:** Lyons & Annoot / **Glazed Ceramics & Curtain Walling:** Schneider / **Louvres Cladding & Internal Blinds:** Levolux / **Ground Floor Glazing:** Seele / **Roofing:** Briggs Amasco / **Dryline Partitions:** BDL / **Suspended Ceilings:** Phoenix / **Raised Floors:** Kingspan / **Internal Stone:** Grants / **Floor Finishes:** Rees / **Metal Doors:** Powershield / **Architectural Metalwork:** PAD / **Ceramic Façade:** NBK

NEW TERMINAL T4 BARAJAS AIRPORT MADRID, SPAIN
RICHARD ROGERS PARTNERSHIP – ESTUDIO LAMELA

Location: Madrid, Spain / **Client and Construction Management:** AENA (Aeropuertos Españoles y Navegación Aérea) / **Design:** 1999 **Completion:** 2005 / **Full Operation:** 2010 / **Gross Floor Area:** 470,000 m² (Terminal), 290,000 m² (Satellite), 309,000 m² (Car Park), 64,000 m² (Access roads) / **Architect:** Richard Rogers Partnership + Estudio Lamela / **Structural Consultants:** INITEC, TPS, OTEP, HCA, AHA / **Main Facade Design:** ARUP Facades / **Fire Protection:** Warrington Fire Research / **Quantity Surveyor:** Hanscomb + Gabinete de Ingeniería / **Acoustic Consultant:** Sandy Brown / **Lighting Consultant:** Jonathan Speirs / **Natural Lighting Consultant:** OVE ARUP and Biosca & Botey / **Landscape Consultant:** dosAdos Arquitectura del Paisatge / **Contractors:** JV Ferrovial, FCC, ACS, NECSO, SACYR, Dragados, OHL / **Finishes Coordinator:** Comsa / **Concrete Structures:** UTEs / **Bamboo:** Lindner / **Indoors Limestone:** Levantina, Luis Sánchez / **Totems and "Dragons" (air-conditioning):** Comsa, Inametal, Trox, NKI Group (Gel coat) / **Glazed Facades:** Folcrá, Inasus / **Glass:** Cristalería Española, Eurocomercial Meyco / **Lighting:** Siteco - Siemens **Metallic Panels:** Gasell / **Lighting Diffusers:** IASO / **Aluminium Frames:** Geze / **Roof Cladding:** Kalzip / **Steel Structures:** Emesa, Horta

AGBAR TOWER – BARCELONA, SPAIN
ATELIERS JEAN NOUVEL AND B720 ARQUITECTOS

Location: Barcelona, Spain / **Client:** Layetana Inmuebles / **Tenant:** Aguas de Barcelona (Agbar) / **Design:** 1999 / **Completion:** 2005 / **Gross Floor Area:** 47,500 m² / **Architect:** Jean Nouvel (AJN), Fermín Vázquez (b720 Arquitectos) / **Design Team:** Jean-Pierre Bouanha, Vander Lemes, Cristiano Benzoni, Pablo Garrido, Alexa Plasencia, Cristina Algás, Francisco Martínez, Elisabeth Farrés, Julie Fernández, Emmanuelle Lapointe **Project Manager:** Argos Management / **Interior Design:** Jean Nouvel (AJN), García Ventosa Arquitectura / **Lighting Design:** Yann Kersalé **Structural Consultant:** R. Brufau & A. Obiol / **Mechanical Consultant:** Gepro, Ibering / **Façade Consultant:** Xavier Ferrés (Biosca&Botey) / **Model:** Étienne Follenfant / **Colour Consultant:** Alain Bony / **Acoustics Consultant:** Higini Arau / **Scenography Consultant:** Ducks / **Renderings:** Artefactory, Mirco Tardio / **Contractor:** Dragados, Axima, Emte, Thyssen-Boetticher, Permasteelisa Group / **Flooring:** Espacio / **Climatization Machinery and Equipment:** Climaveneta / **Executive Plan and Production of Interior Bespoke Cupboards:** Tecno

SOCCER CITY STADIUM – JOHANNESBURG, SOUTH AFRICA
BOOGERTMAN + PARTNERS ARCHITECTS

Location: Nasrec Arena, Johannesburg, South Africa / **Construction Date:** 01 February 2007 – 03 March 2010 / **Client:** City of Johannesburg Owner's Representation: National Stadium South Africa / **Cost:** 325 Million Euros / **Building Area:** Site Area: 254,726 m², Building Footprint: 61,320 m² / **Architects in Partnership:** Boogertman Urban Edge + Partners in Partnership with Populous / **Project Manager and Civil:** Phumaf Consulting Engineers / **Technology:** QA International / **Structural:** PDNA Consulting Engineers, Schlaich Bergermann & Partners / **Acoustical:** Pro Acoustic Consortium / **Fire Protection:** Chimera Fire / **Quantity Surveyors:** Llale & Company, De Leeuw Group / **HVAC:** Dientsenere Tsa Meago / **Mechanical:** Izazi Consulting Engineering / **Town Planning:** Schalk Botes / **Landscape Architects:** Uys & White / **General Contractors:** Grinaker-LTA/Interbeton / **Concrete and Waterproofing:** Grinaker-LTA/Interbeton / **Structural Steel Fabrication:** Cimolai / Grinaker-LTA/Interbeton **Grass Specialists:** Sports Turf Solutions / **Fibre Reinforced Concrete Panels:** FibreC by Rieder

BRANDHORST MUSEUM – MUNICH, GERMANY
SAUERBRUCH HUTTON ARCHITECTS

Location: Munich, Germany / **Design:** 2002 / **Construction:** 2005-2008 / **Gross Floor Area:** 12,000 m² / **Construction Costs:** 48,150,000 Euros **Owner:** Freistaat Bayern, Bayerisches Staatsministerium für Wissenschaft, Forschung und Kunst, Staatliches Bauamt Munich 1 / **Architects:** Matthias Sauerbruch, Louisa Hutton, Juan Lucas Young / **Project Architect:** David Wegener / **Construction Management:** Marcus von der Oelsnitz, Rasmus Jörgensen, Mathias Mund / **Structural:** Ingenieurbüro Fink / **Electrical:** Zibell Willner & Partner / **Climatization:** Ingenieurbüro Ottitsch / **Landscape Design:** Adelheid Gräfin Schönborn / **Lighting:** Arup Lighting / **Acoustics:** Akustik-Ingenieurbüro Moll / **Building Physics:** Müller-BBM / **Glass Façade:** Wicona / **Skylight Glass:** Okalux / **Flooring, Ceilings, Partitions, Doors:** Lindner / **Ceramic Façade:** NBK **Exhibition and LED Lighting:** Zumtobel / **Translucent Ceiling:** Barrisol / **Bathroom Furniture:** Duravit